T0377592

Neoextractivism and Capitalist Development is a brilliant synthesis of economic structures, class relations and state power embedded in a historical analysis. Canterbury provides an insightful critique of the regressive role and impact of international extractive capitalist development. His incisive discussion provides a framework for identifying a progressive and dynamic alternative development model which will be of interest to students, academics and policymakers.

James Petras, Bartle Professor (Emeritus), Binghamton University, USA

Karl Marx chronicled how human activity is essentially the interaction with nature to produce the basic needs for reproduction, and each epoch is characterized by who controls both the process and the outcome of those interactions. Capitalism, as a system of production, is predicated on private ownership of productive forces that appropriates the surplus generated by working men and women. With the expansion of capitalist development worldwide comes the appropriation of natural resources from former colonies masked as beneficial to local populations by a range of development theories. Dennis Canterbury reveals how neoextractivism is but one more iteration of development theory, one informed by neoliberal policies that does little to benefit society. His important case study of Guyana details how neoextractivism creates the false illusion that developing countries have escaped capitalist exploitation through the natural resource extraction of the past, and instead undermines the struggles of working people in their opposition to the ravages of capitalism.

David Fasenfest, Department of Sociology, Wayne State University, USA

This is a work of consummate scholarship that will be of especial interest to members and supporters of left-wing social movements in developing countries. It reveals the limits of progressive development strategies that rely on extracting high world market price raw materials such as oil to finance social projects. The author is interested in development strategies that lead not just to conventional economic growth but also to substantive human progress.

James W. Russell, Lecturer in Public Policy, Portland State University, USA

The book offers a new and innovative perspective on neoextractivism in Latin America and the Caribbean. It uncovers and shares details of the relationships between stakeholders in the region's extractive industries 'space', offering fresh explanations for its underwhelming economic performance. The book promises to be an invaluable tool for researchers active in Latin America, as well international organizations in the donor and NGO communities working on transparency, community development and environmental managerial aspects of the extractive industries in the region.

Gavin Hilson, Chair of Sustainability in Business,
The Surrey Business School, UK

Neoextractivism and Capitalist Development is an exceptional contribution to the scholarly literature on global capitalism, and its influences on development in the Caribbean and other regions in the Global South transitioning from neoliberalism to post-neoliberalism models of capital accumulation. To expound contemporary theories of global capitalism and imperialism in the post-neoliberal phase, Dennis Canterbury operationalizes the concept neoextractivism with its attendant misrepresentations of ideas of development, its promises of social mobility and empowerment, and the alleged enhancement in the quality of life for ordinary citizens. Fundamentally, *Neoextractivism* makes special reference to Latin America and the Caribbean; employing Guyana as a case study, the book aims to provide readers with the analytical tools they need for improving the human condition. This book will be of special interest to academics and students in the fields of international development, political economy, area studies, political science, sociology and globalization, as well as policymakers and political activists engaged in social movements in the natural resources sector.

Darryl C. Thomas, Associate Professor of African American Studies, Penn State University, USA

Neoextractivism and Capitalist Development

The large-scale extraction of natural resources for sale in capitalist markets is not a new phenomenon, but in recent years global demand for resources has increased, leading to greater attention to the role of resource extraction in the development of the exporting countries. The term neoextractivism was coined to refer to the complex of state–private sector policies intended to utilize the income from natural resources sales for development objectives and for improving the lives of a country's citizens. However, this book argues that neoextractivism is merely another conduit for capitalist development, reinforcing the position of elites, with few benefits for working people.

With particular reference to the role of neoextractivism within Latin America and the Caribbean, using Guyana as a case study, the book aims to provide readers with the tools they need to critically analyze neoextractivism as a development model, identifying alternative paths for improving the human condition. This book will be of interest to academics and students in the fields of international development, political economy, sociology, and globalization, as well as to policymakers and political activists engaged in social movements in the natural resources sector.

Dennis C. Canterbury is a Professor of Sociology at Eastern Connecticut State University, USA.

Routledge Critical Development Studies
Series Editors

Henry Veltmeyer is co-chair of the Critical Development Studies (CDS) network, Research Professor at Universidad Autónoma de Zacatecas, Mexico, and Professor Emeritus at Saint Mary's University, Canada

Paul Bowles is Professor of Economics and International Studies at UNBC, Canada

Elisa van Wayenberge is Lecturer in Economics at SOAS University of London, UK

The global crisis, coming at the end of three decades of uneven capitalist development and neoliberal globalization that have devastated the economies and societies of people across the world, especially in the developing societies of the global south, cries out for a more critical, proactive approach to the study of international development. The challenge of creating and disseminating such an approach, to provide the study of international development with a critical edge, is the project of a global network of activist development scholars concerned and engaged in using their research and writings to help effect transformative social change that might lead to a better world.

This series will provide a forum and outlet for the publication of books in the broad interdisciplinary field of critical development studies – to generate new knowledge that can be used to promote transformative change and alternative development.

The editors of the series welcome the submission of original manuscripts that focus on issues of concern to the growing worldwide community of activist scholars in this field.

To submit proposals, please contact the Development Studies Editor, Helena Hurd (Helena.Hurd@tandf.co.uk).

1 **Moving Beyond Capitalism**
Edited by Cliff Du Rand

2 **The Class Struggle in Latin America**
Making History Today
James Petras and Henry Veltmeyer

3 **The Essential Guide to Critical Development Studies**
Edited by Henry Veltmeyer and Paul Bowles

4 **Reframing Latin American Development**
Edited by Ronaldo Munck and Raúl Delgado Wise

5 **Neoextractivism and Capitalist Development**
Dennis C. Canterbury

Neoextractivism and Capitalist Development

Dennis C. Canterbury

LONDON AND NEW YORK

First published 2018
by Routledge
2 Park Square, Milton Park, Abingdon, Oxon OX14 4RN

and by Routledge
711 Third Avenue, New York, NY 10017

Routledge is an imprint of the Taylor & Francis Group, an informa business

British Library Cataloguing-in-Publication Data
A catalogue record for this book is available from the British Library

Library of Congress Cataloging-in-Publication Data
A catalog record has been requested for this book

ISBN: 978-0-8153-5677-6 (hbk)
ISBN: 978-1-351-12734-9 (ebk)

Typeset in Times New Roman
by Wearset Ltd, Boldon, Tyne and Wear

Contents

Acknowledgments viii

Introduction 1

PART I
The debate on neoextractivism 13

1 Neoextractivism and capitalist development: An outline 15

2 Development theory and capitalist development 35

3 Extractivism and neoextractivism 53

4 Neoextractivism: Myth or reality 77

5 Extractive capitalism, extractive imperialism and imperialism 99

PART II
Neoextractivism and development of center-periphery relations 117

6 Natural resources extraction and expanded capitalist relations 119

7 The foundations of post-colonial 'new' extractivism 140

8 The post-colonial authoritarian state 158

9 The criminalized authoritarian state 188

10 Political change and foreign intervention 211

Conclusion 231

Index 237

Acknowledgments

I wish to express my thanks to the people who have helped me along the way, beginning with Henry Veltmeyer and James Petras (my graduate school mentors at Binghamton University), and Clive Thomas and Norman Girvan (my graduate school mentors at the University of the West Indies). Clive Thomas played a critical role in my formative years as a research assistant at the Institute of Development Studies, University of Guyana, and before that Perry Mars and Eusi Kwayana. A special thanks to Henry Veltmeyer and James Petras for introducing me to the debate on neoextractivism and for encouraging me to write this book. Thanks to Randolph Williams, an economist at the Private Sector Commission in Guyana, for the discussions, and to Carmen Cid, Dean of the School of Arts and Sciences at Eastern Connecticut State University, for her constant support. I am grateful to the referees for their useful critical comments on the manuscript and to Helena Hurd and the editorial team at Routledge working behind the scenes. Thanks to my wife Sandra Jennifer for her unstinting support over the years.

Introduction

This book presents a critique of development theory through an analysis of the phenomenon characterized as 'neoextractivism' a twenty-first century development model in Latin America and the Caribbean, but which is really a cyclical occurrence manifested in the resource-rich former European colonies through crisis and reform in global capitalism. Historically, development theory has only promoted capitalist development, as envisioned by the extant dominant branch of the ruling class. Concretely, the class that spearheads and maintains capitalist development vacillates between two dominant strata – industrial and financial capitalists as crisis conditions dictate. The prevailing ideas in development theory, usually reflect the ideas of these two capitalist strata.

Development theory was imbued with ideas about industrialization, when industrial capital was dominant. The nation-states that emerged from colonial domination were encouraged to industrialize as a means to attain capitalist economic development. The focus of development theory at the time was on strategies of industrialization, but that is no longer the case today. Crisis and reform in global capitalism has led to the emergence of financial capital as the dominant form of capital in this moment. Development theory shifted gears with the rise of financial capital and began to focus on the sorts of policy reforms that countries needed to implement to reap the economic rewards of financialization in their pursuit of capitalist development.

The notion of industrialization was evident in the complex of ideas that constituted the origins of development theory in mercantile, physiocratic, and Smithian political economy. In its earliest period, political economy emerged as the mediaeval system disintegrated and elements of a new order surfaced. The formation of strong governments that replaced the spiritual order maintained instead the material balance in society amidst growing intellectual and moral upheaval and as industrial forces grew even stronger, including the insurrections of the working classes, and the rise of armies to suppress them (Ingram, 1915). As manufacturing gained importance, the distinction between worker and entrepreneur became firmly established. Navigation, printing, public credit, industrial development, the opening up of the Americas, all led to the revolutionizing of trade, the establishment of colonies and the preponderance of industrial life and its ultimate universality (Ingram, 1915).

With the rise of mercantilism, European governments became permanently interested in industry which occupied their policy objectives (Ingram, 1915). The mercantile system emerged and attained its highest development about the middle of the seventeenth century (Ingram, 1915). The mercantile school is best characterized by a set of theoretic tendencies namely the significance of processing substantial amounts of precious metals; the acclamation of foreign over domestic trade; the elevation of manufacturing industry over those that produce raw materials to be manufactured into finished products; the promotion of a dense population as a national strength; and the promotion of the state as a means to achieve desirable ends (Ingram, 1915).

Industrialization was key in the subsequent development of political economy albeit the physiocratic school the immediate forerunner to Smithian political economy, regarded it as a sterile activity. The Physiocrats, espoused the positive doctrine which lies at the bottom of all science, by arguing that social phenomena are subject to fixed relations of co-existence and succession (Ingram, 1915). They believed that the manufacturer, merchant, and liberal professions were useful but sterile because they did not produce income themselves but drew it from the superfluous earnings of the agriculturists (Ingram, 1915).

The economic analysis of the Physiocrats takes a particular path beginning with labor being the only productive force that adds to the existing quantity of raw materials available for human consumption. Thus, in their view, the real annual addition to community wealth is determined by the excess of the mass of agricultural products and minerals over their cost of production (Ingram, 1915). Manufacturing gives a new form to the materials extracted from the earth and the value it adds represents the quantity of provisions and other materials used and consumed in its elaboration (Ingram, 1915).

The accompanying political doctrine was that the government should pursue 'laissez faire' an idea that rested on natural rights. All individuals had the same natural rights, albeit not equal capabilities, thus requiring a social union or contract between them. The social contract limits the natural freedom of the individual insofar as such freedom is inconsistent with the rights of others (Ingram, 1915). The government appointed by the consent of individuals is a necessary evil that should be limited in its interference save to secure the fulfilment of the contract (Ingram, 1915). The form of government they favored referred to as legal despotism entailed a combination of legislative and executive functions. The reasoning behind this was their belief that an enlightened government is able to forthrightly implement its programs, in comparison with a government constrained by divergent opinions and constitutional checks and balances (Ingram, 1915).

The individual has a right to naturally enjoy, undisturbed and unfettered, what he/she acquired by their labor and its fruits should be guaranteed to the possessor (Ingram, 1915). The individual must be allowed to make the most of his labor, freedom of exchange ensured, and restriction on competition and monopolies removed (Ingram, 1915). The doctrine of the Physiocrats caused much harm to industrial development and trade, but undoubtedly it consecrated the spirit of individualism, and the state of non-government (Ingram, 1915). It represented a wing of the revolutionary movement against the theological dogma that all movements of the universe, was due to divine wisdom and benevolence to produce the greatest possible happiness (Ingram, 1915).

Smith believed that the annual labor of a nation was the source for its sustenance (Ingram, 1915). Labor, however, whose productiveness lies in its division, is not the only productive factor. The magnitude to which labor is divided is determined by the extent of the market. Once established the division of labor causes individuals to depend on each other, money comes into use as a medium of exchange to facilitate the trade of goods against each other or money, which raises the question of value. Smith believed that exchangeable value of all commodities is measured by labor, which never varies in its own value. Money is the nominal price while labor is the real price of commodities.

These ideas on political economy were formulated in the quest to acquire knowledge on the policies that a nation-state needed to adopt to acquire wealth. Free trade was as centerpiece of those ideas, which would imply the industrial production of commodities to trade. Industrialization was the process by which commodities were produced for trade, as the mercantile era subsided. Indeed, the industrial revolution was in full swing and it created such a stir in society and economy that it brought forth fresh theorizing in political economy on issues such as wealth, value, trade, and progress among others. Subsequent theoretical ideas about development included its social aspects covering a variety of issues such as education, health, gender, social inequality, poverty, etc.

In the period since the late twentieth century, however, in both the developed capitalist countries and former colonies economic and social life seems to revolve around finance and financialization. Capitalist development and its maintenance are in the hands of the finance capitalists, who seem to be at odds with industrialization and more in sync with making profit from financial transactions. These transactions do include those for commodity production from which financial instruments are derived for trading purposes, and trade in other forms of financial instruments. Production seems not to be for the sake of production, but for the financial transactions that can be generated from commodities. The dominance of finance capital has seen the bulk of profit in the capitalist system accruing to the financial capitalists as against the industrial capitalists. The members of the latter group are even themselves becoming engaged in financial transactions for their enrichment rather than by investing in industrial production.

Resource extraction is the constant in the journey of capitalist development, since nature supplies the material conditions of human existence. The significance of nature here must not be construed in a metaphysical sense as containing supernatural powers. It is from nature that raw materials are extracted and converted into commodities for human consumption. The process of resource extraction for commodity production ranges from the simple form of people expending their labor power on nature for their own upkeep, to the more complex form of resource extraction for profit in capitalist society. There is only one concrete way that the latter becomes possible – private property, the private ownership of nature and its products. In the capitalist system, the worker extracts resources from nature not for his own upkeep. He does so for someone else, who pays him a wage to purchase his livelihood in capitalist markets. Generations of scholars have sought to explore the complexities of the processes of resource extraction, as it takes place under capitalism, to upkeep the human race, while simultaneously generating profit for the few. Development theory is an embodiment of the works that explore those processes.

Capitalism has converted natural resources extraction merely for human survival into a profit-making enterprise to benefit a small group of individuals who have made themselves the owners of nature. Capitalist development aided by development theory is about how to make natural resources extraction more efficient to profit individuals who lay claim to nature. Natural resources extraction lies at the foundation of the capitalist economy, since it is from that process that resources become available for manufacturing and upon which rest inter alia commodity production, trade, commerce, and finance for profit. As a by-product people who can afford it are supplied with livelihoods in capitalist markets.

In appearance, development theory is about how nation-states can secure finances to extract natural resources, manufacture commodities from those resources, trade natural resources and the commodities they produce, and speculation, etc., to earn income to improve the human condition. Increases in profit and capital accumulation are described as economic growth and the principal stimuli to economic development. In reality the motivation to engage in productive and speculative activities under capitalism is not to improve the human condition, but to generate profit and accumulate capital. Economic growth takes place amidst the perpetuation of conditions identified as a lack of development. This contradiction exists because development is not about improving the human condition; it is about the capitalist goal to make profit and accumulate capital. Critics of economic growth argue that it alone cannot bring about development; other ingredients of development such as freedom, democracy, gender equality, etc., must be included in the matrix. The case to add social factors to economic development however is made within the framework of capitalist development. Adding the social factors to development does not transform capitalism, it merely occasions the deepening of capitalism in the social realm.

Since the advent of development theory in classical political economy every new addition or extension to it has only deepened the capitalist system of class exploitation. The policy prescriptions by the classical political economists for the nation-state to acquire wealth have been interrogated for several centuries. There have been many twists and turns along the way in this chewing-over of the classical prescriptions for wealth generation and accumulation. These have taken forms such as the neoclassical challenge to the classical focus on single markets for land, labor and capital, by instead atomizing those markets such that there are multiple markets for different types of labor, land and capital. The Keynesian challenge aimed at stabilizing the capitalist system and restoring growth through government intervention.

The Marxist challenge is not to be mistaken to be a development theory, it really provides a critique of political economy, and advanced a revolutionary program of political action to replace the capitalist system of production. Development theories are all in the genre of classical political economy, the point of departure for understanding the capitalist production system as we know it today. The major economic categories analyzed in development theory were all invented by classical political economy.

The dilemma that development theorists face is that they fail to see the reality of their own work – the perpetuation of the exploitative capitalist system; the exploitation of working people by the capitalists. They are fixated on the appearance that their theories will bring betterment to a vast majority of people within the capitalist system. Thus far however their theories coincide with wars for resources and markets, crises, and heightening income and social inequalities.

Concomitant with the deepening of capitalist exploitation, working people have been finding ways to fight back at every stage of capitalist development. This book is fundamentally concerned with the expansion of development theory as a capitalist phenomenon. It explores this observed fact by way of a critical analysis of the cyclical phenomenon identified as neoextractivism in Latin America and the Caribbean.

Structure of argument

The argument is developed in two parts. Part I delineates neoextractivism and the idea that development theory is merely a conduit for capitalist development. It provides an outline and analysis of neoextractivism and capitalist development, undertakes a descriptive assessment of extractivism and neoextractivism, and engages in a critical examination of neoextractivism as a myth or reality. Analytically, it concentrates on different concepts in the debate on neoextractivism in particular extractivism, extractive capitalism, extractive imperialism and imperialism. The objective in analyzing these concepts is threefold.

The first being to highlight in one place for the reader multiple viewpoints on them, while critically analyzing natural resources extraction as an integral component of capitalist development, and appraising the notions of extractive capitalism, extractive imperialism and imperialism as they are considered in the debate on extractivism and neoextractivism. Second it seeks to bring some clarity on the usage of these concepts in the burgeoning literature on the subject of neoextractivism. The goal here is to assist working people and their organizations to understand that despite the fact that neoextractivism improved their social conditions somewhat, in the final analysis it is not really pro-working class but deepens the capitalist stronghold on a country's economy. Third, it situates the debate on neoextractivism within the framework of development theory, which is critiqued on the grounds that it merely fosters the spread of the exploitative capitalist mode of production.

The assumption is that the survival of the human species depends on their ability to eke out a living from nature, but that in the capitalist system a few people have become the owners of nature for whom those who do not own nature must work to make a living while the owners make a profit. This is the origins of the bourgeois problem of distribution; how much of the value produced from nature must go to the owner of nature and how much should the producer receive. Why is development theory, of which neoextractivism is but one of its forms, a conduit for capitalist development? How does development theory, including neoextractivism as one of its current renditions, contribute to the maintenance of the capitalist system?

Part II demonstrates with historical illustrations from Guyana that the phenomenon characterized as neoextractivism is a capitalist dynamic that takes place at different historical conjunctures as capitalism evolves. It is cyclical and produced by certain conditions of capitalism, namely crisis and reform. The historical materialist analysis of natural resources extraction in Guyana illustrates an alternative counter argument to the notion that neoextractivism being associated with progressive regimes in Latin America is a new phenomenon. The political economy relations that developed in the Caribbean periphery after the encounter with mercantile capitalism was founded on an extra-economic extraction of the surplus in the absence of full-fledged capitalist labor-capital relations. This was due to the existence of a slave labor force, which was the dominant form of labor that produced the economic surplus.

The emergence of center-periphery relations was critical to the development of capitalism and the natural resources sector in Guyana. Analyzing this process in comparison with neoextractivism confirms the argument that capitalist crisis heightens nationalist struggle for domestic ownership and or control of natural resources in the capitalist periphery. Specifically, Part II analyzes natural resources extraction and the expansion of capitalist production relations. It explores the foundations of post-colonial extractivism, the post-colonial authoritarian state, the criminalized authoritarian state, and foreign intervention and political change. What is the evidence that neoextractivism is a phenomenon that occurs in historical periods of crisis and reform in global capitalism?

Synopsis of the book

Chapter 1 presents the structure of the central argument being made about neoextractivism and capitalist development, which is that the political economy condition described as neoextractivism is not new. It is driven by capitalist cycles of crisis and reform and as a form of development theory it is merely a conduit for capitalist development.

Chapter 2 elaborates on the relationship between development theory and capitalist development. It explores the central ideas that development theory is a means to capitalist development. It supports the counter argument that in reality neoextractivism merely represents a particular form of capitalist development. It is merely an appearance that neoextractivism is a new progressive development model that improves the economic and social conditions of the poor, as claimed by its advocates. The objective here is to undertake a critique of neoextractivism in the context of an appraisal of development theory or theories of development, which are catalysts for the spread and development of capitalism. In contradistinction to the view that neoextractivism is a new socio-economic development model, the counter idea presented here is that neoextractivism describes a conjunctural phenomenon. It has been manifested at different historical conjunctures in the evolution of the capitalist system of production. It is a capitalist socio-economic development model associated with crisis and reform in global capitalism.

Chapter 3 turns to a discussion on extractivism and neoextractivism to highlight and compare some of the principal existing ideas on the two concepts. It explores different threads in the literature on neoextractivism with the objective to clarify for political activists, social movements and progressive forces ambiguities concerning the concept. It provided these social forces with ideas on some of the central considerations for the development and articulation of appropriate counter analysis and action on extractivism and neoextractivism. The principal assumption is that neoextractivism is a smokescreen for capital accumulation and the exploitation of workers in the extractive sectors. Two key questions to be answered are: what is extractivism and neoextractivism? What is the relationship between extractivism and neoextractivism?

The answers to these questions are intended to provide a clear picture on what both the proponents and opponents mean by extractivism and neoextractivism. The meanings of the terms 'extractivism' and 'neoextractivism' have taken several twists and turns in the recent social science literature. Both concepts are regarded as development models based on natural resources extraction, the exploitation and marketing of these resources as exports. The terms are regarded as models that constitute the foundations for the organization of the economic, political, social, and cultural relations, and class structure, gender relations, the state and public discourse, in the countries or regions where they are in vogue.[1] The pervasiveness of the impact of extractivism in natural resources-rich countries is evident from the major role the production and export of natural resources play in the national economy and the political, economic, social and environmental struggles engendered in the production process. It is necessary to distinguish between 'extractivism' and 'neoextractivism' to clarify the process of capitalist development and exploitation in the periphery via natural resources extraction.

Chapter 4 addresses the problem as to whether it is a myth or reality that neoextractivism is specific to neoliberal capitalism. The analysis brings into focus additional support for the proposition that the dynamic conditions described as neoextractivism really refer to a phenomenon that becomes manifest at specific historical conjunctures as capitalism changes its form rather than being confined to a specific historical period. The myth is that neoextractivism is a phenomenon specific to neoliberal capitalism, while the reality is that it is conjunctural, identified in historical periods when capitalism changes its form for example from colonialism to neo-colonialism or from neoliberalism to post-neoliberalism.

The argument is presented in five parts beginning with an examination of capitalist contradiction and the change from colony to nation-state status in the periphery. The capitalist development models based on national ownership of natural resources in the Caribbean are analyzed as comparable to the conditions described as neoextractivism. Thereafter, analyses are undertaken of neoliberal capitalism and the extractive industries, the development impact of natural resources extraction, and the political foundations of the neoliberal approach to mining. Is neoextractivism new or is the condition it describes merely a social phenomenon that becomes manifest at specific historical conjunctures as capitalism changes its form?

The wrong answer to this question could perpetuate a dangerous myth about natural resources extraction and lead to the continuance of misrepresentations and misunderstandings about neoextractivism that would find their way into class struggle and policy formation on the subject. It would preserve the misallocation and squandering of scare resources expended in the region on a misunderstood phenomenon and jettison the struggle for state power to transform the power structure in resource extraction thereby maintaining the conditions of capitalist exploitation. Alternatively, the correct answer would lead to an exploration of a new realization concerning the subject of capitalist development in general and in particular the former European colonies and clarify hitherto misunderstood important theoretical issues in the literature on the question of capitalist development concerning extractive capitalism.

The object of the analysis is capitalist development, whose subject matter focuses on natural resources extraction. The peripheral capitalist countries in search of a path to capitalist development are the domain where the characteristic features of neoextractivism have become manifest. This is because the dominant form of capitalism in general has succeeded in regenerating underdevelopment in the peripheral capitalist countries by exercising ownership and or control over their natural resources and siphoning off the economic surplus produced from the exploitation of those resources for accumulation in the capitalist center.

In such conditions, at the slightest chance that nationalists have to take control of state power, they seek to reverse foreign domination of their economies by foreign forces. They implement policies to take ownership and or control of their natural resources and to use the economic surplus for the socio-economic development of their peoples and countries. These lofty intentions are scuttled simply because the approach to own and or control natural resources is not transformative but reformist and therefore ends up maintaining the capitalist status quo and perpetuating the capital-labor contradiction, rather than changing it. The struggle between the developed and developing components of the capitalist system is a natural dynamic condition of capitalist development.

Chapter 5 analyzes ‘extractive capitalism,’ ‘extractive imperialism,’ and ‘imperialism,’ with the objective to clarify the veritable confusion in the debate on neoextractivism caused by the interchangeable use of those concepts. Clarification of this confusion requires urgent attention to buttress the understanding of the class struggle from below in the extractive industries. The point of departure in the analysis of these concepts is the counterpoints advanced by Petras and Veltmeyer on the theoretical and political questions concerning the role of the state in their critique of the theory of neoextractivism.

To grasp their counter theoretical arguments on the role of the state in this body of work it is necessary to engage three concepts that are central to their analysis – 'extractive capitalism,' 'extractive imperialism,' and 'imperialism.' Their analysis on the relationship between capitalism and imperialism is of crucial importance as an illuminator of the way extractive capitalism and extractive imperialism are understood. The clarity we seek to provide is contained in the argument that extractivism is merely the embodiment of a particular form of productive activity in the capitalist era that deepens capitalism in the capitalist periphery.

The extraction of natural resources from nature is not a purely capitalist or imperialist process. Humans have extracted their livelihood from nature since the days of primitive communalism up until present-day capitalism. It is not the specific productive activity of extracting natural resources from nature, which is capitalist or imperialist, since capitalism and by extension imperialism are associated with a variety of productive activities. The productive activity has to take place within a capital-wage labor nexus to be of a capitalist variety. Some of the early expositions on the definitions of these concepts are revisited to help the activists have a clear understanding of the debate on neoextractivism.

Chapter 6 is on natural resources extraction and expanded capitalist relations. It presents pertinent evidence in support of the idea that the natural resources sector really began to take hold in Guyana and the wider English-speaking Caribbean in the historical period characterized by the collapse of 'the colonial slave mode of production' in the period between 1834 and 1953. The advocates of neoextractivism argue that the phenomenon arrived on the South America continent in the post-neoliberal period. It is demonstrated with ample evidence however that a similar phenomenon emerged in Guyana prior to the post-neoliberal period, as crisis in global capitalism laid the basis for the advent of a natural resources sector after the colonial slave mode of production collapsed. This crisis in turn stimulated the nationalist struggle for national ownership and or control of natural resources as a means to bring about the capitalist economic development of the country.

The emergence of the natural resources sector depended on the collapse of the agricultural-based colonial slave mode of production, a form of primitive accumulation, which constrained the free movement of labor beyond the boundaries of plantation agriculture into natural resources extraction. As the colonial slave mode of production began to disintegrate, a different official disposition emerged towards natural resources extraction. Property relations changed in favor of full-fledged capitalist property relations and capitalist limited-liability companies emerged. The laws that the plantocracy passed to restrict the movement of labor gradually eased, capital was granted the freedom to diversify out of plantation agriculture, and new capital was invited to enter the country in the natural resources sectors. The analysis demonstrates the extent of the colonial attempt at economic diversification out of the colonial slave mode of production's mono-crop agricultural system, which in essence entailed a transition to capitalist center-periphery relations.

Chapter 7 analyzes the foundations of post-colonial extractivism in Guyana, and contends that the class, race and ideological factors embedded in the peripheral capitalist production relations in the 1953–1964 period continued to shape the essential characteristics of the Guyanese political economy, today. These factors have laid the foundations for the emergence of the post-colonial authoritarian state and post-colonial extractivism between 1964 and 1992. It is demonstrated that there is nothing 'new' about the phenomenon that is taking place in Latin America. Neoextractivism in Latin America pretends to be a part of a dynamic historical process in the struggles for the political, social and economic transformation of peripheral capitalist social formations from a state of dependence on center countries to genuine political and economic independence. In reality, however, it merely serves to deepen capitalist relations in the region.

The foundations for post-colonial extractivism were laid in the crisis of colonial capitalism that spawned the anti-colonial movement, which won power and proceeded to stake a claim for national ownership and or control of natural resources as a development strategy. The anti-colonial struggle was the antecedent of post-colonial extractivism, which was similar to the anti-globalization and anti-neoliberal social movements in Latin America. Evidently, the class and race bases of the social order was apparent in those struggles as well.

Chapter 8 analyzes natural resources extraction as a development strategy pursued by the post-colonial authoritarian state. To varying degrees, the post-colonial authoritarian state followed a natural resources-led development strategy between 1964 and 1992. The phenomenon described as neoextractivism is remarkably similar to the development approach of the post-colonial authoritarian state in terms of the positioning of the natural resources sector as the engine of economic growth and development.

The capitalist political economy conditions in Guyana at the time of the emergence of the post-colonial authoritarian state included the dynamics of race and class conflicts domestically, anti-colonial sentiments in the nation, political and economic nationalist tendencies, divisions in the anti-colonial movement, anti-communist hysteria, and foreign intervention. Looming large among these was the belief that Guyana can take ownership and or control of its natural resources and to redistribute income from the extraction and sale of those resources as raw materials to improve the social and economic conditions of the Guyanese people. The ideal of national ownership and or control of natural resources in order to spread the wealth generated by the sector to the sundry population is a phenomenon, integral to the dynamics of capitalist development in the periphery.

This ideal is rarely ever achieved since peripheral capitalist countries were created. The states that pursue such a strategy often degenerate into various forms of authoritarianisms, due to internal and external political and economic factors. The Guyana-case is a classic example of how the noble intentions of a country to own and or control its natural resources for its self-development, could be degenerated into authoritarianism. Analysis is undertaken of the transition from a post-colonial state to a post-colonial authoritarian state in Guyana. The main purpose is to further demonstrate that neoextractivism, is merely a part of the capitalist development dynamic.

Its focus is on the political economy factors that correspond to those of neoextractivism in Latin America. The anti-neoliberal politics in that region were spearheaded by left-leaning social movements. Progressive politicians depended on these struggles to win power and then to proceed to pursue a political economy agenda to redistribute income generated in the natural resources sector to the poor, while simultaneously taking measures to appease foreign capital. The historical trajectory of the politics of Guyana at the time had more to do with anti-communism and anti-communist coalition politics. It involved the consolidation of power through rigged national elections in the hands of a ruling faction that was handed power by US and British imperialist forces. It included nationalization of the commanding heights of the economy and attempts to redistribute income to the poor, post-colonial authoritarianism, political assassinations, neoliberal structural adjustment, and an anti-dictatorial resistance movement.

Chapter 9 on the criminalized authoritarian state, analyzes the degeneration of the post-colonial authoritarian state into a criminal enterprise and the role of natural resources extraction in that process. The criminalized authoritarian state was characterized among other things by – a ruling clique in which factions of organized crime bosses had a prominent role; a large phantom economy that was a proxy for the economic might of organized crime; and corruption, which served as the willing and able handmaiden of organized crime (Thomas, 2003). It engaged in extra-judicial murders, drug trafficking, money laundering and trafficking in persons, while positioning natural resources extraction as a central plank in its economic development strategy. It used its control over natural resources to enrich its members through rent extraction, and leveraging foreign extractive capitalist seeking to invest in the sector. Interesting, there was an apparent correlation between the predominance of small-scale gold mining and the emergence of the criminalized authoritarian state.

The criminalized authoritarian state was analyzed within the broader problematic of democratization in the twenty-first century. The question is: what is the relationship between democracy and authoritarianism in general and in Guyana in particular? It is argued that in general, democracy and authoritarianism are presented as two ends of a continuum – a country can either be democratic or authoritarian or somewhere in-between those two extremes. Democratization of the colonial state meant granting the plebiscite to the locals by removing the property and literacy restrictions on voting. The post-colonial authoritarian state was meant to inhere democratic practices in the political fabric of Guyanese society. That was not to be, however. Neoliberalism was intended to democratize the post-colonial authoritarian state through free and fair national elections under the watchful eyes of overseas elections observers who would declare the elections result to be either free and fair or unfree and unfair. This is what we call neoliberal democratization, which produced the criminalized authoritarian state.

Chapter 10 is on foreign intervention and political change and broaches the issue of political change in natural resources rich peripheral countries in the historical period, marked by the transition from neoliberalism to post-neoliberalism. The main argument is that neoliberal democratization brought about regime change in post-colonial authoritarian states, but these states were subjected to further foreign intervention in collaboration with domestic forces to deepen democracy. The primary goal of foreign intervention to effect regime change is to maintain control over natural resources in peripheral capitalist states. The imperialist powers believe that neoliberal democratization did not bring sufficient democracy to the post-colonial authoritarian states. There is need for further action by the imperial forces in collaboration with their domestic allies to bring more democracy to the peripheral states. This phenomenon, is distinctly associated with capitalist development in the periphery. Developing countries visited by political change through neoliberal democratization are subjected to further imperial intervention, allegedly to strengthen democracy.

In Guyana, neoliberal democratization represented regime change – the surrendering of the post-colonial authoritarian state to the International Monetary Fund/World Bank/Carter Centre. Then a new form of authoritarianism emerged that degenerated into a criminalized authoritarian state, which prompted further foreign intervention to bring about regime change, but this time under the ruse of strengthening democracy. Installing democracy and strengthening democracy in natural resources rich peripheral countries are ruses for foreign intervention in peripheral states to control their natural resources. The real situation in Guyana however was that the criminalized authoritarian state was not working fully in the interest of the imperial powers namely the US and as such the US needed to bring about regime change to put in place a government that would pay more attention to the interests of foreign capital.

Note

1 For an elaboration on this point see Gensler (2013).

References

Gensler, M. (2013). *Energy policy and resource extractivism: Resistance and alternatives*. Rosa Luxemburg Stiftung: Brussels.

Ingram, J. R. (1915). *A history of political economy*. London: A. & C. Black.

Thomas, C. Y. (2003). 'Guyana and the wider world.' *Sunday Stabroek*, Georgetown Guyana, March 9.

Part I

The debate on neoextractivism

1 Neoextractivism and capitalist development

An outline

One of the most important but surprisingly overlooked facts in the debate on the new extractivism is that capitalist crisis and reform creates the conditions in the capitalist periphery that stimulate demands by the ruling elites in those countries for national ownership and or control of their natural resources – agricultural, mineral, metal, water, marine life, and forest products provided by nature – as a development strategy. The intensity of those demands ebbs and flows with crisis and reform in the global capitalist system. The proponents of the new extractivism nonetheless treats this cyclical phenomenon as a conjunctural event associated with the pushback against neoliberal economic adjustment policies in the current era of global capitalism. Whereas a historical analysis of capitalist development in the Caribbean periphery reveals the presence of the phenomenon at different historical periods; it is therefore not a one-time event caused by neoliberal capitalism.

The large-scale extraction of natural resources for sale in capitalist markets has been ongoing for 500 years. Since the turn of the twenty-first century, however, the growing demand for natural resources has been attributed to increasing global consumption of manufactured goods led by China, India and selected African countries. The World Bank, the International Monetary Fund, Western donor states, and international Non-Governmental Organizations have hailed the increase in consumption as an opportunity for development in resource-rich countries in the capitalist periphery.[1] UNCTAD (2014) justifies its advocacy of natural resources driven development on the grounds that the United Kingdom, Northern Ireland, the United States, Canada and the Netherlands, Australia, Malaysia, Brazil, Argentina and Mexico are all examples of commodity-based development. UNCTAD (2014) stated however that in several developing countries the empirical evidence has demonstrated that the link between natural resources and development is not positive. The negative association of development and resource extraction has led to the idea that the developing countries endowed with natural resources are cursed rather than blessed.[2]

The advocacy of commodity-based development in the developing countries, continues to move apace. In their overview of the geological potential of Africa, for example, Buchholz and Stürmer (2011) set out to show the opportunities for additional tax revenue from the extractive sector that could contribute to further financing the sustainable development of sub-Saharan Africa. Buchholz and Stürmer (2011) observed that the economic rise of emerging economies such as China and India among others had altered international commodity markets. The commodity boom between 2003 and 2008 saw prices increased significantly and the terms of trade turned in favor of commodity exporting sub-Saharan African countries. This phenomenon placed the extractive sector high on the development agenda in terms of its potential to generate revenue for economic development (Buchholz and Stürmer, 2011).

The use of revenue generated from the sale of natural resources is precisely what the new extractivism or neoextractivism in Latin America and the Caribbean is all about. It reflects a complex of state–private sector policies favored by the World Bank and International Monetary Fund (IMF) intended to seize the opportunity for development provided by the growing demand for natural resources to produce consumer products. Moreover, in Latin America and the Caribbean region these measures are described as supposedly the strongest pushback by progressive forces against the failed neoliberal economic policies. They are pointed to as ushering in a post-neoliberal era. The new extractivism seeks to utilize the income a country earns from the sale of its natural resources to improve the standard of living of its citizens.

It is regarded as another development model that is being tried out in the Latin American and Caribbean region. It joins the litany of theoretical expositions on development in the region, such as center-periphery, dependency, plantation dependence, the two-sector model, import substitution industrialization, structuralism, neo-structuralism, neoliberalism, and post-neoliberalism. Like its predecessors however neoextractivism is merely a catalyst for capitalist development, spawned by crisis and reform in different historical periods in the evolution of the capitalist system. Capitalist crisis and reform produce theoretical and policy responses about how development can occur in the periphery. These reactions merely serve to reform the capitalist system and to strengthen it, rather than bring about structural transformation.

The failed neoliberal policies are the motive force behind neoextractivism as a means to stimulate development, and not the idea that increasing consumer demand presents an opportunity for development. The latter idea ascribes more power to buyers than they truly have. A similar mythical idea was debunked in the old debate on consumer sovereignty – the power of consumers to determine what commodities are produced. The idea is associated with Smith (1994) who argued that consumption is the sole end and purpose of all production and that the producer's welfare must be satisfied only for promoting that of the consumer. The falsity of consumer sovereignty has long been established so why bring it back into focus in the debate on commodity-led development? Why argue that a country can develop economically because there is an increasing demand for the natural resources it produces? The consumer is not king and does not determine what is produced. It is the capitalist who decides what commodities are profitable to produce and produces them. After 500 years of resource extraction for sale in capitalist markets, where there is always a demand for extracted commodities, why only now is there an opportunity for economic development in the countries that are endowed with those resources?

The extraction of natural resources in the capitalist system is for profit; the consumers do not determine by their demand what natural resources are extracted as primary commodities to produce consumer goods. It is folly to base a development model on the notion of growing consumer demand for natural resources. To base the development of a country on such an idea merely serves to perpetuate the capitalist system. This is how capitalism works, the investment sharks cash-in on the production of commodities that are trending due to high profit and exit those markets as newer lucrative investment opportunities arise. In their drive for profits the capitalists determine demand for their produce through advertisement.

The notion that neoextractivism is a development model is problematic given the relationship between nature and humans who are also a part of nature. Humans depend on nature for their existence, and given this dependence the real problem concerns capitalist development, which treats nature as the private property of the few to be exploited for profit. This is the issue that has to be addressed and not extractivism or neoextractivism. Also, to question whether natural resource endowment is a curse or a blessing to a country, is undoubtedly a non-issue, misplaced and misleading, but for capitalist development. The problem is not with the quantity of natural resources with which the land is endowed, but with the socio-economic system created by humans to secure the utilization of those resources for their survival. The real issue therefore is that of creating a system of production to exploit nature, not to profit the few, but for the survival of the human species, regardless of their position in the production system.

This issue is not fully addressed in the debate on the neoextractivism in Latin America and the Caribbean. The debate on the new extractivism is less than two-decades old, but in the short period since the concept emerged as a subject for study, it has spawned a voluminous literature in fields such as political economy, sociology, economic development, international development studies, and critical development studies. Arguably, this literature has not produced any grand new ideas about an alternative production system save for the works by James Petras and Henry Veltmeyer,[3] which advance the causes of working people in their struggle against the injustices and inequalities that for them are the hallmarks of the global capitalist system and its peripheral sub-systems.

The intellectual authors of neoextractivism and its critics both on the right and left continue to chew on the same old array of issues and themes of social development that occupied the interests of the social sciences of the bourgeoisie. These sciences, which are really derivatives of the positive philosophy are traced back to classical political economists such as Adam Smith (1994) and David Ricardo (2001), and the utilitarian philosophers and social reformers such as Jeremy Bentham (1907), and John Stuart Mill (1965). The singular focus in the social sciences of the bourgeoisie regardless of their economic, political, sociological, anthropological, psychological, environmental, etc. themes or issues, is on predetermined notions of social development or expansion in social welfare as established in the bourgeois classics. The goal in these sciences is to interpret, explain, explore, investigate, or critically analyze the perceived multiple social problems that thwart or positively enhance the human condition, either hampering or bringing about human progress or social development in the image of capitalism. These various pursuits are necessary conditions of capitalism that emerge in the light of the lopsidedness in the distribution of the wealth it creates by the exploitation of the many by the few.

At the level of ideas, the social sciences of the bourgeoisie have facilitated the transition from theological to scientific explanation of social reality in capitalist society, the positive philosophy. In terms of the organization of society these sciences provided the intellectual foundations for the transition from feudalism to capitalism, a realm in which they are still bogged down. This is to say that the bourgeois social sciences remain stuck in their service to capitalism, explaining how the capitalist system works in its multiple manifestation. They are trapped like water in a gourd unable to escape, but merely to work as handmaidens of capitalist development. The ideas they generate in theoretical expositions such as neoextractivism, continue to push the frontiers of crisis-ridden capitalism to new heights.

Kari Levitt-Polanyi believes however that capitalism is at a cross-roads, but that the direction it takes is yet to be determined.[4] What are the possible directions capitalism may take? Is it going to select a path that deepen its stranglehold on society, would it change into something else on its own volition or, will it require revolutionary action by the downtrodden to bring about its transformation? It seems that the major question faced by working people is for them to determine for themselves whether the fundamental transformation of capitalism is possible through effective government planning, market mechanisms, or revolutionary action?

History has demonstrated repeatedly that fundamental change only comes about by revolutionary action. If this is indeed the case, the central task of working people and their leaders is to decisively confront capitalism at its cross-roads, and in their self-interest to push the human development project in an entirely new equitable and just direction. In this chapter we introduce the big ideas explored concerning neoextractivism and capitalist development.

Neoextractivism is a capitalist dynamic

Six theses on neoextractivism and capitalist development are first the phenomenon referred to as neoextractivism in Latin America and the Caribbean is a capitalist dynamic associated with crisis and reform in global capitalism. Undoubtedly, it is the result of capitalist crisis in the 1970s, which involved the failure of capitalist companies to turn sufficient profit. The neoliberal reforms implemented to restore profitability to global capitalism have reeked economic and political mayhem in the capitalist periphery. The reforms stripped working people of their industrial social welfare benefits, increased unemployment due to job layoffs, retrenchment, or downsizing in the public and private sectors, joblessness, higher levels of poverty, declining economic growth, informalization, and the transference of income from wage earners to profit seekers. The crisis and reform turned the tide on working people by increasing the hardships on them forcing their leaders to resort to neoextractivism as a pushback approach against structural adjustment to alleviate the suffering.

Capitalist crisis heightens nationalist struggles over natural resources

Second, the conditions described as neoextractivism involve the stimulation of political demands in the capitalist periphery for state ownership and or control of natural resources. The state then uses the income earned by those industries to promote social and economic development. The burning question concerning the resource-rich countries in the capitalist periphery is: why do these countries that are well endowed with natural resources have to experience such wretched economic conditions, when their resources are sufficient to bring their people a better life? Their riches in natural resources should be able to bail them out from the negative impacts of capitalist crisis and reform. Capitalism as an economic system does not possess the wherewithal to promote equal development across the global system in which it operates, some countries must be up while others are down. There is no equality in the capitalist system. The train of thought that countries have enough resources to deliver a better livelihood for their people and the corresponding intensification of nationalist struggles to own and or control natural resources, exist in different historical periods of capitalist development.

It encourages the domestic political elites, civil society organizations, and academics in the developing countries, to step up the demands for national ownership and or control of natural resources. The deliberate aim of such demands is to ease the economic hardships caused by capitalist crisis and reform. Neoextractivism, which is in effect reflective of just a particular dynamic of capitalist development, is a product of that line of thinking. The advocates of neoextractivism attack the neoliberal reforms of global capitalism for their failure to improve the conditions of the poor and the powerless in both the advanced and peripheral capitalist states.

A central idea explored herein therefore, is the intensification of the struggle for national ownership and or control over natural resources in resources-rich peripheral capitalist countries in periods of crisis and reform in global capitalism. This is done by investigating the conditions that put an end to the colonial slave mode of production[5] or slavery-cum-capitalism,[6] the form of primitive capital accumulation implemented in Guyana and the English-speaking Caribbean which came to an end between 1834 and 1921. The historical conjuncture characterized by the crisis in global capitalism that led to the collapse of the colonial slave mode of production, stimulated the development of center-peripheral capitalist relations amidst social unrest and demands for political and economic independence. The colonial slave mode of production engaged in natural resources extraction in agriculture, mining, and forestry products. It collapsed simultaneously as nationalist movements staked their claims in their self-interest, to own and or control the natural resources with which their country was endowed, to stimulate the economic development of the country.

Crisis in global capitalism produces reforms that pretend to resolve the crisis but instead create further crisis and heaps more hardships on working people in the peripheral states. This situation generates a dialectical response in the capitalist periphery as the countries there engage in different forms of pushback, whether anti-colonial or anti-neoliberal, against the reform policies. The anti-colonial struggle was in part a response to the crisis conditions associated with the form of capitalism that stimulated wars in Europe, and a fight for political independence and national ownership and or control of natural resources in the European colonies. The anti-colonial struggle was similar to the fight against neoliberal capitalism today, namely a fight for these countries to control their political and economic destinies.

The independent nation-states that emerged from the anti-colonial struggles, like their earlier counterparts in Europe, are merely tracts of nature laid claim to by the class forces that exercise power over them. These forces give the tract of nature a name, establish geographical boundaries around it, and use their political, economic and military powers to protect it from invaders, and as a launch pad to invade other such tracts of nature laid claim to by rival powers. The peripheral capitalist nation-states are faced with the indignity of having foreign powers owning the tract of nature that constitutes their countries. The workers in these states depend on the material products of nature for their survival. They must work for the foreign companies that claim ownership of nature. Thus, the case is commonly made that the economic hardships faced by the people in the peripheral capitalist countries are a direct result of foreign ownership of their natural resources. It follows that if that ownership structure of nature was reversed then the socio-economic conditions in the countries concerned would receive a significant boost.

There were two recent signature developments in Guyana, for example, which were highpoints in the struggle in the capitalist periphery over national ownership and or control of natural resources. The first was the nationalization of agricultural and mining entities in the 1970s, and the second their privatization in the 1990s as global capitalism underwent further crisis-driven reforms. Nationalization and privatization are like dialectical opposites in the fight over natural resources between nationalist and imperial forces. The economic surplus generated from the nationalized entities were socialized to the sundry population through social programs such as free education, health, and improved utility services. The privatization of nationalized entities was supposed to resolve the crisis in global capitalism.

Instead privatization policies stripped welfare benefits to the poor, transferred wealth from the poor to the rich, deepened the income and wealth gap within and between countries and regions, and spawned vigorous anti-neoliberal social movements. These social movements played a significant role in bringing about political change that saw the rise of progressive governments also described as post-neoliberal regimes, which won state power in Latin America in the late 1990s and early 2000s.

The post-neoliberal progressive governments have gone on to do almost exactly the same thing that their anti-colonial counterparts in the Caribbean – Guyana, Jamaica Trinidad and Tobago and Grenada – did in an earlier historical period – take ownership and or control of their natural resources and socialized the economic surplus generated in those sectors. We are therefore witnessing a phenomenon in the peripheral capitalist states that ebbs and flows with crisis and reform in global capitalism. In particular, the phenomenon of state ownership of natural resources and the socialization of the surplus produced from natural resources extraction coincided with the reform of the colonial slave mode of production, and reform in neoliberal capitalism. Indeed, reforms in the colonial slave mode of production and neoliberal capitalism are a part of a singular continuous process of capitalist development.

Neoextractivism cannot explain this process because it fails to recognize the trend for what it really is – a cyclical phenomenon associated with crisis and reform in global capitalisms and not a historical event at a particular historical conjuncture in the evolution of capitalism. Moreover, these are historical events that tend to repeat themselves in the capitalist periphery at various stages of the cycles of capitalist crises and reforms. The anti-colonial struggle coincided with the aftermath of the Great Depression, and the two world wars. Indeed, World War II stimulated capitalist economic growth in the Caribbean, which embolden the nationalists to step up their demands for political and economic independence. The neoliberal reforms implemented in response to the crisis of the 1970s resulted in increasing profits for the few. They, however, plunged working people into deeper poverty due to increased unemployment, flexibilization, job insecurity, poverty, and an eventual financial crash in 2008.

Undoubtedly, the idea of ownership of nature provides the class justification for the exploitation of labor in capitalist society. Those who claim to own and or control nature in the capitalist system are a class of individuals labeled the bourgeoisie and the state elites who run the nationalized entities in the peripheral capitalist countries. The state elites purport to exercise ownership and or control over nature in the name of the people, while the bourgeoisie owns and or controls it as private property. It is in this context that the distribution problem comes to the fore in terms of sharing the wealth generated by natural resources extraction to the constituent parts or classes in society.

Development theory, policy reform and the spread of capitalism

Third, neoextractivism is essential to the reform and maintenance of capitalism; it is not intended to transform the capitalist system into an alternative path of human development. Undoubtedly, neoextractivism promotes capitalist development – it is a product of capitalist exploitation of working people in natural resources extraction and the political and economic systems erected in that process. Nowhere does the advocates of neoextractivism call for the overthrow and replacement of capitalism. Their focus is on increasing the crumbs that fall from the table of the transnational corporations engaged in natural resources exploitation in the periphery that go to those natural resources exporting countries.

Neoextractivism is therefore a capitalist phenomenon that promotes capitalist development, since it does not seek to change the status quo of capitalist exploitation. The problem is that some scholars and policy makers in Latin America and the Caribbean regard neoextractivism as yet another development model in the absence of any recognition whatsoever of its true unspoken role like its earlier counterparts, such as dependency, plantation dependence, import substitution industrialization, and center-periphery theories, as another sorry way to promote capitalist development, while pretending to serve the interest of working people.

The other problem is the ease with which the advocates of neoextractivism, while concentrating their attention on the distribution of the economic surplus generated from natural resources extraction, overlooked the crucial fact of the inseparability of human labor power and nature in wealth creation under capitalism. The impression is conveyed by the exponents of neoextractivism that labor is the sole source of all wealth and therefore should receive its greatest share. Hence the heavy emphasis in neoextractivism is on increasing the amount of the economic surplus that goes to labor through government spending on social programs and increased wages.

The tacit justification for increasing labor's share of the economic surplus seems to be in accordance with the misleading position that the German Social Democratic Party adopted in its Gotha Program. That position, as critiqued by Marx (1970), implied that the sole source of all wealth and culture was labor, and therefore the proceeds of labor belonged entirely and equally to all members of society since it is only in and through society that labor is useful. Marx (1970) argued however that accumulated wealth in capitalism depends on nature in terms of the extraction of natural resources as elements of nature and human labor power as a force of nature.

Furthermore, nature is the principal source of the devices and subjects of labor, but humans treat nature as their property, something that they own and belongs to them. Thus, to regard labor as the source of all wealth, leads unwittingly to the bourgeois justification of the exploitation of labor (Marx, 1970). Marx (1970) believed that the capitalist was standing on good grounds for falsely ascribing *supernatural creative power* to labor, due to the fact that labor depends on nature. The worker possesses no other property but his labor power and must therefore in all conditions of society and culture, slave for the capitalist who made themselves owners of the material conditions of labor (Marx, 1970).

Nature and labor power are both sources of wealth, which the capitalist struggles to share among various social forces – a struggle understood as the distribution problem, rather than as class struggle. The puzzle to share the economic surplus under capitalism in terms of incomes which accrue to the land as rent, capital as interest and profit and labor as wages both the money and social wages, is a perennial problem of capitalist development. This problem will only go away when capitalism is transformed into something else and no individual owns the material conditions of labor.

Instead of focusing attention on what needs to be done to eradicate the distribution problem under capitalism, the primary focus of development theory is on reforming the systems of distribution to increase the share of income that goes to working people. This is otherwise referred to as economic or social development. But, the reforms end up taking from the poor to give to the rich. Neoextractivism is reformist to its core as it is preoccupied with the distribution problem as formulated by the classical political economists.

The real issue is not just to reorganize production to improve the redistribution of the economic surplus. The test is to abolish the capitalist production system itself and the social relations to which it gives rise. It is only under such conditions that the distribution challenge in terms of sharing the economic surplus among the various classes created by capitalist production will disappear. It is the contest to obliterate the need to have to distribute the economic surplus to various classes. The classes that constitute the dialectical forces of capitalist production will disappear when capitalism is eliminated – the worker as proletariat vanishes simultaneously as does the bourgeois as capitalist. When these classes vanish new non-capitalist production relations will emerge in newly constructed forms of social organization. Working people and their allies have to make this happen it will not happen by itself.

Neoextractivism as development theory

Fourth, neoextractivism lies within the general framework of development theory, whose sole purpose since its advent with classical political economy – but which was mistakenly believed to have commenced at the end of World War II – has been to perpetuate capitalist economic relations globally. Development theory is concerned with bringing about desirable capitalist political, economic and social change in a specific nation-state, geographic area, or globally. As a consequence, it is the purview of various social sciences disciplines that focus inter alia on increasing income, freedoms, environmental protection, gender, women, and sustainability. Undeniably, neoextractivism is a development theory if only on the grounds that it represents a genuine, albeit flawed, attempt to improve the social and economic conditions of working people. It is concerned with much more than social and economic improvements that result from increased income. It is also concerned with environmental protection, sustainability, gender empowerment, etc.

Veltmeyer and Petras (2014) posed the question whether neoextractivism is a post-neoliberal development model or imperialism in the twenty-first century? They take the position that it is imperialism in the current era. Indeed, neoextractivism is the new imperialism, but as posited in this book it is definitely a development model within the context of the maintenance and expansion of capitalism. The position taken here is that development is a capitalist phenomenon, designed to further the expansion and maintenance of the global capitalist system. Development theory originated in the capitalist system in the search for ideas to bring about progress in the nation-state system that replaced the system of empires, kingdoms and city-states that previously existed. In the 1940s, development theory took a specific turn to bring into focus the colonies and former colonies of the then European powers to keep the decolonization movement within the ambit of the capitalist system. Neoextractivism is a capitalist development model founded on the new imperialism as outlined by Veltmeyer and Petras (2014).

Global capitalism and political change

Fifth, the forces of global capitalism, whether in their colonial, neocolonial, post-colonial, neoliberal or post-neoliberal forms play a central role in bringing about political change favorable to capitalist development in countries in the capitalist periphery that are rich in natural resources. The policies in the capitalist periphery for those countries to own and or control their natural resources become the counterpoints to the imperial forces. Also, they lead to the emergence of various shades of authoritarianism in those states in the quest by the capitalist powers to maintain a presence in those countries. The global capitalists use different means to maintain a presence in the former colonies to secure the supply of raw materials. The development project is regarded as a principal means through which the imperialist states maintain control of raw materials in the periphery. When not bringing development to peripheral countries the forces of imperialism are seeking to bring democracy to them. They sponsor political change through national elections and illegitimate methods including coups and economic and political destabilization. Their sole purpose is to maintain in power political regimes that are favorable to foreign capital.

Clarification of neoextractivism as means to an alternative path

Sixth, an essential feature of the struggle for alternatives to capitalism requires clarification on the subject of neoextractivism as a development model. Clearing-up existing ambiguities about neoextractivism will guide the activities of policymakers and political activists engaged in social movements in the natural resources sector. The objective is to provide these state and non-state actors with the tools to critically analyze neoextractivism as a development model, with a view to finding alternative paths to improve the human condition in Latin America and the Caribbean. Working people and their representative organizations must therefore avoid the pitfall of investing too much of their resources in a development model that only brings them a little more crumbs from the table of extractive capital. The struggle for neoextractivism is not really in the long-term interest of working people.

Illustrations from Guyana

The historical evidence from Guyana, a Caribbean country by virtue of its colonial relations and culture, demonstrates that as capitalism marches forward, driven by crises and reform, there is a tendency for the elites who control the levers of state power to agitate for national ownership and or control of natural resources. It is envisaged that the state would redistribute to the poor the economic surplus generated from extractive activities in order to counteract the hardships posed by crisis and reform. State takeover of natural resources is only a temporary development because global capitalist forces regain control of the situation and strike back to exact revenge on the recalcitrant peripheral states that dare to challenge the system. This happened after the anti-colonial advances in the capitalist periphery, and we are witnessing the same phenomenon in the anti-neoliberal movement. The agendas of progressive governments in Latin America are being rolled back with electoral victories by right-wing forces. Petras and Veltmeyer (2018) identified this situation as representing the end of the progressive era. Indeed, the progressive era ebbs and flows; the anti-colonial movement was progressive, as is the anti-neoliberal globalization movement.

If the anti-colonial and anti-neoliberal globalization movements were about building genuine alternatives to capitalism it would not be that easy for the global capitalists to scuttle their policy agendas and impose even stronger exploitative economic measures to exact revenge. The ease with which these movements are disemboweled is due primarily to the fact that they are at their very core, capitalist. They have not stepped outside of the realm of capitalist production relations. They still depend on the capitalist markets to sell their produce and use bourgeois social science methods to redistribute income and as bases for the organization of society.

The anti-colonial and anti-neoliberal globalization movements must go all the way to defeat colonial and global capitalism and build alternatives to capitalism. Instead, they employed reformist social movement and electoral practices founded on the liberal democratic tradition. Their struggles occasion periodic changes in government, while the capitalist production system remains intact. The period in which the state in the capitalist periphery appears to have the upper hand to redistribute the economic surplus favorable to the masses is itself a part of the evolutionary process of capitalism. It is a capitalist development produced by crises in capitalism, a function of the 'foundational' and 'moving' contradictions embedded within the capitalist mode of production.[7] The state elites can exercise absolute power over the state-owned entities and use that power to punish their opponents and reward their supporters. These entities are used for the personal enrichment of state elites, their families, and collaborators through both legal and illegal ventures.

In Guyana for example, under the People's Progressive Party-Civic (PPP-C) government, a criminalized authoritarian state emerged in the country between 2000 and 2015. The political elites that controlled the criminalized authoritarian state dictated to the business-owning class in classic Bonapartist fashion; a new low for the country and Caribbean region. The state lost all sense of bourgeois nationhood, with its symbols, culture, and national pride, and became a criminal enterprise (Thomas, 2003, 2012). The criminalized authoritarian state operated purely on a criminal basis for the enrichment of the cabal that controlled it. This was in addition to the state elites leveraging the state apparatus to their benefit by obtaining financial favors from big business domestically, and extracting rent from foreign companies desirous of investing in the country's natural resources sector.

Bourgeois nationhood became a mere aside, a thing of unimportance only to be displayed in a cosmetic manner by state elites in the presence of foreign dignitaries and at national holidays to appease sections of the domestic population. Nationhood became racialized, with East Indians focusing on Hindu religious celebrations. Affinity with Hindu religious deities trumped the identification with state symbols. The state was merely a means to get rich to celebrate Hindu festivals and build Hindu symbols. The African segment of the population concentrated on the symbols of the state along with promoting African cultural traditions. Nationhood was expressed as a competition between the celebration of Hindu festivals and symbols and state symbols and African cultural traditions. There was some paltry appeasement of the aboriginal peoples by publicly displaying some of their symbols as well.

As an instrument of repression, the force and violence that the criminalized authoritarian state inflicted on the masses was illegitimate. The criminalized authoritarian state engaged in the illegitimate use of force and violence, contrary to the Weberian[8] view that the state is the sole source of the legitimate use of force and violence. A criminalized authoritarian state cannot use force and violence legitimately. It would seem that the criminalized authoritarian state pursued power purely for economic reasons, while the post-colonial state chased power merely for the sake of power, albeit the elites in the latter also used the state for personal enrichment and to exert control over the private sector.

The post-colonial state elites used state power to take over the ownership and or control of the commanding heights of the economy the economic foundation from which they rule. The post-colonial state elites themselves did not become private businessmen, a position which they combined with state power to rule. The primary interest of these elites seemed to be to show-off their power, and to use it to threaten and leverage others, and oppress their political opponents. The criminalized authoritarian state seized state property and converted it into private property and engaged in corruption to build an emergent East Indian petti-bourgeois class to accumulate more capital. The criminalized authoritarian state was controlled by criminal elements, while maintaining its bourgeois functions to protect the global capitalist and East Indian petti-bourgeois business interests. Simultaneously, the criminalized authoritarian state was in control of the East Indian elites who featured among the petti-bourgeoisie and who use the state to put themselves into the petti-bourgeoisie. Unlike their post-colonial counterparts, the state elites and East Indian petti-bourgeois private sector elites were almost one and the same.

The historical materialist analysis of the evolution of capitalism in Guyana to show how the phenomenon described as neoextractivism is cyclical associated with capitalist crisis and reform, commences with an examination of the colonial slave mode of production instituted in the country by the European colonial powers. The point of departure is the consolidation of the three colonies Essequibo, Demerara and Berbice in 1814 under British colonial rule. The Dutch were the first to occupy Essequibo between 1616 and 1815, Berbice between 1627 and 1815, and Demerara between 1745 and 1815. Under Dutch hegemony these three colonies came under the control of the privately owned Dutch West India Company. The Dutch allowed British immigrants to settle in Demerara from 1746 and British citizens became the majority in the colony by 1760. This allowed the British planters to take over effective control of the affairs of the colony by 1786, although the Dutch owned the majority of the plantations.[9]

The estranged relations between the Dutch West India Company and the British planters over tax increases to cover the cost of government, was spurred on by the war between the Netherlands and Britain in 1781. That war led the British to occupy Berbice, Essequibo and Demerara. France, however, in alliance with the Netherlands seized control of the three colonies, and governed them for two years. The Dutch regained control of the colonies in 1784, which reignited the conflict between the Dutch West India Company and the British planters. Protests by the planters in this conflict eventually led to far-reaching constitutional reforms that became the basis for the British governmental structure in the colonies.

The constitutional reforms introduced a Court of Policy and Courts of Justice comprising Dutch West India Company Officials and planters who owned a minimum of twenty-five slaves. The charter of the Dutch West Indian Company was allowed to expire in 1792 and the newly formed United Colony of Demerara and Essequibo implemented the new reforms and came under the direct control of the Dutch government, while Berbice remained as a separate colony. The French Revolution and Napoleonic Wars led to the French occupation of the Netherlands in 1795. The British declared war on the French in 1796 and from Barbados led a force to occupy the three Dutch colonies – Berbice, Demerara and Essequibo, although the Dutch administration of the colonies remained untouched. Berbice and the United Colony of Demerara and Essequibo were under British control between 1796 and 1802. The Treaty of Amiens returned the colonies to the Dutch, but with the resumption of war between Britain and France in 1803, the British seized the colonies again. The London Convention formally ceded the colonies to Britain in 1814, and in 1831 they were unified under British rule as British Guiana, until political independence in 1966 when the country was renamed Guyana.

The political economy of Guyana in the period since its occupation by the Dutch and final capture by the British up until 1921 is classified as a colonial slave mode of production. That was the form of primitive accumulation that was the starting point of capital accumulation which took place in Guyana, albeit within a severely backward capitalist mode of production. Eric Williams, the noted Caribbean historian classified this mode of production as slavery-*cum*-capitalism. The slaves were a part of the means of production from which the capitalist accumulated the extra-economic surplus or surplus value as profits. Marx observed that, 'primitive accumulation' played 'in Political Economy about the same part as original sin in theology' (Marx, 1992). Once primitive accumulation is set in train, there is no turning back but to deepen the capitalist production process.

In Guyana it was in the colonial slave mode of production that money was changed into capital, and surplus value made through capital, and from surplus value more capital was made. Colonialism was the intermediatory structure that transmitted the influences of emerging capitalism in Europe to Guyana and the wider Caribbean (Thomas, 1984). Slavery was an essential component of peripheral capitalism but its internal dynamics did not ensure that the economic surpluses were to develop capitalism in peripheral countries such as Guyana (Rodney, 1979).

Marx (1992) observed that capital accumulation assumes that there is surplus value and that surplus value presupposes capitalistic production, which in turn presumes that there hitherto exists a substantial mass of capital and of labor power in the hands of workers. This capitalist dynamic turns in a vicious cycle, which begets a primitive accumulation, which precedes capitalistic accumulation (Marx, 1992). Primitive accumulation is the starting point and not the result of capitalist production (Marx, 1992).

The colonial slave mode of production was the starting point of capitalism in Guyana. But at the same time, it represented an expansion of the capitalist mode of production that was taking shape in certain European countries such as England, France and Holland. It was not necessarily a hybrid system comprising capitalism with slavery as Eric Williams (1994) believed. The colonial slave mode of production was imposed by capitalist states, but it was not necessarily capitalist. It merely served the capitalist interests of the European powers, to facilitate capital accumulation in Europe. It was the method European powers used to expand the capitalist system to the Latin American and Caribbean region. The extra-economic surplus produced resulted from the fact that the direct producers were slaves and not wage laborers in which case the capitalist would earn surplus value. The colonial slave mode of production had to become capitalist, and that transformation only happened as the slave system disintegrated and wage labor became the order of the day.

Crisis in the global capitalist system eventually led to the separation of labor from the means of production. It was at that point that a pure form of capitalism replaced the colonial slave mode of production. But, that separation took place in two distinct movements, a short period of apprenticeship, and a longer period of indentureship. Viewed through the lens of Marx (1992), the end of indentureship represented the total divorce of laborers from all property through which they can realize their labor (Marx, 1992). The capitalist system emerged standing on its own legs maintaining this separation, and reproducing it continually and on a larger scale (Marx, 1992).

Marx (1992) observed that the process, which leads to the emergence of capitalism is one which takes away from workers the possession of their means of production. According to Marx (1992) this is a process of the transformation of the social means of subsistence and of production into capital, as well as the producers into wage laborers (Marx, 1992). In effect therefore, primitive accumulation is the historical process through which the producer is separated from the means of production. It is primitive in appearance because it is the prehistory stage of capital and the capitalist mode of production (Marx, 1992). This is the process that David Harvey identifies as accumulation by dispossession, in the new imperialism.[10]

The colonial slave mode of production took almost a century to collapse between 1834 and 1921. Its collapse was due to crisis and reform in the global capitalist system that favored the development of free capitalist labor markets, versus the maintenance of a slave system. The collapse led to the development of full-fledged capitalist production relations from 1921, which in essence could be represented as a transition to center-periphery relations (Thomas, 1974). The transition to full-fledged capitalist production relations in Guyana involved a number of social developments. These included the domestic political struggles to seize control of the country's natural resources form foreign forces who made themselves owners of those resources, the racialization and radicalization of politics and the accompanying economic policies including a flirtation with socialism and communism, an anti-communist pushback spearheaded by the imperialist forces, the emergence of a post-colonial authoritarian state, the rise and demise of a criminalized authoritarian state, and a current post-criminalized or de-criminalized state since 2015.

Natural resources extraction has played a central role in capitalist development in Guyana. The political economy of Guyana from the colonial slave mode of production through the transition to center-periphery relations to the current post-neoliberal period is characterized by the development of capitalism. The whole period of center-periphery relations was marked by the phenomenon characterized today as neoextractivism in Latin America. The progression is from the colonial slave mode of production to full-fledged capitalist production relations, which is an ongoing process of capitalist development in the country.

The Guyana experience with natural resources extraction portrays a particular pattern that is unique to the political economy relations that emerged with the advent of the colonial slave mode of production and its transition to full-fledge capitalism. This pattern of uniqueness could also be extrapolated to the entire Latin American and Caribbean region. In Guyana for example the initial employment of slave labor in mining was to buttress plantation agriculture, namely sugar, and not to encourage natural resources extraction or to develop the mining industry. Mining was only undertaken to serve the interest of plantation agriculture, as crisis at the emergent global capitalist center threatened the survival of the planter class whose economic activities were located in the periphery. The planter class dominated the state and therefore did everything in its powers to ensure that plantation agriculture trumped all other economic activities.

However, both mining and plantation agriculture were cogs in the wheel of capitalist development in both the center and periphery. The extractive industries were therefore an integral component in the evolutionary development of global capitalism.

The agro-extractivist colonial slave mode of production although dominated by agricultural production engaged in natural resources extraction to buttressed capital accumulation when agricultural prices declined in Europe. Natural resources extraction such as mining and forestry activities were not favored by the planter-dominated state because they competed with plantation agriculture for scarce labor. The focus of capital in the political economic relations in which the direct producers were imported as slaves or indentured labors was on agricultural production the principal economic venture for which labor was assembled. The anticipated and final collapse of the colonial slave mode of production in 1921, led to the take-off of natural resources extraction in earnest.

In 1880 for example, the government even imposed a royalty of 2 percent on gold miners to stem the drain of labor from the agricultural sector to the gold mining districts. Then in 1896 the government published its Mining Regulations that increased the cost of mining on gold miners as a hindrance to discourage them from continuing their mining activities. The miners had to pay fees and to fill out lengthy forms to obtain mining licenses. The Mining Regulations subjected the miners to body searches as they left the gold fields (Josiah, 2011).

The state had an interest in protecting agricultural capital while punishing the small miners who sought to break away from plantation agriculture and establish an independent basis for their survival. Large-scale extractive capital in mining and forestry were not in the picture even though in the 1860s one A. V. Abraham established a gold company with a capital outlay of $75,000 (Josiah, 2011). The state was in sync with the dominant mode of production of the day. Its primary interest was to promote agriculture and in particular sugar, and not the extraction of minerals, metals, and forestry products. The state elites comprised, primarily, sugar planters, who by stifling small-scale mining were acting in their self-interest.

While mining helped to sustain plantation agriculture and advance capitalist development, the economic exploitation of gold in Guyana did not bring benefits to the native peoples although they were the first to engage in gold mining. In the fifteenth and sixteenth centuries many European explorers sought to find El Dorado, the legendary city of gold, in Guyana. During the early 1700s, the Dutch West India Company had ordered the production of gold in Guyana, and African slaves and 'bovianders' (African-Aborigine Mixed Race) were the prime producers. Although at times the owners of slave labor diverted their property to engage in the extraction of gold and forestry products, that act was done merely as a crisis survival strategy for plantation agricultural capital.

International political factors such as the border dispute with Venezuela hampered natural resources extraction in Guyana. The disputed land claimed by Venezuela is located in the mineral-rich Essequibo region of the country. The British and Venezuelan governments had agreed that neither side would occupy the

Essequibo until the dispute was resolved. The 1899 Arbitration award finally settled the land dispute, and the Essequibo was opened up for mining, but Venezuela has re-stated its claim to the Essequibo in the 1960s.

Conclusion

Over the past two decades the debate on neoextractivism has brought to the fore various ideas about the role of resource extraction in the social and economic development of Latin American and Caribbean countries. In tandem with the debate on neoextractivism the leading capitalist global institutions have been calling for resource-rich countries to pursue development strategies based on the revenue earned from the exploitation and sale of those resources. Neoextractivism is also based on the utilization of revenue earned from the production and sale of natural resources to promote social and economic development. These two approaches to development are the same but they differ in an important way. The former is market-driven while the latter is a state-led approach.

Neither are concerned with the transformation of power relations in capitalist society; they maintain the status quo of capitalist development. The ruling elites that control state power operate as mere proxies for foreign capital. Their hold on state power domestically depends on the extent of their collaboration with extractive capitalists in foreign countries. The framework for domestic and international economic policies are set by foreign imperial powers. The ruling elites that fail to collaborate with foreign extractive capital are demonized, destabilized, and ultimately overthrown in a process presumptuously referred to as 'regime change.'

The new rulers continue to do the biddings of foreign capital allowing extractive companies to operate with impunity, while retaining an increased share of income through revenue collection to invest in the improvement of the social services. The ruling elites pursuing a resource extraction development strategy are not revolutionaries, they are reformists. Their strategy is designed to increase the share of income that accrue to the state from resource extraction, while allowing the bulk of the wealth to be siphoned off by foreign extractive companies. They are not in open rebellion against capitalism, instead they are very cozy with it.

Moreover, the phenomenon described as neoextractivism is identifiable at different historical periods in the evolution of the capitalist system. It became evident in the transition from the 'colonial slave mode of production' to center-periphery capitalist relations in the Caribbean. It was also evident in the anti-colonial and anti-dictatorial struggles in Guyana, as it was in the anti-neoliberal struggle in Latin America. These struggles are all reflective of crisis situations in global capitalism and the solutions proffered to the crisis.

Notes

1 For an elaboration on the idea of resource-led development see, among many others, UNCTAD (2014), Shikwati (2011), Buchholz and Stürmer (2011), and Stürmer and Buchholz (2009).
2 See for example Venables (2016), Ross (2015), Haber and Menaldo (2011), van der Ploeg (2011), Polterovich, Popov and Tonis (2010), Carmignani, Andersen and Aslaksen (2008), Boschini, Pettersson and Roine (2007), Stiglitz (2004), Stevens (2003), Auty (2001), Sachs and Warner (2001).
3 See for example Petras and Veltmeyer (2018), Petras and Veltmeyer (2016), Petras and Veltmeyer (2015), and Veltmeyer and Petras (2014) among many others of their publications.
4 Kari Levitt made this observation during her address at the 'Roundtable on Economics, Development and Ideology in Historical Perspective,' at the Canadian Association for the Study of International Development, conference under the theme Scholar/Practitioner Collaborations: Next Generation Leadership for the New Development Paradigm (in collaboration with the Canadian Council for International Co-operation), Ryerson University, Toronto, Canada, May 31–June 2, 2017.
5 For an exposition on the 'colonial slave mode of production' see Thomas (1984).
6 The thesis of 'slavery-cum-capitalism' is elaborated on in Williams (1994).
7 For expositions on the 'foundational' and 'moving' contradictions of capitalism see Harvey (2014).
8 See Gerth, H. H. and Wright Mills, C. (1958).
9 The sources of the data on the early history of Guyana: Daly (1974), Daly (1975), Rodney (1993), Merrill (1992), and Government of Guyana Ministry of Information. Available at: www.guyana.org/ [accessed 9 March 2014].
10 Harvey (2003).

References

Auty, R. M. (ed.) (2001). *Resource abundance and economic development*. Oxford: Oxford University Press.

Bentham, J. (1907). *An introduction to the principles of morals and legislation*. Oxford: Clarendon Press.

Boschini, A. D., Pettersson, J. and Roine, J. (2007). 'Resource curse or not: a question of appropriability.' *Scandinavian Journal of Economics*, 109 (3), pp. 593–617.

Buchholz, P. and Stürmer, M. (2011). 'An overview of geological resources in Sub-Saharan Africa: Potential and opportunities for tax revenue from the extractive sector,' in J. Runge and J. Shikwati (eds) *Geological resources and good governance in sub-Saharan Africa: Holistic approaches to transparency and sustainable development in the extractive sector*. Boca Raton, FL: CRC, pp. 17–32.

Carmignani, F., Andersen, J. J. and Aslaksen, S. (2008). 'Constitutions and the resource curse.' *Journal of Development Economics*, 87 (2), pp. 227–246.

Daly, V. T. (1975). *A short history of the Guyanese people*. New York: Macmillan.

Daly, V. T. (1974). *The making of Guyana*. New York: Macmillan.

Gerth, H. H. and Wright Mills, C. (1958). *From Max Weber: Essays in sociology*. New York: Oxford University Press.

Government of Guyana Ministry of Information. Available at: www.guyana.org/ [accessed 9 March 2014].

Haber, S. H. and Menaldo, V. A. (2011). 'Do natural resources fuel authoritarianism? A reappraisal of the resource curse.' *American Political Science Review*, 105 (1), pp. 1–26.

Harvey, D. (2014). *Seventeen contradictions and the end of capitalism.* Oxford: Oxford University Press.

Harvey, D. (2003). *The new imperialism.* Oxford: Oxford University Press.

Josiah, B. P. (2011). *Migration, mining and the African diaspora: Guyana in the nineteenth and twentieth centuries.* New York: Palgrave Macmillan.

Marx, K. (1992). *Capital: A critique of political economy, Volume I.* London: Penguin Books.

Marx, K. (1970). *Critique of the Gotha program.* Moscow: Progress Publishers.

Merrill, T. (ed.). (1992). *Guyana: A country study.* Washington: GPO for the Library of Congress.

Mill, J. S. (1965). *Principles of political economy: With some of their applications to social philosophy.* Toronto/London: University of Toronto Press, Routledge and Kegan Paul.

Petras, J. and Veltmeyer, H. (2018). *The class struggle in Latin America: Making history today.* New York: Routledge.

Petras, J. and Veltmeyer, H. (with P. Bowles, D. Canterbury, N. Girvan, and D. Tetreault). (2016). *Extractive imperialism in the Americas: Capitalism's new frontier.* Chicago: Haymarket Books.

Petras, J. and Veltmeyer, H. (2015). *Power and resistance: US imperialism in Latin America.* Leiden/Boston: Brill.

Polterovich, V., Popov, V. and Tonis, A. (2010). *Resource abundance: A curse or blessing?* New York, NY: UNDESA United Nations Department of Economic and Social Affairs.

Ricardo, D. (2001). *On the principles of political economy and taxation.* Ontario: Batoche Books.

Rodney, W. (1993). *History of the Guyanese working people, 1881–1905.* Baltimore: Johns Hopkins University Press.

Rodney, W. (1979). 'Slavery and underdevelopment,' in M. Craton (ed.) *Roots and branches: Current directions in slave studies.* New York: Pergamon Press, pp. 275–286.

Ross, M. L. (2015). 'What have we learned about the resource curse?' *Annual Review of Political Science*, 18, pp. 239–259.

Sachs, J. and Warner, A. (2001). 'The curse of natural resources.' *European Economic Review*, 45 (4–6), pp. 827–838.

Shikwati, J. (2011). 'How geological resources can aid Africa's development,' in J. Runge and J. Shikwati (eds) *Geological resources and good governance in sub-Saharan Africa: Holistic approaches to transparency and sustainable development in the extractive sector*, Boca Raton, FL: CRC, pp. 9–16.

Smith, A. (1994). *The wealth of nations.* New York: Modern Library Edition. Sixth Printing edition.

Stevens, P. (2003). 'Resource impact: curse or blessing? A literature survey.' *Journal of Energy Literature*, 9 (1), pp. 3–42.

Stiglitz, J. E. (2004). 'The Resource Curse Revisited, Project Syndicate.' (www.project-syndicate.org/commentaries/commentary_text.php4?id=1656&lang=1&m=contributor)s.

Stürmer, M. and Buchholz, P. (2009). *Government revenues from the extractive sector in sub-saharan Africa: A potential for funding the united nations millennium development goals?* Hannover: Federal Institute for Geosciences and Natural Resources, June.

Thomas. C. Y. (2003a). 'More theses on the criminalized state: Guyana and the wider world,' *Sunday Stabroek*, Georgetown: Guyana, August 17.

Thomas, C. Y. (2003). 'Guyana and the wider world,' *Sunday Stabroek*, Georgetown: Guyana, March 9.

Thomas, C. Y. (1984). *Plantations peasants and state: A study of the mode of sugar production in Guyana*. California: University of California, Center for Afro-American Culture and Society Monograph Series.

Thomas, C. Y. (1974). *Dependence and transformation: The economics of the transition to socialism*. New York: Monthly Review Press.

UNCTAD – United Nations Conference on Trade and Development. (2014). *Natural resources sector: Review and identification of opportunities for commodity-based trade and development*. New York, NY, and Geneva: UNCTAD.

van der Ploeg, F. (2011). 'Natural resources: Curse or blessing?' *Journal of Economic Literature*, 49 (2), pp. 366–420.

Veltmeyer, H. and J. Petras (with Verónica Albuja, Pablo Dávalos, Norma Giarracca, J. Lust, K. Sankey, D. V. Tetreault, and Migusl Teubal). (2014). *The new extractivism: A post-neoliberal development model or imperialism in the twenty-first century?* London: Zed Books.

Venables, A. J. (2016). 'Using natural resources for development: Why has it proven so difficult?' *Journal of Economic Perspectives* 30 (1), pp. 161–184.

Williams, E. (1994). *Capitalism and slavery*. Chapel Hill: The University of North Carolina Press.

2 Development theory and capitalist development

Neoextractivism is a development theory that advocates represent as a progressive development model. It can therefore be appraised in the context of a critique of development theory or theories of development, which go hand-in-hand with the maintenance and spread of capitalism in the periphery. In contradistinction to the view that neoextractivism is a progressive socio-economic development model, it is described as a conjunctural phenomenon that becomes manifest at different historical periods in the evolution of capitalism. It is reflective of conditions that emerge in periods of crisis and reform in global capitalism.

The extraction of natural resources is a historical process, which in its current neoliberal form is exhibited as the best representation of the extant socio-economic realities in Latin America and the Caribbean region. Understanding the evolution of resources extraction, however, is best obtained by analyzing the concrete historical conditions that give rise to it under mercantile capitalism, and caused it to progress through time to its current neoliberal form characterized as post-neoextractivism.

Capitalism has converted the extraction of natural resources merely for the survival of the human species, into a profit-making exercise to benefit a small group of individuals who have made themselves the owners of nature. Capitalist development aided by development theory is about how to make natural resources extraction more efficient to profit individuals who lay a claim to nature. Natural resources extraction lies at the foundation of the capitalist economy, since it is from that process that resources become available for manufacturing and upon which rest trade, commerce, finance, etc.

Development theory is an integral component of capitalist development. It is about how nation-states can secure finance to extract natural resources, manufacture commodities from those resources, trade natural resources and the commodities they produce, speculation, etc. These activities are undertaken for profit and capital accumulation. The increase in profit and capital accumulation is described as economic growth, the principal ingredient in development. Economic growth takes place, however, amidst the conditions specified for a lack of development. Economic growth is then criticized on the grounds that it alone cannot necessarily bring about development. Adding social factors such as culture, freedom, democracy, gender equality, etc., to the economic requirements for development, are done nonetheless all within the capitalist framework.

Capitalist development in Latin America and the Caribbean is like the story of Sisyphus in Greek mythology. They are forced to roll a huge development rock up a hill but every time they make some headway with the task at hand, the rock rolls back down, a futile activity that goes on in perpetuity under capitalism. In this chapter we analyze development theory as a conduit for capitalist development, the central problem under consideration.

Development theory and capitalist development

Development theory is in essence about capitalist development – the hitherto sustained evolution of capitalism. The same is true of sustainable development, which is really about prolonging the development of capitalism as an economic system. It follows then that if neoextractivism is a development theory it is merely an approach to capitalist development. Although capitalism started out as a progressive phenomenon vis-à-vis feudalism, meaning it is an advance on feudalism, neoextractivism is not a new socio-economic system intended to replace capitalism. It is not spearheaded by a revolutionary class, which is bent on smashing the capitalist system as the burghers had intended in the case of feudalism.

Development theory does not seek to establish an alternative system to capitalism it is capitalism – it seeks to understand how capitalism works in order to perpetuate the system and expand it to the furthest regions of the globe. Theories that promote alternatives to development are not in themselves development theories, because they are not intended to prolong capitalism, instead they seek to replace it with a different socio-economic system. The alternative to capitalism however has not been fully formulated.

Capitalist development is a process involving the extraction of the resources of nature by human labor power, itself a force of nature, and their conversion into commodities for sale for a profit in capitalist markets. Capitalist development is not typically understood in this way, where 'capitalism' and 'development' are regarded as one and the same process. Development is construed as an increase in the technical composition of capital[1] – the material alignment of plant, machinery, raw material and labor engaged in production – which is the essence of capitalism.

The increase in the technical composition of capital results from a reorganization of production that raises productivity, which involves either capital or labor or both, being used at an increased rate. The neoclassical economists describe this process as a change in the capital/labor ratio.[2] Marx however analyzed it in terms of the 'value' and 'organic' compositions of capital, in which constant capital is the aggregated value of the factory plant, machinery and raw materials, and variable capital is the aggregated value of the labor employed. In essence, nonetheless, the process of production that constitutes capitalist development is the conversion of the elements of nature by the forces of nature into commodities for sale for a profit.

It is this process that is described as extractivism and neoextractivism rather than as what it truly is – the course of capitalist development. Extractivism and neoextractivism seems to be caught in the general outlook on the *absolute immutability of nature* shared at the very beginnings of the modern natural science (Engels, 1934). This means that nature is remains static, remaining in the same position through time (Engels, 1934). To the contrary, however, the fact is that nature has a dialectical existence everything comes into being and passes away (Engels, 1934). Everything in nature large or small exists in a state of flux in unresting motion and change (Engels, 1934). All nature, as well as the societies that emerge from and are erected on it only have a dialectical existence.

Engels (1934) made the observation that humans alone put their stamp on nature by moving the plant and animal world from one place to another. Humans alter the environment in which they dwell, including plants and other animals and their environs. The effects and significance of human activity will only disappear with the extinction of the terrestrial globe (Engels, 1934). The human hand is the means by which humans place their stamp on nature. Technological innovations depend on the hands, which develop step by step with the brain (Engels, 1934). The growing knowledge of the laws of nature by humans serves as a means for reacting on nature demonstrating the corresponding relations between the hand and brain (Engels, 1934).

Human activity that involves extractivism and neoextractivism have only been possible due to the coordinated development of the hand and brain (Engels, 1934). Nature is natural, and humans are a part of nature but extractivism and neoextractivism are not natural phenomena they are forms of social organization, which are products of the hand and brain. They are merely conduits for capitalist development – the reorganization of production means through which capital accumulation occurs.

Capitalism cannot function without the extraction of natural resources or the conversion of nature into commodities for market exchange for a profit. Labor is a force of nature that has to act on nature and natural resources to create the wealth, which the capitalist appropriates for personal and class accumulation. It should be recognized that nature, just as labor, is a source of use values in which material wealth consists (Marx, 1970). Labor is merely a manifested force of nature – human labor power (Marx, 1970).

The classical political economists asserted however that labor is the source of all wealth. Engels (1934) retorted that labor next to nature is really the source because it is from nature that humans secure materials to convert into wealth. Labor does not only interact with nature of which it is a part to create wealth, it is the prime basic condition for all human existence, and therefore creates man himself.[3] The dispute over how this human labor power is rewarded is settled in neoextractivism by redistributing the economic surplus through social programs to benefit working people.

The expansion in social programs is termed 'development' or at least one aspect of it, through which a greater share of the national income is transferred to working people. The term 'development' however is not always understood as one and the same as capitalist development. Although the classical political economists were concerned to know how a nation-state makes 'progress,' which really meant how capitalism progresses, the claim in development theory is that 'development' is some state of economic and political being that the former European colonies in Africa, Asia, the Caribbean and Latin America have to achieve.

Development became a typical Weberian ideal construct, something to strive for but never to be attained. The impression is conveyed in development theory, which traces its origins to the 1940s and 1950s[4] that 'development' is something other than what it really is – capitalist development. There is a failure to recognize the characteristic feature of 'development' understood as synonymous with capitalism, which is the continuous increase in the technical composition of capital. In that literature on development theory, development is regarded as something that only takes place as a result of economic growth. Capitalism is defined as an economic system in which privately owned production is undertaken for profit. The accumulation of profit, which is identified as the income earned by the capitalist, is used as a measure of economic growth.

The theory of capitalist development was founded by the bourgeois social science classified as classical political economy. The focus was on the social effects of human actions in actually intended production and exchange (Engels, 1934). This is precisely the social organization that social science theoretical expressions reflect (Engels, 1934). It was observed that the individual capitalist engages in production and exchange for immediate profit, but that after he sells the commodity he could care less about what happens to it and its buyer (Engels, 1934). Similarly, in relation to nature and society the existing mode of production is mainly concerned with the immediate and tangible result of production (Engels, 1934). In the capitalist mode of production of necessity, private ownership based on one's own labor is transformed into the expropriation of the labor of others, and wealth is concentrated in the hands of non-workers (Engels, 1934).

False origins of development theory

Existing general surveys on the evolution of development theory showed that development theory owed its origins to various historical events and processes around the 1940s. These events included the end of World War II, the collapse of colonialism, and the transition of former European colonies into newly independent nation-states in the capitalist periphery. The argument in those surveys is that development theory had an independent existence that commenced in earnest in the post-World War II era. The development story is told separately from the historical evolution of capitalism. Diana Hunt (1989) for example commences her book with an analysis of the intellectual frameworks or paradigms of development. The theoretical heritage of development theory is identified to include classical political economy, Marxism, neoclassical theory, and Keynesian theories. Development theory has been mistakenly believed to have developed from the 1940s and is classified in terms of the paradigm of the expanding capitalist nucleus, the structuralist paradigm, the neo-Marxist paradigm, dependency analysis, the Maoist paradigm, the basic needs paradigm, and the neoclassical paradigm and its role in development. If we are to embrace Hunt's classification of development paradigms, then today we may have to add to that schema neoliberalism and post-neoliberalism.

It could be deduced from Hunt's framework that development theory focuses explicitly on the economic, social and political policies that the newly independent nation-states needed to implement to mimic in those aspects the European countries that colonized them. Another point of view that is evident in the general surveys is that development theories were written from the perspectives of different disciplines such as economics, political science, sociology, geography and anthropology – 'the social sciences of the bourgeoisie' – which identify the theoretical contributions of each discipline to the subject (Hettne, 1995; Levitt, 1992; Rist, 1997).

Although the interdisciplinary and multidisciplinary nature of the study of capitalist development is recognizable, the common storyline on development theory is that economists first started to theorize on the subject, but that they overlooked its social dimensions, which needed to be added to make the discipline more realistic. Academics who were not economists claimed that the weakness of theories of economic development was that they overlooked the social dimensions of development. The economists retorted that their critics themselves should add the social dimension through their respective disciplines. Thus, political scientists, sociologists, anthropologists, and geographers, felt obliged to begin theorizing on the subject of the capitalist development of the nation-state, thereby adding the missing social dimensions of development theory. In so doing the focus on capitalist development was broadened from merely a concern with economic issues to embrace the political, cultural, and geographical dimensions of development.

Furthermore, the origins of development theory is said to be associated with Point Four in US President Truman's inauguration speech,[5] which divided the world into developed and underdeveloped countries. The speech recognized the need for the latter countries to pursue economic strategies to catch up with, their developed capitalist counterparts. These events and processes combined to launch development in the capitalist periphery as a subject for study and a national goal pursued by nation-states, necessitating a role for development theory as a body of knowledge separate from hitherto existing disciplines, while drawing on the tools of analysis of existing disciplines.

As theorizing on development in the capitalist periphery took off it was no longer regarded in the same light as the classical political economists' pursuit of progress in the European nation-states. In appearance, capitalist development in the European nation-states and the newly independent nation-states in the capitalist periphery became two separate subjects in their own right, with the study of the latter assuming an existence of its own. The study of progress in the European nation-states became identified with political economy, while the study of development in the peripheral nation-states became identified with development theory. In reality however, capitalist development though multifaceted and uneven is a singular process involving the inseparability of the European nation-states and their former colonies – the newly independent nation-states in the capitalist periphery.

Two cautionary words are necessary here in the light of the observation on the singular process of capitalist development. First, this observation is not synonymous with 'world systems theory.'[6] The major difference has to do with the treatment of class analysis in 'world systems theory' which loses sight of the dynamics of class forces and the consequent struggles at the domestic and local levels.[7] Although development theory and capitalist development go hand-in-hand the observation is not being made from a 'world system perspective,' rather it acknowledges that there is class struggle at several levels, which shape the super-structural architecture of society.

Second, the inseparability of the process of capitalist development in the European nation-states and the former colonies in the capitalist periphery may give the impression that a single theory of development is applicable across all countries. The logic would be that since all countries are pursuing capitalist development then the same theory of development applies. This is certainly not the case since each country has its own unique circumstances. Development theory is multidimensional, but all of its facets are geared towards the advancement of capitalism in whatever its form. The neoliberal approach assumes, however, that development theory as a separate sub-discipline is irrelevant, because the so-called laws of economic social science are universal. This means that the theories of economic social science are universally valid and apply with equanimity to both the European nation-states and the former colonies without distinction. This idea that was popularized by neoliberal theorists, is intended to promote the study and understanding of capitalism as a single process in order to maintain and deepen capitalist economic relations globally.

The argument that capitalist development is a single process is intended to serve a completely different end than those of 'world system theory' and neoliberalism. The neoliberal view is that development theory is a distraction from capitalist development due to the fact that it seeks to fashion an alternative set of theories rather than use standard economic theory to analyze the development process in the former colonies. The neoliberal view wants to abolish development theory to promote a pure free market capitalism. Meanwhile, class conflict which is central to capitalist development at the domestic and local levels are missing in 'world system theory.' The intention here is to establish that development theory as a component of 'bourgeois social science,' promotes capitalist development in the former colonies, rather than seek to find alternatives to capitalist development.

The former colonies now pursue capitalist development not as colonies operating on the periphery of the capitalist system, but in their own right as independent nation-states. Whether they carry the status of colonies or independent nation-states their economic activities are at the very heart of the capitalist system – as markets for finished goods, suppliers of natural resources, or providers of skilled and unskilled labor through migration. To consider the countries in Latin America and the Caribbean as being in the capitalist periphery, or to characterize them as dependent is problematic. The problem with center-periphery and dependency theories is that the center and periphery seem to be in dialectical unity and only exist because of each other. Capitalist development in the center and periphery, however, must be understood as a singular process albeit uneven and multifaceted with multiple nuances of class struggle at domestic, regional and global levels, within the overall class struggle between labor and capital.

The pioneering years of capitalist development theory as a separate endeavor from classical political economy are mistakenly identified as beginning in the 1940s. An assessment of the contributions made by the 'development pioneers' – Rosenstein-Rodan (1943), Ragnar Nurkse (1953), W. Arthur Lewis (1954), Raul Prebisch (1950), Hans Singer (1949, 1950), and Gunnar Myrdal (1944, 1956), among others, show that they were all concerned with bringing about structural change to stimulate the accumulation of wealth in the capitalist periphery designated as developing regions and countries. Levitt (1992), however, dated the origins of development theory in earlier periods such as in the First Five Year Plan in Russia in the 1920s, and in terms of certain aspects of British colonial policy in Asia.

Pains were even taken to distinguish between the classical political economists and development theorists. The former is said to be concerned with 'progress' and the latter with 'development' the economic transformation to full-fledged capitalism in the backward former European colonies. Critics argue that development theory does not belong in the domain of formal economics but lies outside of it and therefore should be purged from economics. If we were to understand capitalist development as a singular process albeit with many forms of capitalism, then the origins of capitalist development must be with the general concerns of the classical political economists about what brings about economic and social progress in a nation-state.

The mistakes in efforts to distinguish between classical political economy and development theory and purge development theory from economics are made because of the failure to recognize the almost simultaneous emergence of the nation-state and capitalism. Traces of capitalism were found in the early city-states, but capitalist forces were only unleashed as the nation-state became consolidated. Capitalism needs a home and the appropriate protection of the state to survive. And what better place for a home of capitalism than the nation-state and agency for its protection than the state as an instrument of repression that manages the affairs of the owners of private property.

The view that the newly created nation-states in the capitalist periphery faced different economic challenges to those experienced by the European nation-states is not as clear as it appears. Yes, the newly created nation-states were colonies of the European nation-states, and were created by them for economic exploitation. The development challenges faced by the nation-state in the capitalist periphery, must therefore be quite different to those faced by the European nation-states.

In another sense, however, the economic challenges between these sets of countries remain the same – capitalist development or alternatives to development. If a nation-state is within the orbit of the capitalist system, it is pursuing and engaged in capitalist development. The economic trajectory of the nation-state is capitalist development. The capitalist continuously increases the technical composition of capital as a means of capital accumulation.

The question the colony, now transformed into a nation-state, faces remains the same as that identified in classical political economy – how best could a nation-state accumulate wealth? Development theory answers this question by propositioning that the former European colonies could best acquire wealth by emulating the capitalist development path of the developed countries in Europe and North America. The capitalist development process has always involved heavy doses of state intervention, coupled with appropriate trade policies. Neoliberalism, however, has taken the notion of free trade to the extreme, eliminating all forms of state involvement in the economy including market regulations.

Should a country insulate itself by erecting protective barriers around its economy or should it engage in free trade. This is the problem of capitalist development faced by all capitalist nation-states, old and new, rich and poor, peripheral or center. It is not an issue merely for countries in the capitalist periphery, but one that is systemic to capitalist development, which varies between the extremes of the state and market. However, the historical evidence showed that protection and free trade are not really two ends of a continuum they are positions taken by nation-states at different periods in the evolutionary development of their respective capitalist systems. The advanced capitalist countries erected protective walls around their economies before they became engaged in free trade and continue this practice on a commodity-by-commodity basis as they deem fit for their own economies.

Latin America and Caribbean in development theory

Latin American and Caribbean scholars have played a major role in the evolution of development theory as something distinct from capitalist development. A series of scholarly works on development theory emerged in what is characterized as the ECLAC School,[8] which takes an approach to development that is classified as 'historical structuralism.' Its focus has been on analyzing the diverse ways that the dynamics of economic development in the former European colonies and the behaviors they generate are different from those of the developed economies. Moreover, 'historical structuralism' seeks to explain how those economic undercurrents have been influenced by the institutional legacy and production structure that those countries inherited.[9]

The first mistake of the ECLAC School was its failure to focus its attention on capitalist development, and the second was its division of the process of capitalist development into two separate processes – one for the developed European states and the other for the former European colonies. The goal of economic behavior in the capitalist periphery and developed capitalist center are the same. They are both pursuing the capitalist development of nation-states by increasing the technical composition of capital.

The ECLAC School has adopted the position that the countries in the Latin American and Caribbean region are 'latecomers to development.' As such, the development dynamics in those countries are different to those of nation-states that developed in earlier historical periods.[10] The ECLAC School therefore rebuffs the idea that there could exist uniform 'stages of development.' Instead, it propositioned that the economies in the Latin American and Caribbean region are better explained by their 'structural heterogeneity.'[11]

Although the dynamics of the development process in the rich and poor countries are different, their goal is the same – capitalist development. Development theory *a la* the ECLAC School does not seek to have the countries in the region pursue an alternative socio-economic system to capitalism. The ECLAC has subdivided the theoretical ideas that characterize its approach to development into five phases originating with the promotion of import substitution industrialization (ISI) in the 1950s. The second phase in the 1960s focused on reforms that facilitated industrialization. Third, during the decade of the 1970s development 'styles' were reoriented in the direction of 'social homogeneity,' and economic diversification to increase exports. Fourth, in the 1980s the focus shifted towards structural adjustment to promote economic growth to pay down the external debt. Fifth, production with social equity became the hallmark of the ECLAC School during the 1990s.[12] Undoubtedly, these five phases are all about promoting capitalist development in Latin America and the Caribbean.

The same is true of the work by Lewis (1950) on the industrialization of the British West Indies, and its critics within the plantation dependence school in the English-speaking Caribbean.[13] The Lewis approach to industrialize the British West Indies and the plantation dependence school did not explicitly set out to bring about capitalist development. They advocated for Caribbean development as if it was something different to capitalist development. It should be noted however that the Lewis (1954) 'two-sector model' explicitly hinges a country's development on the expansion of its capitalist sector. Here again, we notice that the Caribbean countries are not seen as a part of the capitalist development process, but only the economic sector, which is classified as capitalist. Through its expansion, though, the capitalist sector takes over the entire economy of a country. The fact remains nonetheless that development in the Lewis (1954) scheme is construed as the expansion of a country's capitalist sector, which will eventually take over the entire country. If this process occurs in every country, then eventually capitalism will take over the entire globe. Lewis (1950), on the industrialization of the British West Indies and the plantation school, focused on the structural economic changes that were necessary for Caribbean nation-states to mimic their colonial masters – capitalist development, while overlooking that is what they actually did.

Those theories were not constituted to build alternative economic systems to capitalism, albeit they seemingly did not analyze development as a capitalist phenomenon. These theories of development were written specifically for Caribbean countries as the former colonies in the region began to prepare to emerge as, and actually became, independent nation-states. Prior to this the Caribbean merely served as colonial outposts for capitalist development from which European nation-states accumulated considerable wealth. When they became nation-states they were treated as pitiful little infants, to be socialized by their parents into the values of capitalism. They were taught how to behave in the image of the capitalist, knowing when to speak and when not to speak; when to laugh, how to laugh and when and how to cry.

The Caribbean was impacted by the debate on the virtues of protectionism and free trade that took place among the classical political economists in Europe. These impacts can be gleaned from colonial policy in the Caribbean contained in various reports of Commissions of Inquiries conducted by the colonial authorities. Colonial economic activity in the Caribbean was definitely an integral component of capitalist development, as is post-colonial economic policies and practices in the region. The Caribbean countries embraced notions of protectionism versus free trade and inward looking versus outward looking approaches, as they achieved nation-state status.

Caribbean contributions to development theory also sought to bring about the appropriate structural reforms in the region to facilitate the stimulation of capital accumulation by domestic and foreign capitalists. This was the essence of the contributions by Lewis (1950), Best (1968), Best and Levitt (1968, 2009), Girvan (1973), Beckford (1972), and Demas (1965). The Caribbean's 'development pioneers' may have plotted different paths to get there but the goal was the same – capital accumulation in nation-states that translates into economic growth, increases in national income, industrialization, and social development through redistribution with growth. Thomas (1965, 1974), had a different perspective on Caribbean development, which required structural transformation of the region's economy such that the peripheral capitalist dependency relations themselves would be replaced by a self-sufficient socialist alternative.

The 'development pioneers' intensified the manufacture of development theory to expand capitalist relations in the former colonies from the 1940s. Ideas on wealth accumulation ranged from modernization theory to its dependency critique and present-day neoextractivism. The plethora of theories of modernization includes Rosenstein-Rodan's 'big push,' Rostow's 'take-off,' Gerschenkron's 'great spurt,' Hirschman's 'backward and forward linkages,' and 'two-gap' theory, Prebisch's 'center-periphery' model, Lewis's 'two-sector' model (Levitt, 1992), neoliberalism, and post-neoliberal neoextractivism. Dos Santos (1970), Cardoso (1977), Frank (1966), Baran (1957), Magdoff (1969), Sweezy (1942), and Sunkel (1973) have generated a bloc of dependency and Marxian theories that challenged hitherto theories of development. The variant of dependency theory emanating in the Caribbean included the works of Demas (1965), Best and Levitt (1968, 2009), Best (1968), Beckford (1972), Girvan (1973), and Girvan and Jefferson (1971). Thomas (1974) provided ideas for the region's socialist transformation from its state of dependence.

The social dimension as capitalist development

There was no real transformation that resulted from the universal ascension to the argument that development theory focused on economic growth and overlooked the so-called 'social dimension.' The absence of the 'social dimension' was also a mistaken claim, because any study of human behavior, whether in its economic, political or sociological aspects, is social. August Comte (1988)[14] introduced the study of the social dimension as science, which has come a long way through the works of scholars such as Smith (1937), Durkheim (2014), Marx (1992, 1909, 1991, and 1863), and Max Weber[15] among others. Thinking on social development, however, is viewed from the lens of the nation-state and goes hand-in-hand with capitalist development. Studying the social dimension as science only came to the fore as capitalist development took off with the emergence of the nation-state. Thus, the social dimension is enhanced by capitalist development. This means that development theory, albeit mistakenly calling for the inclusion of the social dimension, was in effect advocating for capitalist development.

It was established from the onset of capitalism that social development depended on the accumulation of wealth in nation-states. The accumulation of wealth in the hands of the few however does no good for social development, unless the wealth is redistributed. Hence a central critique in development theory of capitalist development took the form of the idea of 'redistribution with growth.'[16] This means that the problem in the capitalist system is that wealth accumulates only in the hands of the few, and unless it is redistributed, social development will only be minimal. This problem created the urgent need to redistribute wealth to the sundry population through social programs *a la* the new extractivism.

Production and distribution were central concerns in classical political economy. Income distribution among the working and capitalist classes was vital to propel the process of capital accumulation. This idea was embraced by development theorists although they differ on what each class should receive in the distribution process and on the use of their respective shares of the national income in social development. Lewis (1954) saw the need, as did the classical political economists and neoclassical theorists, for the capitalist class as the investing class, to take the bulk of the wealth produced in a country. This was necessary to expand the capitalist system of production across the globe. The counter argument to this view is that if the working class receives a greater share of the wealth they will spend more and that would ultimately result in increased profit for the capitalist. Increased spending, however, could lead to inflation that would eat away profit the neoclassical theorists countered.

Sociologists, political scientists, geographers, and cultural anthropologists entered into the development debate to bring something new to the table – the social dimension. In the economic, political and social organization in the nation-state format, however, capitalist development is inevitably a multidisciplinary phenomenon. Capitalist development does not merely embrace the social dimension. It involves the natural sphere in that humans must extract their livelihoods from nature, which is also a social act. How they organize themselves to carry out that basic act for their survival is what is critical. Engels observed that 'the specialization of the hand' involves the development of the 'tool,' which in turn implies 'specific human activity,' meaning the 'transforming reaction of man on nature, production.'

The specialization of the hand nonetheless is not an activity that is historically done for profit except under capitalism. Should private individuals own nature and due to that ownership have power over others? This is the case at present where humans organize themselves along the lines of capitalist development in which the hand is specialized for profit. Until capitalism is replaced and a different system of social organization emerges the hand will continue to specialize for profit. How could there be social development in a capitalist nation-state without the production and accumulation of capital? The argument by Sen (1983) that the social dimension merely changed the pursuit of economic growth from being the end of development to becoming its means is problematic. The social dimension has always been present in capitalist development – production itself is a social activity, as does how the produce is distributed.

The counter movements in development theory, allegedly feminism, postmodernism, and post-colonialism (Schuurman, 1993), which supposedly emerged from an impasse in development studies in the challenge to existing theories of development, have also missed the mark in their interpretation of capitalist development. The idea on the development impasse claims that development thinking along the lines of the grand meta-narratives of development theory got stuck in a cul-de-sac due to the collapse of socialism and the failure of modernization theory to deliver on the benefits of economic growth (Schuurman, 1993). Indeed, the pursuit of economic growth has generated more ecological, social and economical problems than it has resolved.

There could not have been a 'development impasse' however because nation-states did not abandon the mercantilist/classical political economy goal to accumulate wealth, neither was there a hiatus in theorizing about how nation-states could do so. The neoliberal turn constituted a theoretical framework on what nation-states must do to accumulate wealth in a particular phase in the advance of global capitalism. Neoliberal theories and their critics spread over the whole gamut of capitalist production, distribution and exchange relations including service activities, money, banking, finance, manufacturing, mining, agriculture, governance, social sectors, labor, etc.

The reason for the mistaken argument about a 'development impasse' is the false pursuit of development theory as something that is distinct from capitalist development. The failure to recognize development as capitalist development creates a chasm between the search by the classical political economists for the causes of the progress of the wealth of nations, and the quest for economic development in the capitalist periphery as those countries attained their political independence from their European colonizers. This weakness is carried over into purportedly development alternatives that gained momentum in the 1970s. The so-called alternatives involved ideas about the rethinking of development, the poverty in development economics, the death of development, a development impasse requiring new directions in development theory, cultural studies, gender studies, women studies, sustainable development, post-development, and a range of other posts such as post-modernism, post-structuralism, post-Marxism, and post-neoliberalism. These so-called counter movements are not outside of the realm of capitalist development. The nation-state gives them life to formulate their ideas none of which seek to replace capitalism.

The idea of post-development gives the impression that capitalist development is no longer taking place. If development and capitalism go together then post-development is post-capitalism, but this is not the case. If development and capitalism are separate, then post-development does not take us beyond the realm of capitalism. The post-development theorists argue that the pursuit of economic growth by capitalist and socialist/communist commodity production destroys the environment. Thus, growth-free development is necessary to protect the environment, which in essence requires the evolution of a post-development approach. This means that both the capitalist and socialist/communist approaches must be abolished unless they refrain from pursuing economic growth. In other words, both capitalism and socialism/communism could be entertained so long as they are growth-free. Socialism/communism is lumped together with capitalism as evil because they promote economic growth, which harms the environment.

Growth-free development is an oxymoron, however, since economic growth in capitalist development theory is a necessary condition for development. It is production for profit, which is the evil that stimulates environmental destruction, not the use of natural resources to sustain and improve the human condition. Humans have lived off nature for millennia without destroying the environment, but they were not always engaged in capitalist development. Humans cannot move beyond capitalist development, unless they create another form of social organization. They have to construct their society from the concrete relations that embody existing class struggle. Transcending capitalist development is not an impossible task for the simple reason that humans have organized their social, economic and political activities for a much longer time outside of the capitalist economic system than they did under it.

Conclusion

Experimentation with development in the former European colonies since the 1940s has only strengthened the stranglehold that capitalism has on the globe. The capitalist mode of production continues to spread engulfing even the former socialist/communist countries, which since the Great October Socialist Revolution in 1917 Russia, have thus far posed the greatest challenge to capitalism.

The struggle in the former European colonies for political decolonization and economic freedom from their colonial masters has had two principal effects. It has led to the creation of independent nation-states in the capitalist periphery and the deepening of the capitalist mode of production.

Capitalist development really commenced with concerns about how the newly created nations-states in Europe could achieve economic progress – amass wealth. The production of agricultural, extractive, and manufactured commodities for trade in unrestricted capitalist markets was identified as the best way for a nation-state to progress. The idea of free trade in unrestricted capitalist markets gained strength as a counterpoint to protective trade, which was dominant under the mercantile system. Protectionism, nevertheless, has played a unique role in the development of capitalism – the rich countries engaged in restrictive trade practices, while the poor countries are forced to open their markets to free trade.

The newly created nation-states from the political decolonization struggles were faced with the identical problem. What economic measures should the newly independent nation-states in the capitalist periphery implement to progress or develop? Free trade was placed on the agenda as the best way for these countries to develop. Free trade nonetheless is not understood in the same way by its perpetrators. The basic division among the free traders is what some believe free trade needs to be state-driven, while others take the position that the market must be its driving force. Both versions of free trade however are essentially about the fulfillment of capitalist development. Thus, development in the former colonies, whether state-driven or market-driven, is merely a phase within that overall search for economic progress as capitalism marches on to its final demise.

After running its course, development will reach its saturation point and be replaced by alternatives to development. Development alternatives then are not capitalist development, they refer to the institution of systems of production, distribution and exchange of a different ilk, requiring major structural transformation globally. The principal transformation must be in the relationship between humans and nature. Nature must no longer be the private property of any individual and must return to being free from any form of private ownership.

Integral to the evolution of capitalism is the different forms it takes in various regions operating in the capitalist periphery. These different forms of capitalism have led to the viewpoint that development theory and capitalist development are inseparable. If development means that the former European colonies must 'catch-up' economically, politically and socially with the colonial nation-states that once owned them, then development means the spread of capitalism. To catch-up does not mean structural transformation to an alternative economic system. Development theory provides the theoretical framework for capitalist development in both the capitalist center and periphery. It contains a wide range of theoretical and policy ideas, produced by different disciplines in both the social and natural sciences, which countries in the capitalist periphery are encouraged to implement to bring about the desirable economic, political, and social change that would have them catch up in those respects with their European counterparts.

The chapter on development theory outlined here will not sit well with development theorists – especially those who mistakenly source development theory at the end of World War II. The reality nonetheless is that development theory started with the classical political economists whose central concern was to identify the factors that caused nation-states to progress or become wealthy and what can be done to acquire and retain those factors. Throughout the evolution of capitalism this question has preoccupied the minds of scholars whose central concern was/is about making the system better for profit maximization. This is essentially the same concern that engaged the attention of development theorists whose primary interest was in producing ideas to help the former European colonies in Africa, Asia, Latin America and the Caribbean, and Central, Eastern, and Southern Europe, to acquire the economic conditions to make them wealthy capitalist countries. Development only became an explicit concern of academics and policy makers with the advent of the nation-state system.

The accumulation of capital the principal symbol of development in the nation-state is the *raison d'être* of the relentless quest for profit. It was central to the emergence of capitalism, one of its defining characteristics. The classes to which capital accumulates have the upper hand in shaping the development agenda of the socio-economic systems they dominate by virtue of the sheer size and volume of their riches and the political power they exercise as a consequence.

Marxism presents the nation-states with alternative choices to capitalist development. The pursuit of alternatives to development applying Marxian theory is often misconstrued as Marxian development theory. There is no such thing as Marxian development theory. Marx merely presented a critique of capitalist development, *a la* classical political economy, which could provide the bases for nation-states to fashion alternative societies with non-exploitative systems of production, distribution and exchange that is not based on the profit motive. The idea of Marxian development theory arose as a counterpoint to the dominance of capitalist development theory applied to the peripheral countries since the 1940s.

Notes

1 Marx on organic composition of capital.
2 Cleaver, H. (1992).
3 Engels, F. (1934).
4 See for example Rosenstein-Rodan (1943), Lewis (1950, 1954), Prebisch (1950).
5 Truman, H. S. (1949). 'Inaugural address,' 10 June. Available at: www.trumanlibrary.org/whistlestop/50yr_archive/inagural20jan1949.htm.
6 See Wallerstein, I. M. (2011); Wallerstein, I. M. (1987).
7 See Petras, J. (1981). 'Dependence and world system theory: A critique and new directions.' *Latin American Perspectives*, 8 (3–4), pp. 148–155.
8 Economic Commission for Latin America and the Caribbean.
9 ECLAC – UN Economic Commission for Latin America and the Caribbean. (2016). 'History of ECLAC,' 17 December. Available at: www.cepal.org/en/historia-de-la-cepal.
10 ECLAC – UN Economic Commission for Latin America and the Caribbean. (2016). 'History of ECLAC,' 17 December. Available at: www.cepal.org/en/historia-de-la-cepal.

11 ECLAC – UN Economic Commission for Latin America and the Caribbean (2016).
12 ECLAC – UN Economic Commission for Latin America and the Caribbean (2016).
13 Girvan, N. (2005).
14 Comte, A. (1988).
15 Gerth, H. H. and Wright Mills, C. (1958).
16 For an elaboration on 'redistribution with growth' see Chenery, H., Ahluwalia, M. S., Bell, C. L. G., Duloy, J. N. H., and Jolly, R. (1974).

References

Baran, P. A. (1957). *The political economy of growth*. New York: Monthly Review.

Beckford, G. (1972). *Persistent poverty: Underdevelopment in plantation economies of the Third World*. Oxford: Oxford University Press.

Best, L. and Levitt, K. (2009). *Essays on the theory of the plantation economy: A historical and institutional approach*. Kingston: University of the West Indies Press.

Best, L. and Levitt, K. (1968). *Externally propelled industrialization and growth in the Caribbean*. 4 vols. Montreal: McGill Centre for Developing Area Studies.

Best, L. (1968). 'Outlines of a model of the pure plantation economy.' *Social and Economic Studies*, 17 (3), pp. 283–323.

Cardoso, F. H. (1977). 'The consumption of dependency theory in the United States.' *Latin American Research Review*, 12 (3), pp. 7–24.

Chenery, H., Ahluwalia, M. S., Bell, C. L. G., Duloy, J. N. H. and Jolly, R. (1974). *Redistribution with growth*. Oxford: Oxford University Press.

Cleaver, H. (1992). 'The inversion of class perspective in Marxian theory: From valorization to self-valorization,' in W. Bonefeld, R. Gunn and K. Psychopedis (eds) *Open Marxism: Theory and practice, Vol. 2*. London: Pluto Press, pp. 106–144.

Comte, A. (1988). *Introduction to positive philosophy*. Edited with Introduction by Ferré, Cambridge: Hackett Publishing Company, Inc.

Demas, W. G. (1965). *The economics of development in small countries with special reference to the Caribbean*. Montreal: McGill University Press.

Dos Santos, T. (1970). 'The structure of dependence.' *The American Economic Review*, 60 (2), pp. 231–236.

Durkheim, E. (2014). *The division of labor in society*. (Edited with a new Introduction by Stephen Lukes. Translation by W. D. Halls). New York: Free Press.

ECLAC – UN Economic Commission for Latin America and the Caribbean (2016). 'History of ECLAC,' 17 December. Available at: www.cepal.org/en/historia-de-la-cepal.

Engels, F. (1934). *Dialectics of nature*. Moscow: Progress Publishers.

Frank, A. G. (1966). *The development of underdevelopment*. New York: Monthly Review.

Gerth, H. H. and Wright Mills, C. (1958). *From Max Weber: Essays in sociology*. New York: Oxford University Press.

Girvan, N. (2005). 'W.A. Lewis, the plantation school and dependency: An interpretation.' *Social and Economic Studies*, 54 (3), pp. 198–221.

Girvan, N. (1973). 'The development of dependency economics in the Caribbean and Latin America: Review and comparison.' *Social and Economic Studies*, 22 (1), pp. 1–33.

Girvan, N. and Jefferson, O. (eds) (1971). *Readings in the political economy of the Caribbean*. Kingston: New World Group.

Hettne, B. (1995). *Development theory and the three worlds: Towards an international political economy of development*. London: Longman.
Hunt, D. (1989). *Economic theories of development: An analysis of competing paradigms*. Savage, Maryland: Barnes & Nobel Books.
Levitt, K. (1992). 'The state of development studies.' *IDS Occasional Papers*, 92 (1), Saint Mary's University. Halifax: Nova Scotia.
Lewis, W. A. (1955). *The theory of economic growth*. London: Allan and Unwin.
Lewis, W. A. (1954). 'Economic development with unlimited supplies of labor.' *Manchester School of Economic and Social Studies*, 22, pp. 139–191.
Lewis, W. A. (1950). 'The industrialization of the British West Indies.' *Caribbean Economic Review*, 2 (1), pp. 1–51.
Magdoff, H. (1969). *The age of imperialism: The economics of U.S. foreign policy*. New York: Monthly Review.
Marx, K. (1992). *Capital: A critique of political economy, Volume I*. London: Penguin Books.
Marx, K. (1991). *Capital: A critique of political economy, Vol. III*. (Introduced by Earnest Mandel Translated by David Fernbach). London: Penguin Books & New Left Review.
Marx, K. (1970). *Critique of the Gotha program*. Moscow: Progress Publishers.
Marx, K. (1909). *Capital: A critique of political economy, Volume II The process of circulation of capital*. Chicago: H. Kerr and Co.
Marx, K. (1863). *Capital: Theories of surplus value*. Moscow: Progress Publishers, 1863, from www.marxists.org/archive/marx/works/1863/ theories-surplus-value/.
Myrdal, G. (1956). *An international economy: Problems and prospects*. New York: Harper and Brothers.
Myrdal, G. (1944). *An American Dilemma: The negro problem and modern democracy*. New York: Harper and Brothers.
Petras, J. (1981). 'Dependence and world system theory: A critique and new directions.' *Latin American Perspectives*, 8 (3–4), pp. 148–155.
Prebisch, R. (1950). *The economic development of Latin America and its principal problems*. New York: United Nations.
Ragnar, N. (1953). *Problems of capital formation in underdeveloped countries*. Oxford: Oxford University Press.
Rist, G. (1997). *The history of development: From western origins to global faith*. London and New York: Zed Books.
Rosenstein-Rodan, P. N. (1943). 'Problems of industrialization of eastern and south-eastern Europe.' *Economic Journal*, 53 (210/211), pp. 202–211.
Schuurman, F. J. (1993). *Beyond the impasse: New directions in development theory*. London: Zed Books.
Sen, A. (1983). 'Development: Which way now?' *Economic Journal*, 93 (372), pp. 742–762.
Singer, H. (1949). 'Economic progress in underdeveloped countries.' *Social Research*, 16 (1), pp. 236–266.
Singer, H. (1950). 'The distribution of gains between investing and borrowing countries.' *American Economic Review*, 40 (2), pp. 473–485.
Smith, A. (1937). *An inquiry into the nature and causes of the wealth of nations*. New York: Random House.
Sunkel, O. (1973). 'Transnational capitalism and national disintegration in Latin America.' *Social and Economic Studies*, 22, pp. 132–176.
Sweezy, P. M. (1946) *The theory of capitalist development: Principles of Marxian political economy*. London: Dennis Dobson Limited.

Thomas, C. Y. (1974). *Dependence and transformation: The economics of the transition to socialism*. New York: Monthly Review.

Thomas, C. Y. (1965). *Monetary and financial arrangements in a dependent monetary economy: A study of British Guyana 1945–1962*. Kingston: ISER – Institute of Social and Economic Research, University of the West Indies.

Truman, H. S. (1949). 'Inaugural address,' 10 June. Available at: www.trumanlibrary.org/whistlestop/50yr_archive/inagural20jan1949.htm.

Wallerstein, I. M. (2011). *The modern world system I*. Los Angeles: University of California Press.

Wallerstein, I. M. (1987). *The capitalist world-economy*. Cambridge: Cambridge University Press.

3 Extractivism and neoextractivism

In this chapter an analysis is undertaken of the principal existing ideas on the subject neoextractivism in the social sciences literature. The position is taken that neoextractivism cannot be understood in isolation from extractivism, hence the latter concept is also analyzed. The main goal is to explore the subject neoextractivism in a coherent manner to identify the different ways in which the term is used today. The purpose of this exploration is to unmask neoextractivism as a phase in capitalist development. The belief is that by having a sounder understanding of neoextractivism as a capitalist phenomenon, political activists, organizers in radical social movements, and progressive forces in general will be better equipped to conduct the struggle for alternatives to development.

The objective is to provide these forces with ideas for the articulation of counter analyses and actions on the subject of neoextractivism. The principal assumption is that extractivism and neoextractivism are capitalist economic activities to enhance capital accumulation through the exploitation of working people. In order to formulate and articulate counter arguments and actions in this context, it is necessary to know what extractivism and neoextractivism are all about. It is therefore apposite to provide answers to questions such as: what is extractivism and what is neoextractivism? What is the relationship between extractivism and neoextractivism? It is intended that the answers to these questions will provide a clearer picture on what both the proponents and opponents mean when they use the terms extractivism and neoextractivism. Indeed, the meanings of the terms 'extractivism' and 'neoextractivism' have taken several twists and turns in the recent social science literature. They are both regarded as development models based on natural resources extraction, the exploitation and marketing of these resources as exports.

The capitalist development model based on resource extraction provides the organizational foundations of the political, socio-economic and cultural relations inclusive of the economy and class structure, gender relations, the state and public discourse in the countries or regions where the approach is evident.[1] The pervasiveness of the impact of extractivism in natural resources-rich countries is evident from the major role the production and export of those resources play in the national economy and the political, economic, social and environmental struggles engendered in the production process. It is therefore necessary to distinguish between 'extractivism' and 'neoextractivism' to clarify the process of capitalist development and exploitation in the periphery through natural resources extraction.

Perceptions of extractivism

There are five key perceptions of the term 'extractivism' that could be gleaned from the literature surveyed on the subject of neoextractivism. The first of these is that extractivism is a more general concept that involves a system of natural resources extraction perpetuated in the peripheral capitalist countries by the mature capitalist countries. There is a very long and tortured history of extractive capitalism in countries wherever natural resources extraction for sale in capitalist markets has taken place. This has been especially so in geographic regions such as Africa, Asia, the Caribbean and Latin America. It is a phenomenon that is a direct product of capitalist expansion from Europe to the rest of the globe. Extractivism describes in the broadest sense the removal of large quantities of unprocessed natural resources from a country and to send them abroad as exports (Boron, 2015; Acosta, 2013). Extractivism includes the extraction of minerals, oil and gas that are destined for international markets (Giarraca, 2007). It is not limited to the extraction of minerals, metals and oil, however, but includes farming, forestry and fishing (Acosta, 2013). It is part and parcel of the hegemony of development[2] often leading to relations of dependency between providers and users of resources.[3]

A second point is that extractivism may be classified as a 'mode of accumulation' that had its beginnings five centuries ago as the world capitalist system took shape through the conquest and colonization of Africa, the Americas, and Asia (Acosta, 2013). The demand by the European capitalist powers for raw materials have ever since been the driving force behind the extractivist mode of accumulation. In this process an international division of labor developed in which some geographic regions specialized in the production on raw materials, while others concentrated on the production of manufactured goods (Acosta, 2013). Extractivism has been a mechanism of colonial and neocolonial plunder and appropriation of wealth from the colonies, and has appeared in different manifestations over time (Acosta, 2013).

Extractivism was fashioned by the drive to exploit natural resources for the industrial development and prosperity of the global North (Acosta, 2013). It was oblivious to the sustainability of the extractivist projects, the exhaustion of natural resources (Acosta, 2013), and the disruption of the livelihoods of persons who inhabit communities nearby such production sites. The output of extractive industries has been essentially for export rather than domestic consumption, and has generated very little benefits to resource exporting countries. Furthermore, national companies in extractive zones hardly ever produced the goods, inputs and special services that are utilized by the extractive industries. Usually, these goods, inputs and services are primarily imports (Acosta, 2013).

In the light of the fact that extractivism as a capitalist phenomenon is around 500 years old, it is necessary to analyze the significance and needs of the domestic state which has been in existence throughout that period. There is need to focus on the actions and activities of the state as well as those of the extractive industries in order to derive a better understanding of the extractive process under capitalism. This is a major task to be accomplish in the light of the current debate on extractivism and neoextractivism.

Extractivism has been a 'constant in the economic, social and political life of many countries,' which are characterized as the global South (Acosta, 2013, p. 63). A key point to note is that these countries have been affected to varying degrees by the practices of extractivism (Acosta, 2013). To this day, the dependence on metropolitan centers for the extraction and export of natural resources have remained basically unaltered. Some countries however have managed to transform certain dimensions of traditional extractivism by increasing state intervention in the extractive sector (Acosta, 2013). In this connection, what lies at the very heart of the production policies of both neoliberal and progressive governments is 'the extractivist mode of accumulation' (Acosta, 2013, p. 62).

A third point concerns the advance of the idea that extractivism in the era of progressive governments in the Latin American and Caribbean region represents a second phase of neoliberal capitalism (Zibechi, 2011). This means that the pushback against neoliberalism by progressive governments in the Latin American and Caribbean region is itself within the framework of neoliberalism. Extractivism, however, is said to have taken on a new meaning in recent years under progressive governments in the region. These governments are said to operate the economies of countries endowed with natural resources to the benefit of their citizens. The policies of those governments nonetheless are representative of neoliberal capitalism.

A fourth point is that extractivism is presented in terms of various typologies – predatory, prudent or moderate, and essential or basic.[4] Azamar and Ponce (2014) contend *a la* Gudynas[5] that in its most excessive form extractivism is predatory when it exploits natural wealth for short-term profit without regard to its consequences. The costs of predatory extractivism include the erosion and exhaustion of lands, which have severe negative outcomes for local communities and the environment. These costs do not prevent the state from embracing predatory extractivism. Exporting raw materials at high rates of profit and maintaining an unfavorable style of development based on a heavy dependence on export-led economic growth take precedence over local communities and the environment.

The features of predatory extractivism involving open-pit mining and soybeans monoculture include large-scale extensive operations, the creation of enclave economies, a high level of dependence on foreign investment, and no social control and transparency. Its impacts include pollution and destruction of water sources and forests, displacement of communities, source of rights violations (Conventions 169 and 176 ILO), and semi-slavery working conditions (Aguilar, 2012).

Prudent or moderate extractivism refers to extractive activities that are in compliance with social and environmental regulations. It entails medium- to low-scale activities, the existence of environmental, social and fiscal regulations, more adequate use of technologies, and mechanisms to consult citizens and to encourage their participation. Its impacts include a moratorium on the expansion of extractive activities, linkages with local and regional industries in the productive process, and transparency in investment and social control over the income created (Aguilar, 2012).

Environmental and social benefits have higher values that are defining characteristics of prudent extractivism (Azamar and Ponce, 2014). In this case, political and pecuniary desires are placed on a lower scale in comparison with the high values ascribed to the environment and social development. It would seem that the intension under prudent or moderate extractivism is to shore-up the environment simultaneously as production takes place, utilizing new technologies while improving workers' security.

The procedures for extraction and exploitation of natural resources are subjected to rigorous examination before they are approved by the state. The thorough investigation is intended among other things to guard against the encroachment of natural resources extraction on food production zones. Also, at the bottom of prudent extractivism are concerns such as ecological conservation, working conditions that are healthy and humane, the encouragement of increased state control to create a national market to retain in the domestic economy and society the gains derived from natural resources extraction (Azamar and Ponce, 2014).

Essential or basic extractivism is futuristic in that only essential items will be extracted under alternative forms of development. It involves small-scale extractive activities driven by local and regional market demand, special regulation on health and employment, strong fiscal and environmental legislation, community participation and social control, diversification of the economy and reinforcement of local and regional markets. Its impacts include protection of the ecosystem, decreases in labor accidents, poverty reduction, and diversified exports and investment (Aguilar, 2012).

The notion embraces various locally driven activities in natural resources extraction to meet the basic needs of the people involved (Azamar and Ponce, 2014). These resource extraction activities are devoid of any search for great profit through import-export trade. The profits that are secured through the leasing and using of land for extractive purposes however are defended by predatory and prudent extractivism, as well by neo-developmentalism and communitarian socialism (Azamar and Ponce, 2014). In this connection it is advocated that both public and private developmental objectives could be financed by the profits from natural resources extraction, but only through policies that clearly defend social rights and private capital (Azamar and Ponce, 2014).

It was observed that the increase in foreign capital that resulted from extracting and exploiting natural resources should result in improved living conditions, but that this has not been the case in the Latin American and Caribbean region due to the lack of proper regulations (Azamar and Ponce, 2014). The failure to properly regulate extractive activities has increased the conflict between those who pursue profits and the communities in need of security (Azamar and Ponce,

2014). Furthermore, the location of extractive activities has created added problems in that it allows for the development of enclaves. The technologies imported into these enclaves bring very little benefits to the economies of local communities, while simultaneously royalties that are linked to foreign production and distribution networks have to be paid for them (Azamar and Ponce, 2014). The companies operating these enclaves exploit the labor of persons living in nearby towns due to the poverty conditions and state of ignorance that persist in those communities. Simultaneously, however, the people living in nearby towns harbor the illusion that they could improve their incomes because of their close proximity to the enclaves (Azamar and Ponce, 2014).

Furthermore, the wrapping up of enclave mining hits nearby towns very hard in terms of lost jobs, benefits and desertion. Mining companies, pay scant regards to social, local and national welfare issues concerning their operations and departures. The short-term benefits of extractive activities are due to the repatriation of profits by extractive companies and insufficient state regulation of their activities (Azamar and Ponce, 2014). The extractive industries do not stimulate domestic economic growth. Indeed, the hiring of cheap labor, inadequate private investment policies, and aggression against social movements struggling to improve social rights of workers and land rights of indigenous populations, all combine to work against the stimulation of economic growth in the affected countries (Azamar and Ponce, 2014).

A fifth point is that extractivism is a form of primitive accumulation that portrays a crucial contradiction. The incongruity is that natural resources have reproductive cycles that are affected by the productive capacity of extractive activities, which means that the expansion of reproductive cycles required for the pursuit of ceaseless accumulation cannot be met (Azamar and Ponce, 2014). Nature cannot produce sufficient resources to match the infinite demand for profit. The underdeveloped state of Latin American and Caribbean economies makes them easy prey for capital accumulation based on extractivism. It is for this reason that primitive accumulation dispossesses both people and entire nations of their natural resources. People are turned into mere laborers and the natural ecosystem becomes the means of production (Azamar and Ponce, 2014).

To their folly, rather than building on their industrial and technological capabilities the Latin American and Caribbean countries have hedged their bets on economic development on implementing policies to exploit natural resources to maximize profits. In effect, however, these policies end up negatively impacting social and economic development and cause growth to regress (Azamar and Ponce, 2014). There is therefore a conflict between 'production mechanisms and the development model,' which is why it is extremely important for an alternative development model to be found (Azamar and Ponce, 2014).

Humans cannot survive unless they extract their livelihoods from the natural environment, but it is the way they organize themselves to undertake such extractive activities, and the purpose of extraction, which are problematic. The forms of natural resources extraction in political economic structures in antiquity among the Egyptians, Greeks, Romans, and Akans of West Africa, for example, are not what are referred to as, extractivism. Those earlier forms of extraction were not within a system of commodity production for exchange in capitalist markets. The early empires extracted natural resources for their own consumption, as well as for trade, but they were not necessarily for the purpose of capital accumulation under capitalist conditions. Extractivism and neoextractivism are discussed here as creatures of the capitalist mode of production.

Neoextractivism – progressive, neoliberal or imperial

Eduardo Gudynas (2010, 2013) was one of the first to propose the term neoextractivism in the development literature that stimulated debate on the concept. Since its introduction, the term neoextractivism, or 'new' or twenty-first century extractivism has come to be understood in various ways in the development literature. It is understood as a natural resources-based development model that focuses on economic growth, short production networks and subordinate insertion into the global capitalist system (Gudynas, 2010). The state has a central role in the neoextractivist model and seeks to gain legitimacy by redistributing to the sundry population the rents it appropriates from natural resources. The self-proclaimed progressive governments are associated with the model (Gudynas, 2010).

Gudynas (2010, 2013) argues that neoextractivism is a contemporary version of developmentalism that presents economic growth as a way of overcoming social inequality. It is identified with the state-funding of social programs. The state is no longer exclusively responsible for maintaining the rules of production but has a prominent role in the extractive activities. The principal point here is the significance ascribed to natural resources in the neoextractivist model. In this connection, natural resources extraction is for stimulating economic growth, wealth and jobs creation, and the redistribution of income to the poor (Gudynas, 2010, 2013).

The idea of neoextractivism demarcates a set of stratagems that are attached in a group of economic sectors that remove a large volume of natural resources and export them with very little or no processing (Acosta, 2013; Gudynas, 2010, 2013). It was observed that a rentier mentality has been consolidating in the Latin American and Caribbean region along with patrimonial and patronage political practices in society (Acosta, 2013). Natural-resources endowment however did not always have a positive correlation with positive economic outcomes in the region. This has led to assessments of the relationship between natural-resource endowment and economic outcomes within the *resource curse* framework. In this connection a number of phenomena were analyzed including terms of trade deterioration (Sapsford and Balasubramanyam, 1994),[6] high price volatility for natural resources, ineffectual 'economic diversification, and the *Dutch disease*.'[7]

Explored within the field of critical development studies we may identify three broad theoretical perspectives in the emerging literature on the new extractivism. Albeit the theoretical categorizations presented here do not preclude the identification of others, the new extractivism could be classified as progressive anti-neoliberal, a phase of neoliberal structural adjustment, or as imperialism in the twenty-first century. The pertinent question therefore is whether the new extractivism is a progressive, neoliberal, or imperial order? The 'new' extractivism is a phenomenon associated with countries in the Latin American and Caribbean region that were identified as pursuing progressive socio-economic policies. As we shall see below these policies are quite similar in their essence to neoliberal extractivism.

Neoextractivism as a progressive anti-neoliberal model

The new extractivism emerged in the Latin American and Caribbean region in countries that were characterized as representative of a 'pink tide'[8] due to their progressive anti-neoliberal and pro-nationalist economic and social policies.[9] The new extractivism was said to have been spawned by the dynamics of capitalist development at the historical conjuncture characterized by a combination of several factors. These factors included the failure of the neoliberal structural adjustment model, the concomitant anti-neoliberal social movements generated in the process, and the progressive regimes that won state power while riding the crest of those movements on a political platform to replace the draconian neoliberal policies. Neoextractivism is regarded as an outgrowth of the anti-neoliberal social movements, which the progressive politicians supported and on whose backs they won political power.

The progressive regimes proceeded to pursue a development strategy based on natural resources extraction. This strategy involved a combination of measures including nationalization of foreign companies engaged in natural resources extraction, increasing the state's share in foreign companies extracting natural resources, fiscal measures to increase revenue from the operation of companies engaged in natural resources extraction, and increasing expenditure on social services including education and health, and cash transfers. These measures represented a classic case of resource nationalism.[10] The exercise of state power to increase national ownership and or control of natural resources, was a part of a political economy agenda to implement social protection policies that transferred income from the revenue earned from the extraction and sale of natural resources to the most vulnerable sections of the population.

Progressive governments in the Latin American and Caribbean region therefore are seemingly unquestioning of the part extractive industries play in national development. Instead they develop various justifications such as evoking the national interest and public utility for the adoption of the new extractivist model (Gudynas, 2010, 2013). Also, the enormous natural wealth that these countries possess must be a central factor in the meaningful utilization of these resources for economic and social development (Gudynas, 2010, 2013). The implementation of neoextractivist strategies has intensified, especially at a time when commodities were highly priced in the international market due to the rising demand from Asian countries, especially China, and Africa.

The central ideas that distinguish present-day extractivism under progressive and leftist governments in the Latin American and Caribbean region from the extractivism that took place in previous decades are provided in Gudynas (2010). The new sort of extractivism was identified to have emerged under progressive governments in the region. The new extractivism is said to be characterized by both old and new elements. At the same time however, arguably it has fashioned its own uniqueness especially concerning the role of the state and the new sources of political and social legitimacy (Gudynas, 2010).

The new extractivism is therefore not akin to the earlier neoliberal strategy. At the same time, however, it is not a promising alternative to the neoliberal strategy that transforms the social conditions in society for the better (Gudynas, 2010). There is evidence nonetheless that present-day progressivism offers in many cases substantial improvements in the lives of working people over conservative regimes (Gudynas, 2010). Because of this new development the left in the Latin American and Caribbean region cannot be analyzed using old paradigms. It is worthy of note meanwhile that the new extractivism is not necessarily obsessed with the market ideology, nor does it exemplify a socialist paradise; it is characterized by many tensions and contradictions (Gudynas, 2010). If this is the case, then why not call the new extractivism what it really is – a phase in the process of neoliberal capitalist development. It is not an attempt to build socialism, but merely a state-capitalist phase in the evolution of neoliberal capitalist development.

The new extractivism involves the mining, petroleum, new agriculture, and forestry activities for export (Gudynas, 2010). It is said to maintain a style of development based on the appropriation of nature. It depends on international involvement to produce primary materials for export, which does not represent a diversified framework. The state provides extractive activities with legitimacy due to its redistribution of the surplus from those activities to the poor. State-owned companies involved in extractive activities however, have not eliminated the negative environmental and social impacts associated with earlier extractive endeavours (Gudynas, 2010).

The new extractivism is conceptualized as a version of the classic extractivism, which is characterized in terms of the importance of the raw materials exploited and profits appropriated by the transnational corporations, and the state's preservation of the model internally (Burchardt and Dietz, 2014). The deliberations on neoextractivism have been analytical, critical and normative and 'tends to assume the form of a debate on alternative development.' It embraces 'initiatives such as the post-extractivist strategies' proposed by some scholars in the Latin American and Caribbean region (Burchardt and Dietz, 2014).

The neoextractivist development model invests the revenue earned from natural resources extraction in social programs to help the most vulnerable in the society. The social fund established by the Brazilian government, which is financed by oil revenues was identified as an example state investment in social development. The Brazilian government invested in social programs to alleviate poverty, enhance education and culture, and technological change that have a positive impact on the environment (Moreira, 2010). The improvements in the standard of living of Brazilians that resulted from government investment in social programs, however, should be weighed against the grave environmental and social degradation associated with the extractive industries.[11] These latter challenges however, do not constrain government policy concerning the pursuit of economic growth through the extraction of natural resources for export, which is the hallmark of neoextractivism (Aguilar, 2012).

Neoextractivism is regarded as a resource management system, to protect the forest. The term neoextractivism is taken to have 'evolved from movements of the rubber tappers and other forest-based people' (Diegues, 1992, p. 3). It is seen as a 'resource management system,' which 'seeks to protect the forest and provide secure sustainable, forest-based employment for these different groups of people who are dependent on the Amazon forest' (Diegues, 1992, p. 3). Also, 'it attempts to maintain the socio-cultural identity of indigenous populations' such as the native peoples of the region (Diegues, 1992, p. 3).

Neoextractivism as a neoliberal structural adjustment model

The Ghana-case in Africa is taken to analyze the new extractivism as a structural adjustment model. The Ghana-example is examined in the light of the fact that theorizing on the new extractivism in African countries has not been broached by many scholars (Huber, 2014). The new extractivism in Ghana represents the rapid expansion in natural resources extraction since the implementation of neo-liberal structural adjustment by the Provisional National Defense Council (PDNC) in 1983 (Ayelazuno, 2014; Hilson, 2002, 2004). This view reflects a particular thesis on the new extractivism that Veltmeyer and Petras (2014) advanced. The view is that neoextractivism is imperialism involving inclusive growth based on large-scale foreign investment, private sector development and active state support within the orbit of the Washington Consensus. Neoliberal structural adjustment – imperialism in the twenty-first century involving free market policies, privatization and deregulation has unleashed the forces of the new extractivism that restored prosperity to the natural resources sector in Ghana and Ghana's economy in general.

Arguably, structural adjustment in Ghana has delivered whatever economic prosperity the country has enjoyed in recent years. Ghana has been classified by the international community as a lower-middle-income country since 2010 due to its relatively reasonable level of economic growth. The satisfactory growth figures have even led to the vulgar challenge by Ofosu-Mensah to 'scholars who doubt the transformative, developmental, and poverty-alleviation roles of the mining industry in Ghana' (Ofosu-Mensah, 2016, p. 1).

The empirical data on Ghana's economy however do not substantiate such a brash declaration. The primary reason to doubt the claim is that 'the transformative, developmental, and poverty-alleviation roles of the mining industry in Ghana' is that the structure of Ghana's economy remains dependent on foreign capital. This places Ghana in a subservient position of having to do its best to please external investors, whose sole purpose for investing in the natural resources sector is to generate profit for themselves and not to bring about the economic transformation and development of the country.

In recent years however, 'a fundamental development strategy' (Ayelazuno, 2014) of all Ghanaian governments has been the promotion of large-scale mining spearheaded by transnational mining companies (TNMCs). Ghana's development strategy has been in line with the position taken by the World Bank, International Monetary Fund (IMF) and the international development community about the development potential of extractive industries (Ayelazuno, 2014). The new extractivism in Ghana meanwhile has spawned a substantial amount of horrendous 'injustices against peasants and artisanal and small-scale miners' (Ayelazuno, 2014, p. 292). The injustices included land-dispossessions that were quite similar to the violence of primitive accumulation, which was responsible for the agrarian transformations in European countries that led to the emergence of capitalism and capitalist development (Ayelazuno, 2014).[12] It is undeniable that the peasants and small miners who experience these injustices are a part of the people development seeks to address (Ayelazuno, 2014).

Hilson (2009) argues that the new extractivism is very much present in Sub-Saharan Africa. In his view the new extractivism in Africa resulted from the entrenched presence of a foreign controlled large-scale economy in the continent. The new extractivism is understood in terms of external control of large-scale mining due to neoliberal policies. These policies ensured that there was an increased flow of foreign direct investment (FDI) to the extractive industries; changes in the institutional architecture for governance in Ghana's mining sector, and the increased contribution of mining to Ghana's economy (Hilson, 2002, 2004; Ayelazuno, 2014).

Agbesinyale (2003) established nonetheless that there existed a gold-poverty paradox in Ghana. This paradox led to the conclusion that Ghana is inflicted by the resource curse; its gold wealth is a source rather than the solution to its underdevelopment in the country. Hilson and Potter (2005) also reported that the rampant growth in Ghana's informal mining sector was stimulated by structural adjustment in Ghana, which has also marginalized its impoverished participants. The shift in policy towards structural adjustment resulted in an increased inflow of FDI, which revitalized the extractive industries and produced substantial growth in productivity (Hilson, 2002, 2004; Ayelazuno, 2014).

It is a mistake however to source the emphasis on resource extraction to generate revenue for social development in Ghana, as did Hilson (2002, 2004) and Ayelazuno (2014), to the neoliberal policies of the Provisional National Defense Council (PDNC) and subsequent Ghana-governments since 1983. The Ghana-government in 1957 had expressed the desire to increase revenue from minerals exports to promote development by reducing poverty and inequality, and increasing the sundry population's access to quality education, health, housing and social security (Nkrumah, 1965).

Neoextractivism as today's imperialism

Veltmeyer and Petras (2014) advanced the thesis that the new extractivism is imperialism of the twenty-first century.[13] They argue that the new extractivism of the post-neoliberal state, which supposedly focuses on the economics and politics of natural resources extraction is merely the latest twist and turn in the politics of extractivism imperialism. They investigated this development as an imperialist strategy of natural resources exploitation and its consequences. The outcomes of this strategy include developments such as capital accumulation founded on the pillage of natural and human resources, environmental degradation, the disruption of the livelihoods of people living in communities affected by resource extraction, and increased class struggle from below in resistance (Veltmeyer and Petras, 2014).

Veltmeyer and Petras (2014) presented the argument that the crisis-prone capitalist system is currently in the grips of a deep multidimensional crisis and analyzed the economic and political policy dynamics of natural resources extraction. Their review of FDIs in Latin America under neoliberal globalization has led them to argue that structural adjustment paved the way for the expansion of capital, capitalist development, and imperialist exploitation. They believe that in recent decades the consensus was that there had emerged a post-neoliberal state focused on the economics and politics of natural resource extraction. Veltmeyer and Petras (2014) presented nine theses on extractive imperialism in contradistinction to the new extractivism.

In their view, extractivism is a defining feature of the post-neoliberal state in the current context. The new extractivism takes two different forms, one in which the state follows a neoliberal path towards national development within the orbit of the Washington Consensus and US imperialism as exhibited one time by Columbia and Mexico. The other is represented by 'progressive extractivism' and 'post-neoliberal developmentalism' epitomized by Argentina, Bolivia and Ecuador. There is also a moderate and pragmatic form of post-neoliberal regulationism and progressive extractivism represented by Brazil, Chile, and Uruguay; and a more radical form of progressive extractivism in Bolivia, Ecuador and Venezuela, oriented towards socialism in the twenty-first century (Veltmeyer and Petras, 2014).

Another thesis argues that neoextractivism is contradictory in terms of the unsettled debate on whether extractivism is a curse or blessing. In addition, dependence on foreign investment in a policy of resource extraction is a development trap. It is a fallacy to believe as in progressive extractivism that extractive rents can finance and sustain a process of inclusive development (Veltmeyer and Petras, 2014).

The costs of extractive capitalism exceeded any of its actual and potential benefits. The social and environmental impacts of extractive capitalism are viewed in the literature on the new extractivism from a social and environmental perspective based on cost-benefit analysis rather than from a class-struggle perspective. The resistance in the extractive sector is united in regard to extractivism but divided on capitalism. Finally, there are three models concerning the new extractivism – inclusive growth based on large-scale foreign investment, private sector development and active state support, which Veltmeyer and Petras (2014) termed, imperialism. The second model is in a neo-structuralist mold in the form of progressive extractivism and inclusive development based on a post-Washington Consensus. The third model is under construction by advocates of radical change – the need to move beyond capitalism (Veltmeyer and Petras, 2014).

Critique of progressive and neoliberal extractivism models

The progressive anti-neoliberal and neoliberal structural adjustment theoretical renditions of the new extractivism reveal three important considerations. First, the new extractivism is a development strategy based on the extraction of natural resources for sale in capitalist markets. Second, it is oriented towards the implementation of social protection policies to promote social development, the funding of which depends on the revenue the state earns from the sale of natural resources. Third, it is a state-driven process determined by the state's ownership and or control of natural resources and social development policies to redistribute income in favor of the poor and vulnerable population.

The argument against these two theoretical views on the new extractivism is that resource extraction is not a sustainable basis on which to erect an economic development strategy. In both theoretical scenarios the new extractivism promotes the capitalist exploitation of natural resources. This is really a state-capitalist process to transfer income to the poor through social programs, rather than advancing sustainable development alternatives to capitalist development.

Also, there is nothing new about these two formulations on the new extractivism. The new extractivism is present-day imperialism that perpetuates the transfer of wealth from the countries in the south to the center states in the north.

It relies on the imperial and domestic states to create the institutional architecture of laws and regulations for the smooth operations of foreign and domestic extractive capital. It depends on foreign extractive capital for investments in the natural resources sector. Undoubtedly, the neoliberal policies governing the extractive sector in Ghana for example are merely a return to the kind of imperial policies, which allowed European powers to pillage the country's wealth for centuries. The neoliberal approach to resource extraction perpetuates the mercantilist and colonial or traditional or predatory methods that drained the country of its wealth leaving very little behind. The neoliberal policies on resource extraction in Ghana are intended to and have placed a break on the inward-looking import substitution industrialization strategy that existed between 1960 and 1983.[14]

Resources-based development model

The World Bank, the IMF, Western donor states, and international non-governmental organizations (NGOs) have also promoted a natural resources-based development strategy for resource-rich countries. The World Bank (2011) observed that there was a growing presence of the state-involvement in the mining industry. This development had led to 'new forms of state control' in

Africa, and Russia, China, India, and other emerging economies (World Bank, 2011). The argument advanced was that through public ownership and or control the state managed to increase its revenue from the extractive industries. The state then invested its new-found revenue in projects that are beneficial to the society and environment. The World Bank, the IMF, Western donor states, and international NGOs are not opposed to the use of revenue from resource extraction to promote economic and social development.[15]

Undoubtedly, their concern is over the forms of ownership in the natural resources sector – state or private, and whether there is too much state regulation as opposed to market freedom. They favor the private ownership over state ownership and the free market over government regulations in the natural resources sectors. They however regard the growing demand for natural resources since the turn of the twenty-first century as an opportunity for development in resource-rich countries in the capitalist periphery.

UNCTAD (2014) justifies its advocacy of natural-resources driven-development on the grounds that the United Kingdom, Northern Ireland, the United States, Canada and the Netherlands, Australia, Malaysia, Brazil, Argentina and Mexico are all recent examples of commodity-based development. According to UNCTAD (2014), the empirical link between natural resources and development was assessed to have negative results in several developing countries, leading to the conclusion that natural resources are a curse and not a blessing.

Buchholz and Stürmer (2011) however focused on the opportunities for additional tax revenue from the extractive sector that could contribute to further financing the sustainable development of Sub-Saharan African states. They observed that the economic rise of emerging economies such as China and India among others had altered international commodity markets. The commodity boom between 2003 and 2008 saw prices increasing significantly and the terms of trade turning in favor of commodity exporting Sub-Saharan African countries. This phenomenon has placed the extractive sector high on the development agenda in terms of its potential to generate revenue for social and economic development (Buchholz and Stürmer, 2011).

The fact that the World Bank, IMF, Western donor states, and international NGOs have all been promoting a natural resources-led development strategy, demonstrates that the new extractivism have much in common with neoliberalism. Indeed, the common denominator in the approach by the World Bank group and the new extractivism approach is the use of revenues from resource extraction to promote economic and social development. It is for this and other reasons that the new extractivism is considered as present-day imperialism.

The left turn in extractivism and its challenges

The new extractivism in Latin America and the Caribbean is regarded as a turn to the left and away from neoliberalism. In this instance some of the problems presented by the new extractivism are highlighted, in order to represent the grave challenges faced by the model. The left opposition fostered the belief that once they secured power they would pursue a different approach to development. The major contradiction concerning this progressive extractivism however is that the left governments have implemented the very conventional means of development including the extraction of natural resources by foreign corporations that they vehemently opposed while they were in the political opposition.

The left governments however exhibited many differences while sharing similar platforms with the old extractivism including criticisms of the market, the use of state activism, the advocacy of a fight against poverty, and engagement in a contemporary form of extractivism similar to the old extractivism. The extractivist sectors therefore maintain their importance as a pillar of the development strategies in the developing countries in the Latin American and Caribbean region despite the left turn (Gudynas, 2010).

The states engaged in the left did not seek to abolish capitalist production relations in the natural resources sector and national economies. The struggle between labor and capital remained as the principal contradiction in those societies. Both the old and new extractivism in its progressive and neoliberal variations operate on the basis of capitalist production relations. The role of the state as a means of force, violence, power and domination of others by the group that controls it remains the same.

The false division between progressive and neoliberal approaches hides the underlying conflict between capital and labor relations in capitalist development. Although it is argued that progressive and neoliberal new extractivism are basically the same, a distinction can still be made between them. This is because progressive governments have introduced a number of alternations to the tax and royalty systems, and renegotiated mining contracts. These changes are what have led to the claim that a new style or type of extractivism have emerged in the region, which is different to what existed in the 1980s and 1990s under neoliberal regimes.

The old extractivism under the neoliberal doctrine lowers taxes, tariffs and licenses fees, reducing the surplus collected by the state and subjecting it to a trickle-down effect. In neoextractivism, a substantial change is that the state is much more active in capturing surpluses (Gudynas, 2010). The new extractivism policies allow the state to capture a larger portion of the surplus from resource extraction. This surplus is then invested in social programs that generate legitimacy for both the government and the extractive industries, which in essence helps to pacify local social demands (Gudynas, 2010).

The new extractivism is now regarded as something to combat poverty while the old extractivism was criticized by the left as being the cause of poverty. To this effect the new extractivism is viewed as an engine of economic growth, to combat widespread poverty. This takes place under the assumption that economic growth will trickle down via state action to the poor and vulnerable members of society (Gudynas, 2010).

The new extractivism is therefore presented as a new ingredient in the contemporary Latin American and Caribbean 'version' of development. It pretends to be heir to previous ideas about how a country could achieve modernity and material progress. In reality however, it is merely a result of unique cultural political conditions found in the Latin American and Caribbean region (Gudynas, 2010).

The state is mistaken to have played a limited role under conventional extractivism by transferring business management and relationships to the market. The new extractivism however, is said to be characterized by a much more active interventionist state in the natural resources sector. On close observation however, the association of the interventionist state with the extractive sector as a new phenomenon is definitely not the case at all. The state in these peripheral capitalist societies has always been active in creating the conditions for foreign capital to operate in the extractive sector.

This new extractivism rests on greater international involvement, world trade and capital flows that makes it handy for global business and destined to finance and maintain the subordination of the Latin American and Caribbean region (Gudynas, 2010). As the flow of capital increases, production rises, and profit from natural resources extraction sent outside the region skyrockets. Maintaining the subordination of the region to foreign capital however does not say much about the contradiction between labor and capital in extractive capitalism or how this situation could be resolved in favor of working people.

The exploitation of natural resources under the new extractivism has led to deterritorialization and territorial fragmentation and a monoculture for exploration (Gudynas, 2010). The production enclaves that result from extractive activities are well protected by the state. The enclaves have become a significant ingredient in the process of geographic fragmentation in certain regions (Gudynas, 2010). There is a strong state presence within the enclaves, but it is not guaranteed that the presence of the state will be adequate and homogenous, in the surrounding 'deterritorialized' regions (Gudynas, 2010). Thus, citizens' rights, health care and the administration of justice are severely constrained with limited protections within the deterritorialized areas. In several of these areas the state is weak or absent, but very much present to protect and support extractive activities (Gudynas, 2010). This situation has produced a network of enclaves connected to global markets that exacerbates territorial tensions (Gudynas, 2010).

The problem with this analysis is that the separation of enclaves and the deterritorialized areas fails to properly address the issue as part of the dynamics of capitalist production and the conflict between labor and the capital it produces in natural resources extraction. Besides, the characteristics described as being associated with the new extractivism are not really new developments. As will be shown in a separate chapter, the transition from the colonial slave mode of production to center-periphery relations portrays similar characteristics albeit not necessarily to the same degree. Issues such as deterritorialization and territorial fragmentation, limitations in the protection of rights of citizens, health services, and the administration of justice, the emergence of mining enclaves, environmental destruction, etc., have all been present in that transition.

While there was competition for property under the old extractivism, in the new extractivism the state is predominant and tightens its controls over access to resources (Gudynas, 2010). In spite of the fact that the progressive governments have tightened controls over natural resources, there are certain truths that they need to recognize. The rules of the game of production remains to increase profit while externalizing social and environmental impacts (Gudynas, 2010). In other words, as things change in terms of the ownership structure of the natural resources sectors they remain the same in terms of the production processes, profit maximization criteria, and externalization of social and environmental costs. This is the identical script that is being rewritten from the decolonization phase of global capitalism in the Caribbean.

The severe social and environmental impacts of natural resources extraction have generated much polemic on the subject of the new extractivism. The new extractivism increases social and environmental impacts, and at the same time it generates state actions to confront and address these issues. Many state actions however are ineffective and weak (Gudynas, 2010). The social and environmental impacts and citizen conflicts that abound under the new extractivism, are reminiscent of the decolonization process in the Caribbean.

Environmentalism was not on the agenda in the period characterized by the transition to center-periphery relations in the Caribbean, to the same degree as it is today in Latin America. There were social movements in Guyana however, such as the Reform Association and the Reform Club that had concerns with a number of related issues of the day (Rodney, 1981). This new vision of natural resources extraction is indeed problematic because it is describing a condition of capitalist development identifiable under decolonization, but claiming it is unique to South America.

It is a false idea however that capitalist development is promoted either by the market or the state. This dichotomy is false because the market falls within the protection of the state. It is the state that determines whether the market is free or not – the capitalist market does not have an existence of its own it is completely dependent on the state. The new extractivism as a development model therefore did not result from conditions unique to Latin America and the Caribbean. It is a phase in capitalist development associated with reform in global capitalism.

As global capitalism is reformed it creates conditions for peripheral economies to appear as though they have greater freedom to pursue a different mode of development. In reality however, these countries remain within the capitalist orbit. The advocates of the new extractivism recognize this latter point in that they claim that the more things change the more they remain the same in terms of production profits/efficiency criteria and the socialization of the environmental and social costs associated with natural resources extraction. The new extractivism seems to be an apologist theory for the left governments in Latin America, suffice it to say that the new 'extractivist style as an economic way out' of the present global crisis has historical precedence. The nationalizations in Guyana in the 1970s were also seen as a way out of the situation of foreign domination of the extractive industries.

Acosta (2013) contends that extractivism and neoextractivism are two sides of the same curse.[16] In many countries around the world, poverty is associated with the presence of significant natural resources wealth (Acosta, 2013). Many of the poor countries are rich in natural resources, and their economies are based primarily on extracting and exporting those resources. But, these countries remain underdeveloped despite their possession of an abundance of primary resources (Acosta, 2013).

The new extractivism is described as a progressive post-neoliberal strategy that focuses on the export of raw materials (Ruiz-Marrero, 2011). In this connection, neoliberal extractivism has held the countries in the Latin American and Caribbean region in bondage to the global North and has destroyed the environment. But under the new extractivism the environmentalists have promoted a 'post-extractivist model' that allows natural resources to be used in a rational and sustainable manner primarily for local use. This approach has facilitated a truly national endogenous economic development (Ruiz-Marrero, 2011). The new extractivism is regarded as being 'post-extractivist in orientation.' This orientation is said to reflect the philosophy of sumak kawsay of the indigenous peoples' movements, a term which translates roughly as right livelihood or living well (Ruiz-Marrero, 2011).

In post-neoliberal 'progresismo' or 'twenty-first Century Socialism,' unlike under neoliberalism, the state has a greater role in participating in the economic affairs of the country, directing a part of the foreign exchange funds into social programs. In the same period that the state directs post-neoliberal 'progresismo' extractivism, China has replaced the United States as the main importer of raw materials from the Latin American and Caribbean region (Ruiz-Marrero, 2011). It is a mistake to believe however that the state has a greater role in twenty-first century socialism than under neoliberalism. It is quite obvious that neoliberalism cannot function without the state. The state is what creates the framework of rules and institutions for neoliberalism to materialize.

The 'progresismo' state is capitalist and carries out the functions of a typical capitalist state. The state in post-neoliberal 'progresismo' Latin America cannot be characterized as a 'dictatorship of the proletariat' because it is not the product of a proletarian revolution. The state under neoliberalism and post-neoliberalism capitalism therefore are not two separate entities. In appearance, the former allegedly adopted a hands-off posture towards the economy and the latter has a hands-on position in the economy. Nonetheless, the state under neoliberalism was just as hands-on in the economy as it is under post-neoliberalism. What is different is the class orientation of the state towards the economic surplus produced from natural resources extraction.

While the neoliberal state sought to maintain that the economic surplus remained in the hands of the capitalist, the state in post-neoliberal 'progresismo' is oriented towards having a greater share of the economic surplus redistributed to the poor through social programs. It is really a welfare-type capitalist arrangement being paraded as progressive and leftist. Neoliberalism existed in theory and would remain in that realm, unless the state used its powers to implement and enforce it in practice. The practice of neoliberalism is therefore a creature of the capitalist state. The state was all over neoliberalism; it cannot be said that neoliberalism was anti-state because it could not have existed without the state.

Nothing has really changed in post-neoliberal 'progresismo' except that the label post-extractivism has been replaced by neoextractivism. The extraction and export of raw materials continue as before, but now is justified with a progressive discourse (Ruiz-Marrero, 2011). Undoubtedly, there has not been any structural change to the economy that allowed for a different production system in natural resources extraction. It is only that the state has a greater role in rent generated by natural resources extraction. In this scenario the state exercises some control over the corporations and use social policy to redistribute the income it earns form resource extraction. There continue to exist a paternalistic and clientelist relationship between the state and transnational capital involved in resource extraction. Thus, even though there is some social improvement there is no real change in the pattern of accumulation and wealth concentration (Ruiz-Marrero, 2011).

In the new extractivism, 'endogenous development' is no longer the goal of national development, as economies lose their autonomy in their relations to global markets. There is deindustrialization as some national industries are closed and others fail to recover. The new extractivist style of development does not generate enough employment and large export volume replaces productivity. The large export volume increases the pressure on natural resources and leads to many social conflicts. The increase in exports of natural resources is regarded as a factor that would reduce poverty, but that does not happen. This fact reinforces the need for greater autonomous and endogenous development strategies (Ruiz-Marrero, 2011). Post-extractivism, which is advanced as an alternative to neoextractivism does not reject but rather, establishes the biological and physical constraints of exploitation, and seeks to eliminate poverty and its causes. Arguably, it is moving towards a post-petroleum economy, as the rate of consumption of oil far exceeds its deposits in the region (Ruiz-Marrero, 2011).

At another level, neoextractivism is presented as a new approach to development, and as a progressive but not revolutionary development alternative that favors the poor – neo-developmentalism. Arguably, neo-developmentalism and neoextractivism are variations of capitalist development (Milanez and Santos, 2015). They are post-neoliberal regimes that could face similar long-term challenges (Milanez and Santos, 2015). In other words, there could be more post-neoliberal regimes in the making since neoliberalism is a sort of a barometer against which other spinoff models are measured. But, while neoextractivism is regarded as a post-neoliberal phenomenon in some cases it is treated as a neoliberal phenomenon. The concepts neoextractivism and neo-developmentalism are conjoined, with the latter term representing an alternative development strategy to classic developmentalism and neoliberalism (Milanez and Santos, 2015).

Neo-developmentalism promotes development through industrialization and exports while focusing on the exchange rate, and the structural economic and social impacts of its policies. It is critiqued on the basis of the ambiguities between policy prescription and practice and its focus on the enduring features of neoliberal and monetary policies (Milanez and Santos, 2015). Both neo-developmentalism and neoextractivism originated as strategies in countries that have experienced developmentalism and neoliberalism, and maintain some of the elements of those previous discourses on development (Milanez and Santos, 2015).

These concepts are regarded as post-neoliberal terms that evolved as part of the reaction to neoliberalism in the Latin American and Caribbean region from the mid-1980s to the early years of the new millennium (Milanez and Santos, 2015). Post-neoliberalism concerns the simultaneous achievement of economic growth while deepening democracy (Milanez and Santos, 2015). Post-neoliberalism is not post-capitalism; it is merely a variation of capitalism. Also, capitalism does not have a monopoly on democracy, capitalism exists with a variety of authoritarian political forms including fascism and apartheid.

The post-extractivism debate

The problems associated with neoextractivism have led Gudynas (2013) to put forward the idea that there is need for a transition to post-extractivism in the Latin American and Caribbean region. Post-extractivism avoids predatory extractivism and encourages moderate and basic extractivism (Aguilar, 2012). The view was expressed that the development style being pursued in the region was unsustainable since it depended on the export of raw materials and there were still serious difficulties hampering poverty elimination, and environmental protection.

The economic bonanza from raw materials exports masks the global multi-dimensional economic, financial and climate change problems facing the region. But, the short-term sweet derived from natural resources extraction in mining, oil and gas, and agro-industrial practices lies at the bottom of the development style that allows for that practice to continue despite the grave environmental harm, serious social tensions and protests, and displacement of indigenous communities.

Given this scenario, alternative development has to confront the issue of natural resources extraction since the appropriation of nature for economic growth is at the foundation of the capitalist economic system. Alternative development must be founded on post-extractivism – transition to another development or to '*Buen Vivir*,' an indigenous concept referring to 'good life' (Guillén, 2014). The development goals of ecological sustainability, decent work and social security critical to good living have been unmet in the poor countries.

In this context, Ecuador and Bolivia have embarked on alternative development founded on the indigenous Andean philosophy of the *Buen Vivir* as its national developmental vision (Guillén, 2014). According to this philosophy human wellbeing and sustainable use of natural resources are the goals of development not economic growth (Guillén, 2014). The *Buen Vivir* approach nonetheless does not square well with the dominant neoextractivism approach to development (Guillén, 2014).

Some key arguments to justify the transition to post-extractivism include the impacts of the extractive industries on the environment, the conflict situations they generate, and the limited economic benefits that accrue to domestic economies. Also, there are other issues that justifies the advocacy of post-extractivism, namely that extractivism externalizes social and environmental costs that increase economic costs. It focuses the economy on primary commodities, while thwarting economic diversification, and generating minimal employment. Furthermore, the dependence on non-renewable resources such as oil and gas, and global climate change are some other justifications (Gudynas, 2013; Acosta, 2016).

The post-extractivist alternative is faced with many constraints due to resistance to it by governments and broad sectors of the society and the lack of convincing details on how it can be achieved.[17] Also, it is difficult to achieve the proposed post-extractivism alternative in the light of policies pursued by the developed countries. A case in point for example is the EU's integrated strategy on Raw Materials 2008 (Aguilar, 2012). The raw material strategy brings together a number of policies that focus on securing EU access to raw materials in the international markets. Consequently, it guarantees a more intensive exploitation of raw materials, while simultaneously reducing local industry's dependence on imported strategic raw materials (Aguilar, 2012).

The EU has a strategy that links 'investment to international trade negotiations and European policies of growth and employment' (Aguilar, 2012). The emphasis on linking investment and international trade negotiations has had a debilitating effect on 'sustainable mining.' Indeed, the practices of sustainable mining are abandoned in favor of a strategy that has an explicit goal to 'guarantee competitiveness and growth of the European economy' regardless of 'the social and environmental impact of those measures in other countries' (Aguilar, 2012).

The essence of the problem is that of capitalist development because with private ownership of nature, capitalist countries are going to compete with each other for strategic natural resources to guarantee their hegemonic position in global capitalism. Power is therefore at the very center of natural resources extraction in that the country that controls the extraction of strategic natural resources has more power than those that do not. The big powers engaged in this competitive process are the US, China, the EU and Russia, along with other medium-sized or semi-peripheral powers such as India, Brazil and South Africa.

The control of natural resources is key to the structures of power in global capitalism. The more capital a country accumulates the greater its access to natural resources globally. Historically, in recognition of this fact the Europeans set about to control strategic natural resources such as coal and steel to ensure that no single European country had a monopoly to those critical resources. While under mercantilism control of precious metals or commodity money was a key determinant of a country's power, today it is control over natural resources used to manufacture other commodities.

It was Germany's control over steel and coal that enabled Adolph Hitler to wage war on the rest of Europe. To prevent such a situation repeating itself in the future, the Europeans decided to establish Commissions to regulate coal and steel production thereby taking away the possibility of any single country gaining the upper hand in the consumption and stockpile of those resources. The military and economic significance of natural resources trumps household consumer demand for those products.

This is an important dimension of the profit motive, without which the growth in profit is stymied. Control of natural resources has to do with the economic concerns of their use to feed industry to maintain profit, employment levels, manufactured commodity output, and trade on the one hand, and on the other the maintenance of the means of war to protect profit. Thus, there is an imperialist dimension that lies at the very foundation of the capitalist scramble for natural resources.

Conclusion

Notice that much of the discussion on extractivism and neoextractivism is really about the dynamics of capitalist development. There is recognition in small sections of the literature that neoextractivism is indeed not transformative but remains within the domain of neoliberal capitalism. But, there is compelling evidence that much of the literature focuses on neoextractivism as development theory that can improve the conditions of working people within the domain of capitalist development.

The struggle to achieve the phenomenon identified as development has led to a variety of theorization on what needs to be done to obtain it. Various models and ideas have been put forward on the subject, yet the problems that development is supposed to resolve continue to persist. The real issue, which is the problem of development as capitalist development, has thus far eluded the development theorists. Capitalist development cannot produce the socio-economic transformation in the periphery that the development theorists desire. Capitalist development can only proceed in the exact manner that is has thus far since the advent of capitalism – some states become rich, while others remain poor.

The foregoing discussion sought to define extractivism and neoextractivism as the terms are discussed in various sections of the current literature on the subjects. The main purpose is to reflect on the contradictory nature of the concepts and especially neoextractivism as an alternative form of development. It presents the argument that the debate on neoextractivism is misguided for the simple fact that it deals with surface manifestations of the process of capitalist development, which is mistaken for something new. Neoextractivism is an integral component of capitalist development in the current era of neoliberal capitalism. It must therefore be analyzed for what it is about – capitalist development, and nothing else. This is the most fundamental flaw in the proposition on neoextractivism either as a progressive development because it redistributes income in favor of working people, or as post-extractivism. We now turn our attention to an analysis of the myth or reality of neoextractivism.

Notes

1 For an elaboration on this point see Brand (2013).
2 See Giarraca (2007); Böhm and Brei (2008) for more on the hegemony of development.
3 On the issue of dependence between providers and users see Misoczky (2011).
4 Azamar and Ponce (2014) elaborated on the typologies of extractivism advanced by Gudynas (2010, 2013).
5 See Gudynas (2013, 2010) for more on the typologies of extractivism.
6 For more on the assessment of the terms of trade in the relationship between resource endowment and economic outcomes see Sapsford and Balasubramanyam (1994).
7 For more on this see Davis and Tilton (2005), as quoted in Acosta (2013).
8 The pink tide referred to the Peronists in power in Argentina between 2001 and 2015; the United Socialist Party in Power in Venezuela since 2007 following the election of Hugo Chavez in 1999; the Workers Party in power in Brazil between 2003 and 2015; Evo Morales's Movement for Socialism in power in Bolivia since 2006; and Rafael Correa's PAIS Alliance (Patria Altiva i Soberana, *Proud and Sovereign Fatherland*) in power in Ecuador between 2007 and 2017. See Jorge and Castaneda (2006); Cameron and Hershberg (2010).
9 This process is being rolled back, see Petras and Veltmeyer (2018).
10 On resource nationalism see Bremmer and Johnston (2009).
11 For more on this point see Aguilar (2012).
12 Also see Ayelazuno (2011).
13 See also Petras and Veltmeyer (2016).
14 For a review of industrial development in Ghana see Ackah, C., Adjasi, C. and Turkson, F. (2014).
15 See for example UNCTAD – United Nations Conference on Trade and Development (2014); Shikwati (2011); Stürmer and Buchholz (2009).
16 See Acosta (2013).
17 See the ideas expressed by Aguilar (2012) in this connection.

References

Ackah, C., Adjasi, C. and Turkson, F. (2014). Scoping study for the evolution of industry in Ghana. World Institute for Development Economics Research (WIDER) Working Paper 2014/075, April.

Acosta, A. (2016). 'Post-growth and post-extractivism: Two sides of the same cultural transformation.' *Alternautas (Re) searching development: The Abya Yala Chapter*. Translated by Dana Barblec. www.alternautas.net/blog/2016/4/6/post-growth-and-post-extractivism-two-sides-of-the-same-cultural-transformation.

Acosta, A. (2013). 'Extractivism and neoextractivism: Two sides of the same curse,' in M. Lang and D. Mokrani (eds) *Beyond development: Alternative visions from Latin America*. Permanent Working Groups on Alternatives to Development, Amsterdam, The Netherlands: Transnational Institute, pp. 61–86.

Agbesinyale, P. K. (2003). Ghana's gold rush and regional development: The case of Wassa West District. *Spring Research Series*, 44, Dortmund, Germany: University of Dortmund.

Aguilar, C. (2012). 'Transitions towards post-extractive societies in Latin America: An answer to the EU raw materials initiative.' *Southern Alternatives to EU Trade Policies*. Dublin: Comhlámh.

Ayelazuno, J. A. (2014). 'The "new extractivism" in Ghana: A critical review of its development prospects.' *The Extractive Industries and Society*, http://dx.doi.org/10.1016/j.exis.2014.04.008.

Ayelazuno, J. A. (2011). 'Continuous primitive accumulation in Ghana: The real-life stories of dispossessed peasants in three mining communities.' *Review of African Political Economy*, 30 (130), pp. 1–13.

Azamar, A. and Ponce, J. I. (2014). 'Extractivism and development: Mineral resources in Mexico.' *Problemas del Desarrollo, Revista Latinoamericanan de Economíca*, 45 (179), October – December.

Böhm, S. and Brei, V. (2008). 'Marketing the hegemony of development: Of pulp fictions and green deserts.' *Marketing Theory*, 8 (4), pp. 339–366.

Boron, A. A. (2015). 'Buen vivir (sumak kawsay) and the dilemmas of the left governments in Latin America.' *Climate and Capitalism*, August 31.

Brand, U. (2013). 'Austria and Germany energy policy and resource extractivism: Resistance and alternatives,' in *Energy policy and resource extractivism: Resistance and alternatives*, compiled by Marlis Gensler, Rosa Luxemburg Stiftung Brussels, March 22.

Bremmer, I. and Johnston, R. (2009). 'The rise and fall of resource nationalism.' *Survival*, 51 (2), pp. 149–158.

Buchholz, P. and Stürmer, M. (2011). 'An overview of geological resources in Sub-Saharan Africa: Potential and opportunities for tax revenue from the extractive sector,' in J. Runge and J. Shikwati (eds), *Geological resources and good governance in Sub-Saharan Africa: Holistic approaches to transparency and sustainable development in the extractive sector*. Leiden, Netherlands: CRC Press, pp. 17–32.

Burchardt, H.-J. and Dietz, K. (2014). '(Neo-) extractivism – a new challenge for development theory from Latin America.' *Third World Quarterly*, 35 (3), pp. 392–410.

Davis, G. A. and Tilton, J. E. (2005). 'The resource curse.' *Natural Resources Forum*, 29, pp. 233–242.

Diegues, A. C. (1992). *The social dynamics of deforestation in the Brazilian amazon: An overview*. Geneva: UNRISD.

Giarraca, N. (2007). 'The tragedy of development: Disputes over natural resources in Argentina.' *Sociedad*, 3, pp. 1–14.

Gudynas, E. (2013). 'Transitions to post-extractivism: directions, options, areas of action,' in M. Lang and D. Mokrani (eds), *Beyond development: Alternative visions from Latin America*. Permanent Working Groups on Alternatives to Development. Amsterdam, The Netherlands: Transnational Institute, pp. 165–188.

Gudynas, E. (2010). *The new extractivism of the 21st century: Ten urgent theses about extractivism in relation to current South American progressivism*, Americas Program Report. Washington, DC: Center for International Policy, January 21.

Guillén, M. A. (2014). 'The *buen vivir* in Latin America: An alternative developmental concept challenging extractivism in Ecuador,' in K. Fakier and E. Ehmke (eds) *Socio-economic insecurity in emerging economies: Building new spaces*. London and New York: Routledge, pp. 195–206.

Hilson, G. (2009). 'Small-scale mining, poverty and economic development in Sub-Saharan Africa: An overview.' *Resource Policy*, 34, pp. 1–5.

Hilson, G. (2004). 'Structural adjustment in Ghana: Assessing the impact of mining sector reform.' *Africa Today*, 51 (2), pp. 53–77.

Hilson, G. (2002). 'Harvesting minerals riches: 1000 years of gold mining in Ghana.' *Resource Policy*, 28, pp. 13–26.

Hilson, G. and Potter, C. (2005). 'Structural adjustment and subsistence industry: Artisanal gold mining in Ghana.' *Development and Change*, 36(1), pp. 103–131.

Huber, M. (2014). Extractivism and transition in Africa: Opportunities and challenges. Thesis presented in partial fulfilment of the requirements for the degree of Master of Philosophy in Sustainable Development in the Faculty of Economic and Management Sciences at Stellenbosch University, April.

Jorge, G. and Castaneda, J. G. (2006). 'Latin America's left turn.' *Foreign Affairs*, 85(3) (May–June), pp. 28–43.

Maxwell, A., Cameron, M. A. and Hershberg, E. (eds) (2010). *Latin America's left turns: Politics, policies, and trajectories of change*. Boulder, Colarado: Lynne Rienner.

Milanez, B. and Santos, R. S. P. (2015). 'Topsy-turvy neo-developmentalism: An analysis of the current Brazilian model of development.' *Revista de Estudios Sociales*, 53, Julio–Septiembre, pp. 12–28.

Misoczky, M. C. (2011). 'World visions in dispute in contemporary Latin America: Development X harmonic life.' *Organization*, 18(3), pp. 345–363.

Moreira, S. (2010). 'Dilma Rousseff and Brazil's oil sector.' (An Americas Society and Council of the Americas Energy Action Group Issue Brief), Council of the Americas. www.as-coa.org/sites/default/files/DilmaRousseff_BrazilsOilSector.pdf.

Nkrumah, K. (1965). *Neo-Colonialism: The last stage of imperialism*. London: Nelson.

Ofosu-Mensah, E. A. (2016). 'Mining in colonial Ghana: Extractive capitalism and its social benefits in Akyem Abuakwa under Nana Ofori Atta I.' *Africa Today*, 63 (1), pp. 22–50.

Petras, J. and Veltmeyer, H. (2018). *The class struggle in Latin America: Making history today*. New York: Routledge.

Petras, J. and Veltmeyer, H. (2016). *Extractive imperialism in the Americas: Capitalism's new frontier*. Chicago: Haymarket Books.

Rodney, W. A. (1981). *A history of the Guyanese working people, 1881–1905*. Baltimore: The Johns Hopkins University Press.

Ruiz-Marrero, C. (2011). 'The new Latin American "progresismo" and the extractivism of the 21st century.' *Our Place in the World: A Journal of Ecosocialism*, February 20.

Sapsford, D. and Balasubramanyam, V. N. (1994). 'The Long-run behavior of the relative price of primary commodities: Statistical evidence and policy implications.' *World Development*, 22 (11), pp. 1737–1745.

Shikwati, J. (2011). 'How geological resources can aid Africa's development,' in J. Runge and J. Shikwati (eds), *Geological resources and good governance in Sub-Saharan Africa: Holistic approaches to transparency and sustainable development in the extractive sector*. Leiden, Netherlands: CRC Press, pp. 9–16.

Stürmer, M. and Buchholz, P. (2009). *Government revenues from the extractive sector in Sub-Saharan Africa: A potential for funding the United Nations millennium development goals?* Hannover: Federal Institute for Geosciences and Natural Resources, June.

UNCTAD – United Nations Conference on Trade and Development (2014). Natural resources sector: Review and identification of opportunities for commodity-based trade and Development, Geneva, 2 TD/BC.I/MEM.2/26; http://unctad.org/meetings/en/SessionalDocuments/cimem2d26_en.pdf.

Veltmeyer, H. and Petras, J. (2014). *The new extractivism: A post-neoliberal development model or imperialism in the twenty-first century?* London: Zed Books.

World Bank (2011). *Overview of state ownership in the global minerals industry*. Extractive Industries for Development Series, No. 20, May.

Zibechi, R. (2011). 'Ecuador: The construction of a new model of domination.' *Upside Down World*, August http://upsidedownworld.org/main/ecuador-archives-49/3152-ecuador-the-construction-of-a-new-model-of-domination.

4 Neoextractivism

Myth or reality

Is the 'new extractivism' new or is the condition it describes merely a social phenomenon that becomes manifest at specific historical conjunctures as capitalism changes its form? The wrong answer to this question could perpetuate a dangerous myth about natural resources extraction and lead to the continuance of misrepresentations and misunderstandings that would find their way into class struggle and policy formation on the subject. It would preserve the misallocation and squandering of scarce resources expended in the area, and jettison the struggle for state power to transform the status quo in natural resources extraction thereby maintaining the conditions of capitalist exploitation. Alternatively, the correct answer would lead to an exploration of a new realization concerning the subject of capitalist development in general and in the capitalist periphery in particular. It would clarify hitherto misunderstood important theoretical issues in the literature on the question of capitalist development involving the extraction of natural resources. The object of this analysis is capitalist development, whose subject matter focuses on natural resources extraction.

The underdeveloped peripheral capitalist countries that are in search of a path to capitalist development have been thus far revealed to be the principal domain in which the characteristic features of the so-called 'new extractivism' have become manifest. This is due to the fact that the dominant form of capitalism in general has succeeded in regenerating underdevelopment in the peripheral capitalist countries by exercising ownership and control over their natural resources and siphoning off for accumulation in the capitalist center the economic surplus produced from the exploitation of nature. In such conditions, at the slightest chance that nationalists in the capitalist periphery have to take control of state power they do so and seek to reverse foreign domination of their economies. The nationalist implement policies to take ownership and or control of their natural resources and to use the economic surplus for the socio-economic development of their peoples and countries. But, their lofty intentions are scuttled simply because their approach is not transformative but merely reformist and therefore end up maintaining the capitalist status quo and perpetuating the capital-labor contradiction rather than abolishing it. The struggle between the developed and underdeveloped components of the capitalist system is a natural dynamic condition of capitalist development.

Capitalist development in African, the Caribbean Small Islands Developing States (SIDS), and the Latin American periphery is easily misconstrued as a struggle to bring those geographic regions up to the political, economic and social standards found in the rich capitalist countries. In reality, however, capitalist development in the periphery is really an ongoing struggle for political and economic independence from the economic domination by the rich capitalist states. To achieve the level of political, economic and social conditions that are obtained in the rich states, the peripheral countries must struggle for their political and economic independence. But, the development path they pursue in such a milieu will be capitalist because what they are seeking to do is to mirror the capitalist development of their oppressors rather than struggle for an alternative way of organizing production, exchange and distribution.

The capitalist development struggle commenced in different historical periods in the various peripheral capitalist social formations. It became a central issue especially as the process of political and economic decolonization began in those regions. The transformation from colony to nation-state status in the capitalist periphery has intensified the search for development to replace foreign political and economic control. Capitalist development became a single process characterized by two conflicting zones – the imperial powers and the colonies, the developed and developing countries, or for the want of a better term the center and periphery countries. Capitalist development is therefore the dialectical process of the unity and struggle of the capitalist center and periphery.

The essence of this contradiction is really between capital and labor that only can be resolved when they are both abolished as a direct relation of domination under capitalism. The developed countries only exist because there are developing countries both facing each other as opposite sides of the capitalist continuum. If one is abolished, so too is the other because they only exist because of each other in a dialectical relationship. This outcome will only occur with the resolution of the contradiction between capital and labor, which is at the heart of the struggle between the center and periphery. The struggle for development only produces different means by which center-periphery relations are articulated and the labor-capital dichotomy is perpetuated in capitalist society.

For many years, development was construed as something that only the former colonies needed to achieve, but the capitalist center does not remain static as capitalist relations become advanced in the periphery. The developed countries maintain their power over the developing countries by devising different ways to exploit and subjugate the periphery. Development in its purest sense must therefore mean the economic alternatives that will evolve from the resolution of the contradiction between capital and labor under capitalism – the transformation of capitalism to something else.

The transformation in Europe from the dominion of feudal city-states and kingdoms to the nation-state, the political arrangement for capitalism to prosper, came about only after intense violent struggles. In the peripheral capitalist societies transforming the nation-state to an alternative political economy mode to imperial domination or center-periphery relations has proven to be a much more difficult task. The dilemma of the peripheral capitalist societies is that the historical conditions from which they emerged left them pursuing development models in the mold of their oppressors.

Compounding their predicament is the fact that they are given no opportunity by their former masters to fashion in their self-interest any real alternative forms of economic organization. They are locked into the nation-state and its political, economic and social models handed down to them by foreign powers. At most, they are allowed to carry out tolerable reforms to the economy and polity, but without undertaking any activities that would lead to fundamental transformation of the system itself. They are like honorary servants of the capitalist master plan.

This chapter is intended as additional support for the argument that the dynamic conditions described as the new extractivism really refer to a phenomenon that becomes manifest at different historical conjunctures as capitalism changes its form. The argument is presented in five parts, beginning with an analysis of the transition from colony to nation-state status in the capitalist periphery and some key contradictions of capitalism. The capitalist development models based on national ownership of natural resources in the Caribbean are analyzed as comparable to the conditions described as the new extractivism. Thereafter, analyses are undertaken of neoliberal capitalism and the extractive industries, the development impact of natural resources extraction, and the political foundations of the neoliberal approach to mining.

Colony to nation-state status and capitalist contradictions

The process of transitioning from colony to nation-state status in peripheral social formations such as Guyana involved several steps that commenced with the change from an oppressive 'colonial slave mode of production' to full-fledged capitalist production relations. In essence, this was a change within the capitalist system that deepened capitalist social relations in the former colonies. Simultaneously to expanding capitalist production relations in the periphery, one of its defining characteristics was the attempt by domestic labor to diversify the economy to include small-scale economic activities within and outside agro-extractivism in the form of plantation agriculture and involving natural resources extraction.

The endeavor to diversify the economy was a direct challenge to the status quo of plantation agro-extractivism. The emerging local laboring classes tried to assert their independence from plantation agriculture by resorting to natural resources extraction. In particular, they became involved in gold mining and activities in the forestry industries. As the country changed over to partial self-rule the local middle-class elements that secured limited state power continued the push for economic independence through increased local ownership and control over the economy. They fixed their sights on reining in the foreign owned companies operating in the natural resources sector as well as in plantation agriculture. Finally, when the transition to self-rule appeared to be complete that is as the local middle-class elements secured political independence and full control of the state, they took total ownership and control over major foreign enterprises in the natural resources and agricultural sectors.

An analysis of the transition from colony to nation-state status in Guyana provides the evidence in support of the following observations. First, that capitalist development in peripheral capitalist societies is a struggle by the locals assembled there for capitalist production, to secure political and economic independence from foreign domination. Second, at opportune moments the local elites in control of the state implement measures to take over foreign assets in the natural resources sector. Third, in the light of the poverty conditions in the capitalist periphery, the ideal of such measures is to redistribute income through social spending as a boon to capitalist development. The Latin American scholars who came up with the idea of the new extractivism are merely pointing to a historical phenomenon that is observable at different historical conjunctures in capitalist development.

They mistakenly believe that they have unearthed a political economy phenomenon that is associated only with a specific period in the evolution of capitalism in the Latin America and Caribbean region characterized by the change from neoliberalism to post-neoliberalism. The conditions identified as the new extractivism nonetheless simply represents a conjunctural phenomenon that occurs at times when capitalism changes its form. As capitalism changes its form there is a tendency for peripheral states to secure greater degrees of freedom albeit on a temporary basis. The greater degrees of freedom come from two sources namely domestic political, social and economic agitation by the local elites as the capitalist system is in crisis, and the social, economic, political turmoil created in the capitalist system as it changes its form.

The freedom is temporary because its source is capitalist crisis, but as soon as the crisis is resolved the imperial powers regain control and take measures to reign-in the recalcitrant peripheral states. However, the ruling elites in the periphery fill the space created by capitalist crisis for them to exercise their freedom of action with measures in support of their long-articulated desire for genuine political and economic independence for their countries. These measures take aim at securing ownership and or control of their natural resources and the redistribution of the economic surplus through social spending on the vulnerable population. The independence they seek however keeps the countries within the capitalist system, rather than establish an alternative.

The former colonies in the capitalist periphery have experienced the phenomenon identified as the new extractivism in at least two hitherto historical conjunctures. But, these experiences were part of a continuous process of capitalist development as global capitalism underwent change. The transformation from colonialism to post-colonialism in peripheral societies has witnessed great social and political upheavals accompanied by an emphasis on natural resources extraction as an engine of economic growth, and the eventual nationalization of foreign companies in the natural resources sector accompanied by an increase in social spending.

Spreading the wealth generated by nationally owned and or controlled natural resources extractive companies through social programs was a hallmark of state-capitalist development in post-colonial societies. This is the same phenomenon that was observed in Latin America and the Caribbean, which was labeled the new extractivism, as the region transitioned from neoliberalism to post-neoliberalism. It would seem therefore that what is needed is a deeper understanding of this dynamic capitalist phenomenon. It is capitalist development through state ownership and or control of natural resources along with increased spending on social programs. This capitalist dynamic is what is regarded as a static one-time event associated with post-neoliberalism in the Latin American and Caribbean region.

It is the inherent contradictions of capitalism, which from time to time give rise to this conjunctural phenomenon described as the new extractivism. The contradiction is evident at the capitalist economic base and the political superstructure to which it gives rise. What are the contradictions within capitalism that give rise to situations where peripheral nation-states resort to the promotion of development through domestic ownership and or control of natural resources? Capitalism is a crises-prone phenomenon that is characterized by contradictions and antagonisms at the very heart of the production system. It is the nature of the conflicting elements in crises that must be of concern. This is even more important than trying to find measures to prevent the inevitable (crisis) from taking place.

The nature of the contradiction has to do with purchases and sales of commodities, which represent two opposite phases of an essentially unified process. The independence of purchases and sales however are manifested forcibly as a destructive force (Marx, 1963). The unity of the purchases and sales of commodities are asserted only in crises. Their independence is effectively shattered as the crisis demonstrates that although the two phases are independent of each other they are in unity (Marx, 1963). Crisis would not become manifest if there was no inner unity of factors which are indifferent to each other (Marx, 1963). This is really a crisis produced by the disjuncture between capital and labor.

Such was the nature of the crises in global capitalism that led to World War I and its sequel, World War II. The contradiction between purchases and sales in global capitalism exploded to such an extent that it led to those two wars. As the purchase of commodities decline, sales fell-off and hence so did profit. As purchases wilt away, the stockpile of commodities increased due to the lack of sales. This contradiction is referred to in sections of the literature as the crises of overproduction. As the supply of commodities exceeds their demand crises is manifested in terms of declining profits, which the capitalist interprets as a time to contract their productive activities. As the economy contracts unemployment increases, which ferments social unrest by placing in the hands of working class adversaries the necessary weapons to whip up anti-capitalist sentiments and protests.

Crises in global capitalism strengthen the demands and protests in the capitalist periphery for meaningful economic and political change. The anti-capitalist mass movements in the periphery produced by the crisis in global capitalism in conjunction with the articulation of old domestic grievances against the former colonial masters also weigh heavily on the system. In its weakened state the capitalist is forced to accede even if only temporarily to political demands emanating from the peripheral countries. This leads finally to the installment of local political officials at the helm of the state.

When such a political change takes places in the periphery due to the fallout from those global and domestic crisis conditions, there is a tendency for the newly elected officials to advocate in favor of state ownership of natural resources as a means of economic development and to alleviate the wretched conditions of working people. The outcomes are that the state elites enrich themselves from the leverage they have due to their control over state assets, and the pushback from the imperial powers to restore the old order of domination by foreign capital. The excursion into state ownership is only temporary until crises conditions at another historical conjuncture produces the phenomenon again.

The pressure to break up the colonial system therefore came from two sources – the crisis of overproduction and opposition in the periphery to the unjust colonial social order. The fight against the colonial system was carried over from the two world wars into the golden age of capitalism, which again ended in crisis as the disjuncture between purchases and sales came to a head in the 1970s. The pushback by mature capitalist states against national ownership of natural resources in the periphery came to a head and resulted in the implementation of neoliberal policies in the latter states that dismantled national ownership and reinstated private ownerships of the commanding heights of the economy. Capitalist development in the periphery was thus thwarted and subdued by the dictates of global capital under the general rubric of financialization.

In the Latin American and Caribbean region, the crisis of neoliberal capitalism in the first decade of the twenty-first century created conditions that were similar to those present when colonial capitalism was in crisis. Neoliberal policies have produced a slew of social and economic pathologies in both the peripheral and developed capitalist societies. The culmination of these contradictions in a catastrophic crash in Wall Street in 2007 and its aftermath has led to an about-turn in neoliberal capitalism, in particular concerning the rhetoric on the role of the state.

The *laissez faire* capitalism that is neoliberalism, founded on deregulation, free trade, and a movement from crony capitalism to a plutocracy has been nothing but a failure. It almost put an end to the European nation-state, with the creation of the European Union's global Europe enterprise, which was only halted by Brexit. It has led to the offshoring exports of jobs instead of increased production in the developed capitalist countries. It has demonstrated beyond a shadow of doubt the bankruptcy of the economic theories on which it is founded. Furthermore, it has led to the social, political and economic dispossession in both developed and peripheral societies, and high unemployment. It has created a gigantic chasm in wealth and income distribution within and across countries[1] and has perpetuated fraud by bankers.[2] Poverty, social inequality, militarization and war are other malaise of neoliberal capitalism.[3] Furthermore, the consequences, resistance, and alternatives to neoliberalism have been addressed in various places in the literature.[4]

The period of 'de-neoliberalization' or transition from neoliberalism to post-neoliberalism is hastened by the crisis. It represents a confluence of events and processes that characterize the current historical conjuncture of capitalist development in the first two decades of the twenty-first century. The main current is financialization – the domination of economy and society by the affairs of finance capital.[5] Other developments include the re-emergence of China as a global power that allegedly drives a boom in the demand for natural resources; the new developmentalism in the Latin American and Caribbean region characterized as the 'new extractivism'; the re-colonization of Africa as a culmination of the long decolonization struggles on the continent; growing concerns with the environment and sustainable development; wars that continue to threaten the global peace; and the deepening of class struggles at the domestic and global levels.

The crisis in neoliberalism has opened up a space in peripheral capitalist societies for the locals to actually achieve their demand for national ownership and or control of their natural resources as a means of their capitalist economic development. This historical event is only one aspect of a multilayered process in that in some countries the space for political and economic freedoms remained closed due to neoliberalism. This is especially so in smaller countries like Guyana that lacks the capacity to effectively pursue post-neoliberal policies, despite the fact that neoliberalism is in the process of reform, globally. Guyana had gone through this process that the Latin American and Caribbean region is currently going through, in the post-colonial period, but whose economy has long been re-captured by the forces of neoliberal capitalism. There are of course other factors such as internal political strife that is manipulated by external forces that keep Guyana within the orbit of neoliberal capital.

Thus, rather than abort privatization programs and dig in on national ownership of natural resources, countries such as Guyana continue to implement and depend on neoliberal policies for their false salvation. This situation creates a special anomaly in that the center is changing neoliberal policies while at the same time encouraging such policies as a sort of residual factor in some peripheral economies as others embark on implementing national ownership of their natural resources. This conundrum in peripheral capitalist development is elaborated on in a subsequent chapter.

The crisis in neoliberalism therefore did not produce a uniformed response in terms of the call for national ownership of natural resources in all natural resources-rich peripheral social formations. Similarly, the transition from colonialism to post-colonialism did not have universal effect on all colonial social formations. The degree to which countries were impacted by colonialism and neoliberalism seems to be a deciding factor that determines how they react to the crisis-driven reforms in global capitalism.

There are former colonies such as Guyana that continue to implement neoliberal policies dismantling their national ownership agendas, while in Latin

America some states dismantle their neoliberal programs and implement national ownership strategies. This situation creates the confusion that has led close observers of the Latin American political economy to identify the post-neoliberal national ownership strategy as a new phenomenon. The strategy is associated with crises in the capitalist system, which creates the conditions for peripheral social formations to seize the moment to take over national ownership and or control of their natural resources in their self-interest.

This strategy tends to ebb and flow with crises in the capitalist system, but, so long as it merely takes advantage of capitalist crises to come into fruition, it is reformist and cannot transcend capitalism. As such it becomes an integral component of capitalist development itself in that capitalist crisis is expected from time to time to produce that sort of a response in the capitalist periphery – a model of capitalist development based on national ownership of natural resources.

Thus, what is described as the new extractivism is a historical phenomenon associated with class oppression. As the middle-class leadership in these countries come to the belief that they have thrown off the yoke of their oppressors, whether it is British colonialism or the new imperialism in the form of neoliberalism, they seek to control their national resources for their economic and social uplift. This was the case as Guyana became independent from Britain, as it is the case when Latin American countries believed that they were freed from the yoke of neoliberalism.

But the empire has a way of striking back with a vengeance as we have witnessed with economic and political destabilization in the Caribbean, followed by the implementation of structural adjustment. In Latin America we are witnessing the destabilization of Venezuela, and attempts to dismantle PetroCaribe. In Brazil there has actually been a coup that overthrew the democratically elected Dilma Rousseff of the Workers' Party.

National ownership and or control of natural resources

There is therefore nothing 'new' about the phenomenon described as the new extractivism, which is said to have emerged in the post-neoliberal era in the Latin American region over the last decade. The same phenomenon is observed in Guyana and the Caribbean as the sub-region entered into its post-colonial phase from the 1960s. As Caribbean countries in particular Guyana, Jamaica and Trinidad and Tobago shed the trappings of colonialism their governments placed much faith in their natural resources sectors to play a major role in bringing about the economic and social development of the respective countries. Nationalist experiments in Guyana, Jamaica and Trinidad and Tobago favored state ownership and or control of the natural resources sectors and the socialization of the economic surplus of those entities to the entire population.

The natural resources development model in the Caribbean had four distinctive sides to it. The Guyana government went for a complete 'mortgage-finance type' nationalization of foreign companies, which were forced to sell their assets to the government. The Trinidad and Tobago government went for joint-ownership with the state controlling a majority share in the companies, and it undertook investments on its own to build state companies. The Jamaican government undertook a levy arrangement that saw a greater share of the wealth generated form natural resources extraction remaining in the country. Grenada pursued a non-capitalist path to development that was at the time in line with theoretical works on the subject.

The crisis in global capitalism generated in the Caribbean a 'wave of revolutionary mobilization.'[6] This represented a left turn in the region whose foundations were laid since the labor riots in the 1930s and the developments in Guyana during the 1920s with the formation of the British Guiana Labor Union (BGLU). The BGLU had the explicit goal of building socialism in the British Guiana. The transition from colonialism to post-colonialism, which resulted from the contradiction within colonial capitalism was uneven. It spanned a number of decades since the formation of trade unions in the 1920s and the riots of the 1930s. Undoubtedly, colonial capitalism could not have continued to exist in its then form in the light of the crisis and decolonization.

The post-colonial nationalist movements were determined to seize the moment to bring the natural resources in their countries under the direct control of their respective governments. Jamaica, Grenada, Guyana and Trinidad and Tobago were in the forefront of this development. The US administration however was determined to quell the 'wave of revolutionary mobilization' that swept the region in the 1970s. It resorted to political and economic destabilization, and the military invasion of Grenada that put an end to the Grenada revolution. The Cuban revolution of the 1960s stood out as the only example in the Caribbean of what was possible in terms of national ownership of natural resources.

The democratic socialist government of Michael Manley in Jamaica pursued six principal economic, political and social goals. These goals were designed to bring the Jamaican economy under the ownership and or control of Jamaicans. In essence they represented a struggle for true Jamaican independence and nationhood. First, these policies were designed to reduce the island's economic dependence on foreign powers. Second, Manley's democratic socialism sought to create a mixed economy with the commanding heights of the economy under state control. Third, the government professed that it was doing all in its powers to reduce social inequality. This meant that the wealth generated by state-owned and or controlled companies would be socialized to the sundry population through government spending on social programs. A fourth goal of democratic socialism was to deepen political democracy in Jamaica by garnering a greater level of mass participation in the island's decision-making processes. Finally, the government wanted to forge an independent foreign policy that was more in line with the non-aligned movement.[7]

The policy of the Manley-government towards bauxite fell short of nationalization but there was a much greater protest by the companies operating in the bauxite sector in Jamaica against those measures than what took place in Guyana where the bauxite companies were nationalized. The Jamaican government declared that it wanted a limited disengagement of the ownership and control of the country's bauxite industry from the North American companies that owned it at the time. Also, the government wanted to integrate the bauxite industry more into the country's productive system. The disengagement from foreign ownership and integration of the bauxite industry into Jamaica's productive system was to take place through a series of measures. These actions were to include government playing a greater role in the ownership of the bauxite companies operating in the country, the formation of an international bauxite cartel of bauxite-producing countries, the introduction of a tax levy on bauxite industry, and the establishment of a Jamaica Bauxite Institute. The government also returned to local peasants, lands that the bauxite companies owned but were lying idle. The Manley-government took over '51 percent of the local operations of the bauxite-mining companies.' Also, the government secured 'between 6 and 7 percent of the companies producing bauxite-alumina' (Thomas, 1988, p. 214).[8]

Although Grenada is a small island developing state that depends heavily on the production and export of nutmegs, the revolutionary government in 1979 set out to follow a non-capitalist socialist path to socialist development.[9] This meant that Grenada would bypass the capitalist stage of development and move straight to socialism with the assistance of the socialist bloc of countries. Grenada wanted to utilize its natural environment of sandy beaches, turquoise water, and sunshine to the fullest in the process of building socialism. The principal economic policies were to build an airport large enough to land commercial passenger jets to expand the tourist industry, construct a mixed economy based on the state, cooperative and the private sectors, improve the quality of life of Grenadians by upgrading social services and serving the basic needs of the population, and diversify foreign trade and investment sources by opening up links with the socialist bloc and improving South–South cooperation.[10]

Guyana was declared a cooperative socialist republic in 1970 four years after the country gained its political independence from Britain in 1966. The primary objectives of cooperative socialism were first to nationalize foreign property. Thus, by 1976 the government boasted that it had owned and or controlled 80 percent of the Guyana-economy. The nationalizations under cooperative socialism followed a usual pattern. The government paid fair and adequate compensation for the nationalized entities. Furthermore, the government nationalized the foreign companies when they were in distress and threatened with closure. Finally, the government 'provided post-nationalization contracts to cover management, technology and licensing fees.' The second policy initiative was to feed, clothe, and house the nation by 1976 substituting 'the private profit motive with the social goal of making the small man a real man' (Thomas, 1988, p. 253). Third, the cooperative sector was to become the dominant sector in a tri-sector economy – state, private and cooperative. The fourth policy initiative was to declare that the ruling party stood over all other institutions in the country, including state organizations (Thomas, 1988; Canterbury, 2005).

Trinidad and Tobago is endowed with oil and natural gas sectors and as such its economic development model in the 1970s was hinged on the extraction of those natural resources. Trinidad and Tobago had the largest state sector in the Caribbean and the windfall oil gains that the country earned in 'the good oil years' between 1974 and 1983 led the government to pursue the following policy initiatives and outcomes (Thomas, 1988, p. 279). First, the state intensified its role in the economy through the creation of large-scale energy resource-intensive export industries. Second, the state entered into collaborative arrangements with the transnational corporations to bring these industries into existence including joint ventures, management contracts, consultancies, and suppliers of technical services. The new activities centered on fertilizers, chemicals and iron and steel were centered in the Point Lisas industrial complex. Third, the government encouraged import substitution industries and Export Processing Zone-type investments that were conceived as subsidiaries to the 'large-scale, export-oriented, resource-intensive investments' (Thomas, 1988, p. 285). Fourth, there was a rapid expansion of government revenues from these sources. Fifth, the government used its revenue to improve basic social services provided by the state.[11]

Neoliberal capitalism and the extractive industries

The ascent of neoliberal capitalism represented by the re-emergence of the dominance of finance capital over productive capital came about in response to crisis and the radicalism in the 1970s. The neoliberal turn ushered in a new disposition by global capital towards the extractive industries in the peripheral capitalist countries. Under the hegemony of financial capital there has been an ongoing push to liberalize and privatize state-owned and or controlled natural resources entities in these states. But, privatization has turned out to be unsavory as the peripheral capitalist countries ended-up almost giving away their state-owned natural resources companies to private foreign interests. It is a process that increases national vulnerability to imperial pressure, as countries are forced to surrender their political independence to the multinational corporations (Petras, 2013).

The anti-privatization movements spawned by privatization in the peripheral capitalist states however have succeeded in altering the terms and in some cases have altogether halted or reversed the privatization of some nationally owned entities (Kingstone, 2011). The anti-privatization movement has been central to the left turn in Latin America and the development strategy based on national ownership and or control of natural resources described as the new extractivism. The trajectory of the ownership structure of natural resources extraction in peripheral capitalist societies could be charted as follows: colonialism involving private ownership; decolonization containing national ownership and or control; neoliberalism encompassing privatization; and de-neoliberalization covering national ownership and or control.

The renewed interest in and disposition towards the extractive industries has been evident since the World Bank Group's Mining Department and the

International Financial Corporation published a report on mining and development entitled '*Global mining: Treasure or trouble? mining in developing countries*' in 2002. The views of the neoliberal theorists reflected in the report asserted that the marketization agenda of neoliberal capitalism has created new opportunities for the extractive industries to contribute towards the economic development of the resource-rich but economically poor countries. The positive role that the World Bank ascribed to the extractive industries in economic development was classified as another landmark in the ebb and flow of a long theoretical tradition that seeks to shed light on the role of mineral extraction in capitalist development.

This tradition is traced back to the age of the classical political economists, who focused their attention on answering general questions concerning the nature and causes of the wealth of nations. In their critical reaction to the imprudence and irrationality of the mercantile capitalism in which wealth was measured by the quantity of precious metals, primarily gold and silver that a country owned, the classical political economists focused their attention on wealth creation through commodity production for sale in free-market transactions. They believed that the free market would both generate and spread more wealth throughout society improving the quality of life of the wretched that were entrapped by the backward mercantilist policies.

This was the opening salvo in a long struggle for marketization *á la* classical political economy, which was quite the contrary to the mercantile protectionist system that concentrated precious metals in the hands of a few state elites while the vast majority of the people lived in the misery of abject poverty. The abstraction which was called the 'free market' was identified as the savior of humans and hence a doctrine to fight for because of the perception that it is a conduit for the sundry population to acquire riches and a better quality of life. State protectionism became the villain to be vanquished because allegedly it prevents the rank-and-file from acquiring wealth to overcome their conditions of misery and poverty.

The classical political economy theoretical debates on the nature and causes of the wealth of nations markedly omitted the subject of minerals in the acquisition of wealth by nation-states (Graulau, 2008). But, this claim is arguably spurious because commodity transactions in free markets would inevitably involve trade in minerals from which wealth would be acquired. Even if the classical political economists might not have explicitly discussed the role of minerals in the nature and cause of the wealth of a nation, with very little imagination the link between minerals as raw materials to produce finished commodities and the market is obvious.

All commodities, including minerals are covered in the market transactions proffered by the classical political economists. This would especially be the case for gold and silver that formed the basis for the measure of wealth as commodity money under mercantilism and capitalism. While arguing that the classical political economists omitted to discuss the relationship between the extractive industries and economic development, Graulau (2008) pointed out that David

Ricardo's theory of international trade was the first to broach the issue. Ricardo's trade theory is said to represent a paradigm shift in the theorization on the role of the extractive industries in the process of capitalist economic development. It was identified as the first theory that explicitly had a role for minerals in wealth creation and accumulation by nation-states.

The Ricardian principles of comparative advantage allow for a country to specialize in the production of a commodity in which it has a comparative advantage whether or not this advantage is absolute, and then for it to trade in that commodity. Thus, a country that is endowed with specific minerals must specialize in their production and trade them in order to acquire wealth for itself. But, it is not only that Ricardo is considered a classical political economist, his trade theory is a reinforcement of the free market as the principal means through which wealth is generated, distributed, and accumulated. The extent to which Ricardian trade theory represents a paradigm shift in terms of the study of the relationship between the extractive industries and economic development is highly questionable.

The pushback against Ricardo's principles of comparative advantage is said to represent another paradigm shift in the study of the relationship between the extractive industries and capitalist economic development (Graulau, 2008). This challenge has taken the theoretical forms of Latin American structuralism and the more radical dependency theory. The epitome of structuralism is the Prebisch-Singer hypothesis that presents the classic refutation of the comparative advantage foundation of the Ricardian international trade theory. Radical dependency theory is a critique of structuralism that advocates a break with capitalist development and the pursuit of independence in the periphery via an alternative socialist path.

Latin American and Caribbean structuralism presents the argument that capital accumulation did not take place in sufficient amounts in that region from international trade based on the Ricardian comparative advantage theory. Most of this trade involved the sale of natural resources extracted from the region. The lack of capital accumulation was construed to be the case against the extractive industries playing a positive role in the economic development of the Latin American and Caribbean region. In other words, the minerals, metals, and other commodities extracted from those industries are not traded on terms that are beneficial to the region.

The World Bank framers of the neoliberal perspective on mining and development start off with a paradoxical question that has led to three broad observations on the subject. It commences with the puzzling proposition as to whether a country's mineral wealth is an asset that could be used to stimulate or enhance its economic development, or whether the development of the mineral sector is something to stay away from (World Bank and International Finance Corporation, 2002). The attempt to sort out this paradox from a neoliberal perspective has led to three basic observations.

The first is that countries that depend on mining do much better than their counterparts in their respective regions. The second institutional stability and sound economic management are the reasons that the mineral sector generates economic prosperity in mineral rich countries. These countries are able to effectively manage the revenue generated from mining and manage the sector properly. Third, improved institutional stability and economic management are critical ingredients to be added in mineral rich countries where mining does not generate the appropriate levels of economic prosperity. In the neoliberal perspective mining is good for economic prosperity but there is need for institutional stability and sound economic management of mining revenues and the mining sector. But, the neoliberal perspective on the extractive industries and development is problematic for the following reasons.

First, the World Bank starts off with the wrong question – is mining good or bad for socio-economic development. The issue for the developing countries has never been whether mining is good or bad. This dichotomy is a creation of the neoliberal ideologues seemingly to help to produce the conditions for the exploitation of the natural resources in the developing countries in the present period. It represents a form of neoliberal pushback against the critique by the developing countries that foreign extractive capital takes their natural resources and generates a huge amount of profit for itself, while leaving very little revenue behind in the developing countries for their economic development. To pose the question whether mining is good or bad and then to provide the answers that the World Bank gave places the ball back in the court of the developing countries.

It shifts the blame for the lack of economic development from natural resources extraction in the peripheral capitalist countries from the exploitative capitalist production relations that drains the wealth of those countries, to the developing states themselves. In other words, the failure of the mineral rich peripheral capitalist states to achieve sustained economic development from the exploitation of their natural resources is due to their inabilities in pecuniary management. In the neoliberal view therefore, foreign extractive capital is not the cause of the lack of sustained economic development from extractive industries. It is the disparate institutions and poor management in those countries that are responsible for their lack of development. If the developing countries were only able to strengthen their institutional structures and improve on their money management techniques, they would generate sustained economic development from their extractive industries.

The key points to note here are that, based on the World Bank's prescriptions, the developing countries will blame themselves for their lack of development rather than the operations of foreign extractive capital. Foreign extractive capital will gain a free pass to continue to exploit the developing countries with some minor reforms here or there. This will give considerable leverage to global institutions in the control of finance capital to go into the developing countries to 'help' them create the 'right' institutional framework for the extractive sector. The real purpose of this intervention is to create the institutional structures that would allow foreign extractive capital to continue to operate with impunity in the extractive industries. The institutional structures cater towards the unhindered repatriation of profit, minimizing labor disputes, and creating favorable tax regimes, and duty-free concessions on equipment used in the extractive industries, etc.

Furthermore, management is a science of control. It is in essence the increase in the control over labor and the labor processes by foreign capital in the extractive industries. The primary purpose of this improved economic management is to maximize profit and minimize cost in the extractive industries favorable to foreign capital. This involves a wide range of management techniques including the increasing application of science and cutting-edge technologies to the production process and the minute division of labor in the extractive sectors.

Second, the problem is that the initial development of the capitalist system relied heavily on the expansion of capital from Europe to Africa, Asia, the Americas and Caribbean. This expansion facilitated the unfair production and trade in natural resources as raw materials and their use to produce manufactured commodities. Natural resources production in particular mining has not generated the level of economic prosperity in the colonies as it has in the colonizing states. This is not merely a structuralist argument, it points to the very modus operandi of economic actions founded on the ideals of capitalist commodity production for market exchange for profit. Undoubtedly, the survival of humans has not always depended on their conquest of nature to generate profit for a few individuals. Although, humans have always depended on nature for their survival, their productive activity has not always been for profit. But, the question as to whether mining is good or bad is premised on the idea that the conquest of nature is to generate profit for the few.

The argument here is that although neoliberal theorists critique what is termed the 'structuralist argument' they stand on the same side of structuralism. This congruence is in the specific sense that they both subscribe to the capitalist notion of the conquest of nature to generate profit rather than merely for human survival. The structuralist import substitution industrialization model seeks to generate profit for state or private capitalists. It protects infant industries merely to nurture them until they are strong enough to stand on their own to engage in open competition in the capitalist world markets.

The idea is that the protection of infant industries would eventually lead to the capitalist economic development of the countries in which these industries are located. The profit generated by the protected industries it is believed would be reinvested in the domestic economy thereby spurring capitalist economic development. The structuralist import substitution industrialization model therefore is not really a development alternative to capitalism. Furthermore, the structuralist development argument is not wholly true because capital is usually in search of low production cost to maximize profit, and has a strong tendency to migrate to jurisdiction that would provide it with that outcome. To guarantee that the protected industries reinvest their profits in the domestic economy to stimulate development would require the restriction of movement of profits.

The third reason why the neoliberal perspective on the extractive industries is problematic is because it reduces economic prosperity from mining in mineral rich developing economies to the functions of institutional stability and sound economic management. This view completely overlooks the issue of production for profit versus production for the survival of the species. Institutional stability and sound economic management are about deepening the very capitalist institutional structures and management practices that have placed the developing countries in the positions they are in today. The capitalist institutions and management practices that are touted to be lacking in the mineral rich developing countries must therefore be introduced and or strengthened in these states. Of course, this would make it easier for foreign capital to operate in the extractive industries and repatriate their profit.

Finally, according to the World Bank the reason why the mineral rich developing countries are dithering in their attempt to catch-up economically and socially with the rich countries is not because of their historically exploitative encounters with European and US capitalism. Instead, it is because the developing countries do not have the right institutional and management structures in the mining sector. In one sweep, that claim absolves the imperial countries of any responsibility for the poor socio-economic conditions in the countries in the capitalist periphery and shifts the blame to the victims. The mineral rich economies are poor because they do not know how to manage and lack the wherewithal to create the appropriate institutions for their own development!

Exxon Mobil has found large commercial quantities of oil in Guyana and one of the first things that the Guyana government was encouraged to do by the US State Department was to seek its assistance to put in place the institutional arrangements and management practices to cope with revenue that will flow to Guyana from oil extraction. Under its Energy Governance and Capacity Initiative (EGCI), the US government provided a variety of 'technical and capacity building assistance' that could help Guyana 'to develop financial and regulatory regimes' as well as to 'address capacity issues that would maximize the development potential' from the country's 'offshore oil and gas resources' (US State Department, 2016).

The EGCI is carrying out the World Bank's vision for natural resources extraction in the developing countries. The wide-ranging activities of the EGCI in mineral-rich developing countries include the conducting of seminars on 'revenue management, and regulatory best practices for oil, gas, and mining sectors.' It provides 'in-country advisor support for regulatory agencies' as a means of promoting 'independent energy sector oversight and management.' In addition, 'legal and technical guidance' are provided concerning the implementation of the appropriate 'reforms and policies to create sustainability in the energy sector.' The EGCI is supposed to help to create 'a commercial environment conducive to attracting responsible large scale investment' (US State Department, 2016).

While providing the mineral-rich capitalist peripheral countries with 'specialized assistance and expert guidance in oil and gas revenue sharing and distribution,' the EGCI has a role fashioning 'related financial and tax management' policies. It is involved with creating 'financial tracking systems and other measures to reduce corruption' and undertaking 'technical training in oil and gas resource identification and resource assessment methodology' (US State Department, 2017). It supposedly provides 'modern geological/geophysical data analysis and management,' in addition to helping to build capacity 'on technical and management skills within energy-related ministries and other governmental entities' (US State Department, 2017). Finally, the EGCI provides assistance on 'petroleum engineering, financial advisory services, and environmental studies,' and on 'interagency and public review/comment for oil, gas, and mining sector decision-making' (US State Department, 2017).

The EGCI intends to build technical, financial, legal, and environmental and social capacity in natural resources rich developing countries. The focus on technical capacity concerns 'building expertise in resource assessment and development optimization.' In the area of finance, the concern is with ensuring 'responsible management of government revenues from the sector.' This is evidence that the World Bank and US State Department are on the same page concerning the exploitation of natural resources in the developing countries. The legal concern involves 'embedding international best practices into laws and regulations,' and the environmental and social concerns involve 'protecting people and the environment from sector impacts' (US State Department, 2017).

Whose interests are served by these US State Department activities in the natural resources rich developing countries? Would the US State Department seek to look after the interests of US extractive capitalists or those of the natural-resources developing countries? The answers to these questions are quite obvious. Imagine, the World Bank and US are teaching the natural resources rich developing countries how to regulate US extractive capitalists operating in their countries and manage their financial affairs! This derogatory attitude of the World Bank and US towards the people in the natural resources rich developing counties is taken straight out of the British colonialist playbook. It is an attitude towards the so-called lesser people in the developing world by hegemonic powers that was debated in the nineteenth century.

The British historian James Anthony Froude, in 1888 after his travels in the Caribbean, came to the conclusion in confirmation with the British political elites that elective local legislatures were beyond the reaches of the inhabitants of the Caribbean peoples. The Trinidadian John Jacob Thomas promptly rejected that view in his book *Froudacity*: *West Indian fables by James Anthony Froude explained*. Froude's idea informed British policy towards the region up to the time of the decolonization struggles. The colonial masters believed that there should be a gradual approach to the granting of political independence to the region since the people there did not know how to govern themselves.

The British held the view that they had to teach the inhabitants how to govern themselves. That view is not a far cry away from the idea that the natural resources rich developing countries have to be taught by their very exploiters how to manage their resources and the revenue they generate. While the British position could be interpreted as a political ploy to deny self-rule to the former colonies, the World Bank/US position is an economic ruse to control the natural resources of the developing countries, even as these countries have independent states.

The development impact of natural resources extraction

Mining and development, mining in development, or the development impact of mining, whatever the terminology under capitalism, the process is driven by class forces, the capitalist and the workers. These dialectically opposing class forces are engaged in commodity production in the natural resources industries, one as producer of value (workers) and the other as usurper of surplus value (capitalists), respectively, at any particular historical conjuncture in the evolution of capitalism. It is therefore erroneous to believe that swinging a pendulum on a compendium comprising two moral positions – mining is good or mining is bad – would make the class nature of capitalist production go away or can generate new questions, ideas and theories in that connection. The World Bank's view on whether mining is good or bad is problematic and represents a faulty basis on which to theorize about mining for the following three reasons.

First, it fails to realize that the pendulum is not swinging from one productive system to another, but only within the capitalist system between two moral positions – good and bad. Refutations of social theories founded on moral questions abound in the literature and need not be reviewed here. Suffice it to say however that the general conclusion could be drawn from the debates concerning the explanations of social reality that in every historical epoch, social theories founded on empirical evidence provide a sounder basis for understanding human behavior. The same is true of the political, economic, social and cultural institutions humans create, the social relations they evolve, the production, marketing and consumption of commodities, the production, distribution and accumulation of wealth, where people live, eat and play, and even how they die and are buried.

Second, the social and economic theories produced on mining either represent the ideas of the dominant class forces in society, or those of their opponents. Thus, it is not a question of whether mining is supported in these theoretical expositions as good or opposed as bad for the development process. It is more an issue of conflict between the dominant ideas on natural resources extraction as represented by the class forces that control the means of production and the people who oppose those dominant ideas. Inevitably, the theories on mining at any historical conjuncture will reflect the dialectical relationship between the interests of the dominant class forces in society and their opponents.

Third, new questions, ideas and theories about mining are produced according to which type of capital is dominant – mercantile, agricultural, industrial, or financial/neoliberal. In the current period the dominant ideas on natural resources extraction are those that reflect the interests of finance capital, which heads up neoliberal capitalism. The argument that ideas are formed on the basis of whether mining is good or bad overlooks this important fact. It suggests that ideas on mining are a product of the moral judgment about whether mining is good or bad.

The fact is however that ideas on mining are produced from and by the concrete experiences of humans in the production of minerals within the dominant system of commodity production. In a capitalist society, minerals are not produced merely for the sake of production. Minerals are produced to make a profit either as raw materials or after they are converted into some finished products for consumption by households, firms, or the state. It is from those concrete experiences that we are informed and theorize about the social, political, economic, environmental, community and development impacts of mining and how the financial proceeds from mining are distributed, and which group benefits the most, and who are the winners and losers, in the process.

Framing the debate on mining as one that oscillates between the two moral opposites of good or bad for development allows for the justification of the argument that in the current period the pendulum has swung in favor of neoliberal capitalism. The neoliberal approach to the development impact of mining is that mineral-rich countries must concern themselves primarily with putting in place the right institutional and management structures for them to derive the greatest benefits from mining revenues. On this basis then the mineral-rich developing countries must prostrate themselves before the neoliberal doctrine on mining. This involves surrendering their institutional and management structures to the dictates of the global institutions dominated by finance capital. These global agencies are either established to provide institutional and management support services to 'strengthen' the institutional and management structures in mining in the mineral rich developing countries or they are morphed from already established multilateral Bretton Woods agencies such as the World Bank Group and the International Monetary Fund. Generally, these global agencies operate in an undemocratic manner amidst calls for their democratization.[12]

This is the essence of the neoliberal approach to mining founded on a complex of global institutions that are supposed to 'help' the mineral rich peripheral capitalist countries to attain sustainable development. The neoliberal approach is not merely an issue of imperial military conquest, or the operations of an externally imposed colonial state apparatus in the mining sector in the former colonies. Imperial military conquest and the colonial state have already laid the political and economic foundations for the cooperation by the post-colonial nationalist state in the former colonies with the complex of global institutions currently headed by finance capital in the exploitation of their natural resources. It is pertinent to take a look at some of the political foundations of the neoliberal approach to natural resource extraction in the resource-rich capitalist peripheral countries.

Conclusion

The object of capitalist development with a focus on the subject of the myth or reality of the new extractivism demonstrates that neoextractivism is merely a historical conjunctural phenomenon in the evolution of capitalism. The advance of colonies to nation-state status dispels the myth that neoextractivism is a recent phenomenon by reinforcing the view that peripheral capitalist countries are historically engaged in a continuous struggle for genuine political and economic independence in which they seek to exercise control over their natural resources and to use the proceeds for the social and economic uplift of their peoples. This phenomenon is a direct result of the contradiction in the capitalist production system between the purchase and sale of commodities. The disequilibria between these produce crises, which emboldens the ruling elites in the periphery to take steps to recapture their countries' natural resources from foreign powers. This was evidenced by the drive to national ownership and or control of natural resources as development models, as happened in the Caribbean in the post-colonial struggles for economic independence.

But, neoliberal capitalism has responded to that struggle by formulating policies to recapture control over the natural resources of those countries. The principal stimulus for national ownership of natural resources, namely the inadequacy of benefits from natural resources extraction accruing to the peripheral capitalist countries, is presented to these states as the result of their own doing – poor financial management and institutional apparatuses. This sets up the peripheral countries to invite in the very agencies responsible for the loot of their natural resources to help them to manage their finances from natural resources extraction to stimulate economic development.

This is the exact process that is taking place in Guyana, which is said to be on the brink of becoming an oil producing country. The Carter Center has taken the lead in 'helping' Guyana to put in place measures to manage the finances that will accrue to the country from oil production. Indeed, the US is injecting US$297,000 to help Guyana prepare to become a member of the Extractive Industries Transparency Initiative and ensure 'good governance.' The Carter Center is undertaking a twelve-month project, which the US Ambassador to Guyana, Mr. Perry Holloway said 'will strengthen the work of the Government of Guyana in promoting transparency in the country's extractive industries at a time when Guyana prepares to welcome future growth in the petroleum industry.'[13]

Notes

1 See Piketty (2014) for an in-depth study of wealth and income inequalities in the present period. For a critique of Piketty (2014), see D. Harvey 'Afterthoughts on Piketty's capital,' http://davidharvey.org/2014/05/afterthoughts-pikettys-capital/.
2 See Roberts (2013) for an elaboration of these points.
3 See Chossudovsky and Marshall (2010).
4 See for example Hart-Landsberg (2013).
5 See Lapavitsas (2013) for an elaboration on financialization.
6 See Ambursley (1983).
7 For more on these points see Thomas (1988).
8 See Thomas (1988).
9 For more on the non-capitalist path see Thomas (1978); Mandle (1977); Watson (2015); and Landa (1967).
10 For more on the then economic policies in Grenada see Thomas (1988).
11 For an elaboration on the state-led policy initiatives in the extractive sector in Trinidad and Tobago and the use of the revenue earned to improve the social services in the country see Thomas (1988).

12 For an elaboration on this point see Patomäki and Teivainen (2004); Patomäki (2001); and Murphy (2005).
13 This quote was taken from Chabrol (2016).

References

Ambursley, F. (1983). 'Jamaica: From Michael Manley to Edward Seaga,' in F. Ambursley and R. Cohen (eds). *Crisis in the Caribbean*. New York: Monthly Review Press.

Canterbury, D. C. (2005). *Neoliberal democratization and new authoritarianism*. Aldershot and Burlington: Ashgate.

Chabrol, D. (2016). 'Carter centre is back to help Guyana join global extractive industries transparency watchdog.' *Demerara Waves*, October 7.

Chossudovsky, M. and Marshall, A. G. (eds) (2010). *The global economic crisis: The great depression of the 21st century*. Montréal, Canada: Global Research.

Froude, J. A. (1888). *The English in the West Indies or the bow of Ulysses*. London: Longman, Greene and Co.

Graulau, J. (2008). 'Is mining good for development? The intellectual history of an unsettled question.' *Progress in Development Studies*, 8 (2), pp. 129–162.

Hart-Landsberg, M. (2013). *Capitalist globalization: Consequences, resistance, and alternatives*. New York: Monthly Review Press.

Harvey, D. 'Afterthoughts on Piketty's capital,' http://davidharvey.org/2014/05/afterthoughts pikettys-capital/.

Kingstone, P. (2011). *The political economy of Latin America: Reflections on neoliberalism and development*. New York: Routledge.

Landa, R. G. (1967). 'More on the non-capitalist path of development.' *Soviet Sociology*, 6 (3), pp. 3–10.

Lapavitsas, C. (2013). *Profiting without producing: How finance exploits us all*. London and New York: Verso.

Mandle, J. R. (1977). 'Problems of the non-capitalist path of development in Guyana and Jamaica.' *Politics and Society*, 7 (2) pp. 189–197.

Marx, K. (1963). *Theories of surplus value*. Moscow: Progress Publishers.

Murphy, C. N. (ed.) (2005). *Global institutions, marginalization and development*. London: Routledge.

Patomäki, H. (2001). *Democratizing globalization: The leverage of the Tobin Tax*. London: Zed Books.

Patomäki, H. and Teivainen, T. (2004). *A possible world: Democratic transformation of global institutions*. London: Zed Books.

Petras, J. (2013). 'Mexico: The political cost of privatization of oil and electricity,' http://petras.lahaine.org/?p=1954.

Piketty, T. (2014). *Capital in the twenty-first century* (Translated by Arthur Goldhammer). Cambridge and London: The Belknap Press of Harvard University Press.

Roberts, P. G. (2013). *The failure of laissez faire capitalism*. Atlanta GA: Clarity Press.

Thomas, C. Y. (1988). *The poor and the powerless: Economic policy and change in the Caribbean*. New York: Monthly Review Press.

Thomas, C. Y. (1978). '"The non-capitalist path" as theory and practice of decolonization and socialist transformation.' *Latin American Perspectives*, 5 (2), pp. 10–28.

Thomas, J. J. (1889). *Froudacity: West Indian fables by James Anthony Froude explained*. London: T. Fisher Unwin.

US State Department Bureau of Western Hemisphere Affairs (2016). US Relations with Guyana, Fact Sheet, July 20. www.state.gov/r/pa/ei/bgn/1984.htm.

US State Department Bureau of Energy Resources. (2017). Energy Governance and Capacity Initiative. www.state.gov/documents/organization/264507.pdf, accessed January 1, 2017.

Watson, H. A. (2015). 'Grenada: Non-capitalist path and the derailment of a social democratic revolution,' in W. C. Grenade (ed.) *The Grenada revolution: Reflections and lessons*. Mississippi: The University Press of Mississippi.

World Bank and International Finance Corporation (2002). *Global mining: Treasure or trouble? Mining in developing countries*. Washington, DC: International Finance Corporation.

5 Extractive capitalism, extractive imperialism and imperialism

The interchangeable use of the concepts 'extractive capitalism,' 'extractive imperialism,' and 'imperialism' is the cause for veritable confusion in the debate on the new extractivism in the Latin American and Caribbean region. Clarification of this confusion requires urgent attention for workers, students, and political activists engaged in class struggle in the extractive industries in the region and further afield. It is crucial for these actors to have a clear understanding of the concepts 'extractive capitalism,' 'extractive imperialism,' and 'imperialism' to know exactly what it is they are struggling against. This is a first step in understanding how they may organize in their class-interest. The point of departure in this attempt to clarify the use of these concepts is the counterpoints advanced by Petras and Veltmeyer[1] on the theoretical and political questions concerning the role of the state in their critique of the theory of new extractivism in Latin America. To grasp their counter theoretical arguments on the role of the state in this body of work it is necessary to engage with the three concepts that are central to their analysis – 'extractive capitalism,' 'extractive imperialism,' and 'imperialism.' Also, their analysis of the relationship between capitalism and imperialism (Petras and Veltmeyer, 2015) is of crucial importance as an illuminator of the way extractive capitalism and extractive imperialism must be understood.

The ensuing analysis is intended to bring clarity to the argument that implies that extractivism, which is in essence a descriptor for capitalism is both capitalist and imperialist. Extractivism, capitalism and imperialism are three separate phenomena, which are combined in unique ways by Petras and Veltmeyer in their body of work on the new extractivism. The evidence in support of this observation could be gleaned from the *James Petras Website*, among other sources, which lists a number of articles on the subject of extractive capitalism.[2] In two books by Petras and Veltmeyer however the term 'extractive imperialism' is proffered and explored. They seem to use the concepts 'extractive capitalism' and 'extractive imperialism' interchangeably, and analyze extractive productive activity as both capitalism and imperialism.

But, then in a separate book entitled *Power and resistance: US imperialism in Latin America*, they broached the subject of the relationship between capitalism and imperialism. Perhaps, this later book is intended to reconcile the seeming tension in their earlier works that derives from their interchangeable use of the concepts extractive capitalism and extractive imperialism. In this case they broached the notion of rethinking imperialism by focusing on the intimate relationship between capitalism and imperialism, imperialism in an era of extractive capitalism, extractive imperialism and the post-neoliberal state, and imperialist dynamics of agro-extractivism (Petras and Veltmeyer, 2017).

Petras and Veltmeyer have done an excellent job in delineating labor-capital relations, the class structure, and institutional arrangements that support natural resources extraction under current capitalism in the Latin American and Caribbean region. They have pushed the theoretical envelope on the subject of the new extractivism by among other things subjecting it to rigorous class analysis. Despite their elaborations on extractive capitalism and extractive imperialism and the relationship between the two there still seems to be room for further theoretical clarity in this connection. Their analysis of the political economy of development in the Latin American and Caribbean region seems not to clearly delineate between *capitalism* as a system of commodity production for market exchange and its specific descriptor *extractivism*, the act of natural resources extraction.

The impression is conveyed that the descriptor, *extractive activity*, is the same as the *capitalist mode of production*. Whereas, the Latin American and Caribbean region is characterized by a capitalist mode of production in which natural resources extraction is a dominant economic activity within that mode in some of those countries, but not in others. Also, the natural resources commodities extracted are not the same in every country in the region. Thus, it is not the commodity but the particular mode of production that gives the productive activity its particular meaning. The term 'extractive capitalism' may only be used as a convenience to describe a particular *capitalist productive activity*; it is not the *capitalist mode of production*. It is not the mere act of extraction, which is capitalist – since natural resources extraction took place under hitherto modes of production – but the social organization of production, production relations, property ownership, the state form, etc., under which natural resources extraction is carried out.

Capitalist production in Latin America, whether in the extractive sectors or not, conforms to the formula for the circuit of money-capital: M — C ... P ... C′ — M′. M — C is the first stage in which the capitalist is a buyer on the commodity and labor markets, and his money is transformed into commodities, or it goes through the circulation act of M — C. In the second stage, productive consumption of the purchased commodities by the capitalist, the capitalist is a producer of commodities. Thus, his capital passes through the process of production P resulting in a commodity of more value than that of the elements entering into its production. C′ — M′ is the third stage in which the capitalist returns to the market as seller to turn their commodities into money, where they pass through the circulation act of C — M. The dotted line indicates that the process of circulation is interrupted, and C′ and M′ are an increase on C and M which represents surplus value (Marx, 1909).

This clarification is intended to show what capitalism is – a system of production of surplus value that derives from a particular circuit of money-capital, whether involved in natural resources extraction or the manufacture of a commodity. It is the circuit of money-capital, which is at the heart of capitalism and not merely the commodities produced. The commodity nonetheless is crucial to the circuit of money-capital in that money is transformed into commodities, which in turn are consumed to create more money.

Imperialism, on the other hand, is not defined as precisely as capitalism, there are multiple meanings associated with the concept in the literature. It is understood as an extension of capitalism to incorporate foreign lands within an international or global capitalist production system. To this effect it is understood in terms of Europe's national capital overstepping the shores of Europe in search of profits in overseas territories (Hobson, 1902). It is also regarded as a method of capital accumulation driven by external demand in pre-capitalist economies, through which capitalism meets its realization problem and is plunged into unrecoverable crisis (Luxemburg, 1951).

Capitalism as a system for the production of surplus value must conquer external non-capitalist territories in order to perpetuate capital accumulation. It does so by supplying commodities to these areas and acquiring from them inputs in the form of raw materials and labor power. The system collapses when there are no more non-capitalist lands to conquer, because it is these lands that provide the demand for commodities produced under capitalism (Luxemburg, 1951). Nevertheless, what we are witnessing today is that the capitalist-imperialist system does not collapse but continues to reinvent itself in different forms such as neoliberalism, and neoextractivism.

The lands that are considered non-capitalist do not have to be exhausted to bring an end to imperialism. The capitalist could very well and do develop imperialist relations with countries that are already within the ambit of capitalism as reflected in the center-periphery phenomenon. This is clearly the case in former imperialist countries in Southern Europe, which are themselves capitalist but are being dominated by US imperialism. This is not reverse-imperialism but some kind of an imperialist shuffle where weaker imperialist powers such as Spain, Portugal and Italy are being dominated by US imperialist relations and also by the dominant powers in the European Union.

Some imperialist powers are stronger than others and in the neoliberal era dominate European countries that are considered powers in the capitalist periphery, but are weak among the imperialist states. The contentious world system theory treats this phenomenon in the context of the emergence of semi-peripheral countries where some states gain or lose their core status and others improve their peripheral status (Wallerstein, 1974 and Arrighi, 1994). It is obvious that when we focus on examining the class nature of capitalist society the divisions between core, semi-periphery and periphery is not that useful. What emerges from class analysis is oppressor and oppressed, rulers and ruled. Petras (1981) argues that the innovation of world systems analysis is its use as a unit of analysis, but that its framework is 'strikingly elementary.'

Imperialism is the increasing political and military struggle for control of the non-capitalist territories to guarantee the capital accumulation process under capitalism.[3] Imperialism may be defined as the historical conjuncture at which the separation of money-capital and productive capital is most profound, and refers to the supremacy in economy and society of the owners of capital or the *rentier* capitalists or financial oligarchy. This is a phenomenon in which finance capital dominates all other forms of capital in the capitalist system (Lenin, 1963). Imperialism could even be understood as characterized by stages such as neo-colonialism in the former European colonies considered to be its highest stage (Nkrumah, 1965).

Drawing on these perspectives on imperialism, the view is supported that imperialism is not in itself a mode of production but rather a phenomenon within the capitalist mode of production. But, this phenomenon is particularly associated with the spread of the capitalist mode of production across borders and geographic regions to incorporate territories in the periphery of the capitalist system. It entails an institutional architecture created by the capitalists in collaboration with the foreign and domestic states to facilitate the operations of money-capital in the peripheral countries and the extraction of surplus value realized as profit that accumulate in the money-capital exporting countries.

The method by which natural resources are extracted is not imperialist, but are capitalist. What is imperialist, however, are the associated political and economic arrangements that are put in place in order that capitalist production takes place abroad through the export of money-capital in the form of foreign direct investments from the capitalist center to the capitalist periphery. These arrangements could favor the facilitation of the spread of European or US money-capital in whatever its form – neocolonial or neoliberal – to peripheral economies in search of profits through violent or other means including wars, espionage, etc. Thus, capitalism could exist without imperialism, but imperialism could not exist without capitalism. Imperialism is a product of capitalism and not vice versa.

The clarity we seek to provide here is contained in the argument that extractivism is merely the embodiment of a particular form of productive activity in the capitalist era. It is not capitalism or imperialism. Humans have extracted their livelihood from nature since the days of primitive communalism up until present-day capitalism. It is not the productive activity, which is capitalist or imperialist, since capitalism and by extension, imperialism is associated with a variety of productive activity. We therefore revisited some of the early expositions on the definitions of these concepts to help the activists have a better understanding of the debate on the new extractivism, including the critique by Petras and Veltmeyer, which explores 'extractive capitalism,' 'extractive imperialism,' and views the new extractivism as imperialism.

Primarization and extractivism

What were the political economy conditions that gave rise to the idea that the Latin American and Caribbean region was characterized by a new extractivism?

This question is answered by analyzing the historical trajectory of capitalism and imperialism in the region in terms of 'primarization' and 'extractivism.' The former is explored because of the region's domination by primary commodity production as the growth sector, and the latter is due to an economic development strategy founded on natural resources extraction. Both primarization and extractivism have played a loathsome role in the plunder by capitalism and imperialism of the countries in the capitalist periphery. In this connection the line of argument by Petras and Veltmeyer takes the following trajectory.

The primarization and extractivism associated with the heyday of the British Empire and colonial rule, gave way in the post-World War II period to a new state-led development strategy founded on import substitution industrialization and exploitation of the unlimited supplies of rural surplus labor by incorporating that labor into the capitalist industrial sector. The post-World War II approach collapsed due to a system-wide production crisis caused by the fiscal crisis in the North and debt crisis in the South and ushered in a new world order of free market capitalism founded on financial capital – financialized production and neoliberal globalization. Free market capitalism brought national economies in line with the Washington Consensus, which wrecked the production forces in agriculture and industry and in due course, generated a powerful resistance movement against it which is evidenced by a turn towards natural resources extraction as a development strategy – the new extractivism in the Latin American and Caribbean region.

The new extractivism then, is construed as an alternative development model to free market capitalism. Although its perpetrators tout it as an alternative development model, is that really the case? It would seem that the new extractivism is an integral component of the free market model in the sense that it is because of the free market model that it exists. But, the free market model is merely a sham in that at every turn it is directed by class forces that control the state. It is this same state-led free market model in which the new extractivism thrives. Foreign capital penetrates the domestic economy in collusion with imperial and domestic states to dominate the extractive sector, and export the bulk of the wealth abroad while retaining an increasing amount, domestically. The political economy situation has not been transformed, as the new extractivism maintains the domination over the region by foreign capital. Veltmeyer and Petras (2014) call the new extractivism a new form of imperialism.

The new extractivism is regarded as a form of rentier capitalism, which is not centered as much on the exploitation of labor through the extraction of surplus value (Veltmeyer and Petras, 2014). It is predicated more on the appropriation of monopoly ground rent as profit. Ground rent is value that the capitalist seizes through plunder of the extractive industries by the multinational corporations they control (Veltmeyer and Petras, 2014). It is not value created through the exploitation of labor power. As a defining feature of the post-neoliberal state in the current context the new extractivism represents a shift from classical extractivism. It is characterized by a number of contradictions among which, is whether it is a curse or a blessing, or an economic opportunity to be exploited through good governance and corporate social and environmental responsibility (Veltmeyer and Petras, 2014).

Veltmeyer and Petras (2014) went on to make several other observations about the new extractivism. For example, the new extractivism depends heavily on foreign investment and is caught in a policy of resource extraction development trap. Furthermore, inclusive development is the forte for the new progressive extractivism, which cannot be financed and sustained by extractive rents. Also, the costs of extractive capitalism are in excess of its actual or potential benefits. In addition, the literature on the new extractivism focuses on neoclassical cost-benefit analysis and not class analysis. As well, the resistance movement to which it is united in its opposition to extractive capitalism, is divided in its resistance to capitalism (Veltmeyer and Petras, 2014).

Veltmeyer and Petras (2014) argue that the current debate on new extractivism has given expression to the subject through three contending models. The first is characterized by a search for inclusive growth founded on three factors – large-scale foreign investment, the development of the private sector, and state support (Veltmeyer and Petras, 2014). This is what Veltmeyer and Petras (2014) termed 'imperialism.' The second model is 'progressive extractivism and inclusive development (resource nationalism or inclusionary state activism).' This approach is 'framed within the neo-structural mold associated with the Economic Commission for Latin America and the Caribbean.' It embraces a 'post-Washington Consensus' characterized by a state that is 'an active economic agent promoting an inclusive 'new developmentalism' that brings a better balance between itself and market forces.' The aim of the state as an active economic agent is 'to reduce extreme poverty.' The third model that is still under construction is being framed as a socialist alternative, which represents a transformation from neoliberal capitalism (Veltmeyer and Petras, 2014, p. 246).

On extractive capitalism

The idea of 'extractive capitalism' is investigated in four articles[4] in which we glean some of its characteristic features. The political economy situations in Bolivia, Ecuador, Argentina, Brazil, Uruguay, Peru and Venezuela are analyzed as the locus of extractive capitalism. The conclusion is drawn that these countries were all linked by a common development strategy founded on primary commodity export perpetrated by their progressive regimes (Petras, 2012a). Extractive capitalism is linked to commodity-export based economies and is associated but no longer correlated with neocolonial regimes (Petras, 2012a).

The progressive regimes in those countries pursue anti-imperialist, nationalist and populist rhetoric domestically. These regimes also implement policies to encourage and expand the activities of overseas extractive capital through joint ventures with the state and the emerging national bourgeoisie. The progressive regimes articulate socialism and participatory democracy while their practical policies concentrate and centralize capital and executive power linking them with development.

Their positions are representative of extractive capitalism, but they claim that there are separated from the neoliberal right by the foreign, social, and labor policies they implement, as well as nationalism and state regulations. These policies have caused an almost complete severance of the close ties established between the progressive regimes and social movements. Prior to securing power, the progressive leaders supported the platforms of social movements, which included economic nationalism, ecological conservation, respect for the natural reserves of the indigenous communities, social equality, and the rejection of illegal foreign debts. But, after they won power the progressives appointed government ministers who implemented orthodox economic principles. The ministers adopted the extractive strategy and directed the economies, away from nationalist public-sector approaches that promoted economic diversification, towards mixed economies founded on joint ventures with foreign extractive capital.

Extractive capitalism in the Latin American and Caribbean region portrays significant divergences in economic activity. The nature and character of commodity exports, social polarization, social cohesion, the size and scope of the political opposition, and the sustainability of the progressive and extractive model are divergent (Petras, 2013). The class struggle in extractive capitalism comprises two basic categories of contenders. The first is a ruling class characterized by different sectors of capital that maximize their present and future profits through their social power and control over the economy and state (Petras, 2013). Furthermore, they monopolize the state budget to constrain labor incomes and to displace and dispossess petty commodity producers and local inhabitants from regions that are rich in resources (Petras, 2013).

On the other side of the class divide is located an array of classes inclusive of the employed and unemployed industrial workers (Petras, 2013). Included in this category also are salaried public and private unionized employees and rural landless workers, petty commodity producers and indigenous communities (Petras, 2013). The lower classes demand a greater share of the national income. Also, they want to repossess the land and resources usurped by the state on behalf of agro-mineral corporations (Petras, 2013). Overall, the lower classes are struggling to bring about 'systemic change in property ownership and class relations' (Petras, 2013). The international character of the class struggle has to do with the multinational corporations, international financial organizations and imperial states intervening directly or through their proxies in the domestic class struggle (Petras, 2013).

Extractive capital is the capital invested in the natural resources sector for agro-mineral extraction. Its ascendency was the result of the influential part played by giant agro-mineral corporations in helping to shape state economic policies, which negatively impacted labor, local communities and indigenous peoples. The class forces, the agro-mineral elites directing this process, became partners with the center-left post neoliberal regimes in order to secure the benefits they currently enjoy. The agro-mineral elites accepted increased taxes and royalty payments in return for massive state subsidies and large-scale land grants (Petras, 2013).

A characteristic feature of extractive capitalism, which is founded on a primary export economy, is the reversal of socio-economic gains from import substituting industrialization. Extractive capitalism as represented by Brazil refers to the country's reversion to a primary commodity-export economy based on soya, cattle, iron and metals, simultaneously as textile, transport and manufacturing exports declined. This process has encouraged the penetration of the Brazilian economy by large amounts of imperial multinational corporations and financial flows by overseas banks (Petras, 2013a). Thus, extractive capitalism crowded-out industrial growth and relied on foreign markets and expatriate banks for its success (Petras, 2013a).

The vulnerability of extractive capitalism is its dependence on imperial driven agro-mineral extraction due to alliances between the agro-mineral elite, imperial transnational corporations, local and foreign finance capital, and overseas markets. Extractive capitalism takes place at the expense of the productive forces representing a decline in the relative position of manufacturing, technology and high-end services (Petras, 2013a). Labor earnings, calculated as a percentage of gross domestic product (GDP) declined, foreign capital in the agrarian export and mining sectors were promoted through state subsidies, and credit restraints were placed on small- and medium-size farmers (Petras, 2013a).

Extractive capitalism is destructive of the environment, and involves a privatization (iron and oil in Brazil) swindle (Petras, 2013a). It is regarded as a replacement of neoliberalism or a transition from neoliberalism to extractive capitalism. It de-industrializes the economy that causes an imbalance between manufacturing and extraction. In Brazil this is an indication of the country's reversion to a colonial style of development. Extractive capitalism brings great revenues to the state but at the same time foreign capital exacts great subsidies, tax benefits and profits (Petras, 2013a).

While, the biggest beneficiaries of extractive capitalism are the world's top commodity traders, there has been a decline in working-class struggle against extractive capital. This is due to the co-optation of mass movements, the intensification of extractive capitalist exploitation, and violent dispossession of the indigenous communities. The benefits of extractive capitalism to working people distributed through increased wages are uneven, unequal and distorted. Wealth remains concentrated at the top, as there is a sharp decline in public services and essential life experiences (Petras, 2013a).

The case of Colombia provides added characteristic features of mining and petroleum extractive capitalism (Petras, 2012a). These include heavy foreign investment, energy sector growth, and an increase in the share of minerals and energy as a percentage of exports. Petras (2012) identified other features to include state terror that displaced millions of peasants, Indians and Afro- Colombians. Furthermore, extractive capitalism in Colombia involves land grants to mining and energy corporations, along with lucrative tax-breaks, social inequality, high unemployment, and the formation of a substantial informal sector. Police and private paramilitary death squads are also other characteristic features, as are the suppression of labor demands, poor enforcement of environmental laws, a lack of compensation to peasant communities for environmental damage, and forced relocation (Petras, 2012).

Wealth and power are concentrated in the hands of foreign investors and local collaborators including generals and political elites. The non-extractive sectors, in which the majority of the labor force is located is in decline, and so too is the standard of living of the workers in those sectors. The challenges faced by the extractive model are structural and political, including an over dependence on commodity exports, a lack of diversified markets, discontent among local manufacturers and agro exporters, and the FARC and ELN guerrilla movements (Petras, 2012).

Extractive capitalism is characterized by a capitalist development dynamic, which expands the extractive frontier, and intensifies social conflicts over territorial rights, land, water, and natural resources (Petras, 2012). When viewed from the vantage point of class struggle the new extractivism is associated with political conflict and resource wars. Extractive capitalism is regarded as backward, predatory, and cannot generate the conditions for genuine progress and sustainable development.

Undoubtedly, Petras provides an excellent analysis of the characteristic features of natural resources extraction in Latin America. But, do these characteristic features by themselves constitute a capitalist mode of production? The supposed movement from classical extractivism to the new extractivism does not represent a revolutionary transformation of the capitalist mode of production, it is the same capitalism with a new face. It is merely an intra-capitalist movement, which in essence is indicative of the ability of capitalism to reform itself when it is in crisis. Thus, it is the same capitalist mode of production, which is dominant whether the economy is dominated by primary commodity production or a development strategy is founded on natural resources extraction.

The significance of Petras' works on natural resources extraction in the Latin American and Caribbean region nevertheless are the richness of details, insights, and new knowledge they provide on the characteristic features of the modus operandi of the capitalist reform process. The details, insights and knowledge are presented in the light of the crisis spawned by state interventionist policies of the 1960s and 1970s and neoliberal policies in the 1980s and 1990s. Classical extractivism and the new extractivism operate in the identical capitalist mode of production, which begs the question for a transition to an alternative mode of production. Socialism in the twenty-first century represented a bold attempt to affect that transition, but the recent reversals in those policies in the Latin American and Caribbean region restores the upper hand to capitalism.

The marked shift in capital accumulation and the development project associated with the new extractivism away from the exploitation of surplus labor generated in the agricultural sector, towards the extraction and exploitation of natural resources (Veltmeyer and Petras, 2014), is a key observation. But, there is a difficulty with the characterization of capital accumulation as shifting from the exploitation of surplus labor in agriculture towards the exploitation of natural resources. The exploitation of natural resources also depends on the exploitation of surplus labor understood in a different way to that of Lewis (1954).

The Lewis model advocates the expansion of the capitalist industrial sector by those capitalists reinvesting their profit to employ the surplus labor located in the traditional agricultural sector, where the wage rate is low and the marginal productivity of labor is below zero, among other things. The Lewis model is a development strategy that seeks to enhance the standard of living by employing more people. The extractivist model does not have a specific strategy to generate development by reinvesting profit to employ more people. In this latter case the strategy is to reduce the number of workers to increase profit. While in the Lewis model the growth takes place in the real sector, in the extractive model the growth takes place in the financial sector.

Surplus labor is being exploited in both the Lewis and extractive models. There is a big difference in the meaning of surplus labor as found in Lewis and Marx. In the case of Lewis, surplus labor refers to the un- and under-employed labor in the traditional sector, and people who are working but are not contributing to productivity. In the case of Marx, surplus labor is the portion of labor that the capitalist appropriates as profit. It is the difference between what the capitalist sells the worker's product for and what he pays the worker as wages – unpaid labor. The unemployed in the view of Marx are not necessary surplus labor but the reserve arm of labor, which the capitalist maintains to exercise greater control over the labor process. The finance of both the Lewis and extractive models utilize surplus labor to the extent that reinvested profit and foreign direct investment both originate in unpaid labor.

On extractive imperialism

Extractive imperialism is identified as a phenomenon that turbocharges 'the engine of capitalist development in the region' (Veltmeyer and Petras, 2014). It creates the 'conditions for another period of accumulation by large-scale, long-term foreign investments following dispossession' (Veltmeyer and Petras, 2014). The current system of capitalist production in Latin America, labeled the new extractivism, depends on extractive imperialism to increase its internal efficiency and power by forcing extra energy into the system. Extractive imperialism is a sort of an external stimulus to extractive capitalism. The term extractive imperialism does not say much about the precise form imperialism takes today in terms of the strategies and tactics of the agents of the imperial state (Veltmeyer and Petras, 2014). Thus 'extractive imperialism,' is an imprecise concept, compared with imperialism understood to mean the activities of the agents of an imperial state to facilitate the overseas activities of its domestic capitalists.

In arguing the case for extractive imperialism the idea is advanced that it is necessary to explore the specific and diverse forms imperialism takes today, to promote and support extractive capital (Veltmeyer and Petras, 2014). It would seem that imperialism comes in many forms, but its essence really resides in the precise actions taken by agents of foreign states in support of their domestic capitalist to carry out different forms of productive activities abroad for the purposes of capital accumulation at home.

It follows that the activities of the agents of the imperial state to support foreign investments in agriculture would be defined as 'agricultural imperialism,' logging as 'logging imperialism,' construction as 'construction imperialism' and so on. But, is there a common threat that connects these different forms of 'imprecise' imperialisms? What is it that makes the activities of agents to buttress the overseas economic ventures of the imperial state, imperialist? Could those activities also not be imperialist? Is there a difference between these 'imprecise' imperialisms and precise imperialism? There seems to be many more questions than answers in the presentation on extractive imperialism by Veltmeyer and Petras (2014). But, we could simply say that the imperial state is in the control of transnational capitalist classes.

Lenin (1963) identified imperialism as a special stage of capitalism, its highest stage, which means that imperialism is capitalism. The persistence and progress of the essential features of capitalism in general are directly responsible for the emergence of imperialism. However, it is only at a definite and very high stage of its development that capitalism becomes capitalist imperialism. At that stage certain of its essential features begin to change into their opposites. According to Lenin (1963), this change happens 'when the features of the epoch of transition from capitalism to a higher social and economic system had taken shape and revealed themselves in all spheres.' Imperialism displaces free competition with monopoly, 'cartels, syndicates and trusts,' which are merged with banks to manipulate trillions. Monopoly does not completely do away with free competition, but exist above and alongside it, which leads to antagonisms, frictions and conflicts. Indeed, monopoly represents the transition of capitalism to a higher stage (Lenin, 1963). Thus, it is not all capitalist societies that are imperialist, they have to achieve a mature state before they become imperialist.

It is capitalism that connects the different forms of imperialisms in the suggested interpretation by Veltmeyer and Petras (2014) on the subject. Thus, whatever the era of capitalism the imperialist relations of the day represent its highest stage. Capitalism marches through different historical periods and is characterized by different historical forms, which are turbocharged by different historical imperialisms. However, Lenin's stage theory of imperialism suggests that capitalism has gone through laissez faire, monopoly, and imperialist phases, since monopoly rises above free competition, and monopoly represents the transition of capitalism to a higher stage. Nkrumah (1965) further subdivides the imperialist phase of capitalism identifying neo-colonialism as its last stage. Undoubtedly, neo-colonialism is not the final stage of imperialism, since the new extractivism is associated but no longer correlated with neocolonial regimes.

Veltmeyer and Petras (2014) seem to suggest that different forms of capitalism produce different forms of imperialism. But, in their assessment of extractive capitalism and extractive imperialism it appears as though capitalism and imperialism are two different phenomena. Examining their approach through the prism of Lenin's theory of imperialism, it would seem that extractive imperialism is the highest stage of extractive capitalism. This would mean that extractive capitalism is the dominant form of current capitalism and its highest stage is extractive imperialism. Is extractive capitalism really the dominant form of capitalism in the Latin American and Caribbean region?

There seems to be a general understanding among Marxists that finance capitalism is the most dominant form of capitalism in the current era of global capitalism and that its highest stage, imperialism, is financialization. This means that the economy and society in the Latin American and Caribbean region are permeated by the affairs of finance capital facilitated by the policies and actions of the imperial and domestic states. Banks, non-banks (both non-bank financial intermediaries and firms in the productive sector), households and the state are the principals under financialization (Lapavitsas, 2013). Each plays their part, through their involvement in capital markets, in furthering the domination of economy and society by rentier financial capitalists.

Financial accumulation is the principal means of capital accumulation under financialization. The inseparability of finance from production means however that the current focus on natural resources extraction in the Latin American and Caribbean region is an integral component of the domination of finance capital. It is the productive expression of the domination by finance capital in that the sale of the commodity produced does not bring as much profit to investors as what the related financial instruments bring to the bankers and financial speculators. Natural resources extraction is taking place at the behest of financial capital that fund the production process, but simultaneously whose principals create a variety of financial instruments to make profit, separate from the sale of commodities.

Capitalism and imperialism

Perhaps recognizing the associated conceptual difficulties in delineating the concepts extractive capitalism and extractive imperialism, Petras and Veltmeyer (2017) wrote *Power and resistance: US imperialism in Latin America* in which they investigated the complex and intimate relationship between capitalism and imperialism in the process of rethinking imperialism in the twenty-first century. The era of extractive capitalism assumes its proper place in the relationship between capitalism and imperialism in the chapter entitled 'Imperialism in an era of extractive capitalism.' The order of the connection between imperialism and capitalism in this connection is such that extractive capitalism gave rise to a particular form of imperialism. Thus, each era of capitalism gives rise to its own form of imperialism; capitalism does not come from imperialism but vice versa. Thus, extractive capitalism is associated with a form of imperialism termed extractive imperialism, which only comes into existence because of extractive capitalism, representing its highest stage.

In the article 'Imperialism and capitalism: Rethinking an intimate relationship' (Veltmeyer and Petras, 2015), which reappears in the book *Power and resistance: US imperialism in Latin America*, as 'Capitalism and imperialism:

Notes of an intimate relation' (Petras and Veltmeyer, 2017) the discourse on imperialism and capitalism in the liberal political science literature is critiqued. They identified two problems with the way the terms are used and understood in that literature. The first problem is that imperialism is disconnected from the economic dynamics of capitalism and is reduced to a mere quest for power and world domination. Second, it reduces imperialism to a purely economic phenomenon and confuses the term with capitalism. It is argued that imperialism and capitalism are intimately connected, but each engage the geo-economics and the geopolitics of capital in a distinctly unique manner that needs to be distinguished (Veltmeyer and Petras, 2015).

Veltmeyer and Petras (2015) disputed several aspects of contemporary neo-Marxist and neoliberal theories of imperialism and the imperial state advanced by a number of scholars.[5] It is observed that these theories merely engage in a crude sociological analyses of the class and political character of the imperial state elites and their policies (Veltmeyer and Petras, 2015). Undoubtedly, Veltmeyer and Petras' interrogation of extractive capitalism provides the kind of detailed class analyses of current capitalism and by extension imperialism in the Latin American and Caribbean region. This kind of analysis is absent in the works they critiqued. Most of those theories they critiqued are economic reductionist, which downplay and ignore the political and ideological dimensions of imperial power (Veltmeyer and Petras, 2015).

Also, these theories decontextualized categories such as investments, trade, and markets, and present them as historically intangible things that are similar across space and time (Veltmeyer and Petras, 2015). The dynamics of class relations are then accounted for in terms of general economic categories. These categories include 'finance,' 'manufacturing,' 'banking,' and 'services.' But this account lacks any analysis of the political economy of capitalist development and class formation (Veltmeyer and Petras, 2015). It does not account for the contributions of social patagolies such as the illegal drug trade and money laundering, and real estate speculation, etc., as part of the nature and sources of financial wealth (Veltmeyer and Petras, 2015).

The new world order's institutional and policy framework is shaped on a continuous basis by the power configurations of imperial policy, which is sociopolitical, ideological, and construed through the role of international financial institutions (Veltmeyer and Petras, 2015). Imperial power relations have political and economic dynamics and engage the political apparatus of the state. Marxists understand that imperialism is connected to capitalism and the system of imperial state agencies. Imperialism secures the conditions needed for capital accumulation. It is 'the bearer of capital, an agency of capitalist development' (Veltmeyer and Petras, 2015). But, is the spread of capitalism the same as capitalist development?

Capitalism and capitalist development seem to be two different phenomena, which are presented as the same in the notion that imperialism is an agency of capitalist development. The spread of capitalism is about maintaining capital accumulation in imperial states at the capitalist center. This involves the power configurations of the state that enhances the exhaustion of the countries in the capitalist periphery of their resources and wealth and transferring those to the capitalist imperial states at the center.

The irony of this situation is that both the center and peripheral countries represent the process of depleting the periphery of its wealth and transferring it to the center as capitalist development. In that context capitalist development is construed as a phenomenon associated with peripheral capitalist countries seeking by way of the appropriate policies to catch-up with the technological, economic, social and political advances the mature capitalist states have achieved.

But, this is not the goal of imperialism, which is to secure appropriate environment for capital accumulation. Imperialism does not bear capitalist development but instead creates misery for the conquered countries. Development is bifurcated in that it takes place at the center in a manner that sets the standard for the peripheral countries to achieve, or catch-up. The reality of the situation is that capitalism is in a constant process of development thus capitalism and capitalist development, appears as one and the same process.

Capitalist development must be understood in terms of the ratio of constant to variable capital that is, the organic composition of capital. As the organic composition of capital increases, the rate of profit is lowered. Labor-displacing improvements in technology, which implies the modernization of machinery and materials used in production relative to wage labor is augmented over time, which increases the organic composition of capital. Thus, capitalist development is about increasing the organic composition of capital, although the rate of profit tends to fall in the process implying the crisis prone nature of capitalism. Thus, the increasing organic composition of capital denotes that there is a historic tendency for the rate of profit to fall leading to crisis in capitalism, as profits become more difficult to realize (Marx, 1991).

The policies of the imperial state shape imperial power in the national interest that coincides with the economic and political concerns and interests of the capitalist class and private sector. Imperialism is a matter of politics and political economy, class and state power and as such it is not useful to measure its impact purely in economic terms concerning the volume of inflows and outflows of capital. Furthermore, geopolitical and economic concerns play a role in bringing about change in the relations of domination and dependence. This leads to demands by domestic state elites and politicians in the capitalist periphery for relative autonomy to protect their national interests (Veltmeyer and Petras, 2015).

In the historical materialist tradition, which is the foundations of Marxism as a social science, at each stage in the capitalist development process there is the development of the forces of production. This is associated with a corresponding system of class relations and struggle arising out of the fundamental conflict between the forces and relations of production. Veltmeyer and Petras (2015) have therefore expanded Marxist social science by the argument they present on extractive capitalism. Their argument is that capitalist development in terms of extractive capitalism produces class struggle that is distinct. The class struggle is based on the forces of resistance to extractive capitalism, and imperialism, which in essence is the projection of state power in the service of capital. The projection of state power facilitates the advance of capitalism internationally, and supports its evolution into and as a world system (Veltmeyer and Petras, 2015).

Imperialism to Lenin (1963) however entails merging industrial and financial capital; exporting capital in search of overseas markets; and colonization by dividing up foreign territories of the world by European capitalist powers. Also, it entails the creation of an international division of labor based on a system of exchange of primary commodities for manufactured goods. This comprises the economic dynamic of capital accumulation (Veltmeyer and Petras, 2015). State political power including the use of military force, secured the system's economic structure along with that particular dynamic.

Veltmeyer and Petras (2015) critique Lenin (1963) on the grounds that while he associated imperialism with industrial capitalism, imperialist relations are identifiable in a much earlier period, during mercantilism. Lenin (1963) mistakenly identified the structural features of world capitalism at its stage of development at his time as 'imperialism,' a distinct feature of capitalism. Whereas the earlier phase of mercantile capitalism also projected imperial class-based state power. Under mercantile capitalism the accumulation of merchant capital depended on expropriated natural resources, exploitation of labor and state-sanctioned and regulated international trade. Imperialism was definitely a characteristic feature of mercantilism and an adjunct to capital accumulation in later periods of capitalist development (Veltmeyer and Petras, 2015).

The era of state-led capitalist development in the post-World War II period between 1950 and 1980 has seen a process of productive and social transformation. The transformation, which represented a change from an agriculture-based socio-economic system and pre-capitalist production relations to an industrial capitalist system, resulted from the exploitation of labor in the traditional rural agricultural sector.[6] The transformation was evident in different time periods and unfolded in different ways in the Latin American and Caribbean countries in their struggle to free themselves from colonial subjugation, imperialist exploitation and class rule.

The US and other powerful countries in the Western Hemisphere implemented their notion of development through diplomacy and military intervention to facilitate the entry and exit of their capital at will into peripheral countries. This has led to the development in the periphery of the productive forces that facilitated the capital accumulation process. The institutional arrangements established by European powers and the US to promote development were in essence instruments of imperialism. They were intended to thwart the spread of socialism by diverting the peripheral countries away from revolutionary change.

Veltmeyer and Petras (2015) focused attention on imperialism and capitalism in an era of neoliberal globalization. They argue that neoliberalism was in the making for forty years before the 1980s. That hitherto period provided the conditions for its implementation. The imperial state and its institutions were used to 'reactivate the capital accumulation process' under the Washington

Consensus. The Latin American and Caribbean states became dominated by neoliberal policies, imposed on them as a condition for aid and access to capital markets to address their debt crises. US intervention in the region and economic blockade against recalcitrant states had mixed results, as the imperialist and anti-imperialist struggle assumed different forms in different countries.

International cooperation and the agencies of international development constituted an imperialist offensive front against popular resistance. These agencies used a strategy to dampen the revolutionary movements by providing an alternative to direct collective action and social mobilization that is non-confrontational. This strategy succeeded in some cases but in others such as in Bolivia it did not (Veltmeyer and Petras, 2015).

Conclusion

In conclusion the state as the executive committee of the ruling class serves to facilitate extractive capitalist and imperialist economic ventures in the Latin American and Caribbean region. The question is: are extractive capitalism and extractive imperialism two separate phenomena or are they integral components of an identical capitalist development process, which requires the state as an executive committee of the bourgeoisie to exercise political power to facilitate the exploitation of workers in the extractive industries in the region? Political power is understood to mean the organized power of the ruling classes in the Latin America and Caribbean region to oppress the working classes. Petras and Veltmeyer (2015) cleared up the answer to a foregoing question in their analysis of the relationship between capitalism and imperialism. In their earlier works on extractive capitalism and extractive imperialism, the answer is not that clear.

The capitalist mode of production is a distinct system of producing commodities that sets it apart from hitherto existing modes of production. It represents a specific social organization of production, particular social relations, and production technologies involving a combination of the most advanced scientific knowledge within industry. It comprises privately owned property, market exchange of products, wage-labor, the endless pursuit of profits, capital accumulation, improvements in living conditions with the simultaneous generation and sustenance of the most horrific levels of poverty, and class struggle between the owners of the means of production and working people. Its purpose for existence is the production of surplus value that is fundamental to its reproduction through capital accumulation. The specific commodity produced does not define what the capitalist system of production is all about, even though a capitalist may be delineated in terms of the particular productive activity in which he is engaged.

Thus, for example, we may speak of an industrial capitalist, or an agricultural capitalist, or a commercial capitalist, or even an extractive capitalist. We may even speak of industrial capitalism, agricultural capitalism, commercial capitalism or extractive capitalism in an effort to delineate the capitalist activities surrounding industry, agriculture, commerce, or extraction. But, these are mere descriptive labels, which do not represent the essence of capitalism: what capitalism is in itself.

The extraction of natural resources has no real significance in defining capitalism. Natural resources extraction has taken place under hitherto existing modes of production. What is significant is the extant dominant means by which the economic surplus is produced in support of subsistence labor and capital accumulation, and the derivative social relations that arise. It does not matter whether the form of capitalism is industrial, agricultural, commercial, or extractive, what really does are the labor-capital relations, the institutional edifice including the apparatuses of the state erected in support of the production structure, and the class struggle these produce. The principal antagonistic contradiction in the Latin American and Caribbean region is between *capital* and *labor*.

Notes

1 See for example Veltmeyer (2013, 2015, 2015a); Petras and Veltmeyer (2012, 2015, 2016); Veltmeyer and Petras (2014).
2 Examples of these articles are 'Extractive capitalism and the divisions in the Latin American progressive camp'; 'Colombia: Extractive capitalism and peace negotiations'; 'Latin America: Class struggle and resistance in the age of extractive capitalism'; and 'Brazil: Extractive capitalism and the great leap backward.'
3 For an elaboration on this idea see for example Bellofiore (2009); Bellofiore and Passarella (2009).
4 See for example 'Latin America: Class struggle and resistance in the age of extractive capitalism'; 'Brazil: Extractive capitalism and the great leap backward'; 'Colombia: Extractive capitalism and peace negotiations'; and 'Extractive capitalism and the divisions in the Latin American progressive camp.'
5 See for example Harvey (2003); Magdoff (2003); Amin (2001); Panitch and Leys (2004); Bellamy Foster (2006); and Hardt and Negri (2000).
6 See Veltmeyer and Petras (2015) and Lewis (1954).

References

Amin, S. (2001). 'Imperialism and globalization.' *Monthly Review*, 53 (2), pp. 6–24.
Arrighi, G. (1994). *The long 20th century: Money, power, and the origins of our times*. London and New York: Verso.
Bellamy Foster. (2006). *Naked imperialism: The US pursuit of domination*. New York: Monthly Review Press.
Bellofiore, R. (2009). 'Rosa Luxemburg on capitalist dynamics, distribution, and effective demand crises,' in R. Bellofiore (ed.) *Rosa Luxemburg and the critique of political economy*. London and New York: Routledge, pp. 1–24.
Bellofiore, R. and Passarella, M. (2009). 'Finance and the realization problem in Rosa Luxemburg: A 'circuitist' reappraisal,' in J. F. Ponsot, and S. Rossi (eds) *The political economy of monetary circuits: Tradition and change in post-Keynesian economics*. London and New York: Palgrave Macmillan, pp. 98–115.
Hardt, M. and Negri, A. (2000). *Empire*. Cambridge: Harvard University Press.
Harvey, D. (2003). *The new imperialism*. New York and Oxford: Oxford University Press.
Hobson, J. A. (1902). *Imperialism: A study*. London: Allen and Unwin.
Lapavitsas, C. (2013). *Profiting without producing: How finance exploits us all*. London and New York: Verso.

Lenin, V. I. (1963). *Imperialism, the highest stage of capitalism.* Moscow: Progress Publishers.

Lewis, W. A. (1954). 'Economic development with unlimited supplies of labor.' *The Manchester School*, 22 (2), pp. 139–191.

Luxemburg, R. (1951). *The accumulation of capital.* London: Routledge and Kegan Paul.

Magdoff, H. (2003). *Imperialism without colonies.* New York: Monthly Review Press.

Marx, K. (1991). *Capital: A critique of political economy, Vol. III.* London: Penguin Books & New Left Review.

Marx, K. (1909). *Capital: A critique of political economy, Volume II The process of circulation of capital.* Chicago: H. Kerr and Co.

Nkrumah, K. (1965). *Neo-colonialism, the last stage of imperialism.* London: Thomas Nelson & Sons, Ltd.

Panitch, L. and Leys, C. (2004). *The new imperial challenge.* New York: Monthly Review Press.

Petras, J. (2013). 'Latin America: Class struggle and resistance in the age of extractive Capitalism.' *The James Petras Website.* Available at: https://petras.lahaine.org/latin-america-class-struggle-and-resistance-in-the-age-of-extractive-capitalism/08/06.

Petras, J. (2013a). 'Brazil: Extractive capitalism and the great leap backward.' *World Review of Political Economy*, 4 (4), pp. 469–483.

Petras, J. (2012). 'Colombia: Extractive capitalism and peace negotiations.' *The James Petras Website.* Available at: http://petras.lahaine.org/?p=1910,09/11/.

Petras, J. (2012a). 'Extractive capitalism and the divisions in the Latin American progressive camp.' *Global Research.* Available at: www.globalresearch.ca/extractive-capitalism-and-the-divisions-in-the-latin-american-progressive-camp/30658.

Petras, J. (1981). 'Dependency and world system theory: A critique and new directions.' *Latin American Perspectives*, 8 (3/4), pp. 148–155.

Petras, J. and Veltmeyer, H. (2017). *Power and resistance: US imperialism in Latin America.* Chicago: Haymarket Books.

Petras, J. and Veltmeyer, H. (2016). *Extractive imperialism in the Americas: Capitalism's new frontier.* Chicago: Haymarket Books.

Petras, J. and Veltmeyer, H. (2012). 'The rise and demise of extractive capitalism.' *The James Petras Website.* Available at: http://petras.lahaine.org/?p=1895 July.

Veltmeyer, H. (2015). 'The new geoeconomics of capital in Latin America: Alternative trade and development in an era of extractive capitalism,' in K. Ervine and G. Fridell (eds) *Beyond free trade: Alternative approaches to trade, politics and power.* New York: Palgrave Macmillan, pp. 117–132.

Veltmeyer, H. (2015a). 'Dynamics of alternative trade and development in Latin America.' *Journal of Economics and Development Studies*, 3 (2), pp. 108–123.

Veltmeyer, H. (2013). 'The political economy of natural resource extraction: A new model or extractive imperialism?' *Canadian Journal of Development Studies/Revue Canadienne d'Études du Développement*, 34 (1) pp. 79–95.

Veltmeyer, H. and Petras, J. (2015). 'Imperialism and capitalism: Rethinking an intimate relationship.' *Global Research* Available at: www.globalresearch.ca/imperialism-and-capitalism-rethinking-an-intimate-relationship/5496284December16.

Veltmeyer, H. and Petras, J. (2014). *The new extractivism: A post-neoliberal development model or imperialism in the twenty-first century?* London: Zed Books.

Wallerstein, I. (1974). *The modern world system: Capitalist agriculture and the origins of the European world economy in the sixteenth century.* New York: Academic Press.

Part II

Neoextractivism and development of center-periphery relations

6 Natural resources extraction and expanded capitalist relations

In the analyses of the debates on neoextractivism in Part I the idea was presented that development theory is integral to the development of capitalism and as such could be regarded are one and the same with capitalism. The problem under consideration is the congruence between development theory and capitalism. This problem is examined through the lens of neoextractivism represented as a development theory. This approach is seen as favoring the interest of working people, whereas in reality its true role is to promote capitalist development. The argument is that as capitalism is reformed in its evolutionary development due to crises the struggle in the capitalist periphery over the ownership and or control over natural resources oscillates with that process. Neoextractivism is a part of a capitalist dynamic that takes place at different historical periods in capitalist development as crisis forces capitalism to go into reform mode.

This observation is revealed through the use of the historical materialist method to study neoextractivism. Capitalism was seen to be marching on, driven by crises as the evidence from Guyana showed. The tendency was for the state elites in the capitalist periphery to demand local ownership and or control of natural resources with the explicit purpose of improving the conditions of working people in their countries. The notions of extractivism and neoextractivism were examined, with a focus on their multiple meanings as defined in the burgeoning literature on the subjects.

The issues as to whether neoextractivism is myth or reality was examined. This was done by discussing the transition from colony to nation-state status in the periphery and capitalist contradictions, national ownership and or control of natural resources, neoliberal capitalism and the extractive industries, and the development impact of natural resources extraction. Thereafter, the discussion shifts to an analysis of extractive capitalism, extractive imperialism and imperialism. These concepts, as well as the relationship between capitalism and imperialism, were analyzed.

In Part II on neoextractivism and the development of center-periphery relations, evidence is presented from the Guyana-case concerning natural resources extraction and capitalist development. This evidence supports the theory that neoextractivism is merely a conjunctural phenomenon identifiable at different historical periods of capitalist development. Five interrelated dynamic processes are analyzed in relation to capitalist development and natural resources extraction. These are natural resources extraction and expanded capitalist relations, the foundations of post-colonial neoextractivism, the post-colonial authoritarian state, the criminalized authoritarian state, and political change and foreign intervention.

The transition to capitalist center-periphery relations is analyzed in terms of the administration of the country, and developments in the natural resources sector, in particular the gold, diamonds, bauxite and forestry subsectors. In essence, these developments involved the liberation of labor, capital and the society as a whole from the grasp of plantation property relations. The reforms introduced by the colonial power were designed to favor European capital maintaining control of the natural resources of Guyana. They were intended to facilitate the development of peripheral capitalism in Guyana.

The data presented on productive activities in the natural resources sector at the time demonstrated the extent and commitment of the British government to speed up the transition to capitalist center-periphery relations through natural resources extraction. The colonial slave mode of production had outlived its usefulness, as the indenture system ended. The time had arrived for the colonial authorities to take bold new steps to fashion newfangled economic relations with the colonies through natural resources extraction.

State-led capitalist development

The phenomenon of state-led capitalist development and natural resources extraction is the subject of this chapter. It highlights the issue of the collapse of the 'colonial slave mode of production' and its replacement with center-periphery capitalist relations. The colonial state led the push to expand capitalist relations through natural resources extraction. The focus is on Guyana where the natural resources sector really began to take hold in the economy in the historical period between 1834 and 1953. This period was characterized by a the colonial slave mode of production (Thomas, 1984). It was in that period that the phenomenon described as the new extractivism in Latin America emerged in Guyana. Whereas the Latin American scholars argue that a new extractivism had arrived on the continent in a post-neoliberal period. It will be demonstrated however that the foundations for the emergence of a similar phenomenon in Guyana was laid in a much earlier period with the advent of the natural resources sector after the colonial slave mode of production collapsed.

The British finally took control of the Dutch colonies Essequibo, Berbice and Demerara in 1803 and unified them under the name British Guiana in 1831. In 1966 the country secured political independence from the British and it was renamed Guyana. The British government pursued a serious public relations campaign to attract British capital to the natural resources industries in Guyana. It claimed that there were substantial opportunities for capital to invest in the natural resources sector, characterized by ores and minerals and forestry industries. The British government had established that a wide variety of ores and minerals of economic importance could be found in Guyana.[1] At the time, gold, diamonds, bauxite and kaolin were the only ores and minerals, which were previously discovered in commercial quantities.

The forestry products industries included timber valuable to manufacture paper pulp, and a variety of other valuable and common timbers. Also, they included the production of boards and scantlings, fuel wood, charcoal, shingles, fence saves, vat staves, posts, beams and spars, greenheart and mangrove barks, locus and chicle gums, balata, and other forestry products.

Foreign investment in Guyana for the production any of these products was encouraged, which would deepen the country's capitalist structure. When the question why Guyana remained undeveloped during the 120 years that the British had operated in the country has been pondered, every other reason, except the main one was provided. This was that the colonial slave mode of production served to hold back the full potential of capitalist natural resources industries in the country.

Instead, the British identified a number of other reasons why Guyana remained undeveloped. These included factors such as the small size of the country's population that forced it to depend on imported labor, and the poor sanitary conditions in the country. Furthermore, investors were thought to be ignorant of the country's economic possibilities. Finally, the geographical make-up of the country was not well understood, as many people mistake Guyana for a small island in the Caribbean Sea.

The British government considered schemes to find the best route into the interior of Guyana by train to serve the mining and timber industries. It sought to lure capitalists to diversify the agriculture sector as well as the natural resources sector. It exhorted the capitalists to develop the rubber industries, building on the experimental rubber plantations that had already been established. This attempt to stimulate capitalist development was explicitly a state-led process.

The extraction of natural resources in Guyana for exchange in capitalist markets was mediated by colonial authoritarian politics dominated by the planter class. The planters themselves were not to become engaged in wholesale natural resources extraction. They only did so as a last resort to supplement their incomes when there was a shortfall in profits from the sugar plantations. Sugar profits would decline due to a number of factors, including bad weather or economic crises in Europe that negatively affected the colonies.

As the colonial slave mode of production began to disintegrate between the 1830s and the 1920s a different disposition emerged towards natural resources extraction. The change in property relations in Guyana in favor of full-fledged capitalist property relations led to the emergence of the capitalist limited-liability corporations in the country. The laws that the plantocracy passed to restrict the movement of labor from plantation agriculture to other spheres of economic activity gradually eased. Capital was granted the freedom to diversify out of plantation agriculture, and new capital was invited to enter the country in the natural resources sectors. The ensuing analysis demonstrates the extent of the attempt at economic diversification out of the colonial slave mode of production's mono-crop agricultural system. It starts off with a discussion on the colonial state's concerns with administration, regulatory and costs matters in the natural resources sector as a component part of the transition to capitalist center-periphery relations.

Administration, regulatory and cost concerns

The colonial administration divided the country into mining districts, with each district coming under the authority of a Warden or Sub-Warden who was an appointed officer of the Department of Lands and Mines (British Guyana, 1924). The Warden had powers to settle all disputes concerning mining claims and to continually traverse the district providing help and assistance to miners in adhering to the mining regulations. The mining industry is located in the hinterland where the aborigines inhabit away from the imported populated centers of the country on the Atlantic coast. For mining to take place mineworkers had to travel to the interior, bringing with them their food and other items such as medical supplies. The colonial government sought to regulate that entire process.

The government created regulations that established a scale according to which ordinary laborers in the gold industry were to obtain rations. The regulations granted mineworkers ration allowances that ranged from 1s. 6d. or 36 cents to 1s. 8d. or 40 cents per day in all mining districts (British Guyana, 1924). Mineworkers were given contracts that bounded them to work between three to six months at a time in the goldfields. These workers were typically 'black and colored men, natives of the Colony and the West Indian Islands' (British Guyana, 1924). Laborers who failed to complete their contract were liable to a fine of 10s. or $2.40 or imprisonment.

Miners would buy or rent a boat to travel to the goldfields in the interior regions of the country. A boat capable of holding three tons of provisions, tools, implements, etc., cost about £110 or $528.00 and required a crew of about fourteen to twenty men including the captain, or steersman and the bowman (British Guyana, 1924). It was the duty of these three to steer the boat clear of all rocks through the various rapids and cataracts encountered on the journey. The captain earned a wage between £10 8s. 4d. or $50.72 to £12 10s. or $60.00 a month with food. The bowmen earned £8 6s. 8d. or $41.44 to £11 9s. 2d. $55.36 a month with food. In the event that there was a boom in goldmining the pay of these men would have been increased by 50 percent (British Guyana, 1924).

An investor wishing to prospect for gold first had to obtain a prospecting license. The cost of a prospecting license was $5 or £1 0s. 10d. It was the equivalent to a miner's right to a given plot of land on which to prospect. The prospecting license entitled its owner to prospect over Crown lands for a period of twelve months from the date of issue. The owner was entitled to locate claims by cutting lines to define the boundaries and to erect corner posts, boards or beacons. Once a claim location was established a notice was filed and a claim license obtained at an annual fee of $5 or £1 0s. 10d. for gold and at the rate of 50c. (2s. 1d.) an acre for diamonds (British Guyana, 1924).

The fee for filing an application to obtain exclusive permission to occupy and explore a tract of land for a period not exceeding three years was $10 or £2 1s. 8d. A yearly rent of 7.5 cents or 3.75d. an acre was collected on such lands. The fee was payable half yearly in advance from the date of the first advertisement of the application when the applicant becomes the legal occupant. Companies with titled mining concessions, dredging concessions and mining leases had a slightly higher fee structure. Mining concessions for gold paid a rent of 20c. or 10d, and for diamonds 50 cents or 2s. 1d. per acre. The fee for dredging concessions was 10c. or 5d. for the right to dredge for gold and 20c. or 10d. per acre for the right to dredge for both gold and diamonds. The fee for surveys was 10 cents or 5d. an acre (British Guyana, 1924).

The owner of a single claim license could exercise the right of both quartz and alluvial mining rights, while claims were limited to the size of 1,500 by 800 feet. Over burden or stripping depth varied in the different mining districts but the average size was about four to five feet, while the gravel or 'pay dirt' beneath was about two to three feet thick containing coarse gold, nuggets, or fine gold. Baling of mine pit was done either with buckets or California pumps (British Guyana, 1924). Generally, mining tools and equipment such as surveying instruments, compasses, prospecting drills, air-tight uniform cases, and blow-pipe or assay outfits, were imported, while camp equipment and clothing were readily obtainable locally at reasonable prices (British Guyana, 1924).

To counteract malaria miners were supposed to take at least six grams of quinine every day as a prophylactic. Foreign companies wishing to engage in prospecting had to communicate in advance or on arrival in the country with the Department of Lands and Mines. There they purchased all information and copies of the mining regulations, maps, etc. (British Guyana, 1924).

These costs, regulatory, and administrative reforms were designed to facilitate peripheral capitalist development and streamline capital-labor relations in Guyana. Evidently, free market capitalism was the dominant force during that historical period, but it was the British colonial government's regulations, which were laying the foundations for peripheral capitalist development in the natural resources sector. The colonial state created the rules of the game with which foreign and domestic capitals had to conform in natural resources extraction. The framework of rules included fixing the price for skilled and unskilled labor, as well as the social labor cost for food and health, and a fee structure with which companies had to comply to secure mining rights. The land was referred to as Crown Land meaning that the British Monarch owned it.

The problem really resided in the property relations that emerged in the country. The British Monarch, the state and a few private individuals declared themselves as owners of nature. Those who did not own property now found it difficult to eke out a living for themselves from nature, the property of other. Goldmining was constrained by the regulations, since mining became illegal unless you were licensed to do so. It was illegal to mine on the property of others so in order to survive, property-less miners had to survive by selling their labor power to the owners of nature who hired them to work in the natural resources sector. The gold, diamond, bauxite and forestry subsectors began to attract foreign capital in the period of transition from the colonial slave mode of production to center-periphery relations.

Developments in gold and diamonds mining

The Institute of Mines and Forests of British Guiana, a quasi-government entity was formed in 1890. The purpose of the institute was to recruit, register, and monitor gold, diamonds and forestry workers in the country (Josiah, 2011). The plantation-dominated government controlled the mining industry through the Institute of Mines and Forests. The institute was the means by which capitalist development outside of the agricultural sector was regulated.

The Institute collected data on the mining industry, which it passed on to the government. It pushed back against attempts to organize the mining industry as a competitor with the agricultural sector, although some agricultural capitalists were involved in mining and forestry. There was an individual named B. Howell-Jones, for example, a legislator in the British Guiana Court of Policy who was simultaneously the owner of a sugar plantation and a director of the Barima Gold Mining Company and the Arakaka Placer and Mining Company. The Institute was given permission by the government in 1893, to import migrant labor from Barbados to work in the gold and forestry subsectors (Josiah, 2011).

While the Institute of Mines and Forests looked after the interest of the plantocracy against extractive capital, challenges came from other sources for the genuine freeing-up of the natural resources sector. Domestic capital owned by middle-class professionals such as Andrew Benjamin Brown a black Guyanese lawyer became involved in financing the creation of prospecting crews, to explore the mining sector (Josiah, 2011). Mr. Brown had contested and won the West Coast Demerara seat in the Court of Policy from Howell-Jones (Josiah, 2011). Mr. Brown and middle-class institutions like the Negro Progress Convention (NPC) and the labor unions were influential in forcing labor reforms that contributed to the capitalist expansion and development of the mining industry.

Capitalist development was not restricted to the activities of foreign capital there were middle-class domestic forces that penetrated the colonial political economy espousing ideas similar to the colonial powers in that connection. These forces perhaps represented the earliest expressions of the phenomenon that Nkrumah (1965) identified as neo-colonialism, with the domestic actors being the neocolonialists. The missing factor from Nkrumah's observation was that these forces were not handed state power, which they exercised in the interest of the colonial powers. But, they were the forces that would secure the trust of the colonial powers and handed the rein of government at independence, which was exercised in colonial interests.

Also, various agents began to recruit labor from the wider Caribbean and elsewhere to work in the mining industry. These agents played a significant role in capitalist development by making the mining industry viable through the supply of the appropriate migrant labor to work in the sector. Capitalist development cannot proceed unless there is capital and labor that stand in direct contradiction to each other, which the recruitment agent helped to facilitate. Operating on behalf of mining concerns, the agents acquired shares in various companies and negotiated the purchase and sale of prospecting claims (Josiah, 2011).

In some cases, the agents owned other businesses and managed private gold mining companies, such as the British Guiana Gold Mines, the British Guiana Dredging Syndicate, the Berbice Company, and the Guiana Company (Josiah, 2011). In 1890, it was estimated that there were '3,000 to 4,000' Africans and 'their diaspora counterparts' mineworkers who 'were favorably viewed as recruits in the local gold and diamonds fields' in Guyana (Josiah, 2011, pp. 29–30).

The development of capitalism in Guyana received a boon as global capitalism was altered considerably by global occurrences involving World War I, which carried over into World War II. The Institute had begun to be phased out as bauxite mining began in 1917. The production and the first shipment of bauxite made in 1918 changed the mining sector in a profound manner. Bauxite was needed for military purposes in the production of war planes so its production trumped any attempt by agricultural capital to suppress capitalist development in the natural resources sector.

The rise of social movements and the media also played a role in the capitalist development through advances in the natural resources sector. The Reform Association and the Reform Club, which comprised middle-class elements in the country advocated for social and economic change in Guyana. The members of these organizations identified for themselves the role of reforming and improving the social relations of Guyanese society in order to allow for greater participation in the policy, society and economy of groups other than those who represented the planters' interests. The Reform Association and the Reform Club were joined by the Georgetown Chambers of Commerce to champion the cause of what was described as the 'minor industries.' In consideration in this connection were the non-sugar industries such as those involved in natural resources extraction. Local merchants who operated on a small-scale basis tried to break the planter monopoly on land and labor, which was the main obstacle to the development of alternative capitalist industries.

The media such as the Nugget newspapers launched on August 1, 1888, and the Gold Mining Gazette, which was a special weekly edition of the Echo newspapers, was both part of the domestic middle-class pressure on the colonial authorities for political, economic and social reform. The reform movement held the view that the planters were not in a hurry to bring about settlement to the border dispute with Venezuela because it served their purpose of holding up gold mining (Rodney, 1981). Venezuela had laid claim to the region of Guyana, which is rich in natural resources. The border dispute places a damper on foreign capital from investing in the disputed territory. The reform movement also expressed concern about the poor state of hinterland transportation, which contributed to the underdevelopment of gold mining and other economic activities located in the interior of the country.

The gold industry really took off in the 1880s, which was a clear indication that more capital was being invested in mineral extraction. Investing more capital in mineral extraction with the type of rudimentary technologies employed in the production process meant that the capitalists had to employ larger numbers of laborers. Indeed, the gold industry 'provided a steady means of livelihood for thousands who pursue fortune in the goldfields year in and year out' (British Guyana, 1924).

There was a unique division of labor based on race in that for example 'labor in the diamond fields was provided primarily by the African diaspora in Guyana.' It was believed that 'laborers drawn from the other races [were] rarely satisfactory' (British Guyana, 1924). The East Indians, for example, were seen to be 'not sufficiently robust to stand the rough life of the diamond fields' (British Guyana, 1924). The labor-intensive extractive activities did employ rudimentary technologies to extract gold. These techniques were alluvial washing or panning; sluicing, with the erection of a 'tom' or a 'sluice' in a pit; quartz mining; hydraulicing, the use of water cannons to separate the gold from the gravel; and dredging.

With the exception of the Berbice and Courantyne geographic areas, gold was found in the Essequibo River and two of its tributaries the Potaro and Konawaruk. Also, gold was discovered in the Mazaruni River and its tributary the Puruni, as well as in the Cuyuni, Barima, Barama, Waini, and the Upper Demerara Rivers. Gold was also recovered on the Wenamu River, a branch of the Cuyuni River, which forms a part of the boundary line between the Guyana and Venezuela (British Guyana, 1924). These were the prominent mining districts that emerged in Guyana in the gold rush that took place in the late 1800s. The gold rush occurred only after capital and labor were freed-up to become engaged in natural resources extraction in Guyana. Gold was eventually found in profitable amounts in the 1880s (British Guyana, 1924).

On the order of the British government a number of mineral explorations were carried out beginning in 1836 two years after the colonial slave mode of production had initially began to collapse, and again in 1845 about twenty-four years after the final collapse of the colonial slave mode of production. Then, in the 1860s and 1870s the British government organized geological surveys of Guyana. In 1863 several mining groups sought permission to prospect for gold in a region disputed by Venezuela. The British Guiana Gold Company published a prospectus but ceased operations in 1867.

The depression in England in the 1880s stimulated gold mining in Guyana as profits in the sugar estates declined. Dredging was successfully undertaken in the Potaro River by British mining companies. A sixty-acre mining property at Omai in the Essequibo River produced 95,000 ounces of gold, and gold nuggets were found in the Five Stars District in the Upper Barima River, one weighing 333 ounces, and at Tiger Creek in the Potaro one weighing 1,111 ounces (British Guyana, 1924). Indeed, between 1884 and 1905 an estimated 1,756,630 ounces of gold bullions were recorded in Guyana. Gold bullion recorded declined between 1906 and 1918 to 820,678 ounces. Between 1919 and 1923 gold bullion recorded declined further to 59,843 ounces.

The total quantity of gold bullion recorded between 1884 and 1923 was 2,637,151 ounces at a total value of £9,615,221 or $12,998,432.66 US Dollars[2] (British Guyana, 1924). The available data on the quantity of gold exported and value showed that between 1918 and 1923 Guyana exported 73,984 ounces. The total value of the gold exported was £283,449 or US$1,360,340 in 1924.

The structure of the gold industry involved private companies and/or syndicates that bought claims from the British monarch, laborers who worked the claims for the companies or syndicates, and Pork Knockers. The 'tributor,' 'Pork Knocker' or gold miner who was paid a percentage of the value of the gold he recovered produced the major portion of the gold obtained from the alluvial pan washing method. Generally, the tributor or 'Pork Knocker' started off as a laborer for a claim-holder operating a company or a syndicate. After the claim was abandoned, some laborers remained in the mining districts and continued to fossick on their own. These laborers now 'Pork Knockers' or small miners operated in small groups ranging from about five to ten men. They combined their resources to rummage for gold in the abandoned claims and divided the proceeds among themselves.

Due to the interior location of the natural resources industries it was necessary to establish shops to supply the 'Pork Knockers' and other gold seekers and forestry workers with their daily needs including food, medicines and alcohol. The 'Pork Knockers' would exchange gold for those items at the provision shops that sprang up, which were integral to the development of the gold industry. The micro-entrepreneurs who owned the shops located their businesses in the vicinity of the claims on which tributors were permitted to work. The shop owners were also gold buyers and operated on the understanding with tributors that they received supplies from and sell their gold finds to the shop owner (British Guyana, 1924).

Pork Knocking technologies and processes involved prospecting, digging a pit from fourteen to twenty square feet, until the 'pay dirt' or gold bearing gravel was reached. The 'Pork Knocker' then erected in the pit a 'tom' or a 'sluice' – an open box about eight feet long, three feet wide, and fifteen inches deep, with an open screen inclined at an angle of forty-five degrees affixed at one end (British Guyana, 1924). The box into which the gravel was thrown was hung on pickets driven into the bottom of the pit. The gravel was splashed against the screen with a constant flow of water pumped in through the opposite end to separate the fine particles of gold that pass through the screen and caught in quicksilver in the 'riffles' placed in a small box just below the end of the 'tom' (British Guyana, 1924). Large nuggets remain against the screen to be picked out by hand. The sand and dirt is washed away into a tailings ditch – a major environmental hazard.

The sluicing method was similar to the 'tom' method but had the advantage of allowing a larger number of men to work a much larger pit (British Guyana, 1924). The sluice was a wooden box about twelve feet long and one foot wide and deep. Several of these sluices were placed in the pit from one end to the other. By use of gravity water was flowed through the sluice into which the 'pay dirt' was thrown. The rush of water carried the mass along the length of the sluice and so did the cleaning work, and saved the men having to puddle in the mud as in the 'tom' method. The riffles placed along the length of the sluice caught the gold (British Guyana, 1924).

While the 'Pork Knockers' engaged in the alluvial pan washing method using the 'tom' or the sluice method, some miners engaged in quartz mining, which was another approach to gold extraction (British Guyana, 1924). A quart is a gold bearing rock that is crushed to extract the gold. Quarts were found in several mining districts in the 1890s, which attracted many miners and capitalists who invested in larger mining concerns. Most of the financially successful quarts milling operations were undertaken at Peter's Mine in the Puruni River, the Barima Mine near Arakaka in the North Western District, and the Aremu Mine on the Aremu a tributary of the Cuyuni River (British Guyana, 1924). Peter's Mine was the most successful at quartz mining extracting 39,017 ounces in four years (British Guyana, 1924).

Hydraulicing, which was initially experimented with at the Omai and Tassawini Mines, was another method used to extract gold in Guyana (British Guyana, 1924). This method involved the use of water cannons to wash gravel down sluices in which the gold was entrapped. Hydraulicing was expensive where the energy supply used was steam power, but it yielded remarkable returns. The view at the time was that the availability of cheap hydroelectric power would make the hydraulicing method even more successful.

The dredging method used in gold extraction was attractive in Guyana and was pursued with satisfactory results in the Potaro District since 1906 (British Guyana, 1924). The Guiana Gold Company Ltd., operated four dredges in the Konawaruk River, and extracted a total of 88,343 ounces from the commencement of operations in December 1906, to December 31, 1922. The Minnehaha Development Company Ltd. produced 22,012 ounces during period 1914 to 1922, dredging a total of 16,303 ounces of gold from the Minnehaha Creek, a tributary of the Konawaruk, during 1910 to 1922 (British Guyana, 1924). This encouraged the dredging method of gold mining that is apparently most suitable 'to the widely diffused alluvial values' in Guyana (British Guyana, 1924). The government abolished the royalty on gold extracted by dredging and instituted instead a 5 percent tax on profits from such mining. Alluvial washing dominated by small miners and quartz milling with any equipment smaller than a ten-stamp mill, were charged a royalty rate of 2s. 1d. or 50 cents per ounce on all gold mined (British Guyana, 1924).

The available data on gold mining demonstrated the extent to which gold mining took off after the initial collapse of the colonial slave mode of production. The deliberate colonial policy initiative to explore the country for minerals, which led to the discovery of gold in economic quantities in the 1880s, and the freedom of labor and capital to pursue economic ventures as they see fit outside of the agricultural sector definitely established natural resources extraction as a central plank in the Guyana economy, as gold production exploded between 1884 and 1905.

The significance of natural resources extraction to the Guyana economy as the country transitioned from the colonial slave mode of production to full center-periphery relations can also be gleaned from the magnitude of the quantity of gold exported and its value between 1918 and 1923. The available data on the output of diamonds in terms of number of stones, carat and value between 1916 and 1924 also showed the significance of this mineral. Diamonds were found initially as an accidental product of gold mining in that it occurred, during the clean-up of gold mining. However, the gold expedition to the Upper Mazaruni in 1860 discovered sufficient quantities of diamonds that attracted many diamonds seekers into the area. But, the diamonds seekers who rushed to the area found only small diamonds that did not command high market value.

However, it was in the Upper Mazaruni at Putareng Creek that diamonds mining commenced in earnest. The sterling value of diamonds produced continued an upward trend between 1916 and 1923 increasing from a value of £34,167 in 1916 to £1,033,014 in 1923 (British Guyana, 1924). The number of diamond stones produced increased steadily from 84,466 in 1919 to 1,141,245 in 1923. The carats yielded also increased steadily from 16,707 in 1919 to 241,474 in 1923. The value of diamonds produced also increased from £95,711 in 1919 to £1,033,014 in 1923. The total number of diamond stones mined between 1919 and 1923 was 2,784,224, while the total carats yielded was 563,788 carats. The total value of diamonds between 1916 and 1923 was £2,666,435.

Some diamonds stones weighed up to ten carats, and the average local sale value was £4 3s. 4p. or $20 per carat. The royalty paid on diamonds was 2s. 1d. or 50 cents per carat and all gold, silver and diamonds were to be reported in Georgetown, the Capital City of the country, at the Department of Lands and Mines. Wages in the diamonds field varied from 3s. 4d. or 80 cents to 4s. 2d. or $1.00 per day, and the laborer was fed by his employers as well (British Guyana, 1924).

The take-off of natural resources extraction during the economic crises in the 1880s saw the emergence of firms such as the British Guiana Mining Company, the Essequibo Gold Mining Company, and the Barima Gold Mining Company. These gold mining firms along with others employed various categories of laborers in their productive operations. The location of gold mines in the hinterland and the concentration of the workforce on the Atlantic coast of Guyana, led to the implementation of a system of employment in which workers did three- to six-month shifts at a time in the goldfield away from their homes. Mine workers were recruited on the Atlantic coast and transported to mining locations in the hinterland where they worked to for three to six months at a time.

The gold mining companies had to provide an outlay of social capital as an integral part of their operations cost to support the emergent system of migrant labor that developed. This capital went to finance items such as rudimentary worksite dwellings and supplies, and transportation provided to the mine-workers. Laborers in the goldfields were supplied with rations, which were estimated at a cost of about 32 cents a day, and were paid wages at a rate of about 32 to 48 cents a day (Report of the West Indian Royal Commission, 1897).

In addition to food rations, gold workers' supplies may have included certain medicines, utensils, and other equipment for cooking, appropriate safety booths and clothing, and hammocks for sleeping purposes. Dwelling camps were not usually located at the worksite, so laborers had to walk for miles at a time into what they called the 'back-dams,' where the gold mines were located.

The adequacy of those provisions given to the gold workers was highly questionable. This was especially the case when one considers the fact that many mineworkers returned to their home villages sick with malaria and other diseases they contracted in the goldfield. Also, firms tend to cut their production cost by reducing social benefits when they are faced with an economic crunch. Some gold companies actually closed operations when gold earnings declined at the turn of the century.

Gold miners also took some of their personal effects to supplement whatever supplies they were provided with by their employers. It was not uncommon for supplies to finish while work was in progress or for disputes to erupt over their distribution. In order to address the problem of shortages in supplies, a number of small shops were built near the gold operations. These convenience stores, owned and operated by coast landers (persons, resident on the Atlantic coast), supplied alcoholic beverages and other items at exorbitant prices to the miners stationed in the interior.

The extraction of bauxite

Bauxite extraction also pointed to the deepening and expansion of capitalism and the transition to capitalist center-periphery production relations in Guyana. It helped to cement the extractive sector as a major player in the capitalist development of the Guyana-economy. This was made possible by the then increasing demand for bauxite due to war conditions in Europe and the fact that valuable and extensive deposits of the ore in readily accessible situations were discovered in Guyana. The Christianburg–Akyma District in the Demerara River possessed the most known extensive deposits of the bauxite ore. The foreign corporations that emerged in the bauxite industry had a particular structure, which was vertically integrated, multi-produce, and multinational (Girvan, 1971).

The native peoples used bauxite mud to build their homes long before geologists identified the mineral in Guyana in 1873. Thereafter prospectors, speculators, and investors rushed to acquire property rights to the area where the bauxite deposits were located. The British Aluminum Company and other British mining and commercial interests were not attracted but the Aluminum Company of America (ALCOA) swiftly moved in to prospect for bauxite. In 1914, the Republic Mining and Manufacturing Company of Philadelphia sent its representative George B. Mackenzie, a Scotsman 'to acquire all the workable deposits' of bauxite in Guyana (Quamina, 1987).

The acquisition by American capital of bauxite deposits in Guyana stimulated an intense inter-imperial rivalry between the United States and Great Britain for the ore. The US authorities pressurized the British government to accede to

ALCOA's demands that it acquired the lion share of bauxite deposits in Guyana. To force the British hands on the issue the US withheld its munitions supplies to Britain during World War I, which was in progress at the time, until Britain granted a lease to the Demerara Bauxite Company (DEMBA) an American concern located in Canada. ALCOA won-out in the rivalry and took effective control of 95 percent of the bauxite in the Demerara region of Guyana.

The deepening of center-periphery relations was clearly recognizable in the treatment of domestic Guyanese capital that sought to acquire lands containing bauxite. Foreigners received better treatment compared with domestic applicants for land leases of 500 acres to prospect for bauxite. The applications by the locals 'were rejected for one reason or another' (Quamina, 1987). Local speculators were effectively kept out of bauxite mining in Guyana. This constrained the development of the small miner phenomenon in the bauxite industry and handed over production to foreign companies engaged in large-scale production. Also, it served to confine bauxite production to the domain of foreign capital thereby increasing the dependence of the country on external extractive capital. Indeed, the colonial government issued no other leases for bauxite mining since it leased some 3,000 acres of these deposits to the Demerara Bauxite Company (Northern Aluminum Company of Canada), in 1914 (British Guyana, 1924).

In 1923 in its first year of steady operations the Demerara Bauxite Company produced 100,346 tons of bauxite. Between 1917 when production first started and 1921 the company had produced only 49,980 tons of bauxite. Thus, in total DEMBA produced 150,326 tons between 1917 and 1923. Due to the slump in the metal industries, no bauxite was exported in 1923. The leases granted to the DEMBA stipulated that the company paid 5d. or 10 cents per ton royalty on the ore at the time of export. There was a minimum charge of 5d. or 10 cents a ton per annum for every 5 acres comprised in the lease (British Guyana, 1924).

The production of manganese

Guyana became a producer of manganese in the 1960s albeit for a short period as production ceased allegedly due to global market conditions for the commodity and the threat of nationalization by the Guyana government. The manganese ore is located around Arakaka on the Barima River. After production the ore was transported by railway to a port near Morawhanna for shipment abroad. The operations to undertake manganese production began in 1954. In that year the African Manganese Company, which was a subsidiary of Union Carbide, 'floated a subsidiary, the North West Guiana Mining Company.' This latter company subsequently became Manganese Mines Management Limited. The Barima Gold Mining Company's Exclusive Permission was brought over by Manganese Mines Management Limited, which applied for long-term land leases (Forte, 1999).

The same Union Carbide was responsible for the Bhopal gas disaster in India in December 1984. The Bhopal incident is still considered as the worst industrial disaster every experienced in the world. Manganese production reached 212,000 tons by 1961 (Newman, 1964), and was estimated at 1.6 million tons from 1962 to 1968 (Investing News Network, 2012). Foreign extractive capital has attempted to resuscitate manganese production in recent years but the fall in demand for steel of which manganese is a ferroalloy utilized as a deoxidizer in its manufacture, has stymied its revival. But, there is still talk in Guyana about resuscitating the manganese industry in the country.

The forestry industries – timber

The expansion in natural resources extraction included the spread of capitalist development to the forestry industries. These included timber, paper pulp, balata, and other forestry products including gums, oils, fruits, rubber, scantlings, fuel wood, charcoal, shingles, fence staves, vat staves, posts, beams and spars (British Guyana, 1924). It was estimated that 87.4 percent of the total area of Guyana or 78,180 square miles was covered with forests that contained valuable timber. These timbers were dyewoods, resinous trees, mahogany and other cabinet woods and timber such as greenheart and mora suitable for wood paving, railway sleepers, and harbor work, and many more (British Guyana, 1924).[3]

The forestry situation in Guyana was investigated at a meeting held by experts at the British Empire Forestry Conference in Canada in the summer of 1923. The meeting reported that Guyana's 'forests are the sole known source of the world's supply of Greenheart.' It was reported that Greenheart was 'one of the most important utility timbers of the world and [was] in special demand for shipbuilding, wharf construction, fishing rods and other purposes' (British Guyana, 1924). The report considered Guyana's forestry sector as possessing considerable potential value, which was boosted 'by their propinquity to the large and expanding markets of the United States of America.' Another important factor that augured well for Guyana's forestry sector at the time was the fact that those markets were 'turning more and more to Central and South America and other tropical markets to supply their own deficiencies in hardwoods' (British Guyana, 1924).

Expansion in the forestry sector was therefore considered in the context of raw materials for exports to the US. The forestry sector was not necessarily envisioned to develop the manufacturing and forestry sectors in Guyana. But, it was fundamental to capitalist development through natural resources extraction. The forestry sector however, perpetuated Guyana's dependence status quo. The country's position in the international division of labor in the forestry sub-sector would be to produce timber as raw materials for export to the US. The US would then convert the timber into finished products, for re-export to Guyana.

This was not the only consideration in the forestry sector, imperialist rivalry was very much present as well. The thinking at the time was that in the light of expanding US markets the British capitalists needed to 'turn their attention to the development of the potential wealth of the British Guiana forests,' otherwise, 'they may be forestalled by the United States' (British Guyana, 1924). To this effect the British government changed the organizational structure of the forestry sector, so that it would reflect the interest of the British state, which was to attract British capital to engage in forestry extraction in the Guyana.

The British government created a Forestry Branch, which was placed under the control of the Commissioner of Lands and Mines. In 1924 an independent Forestry Department was inaugurated to separate forestry as an autonomous capitalist activity from that of mining. The government bureaucracy in the forestry sector comprised a Conservator of Forests and Assistant Conservators; a Superintendent of Forest Surveys, Forest Surveyors and the necessary clerical workers who staffed the Forestry Department.

Investments in the forestry sector focused on the transportation of timber to the markets through the Essequibo River and a railway service to Wismar, a navigable point on the Demerara River for ocean-going vessels. The sector was basically set up for exports. The height of the Guyana-forest ranged from 125 to 200 feet, while the boles of the trees reached lengths of sixty to seventy feet allowing for long and large logs (British Guyana, 1924).

Ninety-nine percent of the forest area was owned by the British Monarch, which granted two-year licenses for a period of woodcutting with the possibility of an extension. The annual rent for 5,000 acres was 2½d. or 5 cents per acre up to 2,000 acres, and ½d. or one cent per acre above that, with a minimum charge of £1 0s. 10d or $5.00. Woodcutting also took place under leases for longer periods under special terms for areas above, 5,000 acres (British Guyana, 1924). Woodcutting was undertaken for greenheart and other woods for timber, lumber and railway sleepers, wallaba shingles, vat and fence staves, posts and poles, and charcoal and fuel.

The timber production data for Guyana available for the years 1915 and 1919 showed that the forestry sub-sector had begun to make an impact in the country's economy. In the five years 1915–1919 the output of greenheart, mora, and other hardwoods was 414,281 cubic feet. Greenheart was 92 percent of hardwoods output and mora 6.5 percent. The output of mahogany and other soft woods in the period was 87,189 cubic feet, which was 21 percent of hardwood output. Mahogany represented 85.7 percent of soft wood production. Thus, the two key timbers were greenheart and mahogany. Over three million shingles and one million pounds of balata were produced, as well as 528,251 lbs. of greenheart and mangrove bark.

Greenheart production was 381,311 cubic feet in the period. This was by far the largest output of timber followed by the output of mahogany at 74,723 cubic feet, mora at 26,936 cubic feet, other soft wood 12,466 cubic feet, and other hard wood 6,034 cubic feet. A total of 61,292 tons of fuel wood was produced, and 4,799 tons of charcoal. Also, 9,980 feet of boards and scantlings were produced, as well as 3,533,600 shingles, 76,855 fence staves, 16,968 feet of vat staves, and 34,569 feet of posts, beams and spars. Furthermore, 5,450 lbs. of locust and chicle gums and 1,136,162 lbs. of balata was produced in the period (British Guyana, 1924).

The technologies in the forestry industries were based on manual labor or oxen-hauled timber logs to navigable water for shipment. Only a few motor tractors were in use at the time. One timber grant used a winch and cable haul for about a mile and adopted rail to river for about three and a half miles. Punts were used to transport heavier woods slung to their sides, while lighter woods were floated down the rivers in rafts (British Guyana, 1924). Carts conveyed charcoal, fuel wood and other articles to a navigable stream for transport by punts to the market.

The industry employed laborers for a period of three to four months at a time. General workers were paid a daily wage, while labor employed in felling and squaring timber were paid at a rate agreed on per cubic foot of the timber felled. Most of the charcoal was produced in the Berbice and Demerara Rivers, using the covered pit method although brick ovens have also been used to burn coals. Manual labor dominated the sawmilling industry and woodworking factories although some sawmills were power-driven. The manual-labor dominated sawpits dealt with timber for local use and exports. Fuel woods, sold by the cord or by the ton were made primarily from Wallaba and Manabadin, Kurida (Avicennia nitida), and Mangrove (Rhizophora mangle) (British Guyana, 1924).

The available data on output, exports and domestic consumption of shingles, fuel wood, charcoal and balata in 1924 showed that all the balata was exported. However, domestic consumption and exports of shingles and charcoal were almost split half and half. The bulk of the fuel wood was consumed domestically. The country exported 51.4 percent of the shingles and 100 percent of the balata it produced. The domestic consumption of fuel woods was 89.9 percent of total output the rest was exported. Charcoal output was mostly exported, 55.5 percent. The country exported only 12.6 percent of its fuel wood and charcoal combined and consumed domestically 87.4 percent. There were some imports of forestry products such as oak shooks, staves and headings from the UK, US and Canada.

The raw data showed that 5,686,145 shingles were produced in 1924, of which 2,920,862 were exported and 2,765,283 consumed domestically. Fuel wood production was 78,560 tons, of which 7,945 tons were exported and 70,615 tons consumed in the country. The total out for charcoal was 4,556 tons, of which 2,530 tons was exported and 2,026 tons consumed domestically. The entire 1,407,272 lbs. of balata produced in that year was exported.

The average value of output per annum of timber of all kinds was $313,065 or £65,222, and all other forest products, including Balata, $866,315 or £180,482, or a total value of $1,179,380 or £245,704 (British Guyana, 1924).

The paper pulp, balata and rubber subsectors

In 1923 the Imperial Institute examined a number of timbers in Guyana to determine their value for the manufacture of paper. The results were established to be very encouraging in the light of the good yields of pulp that had been obtained from a number of timbers. Fotui or *Jacaranda copaia* had the highest yield of dry pulp expressed on material containing 12 percent of moisture (British

Guyana, 1924). Fotui and Kaahora unbleached percentage, were both above 50 percent, while only ite palm and mukka mukka had an unbleached percentage below 40 percent (British Guyana, 1924).

The production of wood pulp to make paper was not envisioned to expand the manufacturing base in the Guyana-economy. Guyana was merely to produce the raw material to feed the wood pulp factories in Britain and the US. The view was expressed at the time when due to salubrious climatic factors soft wood trees grew exceedingly quickly in Guyana. It was believed that with judicious planting wood pulp factories would be in a position to obtain an inexhaustible supply of their raw material.

As we have seen above, balata production in Guyana was exclusively for export. The first sample of balata was sent from Guyana to England in 1859. Six years thereafter in 1865 the country exported 20,000 lbs. (British Guyana, 1924). In 1917 Guyana exported 1,595,888 lbs. of balata, the largest amount in the early period of its production in accordance with the steadily increasing demand for the product (British Guyana, 1924). Balata is the trade name of the coagulated latex of the balata tree. It is used largely in the manufacturing of belting and boot soles. Based on the value of its exports, the balata industry was very important to the country. Its earnings were right up there with gold, diamonds, and timber. Guyana produced a total of 6,949,730 lbs. of balata in the years from 1918 to 1924. The total value of the balata produced in that period was the equivalent of £993,581 or $4,769,190.

Balata producers obtained licenses with the right to tap only balata trees for a period of five to fifteen years for forest covering from fifty up to 250 square miles. Balata operators paid a fee of $8 or £1 13s. 4d. to file an application, and an annual rental of the balata licenses of $20 or £4 3s. 4d. The royalty rate for balata was 2c or ld. per lb. payable on the dried gum produced. At December 31, 1920, there were in existence, or awaiting issue of, 749 licenses (British Guyana, 1924).

Laborers in the balata field were usually black, colored, and aboriginal and had to be registered by the government. They were paid in accordance with the weight of dry balata collected. The laborers were advanced some money at the time of employment to buy food, clothing and tools. An average of 4 to 6lbs. of latex is yielded from a tree on first tapping, but there were considerable variations in returns depending on the weather and other conditions. Re-bleeding a tree on the same spot after five years yielded only about one-third of the first tapping (British Guyana, 1924).

Located most abundantly in the Berbice and Rupununi districts in mixed forest areas the balata tree was not to be cut down. Operators could only cut down a balata tree with the written permission of the state. Also, no tree was tapped which had a girth of less than thirty-six inches at 4.25 feet from the ground (British Guyana, 1924). The trees were milked by means of a cutlass with which 1.5 inches wide incisions were made on the bark. The incisions were made ten inches apart in a featherstitch pattern up the clear bole of the tree and around only one-half of its girth. Also, by means of leg-irons or 'spurs' the operator was able to tap from the base of the first forking of the trunk, at a height of about fifty to seventy feet above ground. Unless cuts were entirely healed in up to four or five years, trees were not to be re-bled (British Guyana, 1924).

A calabash or gourd made from the calabash tree *Crescentiacujete*, was set to catch the latex flowing down the cuts, which was then removed in tins to a separate location where the latex was poured into shallow trays or 'dabrees' that hold between five and thirty gallons or more (British Guyana, 1924). The latex partially dries on the surface of the tray into thin sheets that are removed and hung up in a shed until dry.

As the economy and country opened up as the colonial slave mode of production collapsed, several sugar estates in different parts of Guyana experimented with the cultivation of para rubber. Rubber extraction was placed on the agenda in a serious way. A few small rubber plantations were established, grown in conjunction with cacao and coffee. The government established plantations of rubber-producing trees in different parts of the country to determine the rate of growth, the best cultural methods and tree-yields. In 1905 the cultivation of these rubber-producing Sapiums was undertaken, with about 500 acres of the trees planted. Guyana rubber was valued at the top price of the market by April 1910. Also, the 1911 International Rubber Exhibition in London awarded a silver cup to rubber from an estate in Demerara for the best sample of West Indian plantation rubber (British Guyana, 1924).

Other forestry products

The foray into the extraction of natural resources as a means of capitalist economic development and diversification saw extractive capital venturing to produce several other forestry products including gums, oils, fruits and fibers. A hard, translucent, amber-colored gum, called gum animi, was extracted from the locust tree, *hymenoeacourbaril*, with government written permission to make varnishes (British Guyana, 1924). Also, chicle gum used to make chewing gum was extracted from the Sapotaceae tree and exported (British Guyana, 1924). The balsam of copaiba which was used medicinally was extracted from the *Copaijera Guyanensis* tree found in the Upper Essequibo and Rupununi districts. The Haiawa tree, *Protium heptaPhyUum*, produced Haiawa gum, an aromatic, resinous, white gum used for incense by the locals and to scent oils used by the natives (British Guyana, 1924).

The fruit of the mahogany or crab wood tree, *Carapa guianensis*, produces crab oil that is used medicinally and in oil lamps (British Guyana, 1924). Edible oils were extracted from the fruits of the following palm trees – 'kokerit' *Maximiliana regia*, 'kuruwa' *Attalea spectabilis*, 'akuyuro,' and 'awarra' *Astrocaryum spp* (British Guyana, 1924). Also, certain vines, shrubs, barks and fruits of trees produced medicinal substances – these were, for example, sarsaparilla, quassia and bibirine from greenheart (British Guyana, 1924). Also, tanning material was extracted from the bark of many trees including the greenheart and mangrove *Rhizophora mangle* (British Guyana, 1924).

Fruits used in the production of perfume included those from the Kumara or Tonkabean tree, *DiPteryxodorata*, the dried seeds of which contained cumarine and were used for perfumery (British Guyana, 1924). Sawarri nuts from the tree Caryocar tomentosum, Brazil nuts from the tree Bertholletia execlsa, monkey pot nuts of the wadaduri tree *Leeythis sp.*, and vanilla, the fruit of an Orchidaceous vine are forestry products to which extractive capital was induced to invest in. The situation was the same for fibers obtained from the unopened leaves of the palm *mauritia flexuosa*, the natives used to make cordage and hammocks. Also, small quantities of silk cotton, a light brown silky fiber surrounding the seeds of the Kumaka tree *Bombax sp.*, were exported (British Guyana, 1924).

Conclusion

The colonial slave mode of production placed a damper on the development of the natural resources sector in Guyana. And by so doing it held back peripheral capitalist development in the country. The state dominated by agricultural interests prevented the capitalist foray into natural resources development because that would have led to a competition with agriculture for scarce labor. As capitalism strengthened in Europe the colonial authorities were forced to embrace capitalist production relations in the colonies rather than uphold a form of semi-capitalism or primitive accumulation in the form of the colonial slave mode of production. This capitalism could be defined as capitalism-cum-slavery representing a mixture of un-freed labor with freed labor in the dominant form of production and capital accumulation.

The foregoing was an examination of developments in the natural resources sector – gold, diamonds, bauxite and forestry product, in Guyana in the period characterized by the initial development of capitalist production relations as the colonial slave mode of production collapsed. The key factors to note here are first the British state were keen on diversifying the mono-crop economy by encouraging the extractive capitalist to invest in the natural resources sector in Guyana. Second, the British government undertook experiments in the extraction of forestry products to encourage extractive capital to invest in the forestry sector. Third, the British government developed regulations to control and mediate capitalist-labor relations in the natural resources sector. Fourth, labor in the extractive sector was made up primarily of blacks, coloreds and native peoples. The East Indians were wrongfully regarded as 'inferior' to endure the physical strains of working in the natural resources sector. Fifth, there was push-back against economic diversification in that the interest of the local planters and those of the British government seem not to be the same. The planters fought to maintain the status quo of the colonial slave mode of production while the British government wanted the situation to change.

The transition to capitalist relations had a particular effect on labor in that the small miners who dominated the mining sector were subjected to considerable regulation. The transition from the colonial slave mode of production to capitalist center-periphery relations led to a rush of independent small miners to the mining sector. Large-scale mines also went in, but the bulk of the miners operated on a small-scale basis. This was largely due to the fact that depending on one's location gold mining can even be done in one's backyard. This pattern continues until today where the sector is dominated by small miners. Historically, large mines owned by foreign extractive capitalist tend to operate in berths that stretch over a few years depending on the lifespan of the mines before they leave or close down. Small miners then move in to work the tailings left behind by the large mines.

The British government's policy to encourage foreign extractive capitalist to invest in Guyana was in essence a failure. In retrospect the forestry sub-sector continues to fail to achieve its full potential in terms of the varieties of commodities it could produce. The same is true of mining and quarrying. This sub-sector is focused more on gold and diamonds, and the other precious metals are not major contributors to the economy. The bauxite industry continues to limp along, while the promise of manganese remains.

In essence, the colonial state-led natural resources approach to peripheral capitalist development in Guyana was a failure. The colonial state-led natural resources approach to development is currently being recycled as neoextractivism in the Latin American and Caribbean region and by the global institutions such as the World Bank that advocate such an approach for natural resources-rich countries. The crisis in capitalism in that the early period forced the British state to take measures to hasten the development of capitalist 'free markets' at the expense of unfree ones associated with the colonial slave mode of production. But, their success in doing so brought about reforms that helped to put in place center-periphery capitalist relations involving Guyana becoming a supplier of raw materials in an international division of labor on which its economy depended.

Notes

1 These were gold, kaolin, platinum, gibbsite (crystalline), silver, bauxite, copper, cliachite (amorphous), gold telluride, mica (muscovite and sericite), diamond, auriferous quartz, bort, stibnite, graphite, galena, micaceous iron ore, pyrite and marcasite, hematite, arsenical pryites, magnetite, chalcopyrite, ilmenite, garnet, limonite, monazite, rutile, pyrolusite, zircon, psilomelane and wad, scheelite, beryl, tourmaline, corundum, sphene, bitumen, cobaltiferous wad, lignite and feldspars (British Guyana, 1924).
2 The US dollar amount was calculated on January 1, 2018.
3 They included valuable and common timbers with vernacular names such as awasakuli, balata, bania or ebony, baramalli, mahogany or crab wood, red cedar or kurana, dakama, fotui, greenheart, hububalli, kabukalli, karting, kauta, kauta-balli, locust or simiri, mora, morabukea, purpleheart, tauroniro, wadaduri of monkey pot, waikey, wallaba, wamara, and yaruru or paddle wood (British Guyana, 1924).

References

British Guyana. (1924). British Guiana – British empire exhibition. London: The Baynard Press. www.saints.edu.gy/History/BRITISH-GUIANA-1924.pdf.

Forte, J. (1999). 'Karikuri: The evolving relationship Karinya people of Guyana to gold mining.' *New West Indian Guide*, 673 (1 and 2), pp. 59–82.
Girvan, N. (1971). 'Why we need to nationalize bauxite and how,' in N. Girvan and O. Jefferson. (eds) *Readings in the political economy of the Caribbean*. Kingston, Jamaica: New World Group.
Investing News Network. (2012). 'Guyana aims to become a top manganese producer,' May 24, Investingnews.com.
Josiah, B. P. (2011). *Migration, mining and the African Diaspora: Guyana in the nineteenth and twentieth centuries*. New York: Palgrave Macmillan.
Newman, P. (1964). *British Guiana: Problems of cohesion in an immigrant society*. London: Oxford University Press.
Nkrumah, K. (1965). *Neocolonialism the last stage of imperialism*. London: Thomas and Nelsons, Ltd.
Quamina, O. T. (1987). *Mineworkers of Guyana: 'The making of a working class'*. London: Zed Books.
Report of the West India Royal Commission, with subsidiary report by D. Morris, Esq., D.Sc., C.M.G. (appendix A) and statistical tables and diagrams, and a map (appendix B). (1897). London: Her Majesty Stationary Office.
Rodney, W. A. (1981). *A history of the Guyanese working people, 1881–1905*. Baltimore: The Johns Hopkins University Press.
Thomas, C. Y. (1984). *Plantations peasants and state: A study of the mode of sugar production in Guyana*. California: University of California, Center for Afro-American Culture and Society Monograph Series.

7 The foundations of post-colonial 'new' extractivism

In the previous chapter it was argued that natural resources extraction played a significant role in the transformation from the colonial slave mode of production to center-periphery relations in which peripheral capitalist production relations became fully developed in Guyana. It is contended in this chapter that embedded within the peripheral capitalist production relations in the 1953–1964 period were class, race and ideological factors that continued today to shape the essential characteristics of the Guyanese political economy. These relations have laid the foundations for the emergence of the post-colonial authoritarian state and 'post-colonial new extractivism,' thereby demonstrating that there is nothing 'new' about the neoextractivism phenomenon in the Latin American and Caribbean region. The 'new extractivism' in the region appears to be a new phenomenon, but in reality, is not. It is merely a part of a dynamic historical process in the struggles for genuine political, social and economic transformation of peripheral capitalist social formations from a state of dependence on center countries. The problem is however that these struggles for genuine independence are not intended on constructing alternatives to capitalism. They are merely concerned with deepening exploitative capitalist production relations. However, perhaps the only major difference in the phenomenon described as neoextractivism in Latin America and what took place in Guyana is that they are occurrences in different time periods.

The countries in Africa, Asia, and the Latin America and Caribbean region are in a constant fight to rest the control of their natural resources from foreign-owned transnational corporations. In a real sense the 'new extractivism' in the Latin American and Caribbean region today is a part of a historical process that commenced with the struggle for political and economic independence in the hemisphere. The capitalist political economy relations associated with the 'new extractivism' are not static processes that relate only to the historical conjuncture characterized by the transition from neoliberalism to post-neoliberalism. It is a dynamic historical phenomenon identifiable in the evolution of peripheral capitalist societies. Rather than analyzing the 'new extractivism' in a static manner, it is better to explore the dynamics of the process in order to unearth its true modus operandi and formulate strategies to transform peripheral capitalism itself. The 'new extractivism' must be understood as a process of liberation of peripheral capitalist social formations from the clutches of capitalism.

The political opposition to colonialism in Guyana is identified as the antecedent of post-colonial new extractivism. In many respects this opposition was similar to the anti-globalization, anti-neoliberal social movements in the region. The political opposition in the anti-colonial movement wanted to rid the region of foreign domination and so too was the anti-neoliberal social movements. In both periods the nationalist movements wanted to control the natural resources of their respective countries and to use the economic surplus generated from their exploitation to improve the social and economic conditions of the underprivileged masses. Several positions taken up by the anti-colonial movement are identified and discussed as the evidence that the radicals in Guyana shared similar positions as the anti-neoliberalism social movements in the wider Latin American and Caribbean region.

The discussion on the antecedents of 'post-colonial new extractivism' is followed by an analysis of the class and race bases of the social order that emerged. This is critical in furthering understanding of the foundations of Guyanese politics, which are based on class manipulation of racial differences, and foreign intervention. The two dominant political parties that emerged in Guyanese politics, the People's Progressive Party (PPP) and the People's National Congress (PNC) are both based in different racial sections of the population. Inevitably the educated elites in control of both political parties who are in pursuit of state power are able to manipulate their mass supporters who are also members of their race camps. External forces that helped to create the political divisions along race lines are also able to maneuver the race divide in their self-interest.

Analysis of the class- and race-based social order is followed by an examination of relevant economic indicators for the period 1953 to 1960. This is done to demonstrate that, despite the political repression in the country by the British in the early 1950s and the concerns of foreign-owned companies that they would be nationalized, the Guyana-economy still performed at a fairly consistent level. The split in the nationalist movement and the role of foreign intervention are analyzed to demonstrate the manner in which the imperialist forces pushed back against the aspirations of a colonized people to attain their freedoms. But, despite the challenges coming from the imperial forces the PPP was steadfast in its policies as can be gleaned from its budgetary measures in 1962. Furthermore, the difficulties created for the government by the 1962 budget did not prevent the economy from holding its own between 1961 and 1964. In addition, the 1960–1964 development plan remained on track despite the social unrest that followed the 1961 budget.

Anti-colonial antecedents

Undoubtedly, the immediate antecedents of the 'post-colonial new extractivism' are located in the opposition to colonialism that swept the radicals to power in Guyana in 1953. There were 130 candidates that contested the April 27 national elections for the twenty-four seats in the House of Assembly. Of those 130 candidates there were twenty-two from the PPP, twenty-nine from other parties and seventy-nine independent candidates. Due to universal adult suffrage introduced in that year by the Waddington Constitution,[1] which removed income, property and literacy qualifications to vote in national elections the electoral list comprised 208,939 persons, about 150,000 who were newly enfranchised (The Robertson Commission, 1954). The PPP's demand was for full self-government on the basis of a new constitution written by the people of Guyana for themselves. The PPP's position was that the people of Guyana alone were capable of determining a constitution for the country. It proposed that a constituent assembly elected on the basis of universal adult suffrage should be entrusted to draft an acceptable constitution for Guyana.

The PPP leaders argued that the Waddington Constitution merely gave a new form or appearance to the old reality. The constitution maintained power in the hands of the colonial authorities while in appearance it gave the semblance that the country was a democracy. The then chairman of the PPP Mr. Forbes Burnham was accused by the authors of the Robertson Commission (1954), of 'adapting the language of Karl Marx' in an article he wrote in the party's newspaper *Thunder*. The Robertson Commission (1954), observed that Mr. Burnham pointed out in the article that the Waddington Report succeeded in demonstrating that the ruling class used the state to exercise its power and dominance over the working man.

The Robertson Commission (1954) maintained that Dr. Jagan the vice-chairman of the PPP attacked the Waddington Constitution as being ingenuine, a trap and another tactic of British imperialism to propagate exploitation and to maintain the old order. Dr. Jagan 'urged the struggle for immediate self-government and the setting up of a People's Government.' The view was expressed that 'the agents of vested interests and their stooges is a real indication of the worthlessness of the Constitution' (The Robertson Commission, 1954).

Mr. Eusi Kwayana (then known as Sidney King) the Assistant General Secretary of the PPP was also quoted by the Robertson Commission (1954) as saying that 'the British will write any constitution for a colony except a free constitution.' Mr. Kwayana was quoted as saying that 'a free constitution never descends from an Imperialist overlord into the arms of an exploited people', it has to be 'won and written by the people themselves in the face of battle.' Furthermore, in the view of Mr. Kwayana, it was 'more likely for a dog to surrender a bone, more likely for a crow to relinquish carrion than for an imperialist power voluntarily to hand over control to the people of the colonies' (The Robertson Commission, 1954).

Economic nationalism, fairness, justice, constitutional change determined by the locals were all part of a political platform that appealed to the masses but which signaled bad news to the colonial capitalists. The ideas harbored by the radicals included national ownership of the country's natural resources, and the use of the economic surplus to lift the masses out of their conditions of abject poverty. What a remarkable similarity between the goals of the nationalist in 1953 in the anti-colonial struggle in Guyana, and the champions of neoextractivism in the Latin American and Caribbean region in the struggle to replace neoliberalism. The position adopted by the radicals was quite natural given the appalling socio-economic conditions in the country. They wanted to share the country's wealth with its underprivileged classes. The radical leaders themselves came from the ranks of the poor and neglected and had moved up the social ladder through the education process having studied abroad in the UK, the US or by correspondence courses with overseas educational institutions.

The conditions that characterized the transition from colonialism to post-colonialism were quite similar to those of the transition from neoliberalism to post-neoliberalism. The economic and political chasms between the suffering masses and the wealthy imperialist and their domestic cronies were sufficiently repulsive to galvanize the former into action. The social unrests took the forms of anti-colonial mass political movements and anti-neoliberal/anti-globalization mass social movements.

The key point about these mass movements although they took place in different time periods is their opposition to foreign political and economic domination and the unity in the resolve by the locals to take control of their own destiny in terms of poverty alleviation through national ownership of their country's natural resources. The sad reality however is that both the anti-colonial and anti-neoliberal struggles are integral components of the expansion of and sustenance of the capitalist system.

The 1953 elections manifesto of the PPP made frequent references to the intention of the party to proceed with extensive financial and economic reforms. However, with the possible goal to appease the colonial authorities the PPP claimed that it was fully conscious of the role which private capital would play in the development of Guyana, and that it would take steps to encourage and attract private capital to the country. But, simultaneously the party pointed to 'imperialist exploitation' and was complaining about the use of the surplus from gold mining by the British Guiana Consolidated Goldfields Limited. In 1952 the party questioned in *Thunder* the duration of imperialist plunder in Guyana to enrich a foreign power (The Robertson Commission, 1954).

The popularly elected government in Guyana in 1953 was the first in the Latin American and Caribbean region in which several of its leaders had publicly embraced the socialist/communist ideology. Some leaders of the PPP declared themselves as socialist, although the party had not been an avowedly communist party. But, the colonial authorities believed that it was expediency and not principle that had restrained the PPP leaders from forming and leading an openly communist party (The Robertson Commission, 1954). The colonial authorities held the view that the radical leaders in the PPP as a matter of tactic decided to remain associated with others who shared similar objectives in the popular anti-colonial movement, to speedily achieve their most important and immediate goal to rid the country of British rule and influence (The Robertson Commission, 1954).

In the assessment of the Robertson Commission (1954), there was no evidence that the radicals in the PPP were going to abandon or modify their view that British governments were all imperialist and capitalist and would never concede full self-government to a colony of non-European peoples. Furthermore, the radical leaders did not believe in the achievement of self-government for British Guiana through a gradual process that demonstrates their ability to govern responsibly. They were of the view that self-government could only be won through violent action. In addition, the radicals figured that Great Britain was due to its role in the recent world war was weak economically, tired of conflict, and on the defensive morally. They believed that the British Government would concede self-government to British Guiana, under an unwavering threat of sustained social unrest and violence (The Robertson Commission, 1954).

Indeed, the colonial authorities were confident they had the evidence of the degree to which the PPP leasers were involved with the international communist, or communist controlled organizations and their local branches (The Robertson Commission, 1954). This supposed evidence forced the colonial authorities to conclude that PPP leaders were involved with the international communist, or communist controlled organizations and their local branches. The colonial authorities identified six prominent leaders of the PPP who unreservedly embraced the doctrines of Marx and Lenin. These leaders were supposedly strong supporters of the modern communist movement, and contemptuous of the British Labor Party and other social democratic parties in Europe (The Robertson Commission, 1954).

The Robertson Commission divided the PPP leadership into communists and socialists. The Commission noted that four of the seven principal officers of the PPP and the editor of *Thunder* Mrs. Janet Jagan were communists. Also, the Executive Committee members of the PPP were evenly divided among communists and socialists. The communists were said to be a minority on the party's general council, but they were said to probably have the greater influence and followers among Party membership. The Robertson Commission recognized Mr. Burnham as the leader of the socialist wing in the PPP. This wing included Mr. Ashton Chase, who was a member of the Executive Committee of the party, Mr. Clinton Wong, one of its senior-vice chairmen, and a number of its less prominent leaders. The socialists were said to be strongly opposed to British colonial rule as their communist counterparts, but they were not communists. The colonial authorities believed that the socialists had knowledge of communist theories on imperialism and capitalism, and approved of many of them (The Robertson Commission, 1954).

The socialists' dislike of imperialism and capitalism was not so much based on Marxist historical materialism, but on their own interpretation of the history of colonial rule. They based their interpretations of history on their own experiences with capitalist development in British Guiana (The Robertson Commission, 1954). The Commission concluded that the socialists in the PPP were the democrats, who wanted the party to pursue its constitutional objectives through peaceful means (The Robertson Commission, 1954). But it doubted whether the socialists had the wherewithal to distinguish themselves from the communists (The Robertson Commission, 1954). This was regarded as the dilemma of the non-communists in the PPP. In the view of the Commission the difference between the communists and socialists placed Dr. Jagan and Mr. Burnham in direct rivalry for the moral leadership of the PPP (The Robertson Commission, 1954).

The imperialist forces invented this division among the nationalist leadership in Guyana and exploited it to split the nationalist movement in the country. Once the seeds of discord were sown in the nationalist movement it was difficult to bring the leadership of the PPP back to a united position. Indeed, the PNC emerged as a new party from the PPP, and Guyanese politics took on a decidedly race and class character. More aptly put, class manipulation of race came to dominate politics in Guyana. The East Indian and African middle classes manipulate the members of their respective races to fight their battles. After the race-based middle class win power it proceeds to enrich its members at the expense of the masses.

The East Indians are the majority race in the country and can hold power indefinitely at fair elections. The exceptions were if their vote was divided or East Indians failed to turn out at the polls in which case their middle-class leaders will resort to electoral fraud. The Africans as the minority has to form alliances to secure power, and if the alliance breaks down the only way they can hold on to power is by electoral fraud. The political landscape is open to foreign intervention in support of both the PPP and PNC when either side forms the opposition and the other side is in power for extended periods. The PPP was installed in power by foreign intervention at the 1992 national elections after the PNC was in power for twenty-eight years. Foreign intervention assisted in bringing about political change in Guyana in 2015, after the PPP was in power for twenty-three years.

The PPP of 1953 was quite in the vanguard of the left movements in the Latin American and Caribbean region. Although the attack on the Moncada Barracks in Cuba took place in 1953 the Cuban Revolution had not yet been made. The PPP in 1953 was ahead of Salvador Allende in Chile, Hugo Chavez in Venezuela, and the 'pink tide' in Latin America. The PPP in 1953 was continuing in the tradition of the great liberators of South America and the Caribbean. It was a part of a global anti-colonial movement that was taking place in Africa and Asia, similar to the global anti-neoliberalism social movements of the day.

The radical PPP in 1953 whose leaders espoused a socialist/communist ideology should not be confused with the PPP today. The PPP today is no longer a radical party it has morphed into something else, as will be demonstrated when the criminalized authoritarian state is analyzed below. The current leaders of the PPP embrace the very neoliberal policies that the Latin American left-leaning parties oppose and espouse race rather than class politics as the basis for securing power domestically.

The radicalism of the democratically elected 1953 government evoked an imperialist backlash, which continues to blight Guyana until today. The UK overthrew the Guyana government and appointed a new government handpicked by the colonial authorities and wrote a new constitution for the country.

The new constitution reduced the powers of the elected officials supposedly as a safeguard against government excesses. Increasing the powers of the British appointed governor, who was given the veto over government policies, was the means through which the colonial authorities intended to maintain control over the state.

The holding of national elections under the new constitution contested by different factions of a divided nationalist movement produced the inevitable in an immigrant dominated social formation – race-based politics and conflict. Thus, although the development of peripheral capitalist relations in Guyana allowed for greater freedom of movement of labor and capital, it simultaneously developed a very unsavory political under-belly – race politics and violence.

The social and political developments in this period were a direct consequence of the class and race character of the immigrant-based population. Politics in such a society is subject to manipulation on the basis of race by the dominant race-based classes in the country. Equally so external capitalist forces in center states that have an eye on the country's natural resources can and have also exploited the race differences to their benefit. This situation only became possible with the development of peripheral capitalist production relations. Class manipulated race conflict to control the reigns of state power was not evident under the colonial slave mode of production.

This phenomenon became manifest in the period in which peripheral capitalist production relations were being cemented in Guyana. Even up to 1950, this was not the case as was noted by the Waddington Constitutional Commission 1950–1951. The Commission commented as follows: 'We were, however, impressed by the amity with which peoples of all races live side by side in the villages, where mutual dependence is, of necessity, recognized.'[2] Earlier in 1927 Mr. H. Snell, a member of the Wilson-Snell Constitutional Commission[3] had made similar remarks (Hubbard, 1969).

The form of the state had changed in that it was now possible for locals to occupy positions of power without merely serving at the pleasure of the colonial office. But, the nature of the state as an instrument of repression had not changed. With local control of key state positions, however, the object of state power also changed. In such a situation, the object of state power became that of fortifying race and class interests, enrich state elites and their acolytes, maintain control of the government, and subordinate the private sector to the dictates of the state, among other things.

These developments became even more entrenched in and associated with the post-colonial period. In the period under consideration, once the locals obtained state power they would argue for the use of the country's natural resources to elevate the social and economic status of the poor. The options available to garner natural resources for national development included greater participation in the ownership and control of the industries operating in the sector, the outright nationalization of foreign entities, and state–private partnerships.

The development of peripheral capitalist relations simultaneously created a situation in which there was greater freedom of movement of labor and capital, and the transfer of economic control from the plantocracy, which engaged in the extra-economic extraction of the surplus, to the profit maximizing multinational corporations that operated on the basis of wage labor. The sheer size of these corporations in the local economy and the fact that they were foreign owned led to the development of the dependency syndrome. As peripheral capitalist relations expanded in Guyana the country became increasingly dependent on foreign sources for its survival. The domination of the Guyana-economy by foreign corporations produced local resentment and laid the basis for arguments in favor of local ownership and control of the country's natural resources and economy as a whole.

The social order and politics

A crucial aspect of the social order that developed in Guyana as peripheral capitalist production relations became cemented in the country was its unique class and race character. This development tended to undermine the unity of the worker class-led mass movement in its quest for self-determination and control of the country's natural resources. The government was seen to be under the influence of a particular race and so members of the other race did not support it. A major consequence of this division was the severe negative blow it struck at the heart of any attempt to pursue national ownership of the country's natural resources. The same was true of economic development policies pursued by the government under the perceived domination of either race group.

The abolition of slavery saw the African former slave living side by side with his European former master, with both groups being distrustful of each other. The resultant labor crisis on the plantations due to labor shortages came about as a result of the migration of African-Guyanese into the natural resources and other sectors. The workers of African origin withdrew their labor services from plantation work, unless their wages were increased. That action led to the commencement of immigration of indentured labor in 1835 until 1917.

During this period 30,800 Portuguese were brought into the country to join the agricultural proletariat as indentured laborers. By 1891 only a little over 12,000 Portuguese remained in the population due to harsh working conditions and migration to Brazil. Between 1853 and 1879 a total of 14,000 Chinese immigrants, of which there were 11,900 males entered the country as indentured laborers. By 1917 the Chinese numbered a little more than 2,800 of whom 1,570 were males. The disproportion of the sexes among the Chinese was given as a factor in the decline in their population. Then, from 1838 to 1917 a total number of 238,979 East Indians were imported into the country as indentured servants. It was reported that a total number of 65,538 East Indians repatriated to India from where they were recruited (Hubbard, 1969).

The emergent class and race character of the social formation has had a major negative influence on political development that persists until today. Although the state in the period of the transition to center-periphery relations continued to be dominated by the colonial authorities there were powerful groups comprising different sections of the Guyanese population based on race, color and class that had begun to emerge.

The color composition of the social order was such that the lighter-skinned peoples controlled the top positions in the economy and society while the darker-skinned people worked for them. The social hierarchy based on color was further subdivided, such that whites were at the top followed by Portuguese, mulattoes, light-skinned blacks and East Indians, and dark-skinned black and East Indian workers. The locals who were effectively locked out from the power structure resented the social order and wanted it to change.

The local educated elites of all shades and class positions wanted to have a greater say in the political and economic affairs of the country. The colored elites who did secure some semblance of political and economic power served at the pleasure of the colonial authorities. They had to toe the line of the colonial administration, headquartered abroad in England. The resentful social and economic organization, British and US imperialisms, and the reactionary light-skinned middle classes that oppose social and economic reform, stimulated the nationalist independence movement. This resentment served to bring together a group of local politicians led by the East Indian Dr. Cheddi Jagan and the African Mr. Forbes Burnham among others in a struggle for political and economic independence. The African and East Indian working classes became united in a single political party – the PPP.

The domestic classes and race groups prevailing at the time were the urban African/colored middle classes, a rural Indian middle class, African and East Indian working classes, and Africans and East Indians as the dominant race groups. The rural East Indian middle classes did not all support the left tendencies of Dr. Jagan, but supported him on the basis of race, and disliked the African/colored urban middle classes. The same was true of the African/colored urban middle classes in their disposition towards the rural East Indian middle classes. Dr. Jagan and Mr. Burnham, once they were together, united the African and East Indian working classes to oppose colonial rule.

That unity was destroyed soon after they won power in 1953 and was replaced on the one hand by an alliance of sorts comprising an urbanized African/colored with the urban multi-racial bourgeoisie, and on the other East Indian sugar estate workers and rice farmers (Robertson Commission, 1954). The balkanization of the population into those diverse race and class groups thwarted the emergence of a straightforward class struggle between labor and capital and a coherent stable social order in Guyana. Rather than coherence and stability the society was and remains divided down the middle between Africans and East Indians and manipulated by forces associated with three groups the African and East Indian elites, and external powers.

The seeds of this race and class divisions were sown during the colonial slave mode of production in the manner in which the immigrant society was assembled. The former African slaves, the East Indian, Portuguese and Chinese indentured servants, the aborigines, and the Europeans were all in the social milieu.

As it turned out politics in such a taxonomic immigrant society produces much racial hostility over the control over the state and economy.

It must be noted that the British colonial power, which pursued a divide and rule tactic were first to pit the Africans and East Indians against each other. Race politics between Africans and East Indians in Guyana was a learned behavior from the colonial authorities. This politics is subject to external manipulation by the capitalist forces determined to control the economic resources and the domestic elites who control state power. Such was the social order in which local groups and their institutions sought to control the natural resources of their country in their self-interest.

Economic considerations 1953–1960[4]

Considering the conditions outlined above, the major concern of foreign companies that controlled the Guyana-economy, was what would become of them, as the locals took over the reins of power. Would they be left to operate as they pleased, as was the case under colonialism, or would they be held to a different standard, or be all together taken over by the domestic state? These dynamics are very present in the new extractivism as the state struggles with foreign capital to hold them to a different standard compared to when they operated with carte blanche under neoliberal capitalism.

The view was expressed that these firms operated on a very large-scale in both absolute terms and in the context of the Guyana-economy and would have incurred considerable economic losses were they to operate on a smaller scale. The transnational corporations, Bookers Bros., and Sandbach Parker controlled the sugar industry, while Aluminum Company of Canada (ALCAN), Reynolds Metals and the North West Guiana Mining Company respectively dominated the bauxite and manganese mining industries. These five firms accounted for nearly 80 percent of Guyana's exports, which totaled around £30 million a year (Newman, 1964).

The domination of the Guyana-economy by foreign capital produced local opposition to the free enterprise system that the Western democracies idealized. The view held by foreign forces was that the conditions in Guyana would naturally lead the locals to call for national ownership and control of the domestic economy. That a call would be unrealistic in the short-term because the Guyanese economy did not possess the skills to effectively manage such large-scale business enterprises.

External economic domination, domestic resentment of that situation, and the lack of locally skilled personnel to properly manage large-scale foreign entities produced a dilemma for the nationalists. The situation was not as easily resolvable politically as well as the other tensions between the domestic radicals and foreign capitalists. The radicals developed an all or nothing attitude towards foreign capital, while the capitalists entertained a wait-and-see attitude towards expansion due to the risk of nationalization. The disposition of the locals who were at the doorsteps of domestic political power as colonialism collapsed was to nationalize foreign companies. This attitude continued into the post-colonial period when the foreign-owned companies were indeed nationalized.

The period between 1953 and 1960 was characterized by a tug of war over the Guyana-economy between the nationalists and the colonial authorities as the country continued in its transition to center-periphery relations. The selected economic indicators for the Guyana-economy in that period demonstrated that there was some economic progress as the country continued in its transition to center-periphery relations, despite the struggle between the nationalists and the colonial authorities. Who should control the economy and in whose interest? Were the nationalists to be left alone to manage their own affairs, the country would have made even greater economic progress. This in turn could have translated into improved social conditions for the underprivileged masses. In the same manner however that the neoextractivist in the Latin American and Caribbean Region are being stymied by neoliberal capitalism, the nationalists were thwarted in their endeavors by the colonial capitalists.

The selected economic indicators reviewed for the period indicated that the Guyana-economy depended heavily on exports. As a percentage of the national income, exports was 50 percent and above in each year from 1950 and 1960. Personal consumption expenditure increased steadily and was the highest in 1960. The same was true of government current expenditure and gross public and private capital formation. The latter only experienced a decline in 1959, but it was still above what was achieved between 1953 and 1956. It shot back up to its highest point in the period in 1960, which was almost three and a half times the level it achieved in 1953 (Newman, 1964).

The export of goods and services only declined in 1958 but increased again in the following two years. Exports in 1958 and 1959 however were below the 1956 level, but well above the points reached between 1953 and 1956. Imports of goods and services declined in the years 1958 and 1959, but in 1960 returned above the level attained in 1957. The terms of trade were favorable, except in 1955 when the value of imports was greater than the value of exports. But, as net direct taxes and GDP at factor cost continued to rise in the period, net income paid abroad tended to fluctuate and was unstable. Depreciation allowances rose steadily except for the years 1957 and 1958 when it remained constant (Newman, 1964).

National income increased consistently in the period except in 1955 when it declined, with the same pattern portrayed by household net income. The cost of living index showed a slight increase between 1959 and 1960, but the rise was 10.4 percentage points higher than what the index was in 1953. Net per capita household income at constant prices declined by 4.6 percent between 1953 and 1955, but overall it increased 3.2 percent. The increase in per capital household net income however did not compensate for the rise in the cost of living index. The population grew by 107,800 in the period, although it declined in 1955. The growth rate of the population increased consistently except between 1959 and 1960, when it declined. The largest increase was between 1958 and 1959 and the lowest was between 1953 and 1954 (Newman, 1964).

The bulk of the export earnings came from sugar and its by-products molasses and rum, and metalliferous ores and metal scrap. The export of timber also contributed albeit a small part to export earnings. But, when timber was combined with metalliferous ores and metal scrap the natural resources sector contributed an average of 28.1 percent to the value of exports between 1957 and 1960. Sugar and its by-products and rice combined to contribute 64.5 percent to the value of exports. Guyana had stepped up its dependence on the natural resources sector, which contributed more than a quarter of its export earnings. Although the agricultural sector and sugar in particular occupied the top spot, the trend indicated that it was in decline from the commanding position it occupied during the colonial slave mode of production (Newman, 1964).

The output of dried bauxite reached 2,426,000 metric tons in 1952, and Guyana became the world's second largest producer of the commodity, after Suriname with 3,224,000 tons. Guyana fell to third place by 1956, producing only 2,521,000 tons, behind Jamaica with 3,134,000 tons and Suriname with 3,483,000 tons. Jamaica produced the largest amount of the commodity by 1960, 5,837,000 tons, followed by the U.S.S.R. with an estimated 3,500,000 tons, Suriname with 3,455,000 tons and Guyana in fourth position with 2,517,000 tons (Newman, 1964).

The high production cost of bauxite in Guyana, coupled with greater shipping cost due to the length of time to the markets and sandbars on the Demerara and Berbice rivers were identified as the major stumbling block in the way of using the bauxite surplus for economic development in the country in comparison with Jamaica. Manganese production, which began in 1960, was put forward as a partial reward for the reduced surplus from bauxite production.

Overthrowing the PPP government 1960–1964

Even in the years when the social unrest to overthrow the PPP was at its highest point the economy continued to perform reasonably well. The budget presented to the national assembly in 1962 was used as a catalyst for the rioting, burnings, looting and the second British military occupation of the country in nine years – 1953 and 1962. But, undoubtedly, the budget put forward by the PPP government in 1962 was in line with the positions adopted by the radicals nine years earlier in 1953. The opposition to the budget was the Trojan horse conjured up by the imperial forces to create a state of social unrest, militarily occupy the country, rest power from the PPP, and install a pro-West PNC–United Force (UF) coalition government in Guyana in 1964.

The wider consideration was to prevent Dr. Jagan from obtaining political independence for Guyana. But, 'there was nothing deeply vicious or destructive of economic security in the budget' (Commission of Inquiry, 1962, p. 15). Indeed, the budget 'had been drawn up on the advice of an experienced economist, who could not be said to have any Communist prepossessions' (Commission of Inquiry, 1962, p. 15). Both the *New York Times* and *The London Times* newspapers hailed the budget as 'courageous,' economically sound, and what was necessary for Guyana at the time. But, the local newspapers the *Daily*

Chronicle, which was effectively controlled by Mr. d'Aguiar, the leader of the Portuguese-based UF party, and the *Argosy* newspaper, attacked the budget claiming that it would take bread out of the mouths of the workers. Headlines such as 'Tax avalanche will crush working classes,' 'Slave whip budget,' 'Budget is "Marxist"' and 'Iniquitous budget' appeared in those newspapers (Commission of Inquiry, 1962, p. 15).

The riot in 1962 led to the deaths of one policeman and four civilians, and the reported injury of thirty-nine policemen and forty-one civilians. Rioters destroyed by fire fifty-six business premises, damaged twenty-one by fire, and damaged and looted sixty-six. A total of twenty-nine market stalls were damaged and looted. Two police cars were damaged by fire and three otherwise damaged. Five private vehicles were damaged by fire, and fifty-one road traffic signs were also damaged. The total claims made on insurance companies amounted to $11,405,236. The police used up sixty LR tear smoke shells, sixty-two SR shells, 115 speed heat and CS grenades, twenty-four three-way grenades, and thirty-five 1.5 cartridges (Commission of Inquiry, 1962).

On Friday February 16 the British government dispatched to Georgetown, Rifle Company A of the 1st Royal Hampshire Regiment, with reinforcements from the Jamaica Tactical Headquarters and two Rifle Companies of the 1st Royal Hampshire Regiment (Commission of Inquiry, 1962). Then on Saturday February 17 reinforcements from Jamaica arrived – two Rifle Companies of the 1 East Anglian Regiment and one Rifle Company of the 1st Duke of Edinburgh's Royal Regiment. On Friday February 16, HMS *Troubridge* commanded by T. A. Q. Griffiths of the Royal Navy, and HMS *Wizard* commanded by D. J. Farquharson of the Royal Navy arrived outside the 'bar' to Georgetown harbor (Commission of Inquiry, 1962).

HMS *Troubridge* moored at the Sprostons No. 1 jetty and immediately dispatched an internal security platoon to Police Headquarters. HMS *Wizard* dispatched an internal security platoon to the Power Station in Georgetown. On February 17, HMS *Vigilant* commanded by Lieutenant Commander J. D. B. McCarthy of the Royal Navy berth alongside Sandbach Parker Wharf and dispatched an internal security platoon to relieve the platoon from HMS *Troubridge*. HMS *Urchin* commanded by Captain T. T. Lewin, M.V.O., D.S.C. of the Royal Navy berthed alongside HMS *Vigilant* (Commission of Inquiry, 1962).

What were the key budgetary policies[5] that the then pro-West political parties opposed and saw the need for a change in government? The budget in essence was of an import substitution type, in that it sought to restrict the imports of commodities that could be substituted locally, and to increase earnings from natural resources extraction for exports. It increased import duties on non-essentials such as alcoholic drinks, tobacco, concentrates for non-alcoholic drinks, tea, motor parts, perfumery, cosmetics, dress fabrics, footwear, glass wear and chinaware, jewelry, radios, refrigerators and household electrical appliances and motor cars (Commission of Inquiry, 1962).

It increased import duties on items for which adequate substitutes could be supplied from local production such as meat, fish, butter, milk (excluding condensed milk and milk-based infant foods), cheese, fruit, fruit juices, jams, coffee, confectionary, prepared paints, toilet soap, paper bags and some varieties of clothing. An export duty of about 4 percent free on board (f.o.b.) was imposed on the export of greenheart timber. Excise duties on rum and other spirits were increased from $9.60 to $14.40 a proof gallon, and on beer from 75c to $1.40 a liquid gallon. License duties were increased for motor vehicles drivers, money-lenders, pawnbrokers, bonded warehouses, and liquor. There were also increases on auction and stamp duties (Commission of Inquiry, 1962).

The budget introduced important changes to the tax rates for individuals and companies. Personal allowance was reduced from $900 to $750 and wife allowance from $750 to $600 and a flat rate child allowance of $300 was put in place of the existing three-tier system of $250/350/500 according to age. A limit of four was placed on the number of dependent relatives and children for who tax allowances could be had (Commission of Inquiry, 1962).

The minimum income tax payment for companies was to be based on an assumed income of 2 percent of turnover in the case of mining, manufacturing or mercantile business (not agriculture) even where a loss occurs, but adjustable against future profits. The budget placed restriction on provisions regarding trade losses to allow only the indefinite carry-forward of loss from the same source but disallowing the set-off of loss against other income in the same year (Commission of Inquiry, 1962).

The existing tax concessions for new enterprises were removed and new provisions were introduced. The fresh budgetary provisions allowed new companies involved primarily in mining, manufacturing or processing activities to write-off 70 percent of any capital expenditure incurred during the first five years of their operations in the country as a charge on their current profit. The initial allowances for non-tax-holiday companies were reduced from 40 percent to 20 percent. There was a disallowance of entertainment expenditure and a limit of one-quarter of a 1 percent of turnover placed on allowance on expenditure on advertising, excluding general or 'prestige' advertising. Also, the budget disallowed expense of any excessive changes in respect of directors' emoluments (Commission of Inquiry, 1962).

Capital Gains Tax was introduced on net property at ordinary income tax rates, with the highest rate fixed at 45 percent. The budget introduced an annual tax on net property at rates increasing from 0.5 percent per annum on the first $150,000 of property in excess on $50,000 to 1.5 percent on property in excess of $1M. It introduced a gift tax on transfers of property *inter vivos* at rates similar to the existing estate duty (Commission of Inquiry, 1962).

It introduced a Compulsory Savings Scheme of 5 percent of wage and salary income and 10 percent of other income. The income of self-employed in excess of $5,000 was regarded as being in a category of saving, while income under $1,200 per annum was exempted. Companies were to make a contribution of 10 percent flat on all profits with no exempt income. Government bonds were to be issued to contributors, repayable at the end of seven years with tax-free interest at 3.75 percent (Commission of Inquiry, 1962).

The social unrest forced Dr. Jagan to announce modifications to the budget in his broadcast to the nation on February 14, 1962. The government removed the increase on duties on most of the imported commodities listed. This would have had the effect of reducing government revenue and humbug the funding of its social programs. The imported commodities on which tax remained were motor-cars, spirits, tobacco, coffee extract and concentrates. The Compulsory Savings Scheme was modified, by raising the lower limit from $1,200 per annum to $3,600 per annum (Commission of Inquiry, 1962).

Selected economic indicators and the development program data between 1960 and 1964 showed that in the period of social unrest the value of sugar exports including its by-products increased between 1961 and 1962. The value of rice exports also increased in those two years, as well as that of metalliferous ores and metal scrap. The value of total exports increased by 11.2 percent between 1961 and 1963, but the value of total imports declined by 15 percent. The quantities of sugar and bauxite exported declined, while that of alumina increased in those years. The GDP at factor cost declined between 1961 and 1963 and was unchanged between 1962 and 1963. Prices were on the rise as indicated by the increasing trend in the consumer price index (Newman, 1964).

The PPP forged ahead with its development program in the tumultuous 1961–1964 period. In 1960 the actual expenditure on the development program was below the estimated and revised amount for that year. This was the pattern in each of the years under review (Newman, 1964).

Imperialist foreign intervention

The social unrest was a sort of culmination of the split in the PPP in 1955, which led to each of the two factions, one led by Dr. Jagan and the other by Mr. Linden Forbes Sampson Burnham, both factions calling themselves, the PPP. The Burnham faction considered as socialist and moderate by the imperialist forces eventually became the People's National Congress (PNC) in 1957. The Jagan faction retained the name PPP and was considered communist. Mr. Burnham fell for the bait thrown out by the imperialist forces that he represented the 'moderates' in the PPP and should take over the leadership of the party from Dr. Jagan. This he did while the British imprisoned five of the executive committee members of the PPP and held three others under house arrest.

Mr. Burnham called a party congress in 1955 against the wishes of the imprisoned executive members, changed the congress venue from Berbice where East Indians are in a majority to Georgetown where Africans are in a majority, and had a new leadership of the PPP elected with him as leader. The new leadership included individuals who were supporters of Dr. Jagan, which undoubtedly was a ploy to show that Mr. Burnham was indeed the true leader of a united PPP. The majority of the party's membership comprising mainly East Indians and a smaller number of Africans refused to follow Mr. Burnham. The party was effectively split with two PPP's one under Burnham and the other led by Dr. Jagan.

The US and British administrations continued their support and encouragement of leaders and political organizations that were in opposition to the PPP and had adopted a pro-West stance. Dr. Jagan regained power in subsequent elections held under the Robertson Constitution in 1956 and 1961. In the early 1960s, however, the US administration established a Special Group/303 Committee to oversee US covert operations in Guyana. The Special Group/303 Committee approved approximately US$2.08M for covert actions programs between 1962 and 1968 in Guyana. Between November 1962 and June 1963, a part of the US$2.08M was used to help the pro-West opposition political parties in their campaigns to rest power from the PPP government. These parties were the PNC backed mainly by Africans, and the United Force (UF), followed primarily by the Portuguese, light-skinned mixed-races individuals, and the native peoples.

Curtis (2004) noted that the anti-Jagan protests in February 1962 were organized and financed by the CIA. The externally funded anti-Jagan protests involved strikes and riots and resulted in British military intervention to restore order (Curtis, 2004).[6] The CIA's covert operations centered on funding the 80 days general strike that began in April 1963. Indeed, the CIA had allotted US$1 million for that purpose and advised labor union leaders in British Guiana how to organize and sustain the strike. The CIA provided the funds and food to sustain the striking workers. British officials cited the strike as evidence that Dr. Jagan could govern the country (Curtis, 2004).

The US encouraged the British government to impose a system of proportional representation (PR) to replace the first-past-the-post constituency politics that was in place, and to delay granting independence to Guyana until the anti-Jagan forces were strengthened. The implementation of these requests decidedly favored the political parties that opposed the PPP government.

The US supported the PNC and the UF with money and campaign expertise, which played a decisive role in the registration of voters likely to vote against the PPP. The registration of the supporters of the PNC and the UF helped to elect the anti-Jagan coalition government. The US continued to provide substantial funding to both the PNC and the UF after they formed the coalition government in 1964. The US government turned a blind eye to Burnham's plans to use fraudulent means to stay in power in the 1968 and in subsequent general elections.[7]

Conclusion

The foundations of post-colonial new extractivism were laid in a period characterized by the expansion of center-periphery capitalist production relations in Guyana. It incorporated a number of antagonistic and non-antagonistic contradictions in a race- and class-based social order. The non-antagonistic race contradictions in the political process are yet to be determined in an amicable manner, while the antagonistic class contradictions will only be resolved by revolutionary action. Indeed, the race and class conflicts have been a part of the social milieu as the post-colonial authoritarian state emerged in Guyana and its foreign enterprises were nationalized. The notions of national ownership of natural resources as a means to social and economic development were present in periods before the post-colonial authoritarian state and the emergence of post-neoliberal neoextractivism.

It would seem that it is a historical law of capitalist development that subjugated peoples in the capitalist periphery will always struggle to control their natural resources to bolster their chances of social and economic improvement, measured by capitalist yardsticks. Because of this observable historical phenomenon, it is difficult to argue that the 'new extractivism' in the Latin American and Caribbean region is given only to the historical period characterized by the change in capitalist policies from neoliberalism to post-neoliberalism. That position is ahistorical and static, because it does not take into consideration the dynamic and cyclical nature of capitalist development through the exploitation of the natural resources in foreign lands. The key point to note here is that the phenomenon identified as the new extractivism in that region is a part of a dynamic historical process of capitalist development, which is not transformative but reformist. It merely operates within the confines of capitalist production relations but seeks to retain a higher share of the economic surplus to fund social and economic improvements in the respective countries.

In a different historical period, the situation in Guyana illustrates this observation even under the original PPP whose leaders the colonial authorities divided into 'communists' and 'socialists.' The first thing the locals had to do was to take political control of the state. Thereafter, they could proceed to implement economic policies that would allow the state to capture a greater share of the economic surplus, with the aim to redistribute it to the poor. This is not a revolutionary agenda, but a common sense one in the circumstances of colonial domination. As capitalist development ebbs and flows in the throes of crises in the spheres of production and consumption the oppressed peoples in the natural resources rich capitalist periphery seek to exact a greater share of the capital accumulated in the system, which is used to improve their social and economic needs.

Notes

1 The British government appointed a constitutional commission on October 8, 1950 to review the electoral system in Guyana and the composition of the legislature and to make recommendations. The commission visited Guyana in 1951 and recommended sweeping changes to the constitution a most important one being universal adult suffrage. The constitutional commission was chaired by Mr. E. J. Waddington. The commission became known as the Waddington Commission. The constitution that was a product of the report of the commission became known as the Waddington Constitution.

2 See Report of the constitutional commission, 1950–51 and dispatch from the secretary of state for the colonies to the governor of British Guiana dated October 6, 1951.

3 See Report of the British Guiana commission, 1927. (1927). London: Her Majesty's Stationary Office, Cmd 2841.

4 The economic analysis for the period 1953 to 1960 is based on data provided in Newman (1964).

5 The analysis on budgetary policies is based on data that can be found in (Commission of Inquiry, 1962).
6 See also Rabe (2005).
7 See U.S. State Department. Archive. Foreign Relations, 1964–1968, Volume XXXII, Dominican Republic; Cuba; Haiti; Guyana. https://20012009.state.gov/r/pa/ho/frus/johnsonlb/xxxii/44659.htm.

References

Curtis, M. (2004). *Unpeople: Britain's secret human rights abuses*. New York: Vintage Publishing.

Hubbard, H. J. M. (1969). *Race and Guyana: The anatomy of a colonial enterprise*. Georgetown: Guyana.

Newman, P. (1964). *British Guiana: Problems of cohesion in an immigrant society*. London: Oxford University Press.

Rabe, S. G. (2005). *U.S. intervention in British Guiana: A cold war story*. Chapel Hill: The University of North Carolina Press.

Report of a commission of inquiry into disturbances in British Guiana in February 1962. (1962). London: Her Majesty's Stationary Office, Colonial No. 354.

Report of the British Guiana constitutional commission resented by the secretary of state for the colonies to parliament by command of Her Majesty September 1954. (1954). London: Her Majesty's Stationary Office Cmd. 9274 [The Robertson Commission, 1954].

Report of the constitutional commission 1950–51 and dispatch from the secretary of state for the colonies to the governor of British Guiana dated 6th October 1951. (1951). London: Her Majesty's Stationary Office.

Report of the British Guiana commission, 1927. (1927). London: Her Majesty's Stationary Office, Cmd 2841.

U.S. State Department. Archive. Foreign Relations, 1964–1968, Volume XXXII, Dominican Republic; Cuba; Haiti; Guyana. https://20012009.state.gov/r/pa/ho/frus/johnsonlb/xxxii/44659.htm.

8 The post-colonial authoritarian state

In this chapter we analyze the rise of the post-colonial authoritarian state between 1964 and 1992. The post-colonial authoritarian state is a political economy phenomenon that is manifested in the colonial phase of capitalist development in the periphery. The key capitalist political economy circumstances in Guyana at the time of the emergence of the post-colonial authoritarian state in that country included the dynamics of race and class conflicts domestically, anti-colonialism sentiments in the nation, political and economic nationalist tendencies, divisions in the anti-colonial movement, anti-communist hysteria, and foreign intervention.

Looming large among these was the belief that Guyana can take ownership and control of its natural resources and to redistribute income from the production and sale of those resources as raw materials to improve the social and economic conditions of the people living in the country. The ideal of national ownership and control of natural resources and to spread the wealth generated by the sector under national ownership and control to the sundry population is a phenomenon, integral to the dynamics of capitalist development in the periphery. This ideal is rarely ever achieved since peripheral capitalist countries were created. The peripheral states that pursue such a strategy degenerate into various forms of authoritarianisms, due to internal and external political and economic factors. The Guyana-case is a classic example of how the noble intentions to own and control a country's natural resources for its self-development, degenerated into authoritarianism.

The ruling elites of the post-colonial authoritarian state secured power with the support of imperial forces in opposition to their nationalist counterparts who forced their way into political office with mass support against the colonial power. The leaders of the post-colonial authoritarian state in Guyana participated on the side of the imperial forces that engineered a split in the anti-colonial mass movement. To win mass support domestically and in the developing world they sought to carry out the nationalist agenda of the anti-colonial mass movement including nationalization and income redistribution while being financially supported by their imperial backers. This alliance of convenience – the imperial forces behind the anti-communist propaganda and the renegade leaders who would do anything to secure power – was doomed to failure and degeneration into post-colonial authoritarianism. The same thing happened when the victors in the struggle against the post-colonial authoritarian state secured power with foreign support and then degenerated into a criminalized authoritarian state.

The post-colonial authoritarian state had similar economic policy trappings to the capitalist phenomenon characterized as neoextractivism in the Latin American and Caribbean region. This is mistakenly understood as a historically specific event that is taking place in the region characterized by a shift from neoliberalism to post-neoliberalism. Contrary to that understanding however an investigation into the rise of the post-colonial authoritarian state in Guyana showed that the political economy features, which are identified as distinctive of neoextractivism, were also present in that country in the historical period under consideration between 1964 and 1992.

As capitalism restructured from colonialism to center-periphery relations it set in motion a series of events and processes in Guyana that culminated in the rise of the post-colonial authoritarian state, which portrayed certain features. First, as in Latin America under neoextractivism, the post-colonial authoritarian state took control of the commanding heights of the economy through a process of nationalizations of foreign entities the biggest being in the natural resources and agricultural sectors. Second, as in Latin America the post-colonial authoritarian state sought to socialize the wealth from the nationalized entities by creating programs to alleviate the poor economic conditions of the masses. Third the post-colonial authoritarian state worked in close collaboration with imperial forces as it provided the best alternative to the presumed communist threat emanating from its political opposition in the country. The neoextractivist state also work in close collaboration with imperial forces. The nationalizations of foreign entities were not outright confiscations, but of a mortgage finance type or involving some other form of purchase.

In this chapter we analyze the transition from a post-colonial to a post-colonial authoritarian state in Guyana. The main purpose is to further demonstrate that neoextractivism, which is considered, as a new phenomenon in the Latin American and Caribbean region is merely a part of the capitalist development dynamic. Its focus is on the political economy factors that correspond to those of neoextractivism in the region. The politics in the region were anti-neoliberalism in nature spearheaded by left-leaning social movements, which progressive politicians seized upon to win power and then to proceed to pursue a political economy agenda to redistribute income generated in the natural resources sector to the poor, while simultaneously taking measures to appease foreign capital. The historical trajectory in Guyana had more to do with anti-communism, coalition politics, the consolidation of power through rigged national elections in the hands of the faction of the ruling elites handed power by US and British imperialist forces, nationalization of the commanding heights of the economy and attempts to redistribute income to the poor, post-colonial authoritarianism, political assassinations, neoliberal structural adjustment, and an anti-dictatorial resistance movement. Underlying these processes was the notion of appeasing foreign capital as a means to retain power domestically.

Ever since the collapse of colonialism, as global capitalism was restructured after World War II, there have been several analyses of the origins, nature and role of the state in post-colonial capitalist societies (Alavi, 1972; Saul, 1974; Leys, 1976; Gittens, 1982; Thomas, 1984; Petras, 1988). A feature of this body of work on the post-colonial state is the inquiry into its authoritarian dynamics in particular its relationship with the economy and politics, and the classes that dominate it and which it dominates. The development of the post-colonial authoritarian state is investigated in the context of the debate on neoextractivism in which the state takes the lead to nationalize foreign assets of multinational corporations in the natural resources sector with the explicit purpose of transferring wealth to the poor. The capitalist phenomenon described as neoextractivism is a state-driven process, similar to its earlier versions in Guyana.

It is illustrated how the political party that set about to build a post-colonial authoritarian state came to power beginning with an analysis of the support of imperial powers and a coalition government forged to unseat the (People's Progressive Party) PPP government, which was unpopular with the imperial forces. The economic policies of the coalition government are analyzed, before we examine the actual steps taken by the PNC between 1968 and 1985 including the dissolution of the coalition government and rigged national elections to create the post-colonial authoritarian state.

Thereafter the capitalist economic policies of the PNC government between 1966 and 1972, are assessed before tackling economic policies of the entrenched post-colonial authoritarian state in the 1970s. It was in this latter period that we identify similarities between economic policy in Guyana and the period described as the new extractivism in the Latin American and Caribbean region. The government nationalized foreign assets in the natural resources sector, with a view to redistribute the wealth generated to the poor. The government claimed that it was building a Cooperative Socialist Republic that would make the small man a real man. That required national ownership of the country's natural resources, and centering the cooperative sector as the dominant sector in a tri-sector economy – cooperative, state and private.

The pushback against this state-led approach in the form of neoliberal structural adjustment coincided with the reform in global capitalism plunged into crisis as the 'golden years of capitalism' came to an end in the 1970s. Finance capital emerged as the dominant form of capital under structural adjustment, replacing productive capital, and with it financialization and financial accumulation.

The post-colonial authoritarian state embraced structural adjustment, then rejected it publicly as it implemented neoliberal policies quietly. It then openly invited the (International Monetary Fund) IMF and World Bank back into the country through the Economic Recovery Program (ERP) in 1988. The effect of the ERP was such that there was economic growth primarily from the privatization of state assets, but social welfare benefits declined. This is the problem that neoextractivist regimes in the Latin American and Caribbean region is responding to by nationalizing foreign assets and to use the proceeds to fund social welfare developments. It seems that the peripheral capitalist countries nationalize private companies to improve social welfare, but the privatization of these companies decrease welfare, which seems to be a pattern of capitalist development in peripheral countries.

People's National Congress–United Force (PNC–UF) coalition politics

The formation of the PNC–UF coalition government represented a significant step in the capitalist development dynamic towards the emergence of a post-colonial authoritarian state. The state implemented nationalistic policies with the aim to redistribute income to the poor, while simultaneously seeking to appease foreign capital. Indeed, it was merely the continuation of a political economy process to deepen capitalist center-periphery relations that commenced with the collapse of the colonial slave mode of production. This process was driven by factors that were internal and external to the Guyanese social formation.

The domestic elites in control of local manufacturing, commerce, agriculture, etc., along with an intellectual stratum comprising the educated elites, sided with foreign capital to encourage the exploitation of Guyana's natural resources for export. This deepened the country's position in the capitalist periphery, as it depended on the manufacturing centers in Europe and the US to purchase its raw materials produced by transnational corporations headquartered in the capitalist center.

But, the coalition of convenience instigated by US and British imperial forces to oust the PPP from office, was not built on a strong foundation. Differences in opinion on politics, public and economic policy are accredited for the collapse of the coalition government (Burrowes, 1984; Jeffrey, 1986). The truth of the matter was that those differences were only symptom of a much deeper problem. The more fundamental cause of the demise of the coalition government was revealed after 1968. The PNC's real ambition was to exercise authoritarian control over the Guyanese state. The PNC used the coalition government to build-up its rank-and-file in supposedly PPP strongholds, in anticipation of going it alone in future elections. However, the PNC miscalculated the power of race in Guyanese politics that it along with the PPP and colonial forces had hitherto shaped. By no stretch of imagination could the African-Guyanese-based PNC have won over East Indian votes in a racially charged electorate. Thus, the continuous campaigning by PNC ministers to expand the base of the party, after the coalition government accented to power, was to no avail.

The UF accused the PNC of not adequately performing its governmental duties (Despres, 1967; Burrowes, 1984; Jeffrey, 1986). This problem caused the leader of the UF to threaten to resign his position as Minister of Finance. The rift between the PNC and the UF escalated as the PNC accused the UF of engaging in behaviors that constrained the former's social and economic programs to improve the standard of living of working people. The coalition government's failure to transform the social and economic conditions of working people was blamed on the UF.

The PNC took control over the government bureaucracy by filling vacancies with qualified re-migrants who were its supporters, much to the trepidation of the UF. The dispute over this issue among other things led to the resignation of the Minister of Finance in 1967, who proceeded to take up a back-seat position in the Parliament. The PNC then poached the UF Minister of Works and Hydraulics, who crossed the floor to become a PNC minister, instead. The minister was under pressure from his UF party to resign his position due to corruption. The PNC publicly supported the corrupt minister and lured him away from the UF.

Arguably, the case concerning the corrupt Minister of Works and Hydraulics was an early indication of an essential feature of the post-colonial authoritarian state. The leader of the PNC pardoned the corrupt minister and made him into his loyal servant. This phenomenon was to become a central feature of the post-colonial authoritarian state.

Economic policy between 1964 and 1966

The troubles that the PPP faced with the Western powers was due to the sympathies its leaders showed towards the communist bloc and its ideology. The purpose of the PNC–UF coalition government was to counteract the left-leaning PPP, and to place the country squarely in the fold of the capitalist bloc. To that effect the economic policies of the coalition were pro-West and founded on deficit financing. The increase in government spending was financed through a combination of borrowing in capital markets and increased taxation. The coalition increased current and capital expenditures by 50.2 percent of which in excess of 33 percent was to be funded through borrowing. There was still a hefty increase in taxation by 68.5 percent, while domestic and foreign borrowing rose by 20 percent and 16.3 percent. Also, the imperial forces provided the coalition government with various grants. The government established a national lottery and national radio bingo to raise additional revenue (d'Aguiar, 1965).

The country's public debt was US$134M comprising US$29M internal and US$105M external at December 21, 1964. The per capita debt was US$211, which increased from US$74 in 1955. The public debt began an upward trend under the coalition government, such that for the period 1967–1969 borrowing was 50.6 percent of total loans to government between 1960 and 1969 (d'Aguiar, 1965). The overall tone of economic policy under the coalition government was to enchant the rich.

First, it implemented a regressive tax system in 1965, which rewarded the rich and punished the poor by transferring the tax burden from the former to the working people. Second, the extension of duty-free concessions to all imports, enabled the business strata to increase profit, while price volatility removed any anticipated sustained benefits to the poor. Third, depreciation and initial allowance were expanded to cover all buildings, rather than only buildings that housed machinery.

Fourth, advertising and entertainment expenses were restored as proper expenses for income tax purposes. This measure allowed businessmen to deduct those expenses for income tax determination. Measures taken to strengthen the capitalist foundations of the economy involved the elevation of the money and banking sector, the nerve center of a capitalist economy. To this effect a national currency board, a monetary authority, and a suitable framework for commercial banking were promoted.

To strengthen the government bureaucracy, the coalition implemented a wages policy to attract qualified individuals to fill professional and administrative positions in the public sector. It increased basic pay rates in the public sector marginally, while substantially increasing the pay grades for professional and administrative staff. The IMF employed this very strategy in Guyana during the late 1980s and the 1990s. The view was that the professional staff needed to be remunerated at a higher rate. The workforce was even divided into core and peripheral, with the former receiving higher wages and the latter subject for redundancy during the 1980s and 1990s.

The social and economic programs of the coalition government focused on the completion of drainage and irrigation, roads, airport facilities, land development, the construction of schools, homes and public buildings. Coalition government policies increased the tax burden on the poor, were favorable towards the propertied classes through tax concessions to increase profitability, grew the domestic and foreign debt, and started the trend of Guyanization in the public service by employing party supporters and friends. These tendencies continued as the PNC constructed a post-colonial authoritarian state after the collapse of the coalition government in 1968. They were especially manifested through the 1966–1972 Development Plan (GOG, 1966), and the draft second development plan 1972–1976 to feed, clothes, and house (FCH) the nation (GOG, 1973).

Creating a post-colonial authoritarian state, 1968–1985

The essential characteristic of the post-colonial authoritarian state was the concentration of the powers of the state into a single political party. The principal processes through which the PNC seized state power were electoral and referendum frauds and the creation of a de facto one-party state. The post-colonial authoritarian state produced a sort of a social movement representing a multiracial and multiclass struggle to defeat it. But, there were several factors that served to maintain the post-colonial authoritarian state chief, among them was the notion that its Cold War allies believed it served to keep the allegedly communist PPP out of power.

The PNC stripped the electorate of their voting rights between 1968 and 1985. These rights were won through political struggle that culminated in the colonial authorities granting universal adult suffrage to the country for the national elections in 1953. The race-based political culture and the proportional representation electoral system combined to impact the development of the post-colonial authoritarian state. The majority East Indian electorate would ensure that the East Indian-based PPP would win national elections thereby creating a *de jure* one-party state. The minority African-based PNC could only secure power through electoral fraud or coalition politics. The PNC won power through a coalition in 1964 then maintained itself in power through electoral fraud until 1992. The PPP won power through its race-based electoral majority in 1992 and maintained itself in office until 2015 when it lost to a PNC-led coalition government.

Guyana was on its way to become a de facto one-party state after the PNC enacted a new law and amended existing laws relating to voter registration and the Election Commission. The 1967 National Registration Act provided for the national registration of all citizens, the issuance of national identification cards, and for the creation of the register of voters from the national registration list. The Representation of the People (Adaptation and Modification of Laws) Act 1968 amended the laws relating to the registration of voters and elections before the national elections in 1968. This latter Act reformed the powers of the Elections Commission, which was empowered by the Elections Regulations of 1964 to appoint the senior officials in the national registration and elections processes. Those powers were transferred to the Public Service Commission (PSC) through the Representation of the People (Adaptation and Modification of Laws) Act 1968 (Fitzpatrick and Rockcliffe, 1991). The PSC was now placed under the control of a government minister who could interfere in the appointment of senior officials of the election machinery.

The Minister of Home Affairs took over responsibility for national elections through the 1968 Act. But, those responsibilities belonged to the Election Commission as stipulated in the Guyana Independence Constitution 1966. The 1968 Act granted voting rights to non-resident citizens and expanded the proxy vote, from three to five (Greene, 1974). The powers of the Election Commission were eroded as a result of these changes, which were implemented in the national elections in 1968.

There were 68,000 overseas voters in addition to 369,088 electors on register in 1968. The PNC 'won' the elections by a clear majority, twenty-seven seats, followed by the PPP, twenty-one, and the UF, four, such that a coalition by the latter two parties could not have defeated it. Thus, commenced the process of rigged national elections that propped up the post-colonial authoritarian state. The laws that governed the 1968 national elections prevailed in the plebiscite in 1973.

The most contentious issues for the political opposition in the 1973 elections were the restoration of the powers of the Elections Commission, the compilation of a new and accurate voters list, scrapping overseas and proxy voting, counting of votes at the polling stations, and the lowering of the voting age from twenty-one to eighteen years. The PNC agreed only to lower the voting age, because it could have used that provision to its advantage. Recognizing that reality, the PPP opposed the bill to lower the voting age thus refusing to subscribe to the two-thirds majority vote in the parliament required for it to pass. The voters' list was kept a secret by the government, but the political opposition found out that while the number of overseas voters decreased by 51 percent from 68,558 to 33,546, the number of voters had increased by 75,000 since 1968, which in essence represented an increase in the entire population and not the electorate (Morrison, 1997).

Two opposition political activists who tried to protect the ballot boxes that were being taken to the officially designated, counting places were fatally shot by the military. The results of the elections were announced three days after it was held and the PNC declared that it had won by a two-third majority landslide – 243,803 or 70.09 percent of the votes cast domestically, and 29,031 or 97.9 percent of the 29,643 overseas votes. The PPP was awarded 92,374 or 26.56 percent of the votes cast the equivalent of fourteen parliamentary seats.

The PNC now had the kind of majority to implement whatever constitutional changes it desired without having to seek the votes of the parliamentary opposition. The political opposition claimed that the ballot boxes were diverted to the compound of the Guyana Defense Force (GDF), where they were tampered with. The PNC then took a number of repressive measures against its political opponents, as the country began its travel further down the ominous path of building a post-colonial authoritarian state.

The path to a post-colonial authoritarian state included the holding of a fraudulent referendum to postpone the general election that was constitutionally due in 1978. The PNC was still constrained from exercising absolute power although it had a two-third majority in the parliament, as certain provisions in the Independence Constitution could only be changed by referendum. The Constitution (Amendment) Bill passed in 1978 removed 'the requirement for holding a referendum' and enabled 'provision of that kind to be amended by a Bill, which had been supported by not less than two-thirds of all elected members of the National Assembly' (Morrison, 1997, p. 109).

Civil society organized a broad anti-referendum alliance that was multiclass, multiracial and multiparty, which called on the electorate to boycott the referendum, which it did overwhelmingly (BPGHR,[1] 1980; Darshan, 1984). The PNC announced however that the voter-turnout was 71.45 percent, of which 97.7 percent voted in favor of the postponement of the elections. The independent monitors of the referendum estimated the voter-turnout at 14 percent. The 1978 elections were postponed until December 1980.

The post-referendum national elections maintained a similar pattern of disenfranchisement of the Guyanese electorate. The 1980 elections were described as 'Something to Remember' by the British Parliamentary Group on Human Rights (BPGHR, 1980). The BPGHR was an international observer at the elections under the leadership of Lord Avebury. The International Team of Observers stated in their report that the PNC resorted to coercion and intimidation in the build-up to the elections; there was considerable political pressure on employees in the public sector who were coerced to vote for the PNC; and there were a great number of irregularities on the day of the elections.

The 1985 national elections were characterized by significant irregularities including military personnel voting six days before the civilian population and without supervision by opposition election scrutineers. The elections were also massively rigged in a blatant, clumsy and open fashion. On the day after the elections a statement on human rights[2] was issued by several organizations condemning the PNC's actions.[3]

The next general elections took place in 1992, under the overall supervision of the Carter Center headed by former US President Jimmy Carter, and several international observers. The PPP emerged victorious at that election, which the local, regional and international communities declared as 'free and fair.' These elections were delayed by two years in order to put in place the election machinery that was acceptable to the contestants.

Four years after Guyana secured its political independence, the PNC declared the country a Republic in 1970 severing ties with the British colonial system. On attaining Republican status for Guyana, the PNC proceeded to embark on its program of 'cooperative socialism.' The essential principles of cooperative socialism were the nationalization of foreign assets; the promulgation of the doctrine of paramountcy of the party; the repositioning of the cooperative society as the vehicle to effect socialist transformation; and the drafting of a development plan to feed, house, and clothe the nation by 1976.[4] The PNC moved rapidly under cooperative socialism to take the necessary steps to control the government, military, judiciary and economy. It nationalized the Demerara Bauxite Company (DEMBA) the Canadian multinational in 1971, Reynolds the American owned bauxite multinational in 1975, Jessel sugar in 1975, and Bookers sugar in 1976. As a result of those nationalizations the government then owned and or controlled over 80 percent of the Guyana economy.

Capitalist development plan 1966–1972

Prior to the plan to feed, clothe, and house the nation in which the proceeds from the nationalized industries would have a central role, Guyana embarked on a full-blown capitalist development plan between 1966 and 1972 after the country attained political independence in 1966. The main objectives of the 1966–1972 development plan formulated by Sir W. Arthur Lewis[5] and its underlying development strategy were to raise real income and living standards, reduce unemployment, and improve the economic infrastructure (GOG, 1966; Brotherson, 1983; Hope, 1979). Cambridge economist Kenneth Berrill had directed economic planning in the country between 1960 and 1964 (Jagan, 1967).

The Lewis plan expanded government expenditure by 2.7 times compared with the Berrill plan, and allocated very little to social programs. It proposed to combine expenditures on education and training; housing, urban and rural community development; and health, sanitation, and water supply, were only 19.4 percent of total expenditures, whereas planned spending on transportation was 22.1 percent of total expenditures, compared with 20.1 percent for agriculture and fishing (GOG, 1966). Domestic borrowing was 20.8 percent of the funds raised in the international capital markets. The goal of the Lewis plan was to create an institutional framework to stimulate the take-off of the private sector into a process of sustained economic growth. But, the reality was that government expenditure was supposed to stimulate private-sector economic activity.

The Lewis plan was based on his theory that the capitalist sector, the engine of economic growth reinvests its profits to absorb surplus labor from the traditional sector (Lewis, 1950 and 1955).

The plan did not bring about the desired results; gross national savings (GNS) peaked in 1970, but between 1966 and 1971 when the plan was abandoned its overall increase was 10.9 percent. The average annual growth rate in national savings was 3.75 percent in the overall plan period, albeit it was negative 13 percent in 1968 and negative 21.07 percent 1971. The average annual growth rate in gross national product (GNP) at factor cost was 7.13 percent, while GDP grew by 6.58 percent, and domestic expenditure 6.35 percent in the plan period.

The average annual growth in per capita income was 5.32 percent compared with 6.72 percent for consumption. Private consumption was 5.70 percent and public consumption 10.35 percent was almost twice the growth rate in private consumption. The average annual growth rate of fixed investment was 2.65 percent, comprising private fixed investment, which grew at negative 9.55 percent, compared with public sector investment, which was 9.5 percent. The national income grew on average at a rate of 6.16 percent during the plan period compared with 4.92 percent for total investment. However, the annual average change in the all-items index was 2.68 percentage points over the plan period.[6]

The indices of import and export prices, and the terms of trade also demonstrated how difficult the situation became for working people during the plan period. The average annual rate of growth in import prices was 5.6 percentage points, but the data showed an escalation in these prices between 1970 and 1972.[7] Brotherson (1983) observed that community welfare declined during the plan period due to a lack of unemployment benefits. Private investors contravened public health regulations by failing to provide basic amenities in the housing sector. The inadequacy in land allocation for schools and recreation facilities, constraints on small farm output, and institutional conflicts between local governments and the housing authority were other factors that had a negative impact on community welfare.

The plan failed to achieve its stated objectives to raise real income and the standard of living, reduce unemployment estimated at 21 percent in 1965, and to improve the economic infrastructure. The failure of the plan resulted from factors such as the lack of sufficient teamwork between the public and private sectors, relentless political opposition to its macroeconomic policies, and the dysfunctional system in place for its administration (Brotherson, 1983). The state abandoned the plan during 1970 and 1971 as it pursued its authoritarian economic policies. The conclusion to be drawn however is that the state sector started to become dominant in the economy during the plan period, under conditions of a relatively high rate of nominal economic growth. A similar development took place in Latin America. Cardoso (1979) observed that the 'new authoritarianism' in Latin America came into existence in the midst of a period of high economic growth in the region.

Post-colonial state authoritarian economic policies

The economic policies of the post-colonial authoritarian state were similar to those associated with the neoextractivist regimes in Latin America. In 1970, the government declared its intentions to build a cooperative socialist republic under the banner of cooperative socialism (PNC, 1970).[8] This was similar to the policies of socialism in the twenty-first century pursued in Venezuela as a part of the new extractivism. The state-led economic policies of cooperative socialism reinforced the political power of the post-colonial authoritarian state. The annual conferences of the ruling PNC became the venues for the formulation of national economic, social and political policies. The party was regarded as the vehicle for economic, social and political change.

The state promoted 'self-help' as the basis for economic development and rejected foreign aid as the solution to the conditions of underdevelopment. It identified the cooperative as a vehicle for national unity and the principal institution for national development. Workers were taught the philosophy and ideology of 'cooperative socialism' as promulgated by the state. They were trained in practical skills and were encouraged to save in the indigenous state-owned Co-operative Bank. The state set a goal to build a new city in the hinterland of the country. It established a Ministry of Cooperatives and pronounced cooperative socialism as the essential method of working-class control of the economic and society. It believed that the cooperative would bring about maximum people's involvement in economic decision-making, and socialist development (Johnson, 1981). The Guyana Constitution 1980 stated that the cooperative 'shall be the dynamic principle of socialist transformation' that pervades and inform all inter-relationships in Guyanese society (GOG, 1980: Article 16).

The PNC announced at its party congress that it was preparing a ten-year development plan from 1971 to 1981 and a shorter detailed five-year plan for the period 1971 to 1975. The main objectives of the FCH plan were to obtain full employment, economic independence and self-sufficiency, egalitarianism, and a growth rate in GDP of 8.5 percent per annum. The plan required substantial amounts of investment, domestic savings, and external capital inflow. The total projected planned expenditure was 3.9 times greater than that proposed for Lewis plan (GOG, 1973).

The data showed that the Lewis plan placed more emphasis on agriculture and fishing, inclusive of drainage and irrigation and river and sea defense, which represented 24.84 percent of the planned expenditure compared with 16.67 percent for the FCH plan. Transport and communication was 22.11 percent of proposed expenditure between 1966 and 1972 and only 18.05 percent between 1972 and 1976. The planned expenditure for housing in the Lewis plan was 21.7 percent, compared with 8.61 percent in FCH plan, which proposed to build 5,000 housing units in 1972; 8,000 in 1973; 13,000 in 1974; 17,000 in 1975, and 22,000 in 1976.[9] The Lewis plan expended 6.62 percent of its total expenditure on health, sanitation and water supply, while the FCH plan for the period between 1972 and 1976 expended less than 0.4 percent in those sub-categories.

An assessment of the FCH plan against its stated objectives showed that it was a failure. By 1977, there was a calamitous shortfall in agricultural output from self-help and cooperative farming, an indicator of the failure of the food program (Four Unions, 1977). Only 6,000 of the total 65,000 housing units targeted to be built between 1972 and 1976, were completed, or just 1,000 more than the 5,000 target set for the first year of the plan, leaving a 90.77 percent shortfall in the housing target (Four Union, 1977).

Malnutrition and poor sanitation had combined to make gastroenteritis a serious scourge among children. By 1977 the nutritional intake of the population had not improved from levels identified by the Caribbean Food and Nutrition Institute (CFNI) in 1971. A survey conducted by the CFNI in 1971 established that 18 percent of children younger than five years had moderate to severe signs of protein and calorie malnutrition, and 43 percent more had mild signs. As much as 54 percent of urban households had inadequate protein intake, while in the rural areas the figure was 60 percent. Furthermore, 66 percent of urban households had inadequate calorie intake, while in the rural areas the figure was 74 percent (Four Union, 1977).

There was no evidence that unemployment declined. A conservative estimate placed unemployment at 25 percent, with the figure for young people between the ages of 18–23 years in urban areas being over 60 percent (Four Unions, 1977). The poor socio-economic conditions set the post-colonial authoritarian state on a collision course with the labor unions that demanded improvement in the economic and social conditions of working people. But, the labor unions were repressed and several of them became mouthpieces of the ruling PNC, which had declared itself as the paramount institution in the country under the doctrine of the 'paramountcy of the party.'

The failure of the FCH plan reflected in the poor economic conditions, which prevailed by 1977 forced the PNC to seek a financial bailout from its allies in the IMF and World Bank for 1978, 1979 and 1980. The government formulated a new set of policies to build a socialist economy through agricultural, industrial and technical development. The IMF and World Bank were now financing 'cooperative socialism' a state-capitalist enterprise. The government merely rolled over the FCH plan in combination with the policy measures associated with the IMF and World Bank. In this approach the government emphasized that agricultural production, fishing, forestry, and mining should be linked to manufacturing and industry. It advocated appropriate technology to satisfy domestic needs in manufacturing, and which fits in with the country's natural resources and environment and is readily understood and utilized.

Food production for exports and the production of nutritional foods, were the new goals for agriculture. Energy policy focused on the production and use of wood, charcoal, and hydro-power, as the authoritarian state saw the need to develop a highly competent and motivated scientific community, and to build institutions to facilitate scientific research (Hoyte, 1979). In the immediate post-FCH period the focus of the capitalist development process shifted from self-help and cooperatives to one that emphasized an attachment to the land, a team or group approach, the simultaneous improvement in the material and the cultural conditions, and the harnessing of the social arrangements and the cultural experiences of the people (Hoyte, 1979).

The government proposed new spending on education and culture, scientific and technological research and development through the National Science Research Council (NSRC), and on scholarships and training programs to prepare workers in a wide range of skills. Expenditure in the health sector focused on upgrading the referral hospital system, and improving the infrastructure, equipment and supplies to rural hospitals between 1978 and 1982. Government spending focused on rural water supply to filter and provide water to houses, and to investigate the base lands in the coastal region for their water bearing potentials.

The investment code (GOG, 1979) published in 1979 was intended to attract and stimulate foreign and domestic investments in the country. It outlined the economic policy of the post-colonial authoritarian state, which indicated a shift from its cooperative socialism rhetoric. It stated that the country was characterized by a tri-sector economy comprising a public sector, the cooperative sector, and the private sector. It described the public utilities sector as comprising, road, air and water transportation, telecommunications, water supply and electricity supply.

The investment code claimed that a fundamental principle that guided investment was that the ownership and control of the country's natural resources should remain in the hands of the state, which must be in effective control of the national economy on behalf of the citizens. The contradictory signals of the investment code did not give much encouragement and confidence to private and foreign investors. As a consequence, the investment climate remained volatile and the state continued as the main investor exercising control over the economy.

The state-led economic policies of cooperative socialism were supposedly based on the principles of self-help, self-reliance, and subsequently, measures to promote agricultural, industrial and technological development. To realize the self-help and self-reliance objectives the state implemented a regime of price controls (GTUC, 1973) and food bans (GHRA, 1982). Price control was the principal public policy instrument to regulate inflation (GTUC, 1973), but it exacerbated the plight of working people, negatively affected their social welfare, and was another source of food shortages, inflation, and the development of a black market.

The price control ordinance listed an exhaustive number of items that were subjected to price controls from 1971. It fixed the maximum wholesale and retail prices of these items on the basis of changes in their cost. While price controls were introduced in the English-speaking Caribbean during World War II, by the colonial authoritarian state as an economic policy option to combat the enormous shortages created by the war the post-colonial authoritarian state introduced the controls purely to satisfy its ill-advised self-reliance and self-help strategies.

Under the price control system, the maximum price fixed by the state became the uniform price, which had the effect of distorting the competitive market price, thereby giving sellers monopoly and quasi-monopoly power. The state needed to have knowledge of the operating costs of private businesses before it could effectively fix prices that would be sufficient to cover those costs, but it was virtually impossible for the state to obtain that information. The black market pushed prices above their maximum legislated levels, created even greater hardships for working people, became the only means by which important commodities were obtained, and was the source for the emergence of the *nouveau riche.*

The price of potatoes recorded an increase of 140 percent, while the price of pickled beef went up by 104 percent, between 1971 and 1973. The prices of cooking and table butter were increased by 92 percent and 73 percent, respectively. The price of evaporated milk went up by 50 percent and powdered milk by 54 percent. The prices of baby foods, onions, cheese, and chickpeas all increased by over 50 percent (GTUC, 1973). These are foods that the working people consume daily, and there was no corresponding increase in wages. There were 271 items subjected to price controls by 1978, although the number was subsequently reduced due to the banning of imports (GHRA, 1982).

Sugar, rice and chicken were the only items available in shops at their controlled prices in 1981. The same was true as well for mosquito coils, gasoline, aerated drinks and beer. A large number of items were unavailable or available only for short periods or on the black market.[10] The food shortages that resulted from the price control policies were compounded by the measures to ban a large number of food and non-food items to stimulate the self-help and self-reliance objectives. The food ban was wide-ranging, covering a majority of items consumed by working people. The list of prohibited goods was prepared and tabled by the Ministry of Trade in August 1982.

Anyone caught in the possession of the banned items were liable to be charged, tried, imprisoned or made to pay a fine. The banning of foods and other items however led to the development of a thriving black market for those commodities in which even state officials participated as sellers and buyers. The food-ban policy led to the criminalization of the population, as many people bought banned items on the black market. The severe food shortages contributed to the moral decay in the society, as decent citizens were forced to physically fight in food lines to get the opportunity to buy scarce items. Some people were trampled to death in the process. The phenomenon of human scavengers in refuse dumps emerged, as land-fill sites were locations where droves of workers and unemployed poor searched the refuge to secure food and other items.

The economic institutions created by the government to execute its policies of ‘cooperative socialism’ were the External Trade Bureau (ETB), the Knowledge Sharing Institute (KSI), and the Guyana National Cooperative Bank (GNCB). The ETB had an important role in the administration of the distribution of all imports, while the KSI was a semi-state distribution chain owned by the PNC, and the GNCB was to mobilize domestic savings to finance ‘cooperative socialism.’ The state claimed that it controlled all import trade in order to diversify the country’s trade routes to include the socialist countries, and to benefit from the advantages of buying in bulk. The ETB established a Sino-Soviet department, but there was no significant trade diversification. The state remained heavily dependent on its traditional European and North American trade partners. The ETB prepared and distributed a list of commodities it imported to wholesale directly to the public, or on behalf of local private business enterprises.

The division of imports between the state and the private sectors was quite arbitrary, as there was no rationale for the state selecting certain items for itself and giving others to the private sector. The ETB did not significantly improve on the importation of important food items and was saddled with a number of problems that interfered with its efficiency. The organizational structure and function of the ETB caused confusion as to whether it was an arm of the ruling party or a state entity. The ETB was incapable of providing imported foods to match the demand for such products, which resulted from shortfalls in locally produced foods.

The centralization of imports meant that distributors had to queue at the ETB to make their purchases. The ETB did not establish an orderly queuing system, since political and other considerations determined who received imports. The 'fair rota system' for the distribution of goods established by the merchants in collaboration with the ETB was frequently violated, as bribery and corruption became the order of the day at the institution (GTUC, 1973).

The KSI was an economic institution operated by the PNC that functioned as a retail and in some cases a wholesale commercial institution. Customers had to produce a PNC party card to purchase commodities sold at the KSI, which became the main distribution center, replacing the wholesale cooperatives in many areas. The retail cooperatives purchased their goods wholesale from the KSI. But the financial proceeds of the KSI remained a mystery since there was no financial accountability (GHRA, 1982).

The GNCB, created in 1970, was considered the people's bank intended to garner their savings, apply them to national purposes, and grant credit to poor people and their institutions (Bascom, 1969 and 1970; Burnham, 1970). The government was the largest shareholder in the bank, but it was envisaged that cooperative societies and working-class groups would eventually become the majority shareholders (Bascom, 1969).

The bank operated on a strict commercial basis and the bulk of its loanable funds went to the cooperative sector (Bascom, 1969). Albeit there was a contradiction between its commercial operations and the supposedly cooperative socialist objective of the state. The profit motive was not the driving force behind cooperative socialism but it sure was behind the operations of the CNCB. The GNCB performed the entire gamut of functions associated with commercial banks for profit (Bascom, 1970).

There was no real gain from cooperatives doing business with the bank, it was better for cooperative societies to take loans from any bank that offered the lowest interest rate. A major problem was that some cooperative enterprises operated like joint-stock companies, abandoning the intended principles of the cooperative. Commercial firms merely took on the name of a cooperative in order to benefit from the tax and other gains associated with cooperatives, while continuing to operate like the regular microenterprise, partnership, or even private limited company.

Economic policy under cooperative socialism included plans to diversify the economy through hinterland development (Jack, 1970). These were contemplated in order to improve employment, production and income, and the social conditions of working people. The level of unemployment was estimated at being between 15 percent and 20 percent in 1970. It was believed that the development of the natural resources rich hinterland was key to resolving the unemployment situation.

Colonial hinterland development policy included plans to resettle Syrians there in the nineteenth century. Also, the Moyne Commission[11] recommended that Jews be settled there, but that project was thwarted by the outbreak of World War II and events thereafter. In 1949 the Evans Report recommended that Europeans and West Indians should be settled in the hinterland (Jack, 1970). The PNC government sought to resettle people from Guyana's Atlantic coast in the interior locations as a part of its hinterland development strategy. Also, the government had a plan, which was halted, to settle Hmong refugees from Laos in Guyana's hinterland near to location of the notorious Jonestown settlement. The Hmong or 'free men' were enlisted by the CIA as surrogate soldiers in its 'secret war' against North Vietnamese troops in Laos in the 1960s. When the war ended the Hmong could not have returned to Laos.[12]

The government believed that the drainage and irrigation problems on Guyana's Atlantic Coast made it difficult for agricultural production to expand, but that there were better opportunities for agriculture in the hinterland. The security argument for hinterland development was that it would counteract Venezuela's claim to two-thirds of the country. In addition, it was believed that hinterland development would promote general economic expansion. The government argued that the economic development of the country depended on the occupation of the hinterland. It established a 'Hinterland Development Corporation' to develop criteria to select people to settle in the hinterland and to administer hinterland development. Initially, the state would provide land clearance, shelter based on materials from the areas to be settled, and supply basic foods, the basic necessities for hinterland development.

The speedy construction of roads was envisaged as important to hinterland development, as well as the clearing of waterways for communications purposes. Schools with qualified personnel and medical services were also identified as basic necessities to encourage permanent settlement. It was envisaged that a settlement scheme in the hinterland would take between five to ten years to be established. The elaborate hinterland development policy was like a fairy tale, based on unsound economic reasoning, simplistic observations about people's needs in relocation, and depended heavily on government financing, rather than incentive schemes to attract people to the interior.

In 1992 when the PNC was finally removed from office the social services were in a state of disrepair. The housing shortage had reached critical proportions and many working people in the urban centers were forced to resort to squatting on unoccupied lands where they built shacks for dwellings developing many small shantytowns in and around Georgetown, the capital city, and in rural districts. The education system was in poor shape, as many teachers fled the country to work in the Caribbean islands and other locations. The national science and technology policy was a failure, as the country could not stem the tide of migration of its top scientists who were poorly paid and treated shabbily.

The scholarships program was a disaster since most people who were sent abroad for training did not return. The health sector was in a state of ruin, understaffed, under-equipped, and workers underpaid (Baker, 1994). Diseases, such as yellow fever, dengue fever, and malaria that had hitherto been eradicated from the population centers had reappeared. The hospitals were without adequate drugs, bandage, equipment, etc. The water situation had become a nightmare, as the state had failed to supply pure water on a secured basis to a vast majority of the population. People had to make provision for the private supply of water, by installing overhead tanks to catch rainfall, and electrical pumps, although they were called on to pay water rates. The electricity situation was outrageous and citizens also had to make their own provisions for that item by buying electrical generators or large batteries to supply their homes with power.

The post-colonial authoritarian state faced two major problems regarding its economic policies. The first problem was political in that the state was illegal and people would not co-operate with its economic policies no matter how sensible and well-meaning they were. The tension between the economic and political realms was great and worked against the success of government economic policies. Second, the economic policies were unsound, lacked proper economic analyses, and were driven by political considerations. The authoritarian state had hoped to legitimize itself through the economic realm, thus, its economic policies had political rather than clear economic objectives. Expectations of political legitimacy, served to subordinate economic objectives that were relegated to a secondary status.

Post-colonial authoritarian state versus global capitalists

The global capitalists supported the government of Guyana during the heyday of the Cold War, but had begun to change their policies towards the country in the 1980s. The significance of the authoritarian states supported by global capitalism had begun to diminish as the Cold War began to thaw. The Washington Consensus replaced the Keynesian Consensus as the dominant economic paradigm supervised by the IMF and the World Bank (Singer, 1997).

The Guyana government had abandoned the first full-fledged structural adjustment program it implemented in 1980. That development ruptured the relationship between the PNC and its global capitalist allies (Burnham, 1983). The PNC was adamant that it had the 'will to survive' the pressure the global capitalists brought to bear on the country. The leader of the PNC complained in one of his addresses entitled '*Will to Survive*' to the fifth biennial congress of his party that the US administration at the time 'as a matter of theology and ideology, disagrees violently with' his 'economic policies generally, and would have them "corrected"' (Burnham, 1983, p. 9). The PNC leader told his followers that the country was not free to pursue its own development path, nor have the right to make its own policy decisions (Burnham, 1983).

The PNC leader protested that the US administration wanted the Guyana government to hand back all the nationalized industries to foreign corporations. The party members and followers were told that they did not win their independence to yield to or accept re-colonization, and that they must be self-reliant in food, regardless of whatever happens. That task was to be achieved by the farmers, the military and paramilitary forces, and the education system (Burnham, 1983).

There was a turn in economic policy after the conflict between the government of Guyana and its imperialist backers erupted. Although the 1980 structural adjustment program was abandoned (Harrigan, 1991; Canterbury, 1997; Thomas, 1982), the government's economic policies continued to reflect structural adjustment measures. Indeed, the Guyana government had top level discussions with the IMF in 1983 that left the door open for future talks between them. No new program was negotiated with the IMF until 1988 when the economic recovery program in place today was introduced.[13] The observation that the state abandoned structural adjustment but continued to implement some adjustment policies is gleaned from the annual national budget in 1985 (Greenidge, 1985).

The development priorities identified in 1985 were food, agriculture and forestry; manpower training; export promotion; energy; technology; mining and quarrying; and regionalism and cooperatives. Food, nutrition, health, education, recreation, culture, housing, clothing, employment, equitable income distribution, security of individuals and their property were identified as national welfare priorities. The government's rhetoric was shifted from cooperative socialism to social welfare. The national welfare priorities recognized that development is the precursor of welfare, and welfare is the *raison d'être* of development. In typical neoclassical welfare theoretical tradition however, the state argued that its provision of welfare benefits to working people was unsustainable. The neoliberal argument was used to cut back the state-provided welfare benefits.

The state identified two types of constraints regarding the reduction in welfare benefits. The first concerned the political judgment of persons, and the maturity of the nation. The populace should freely give up certain welfare benefits that would generate more savings for the country. If people agreed to a cut in welfare, that would have demonstrated sound political judgment and maturity. The second constraint had to do with the identification of the welfare items that were fundamental to development. The Guyana government argued that education was the first welfare priority, which was crucial for development and that the second was employment. The government contended that improvements in housing, food, and employment were parts of the welfare function that the workers could be persuaded to give up. It was clearly an anti-working-class idea to want to persuade people to ease their demands for food, better housing and more jobs!

The economic idea to separate the welfare function into items that the people could agree to give up and those that are crucial for development is a neoliberal prescription to cajole people to accept fewer benefits, even as they worked harder. The government was quietly implementing an IMF/World Bank neoliberal agenda. In 1988 the full-fledged structural adjustment program that was implemented resulted in some economic growth, but was due to the sale of state assets (Canterbury, 1998). The 1980 structural adjustment program was not totally abandoned. The government restructured state corporations, and the rice and bauxite industries, which was a part of the structural adjustment program it had supposedly abandoned. The price mechanism was restored as the main means of resource allocation, rather than state planning. The government had hoped to win back favor with the global capitalists by quietly implementing structural adjustment, while at the same time creating an appearance of strength to its supporters by publicly opposing the IMF/World Bank.

The effect of these policies was that performance in the social sector had been severely constrained as government spending declined from 15 percent to 12 percent, between 1970 and 1980, while its disbursement on health fell from 8 percent to 6 percent in the same period. Simultaneously, the government's disbursement on personal emoluments declined from 40 percent to 26 percent of its total expenditure.[14] That was an indication of the success of government's stabilization and structural adjustment labor market objectives in the 1970s to reduce employment in the public sector.

By 1980, social service and utility standards had deteriorated badly in areas such as electricity supply, which became erratic and unpredictable, and the water and sewerage systems, which collapsed. Water in many parts of the capital city became unfit for human consumption. The sanitary situation degenerated rapidly as many mosquito-borne diseases, such as malaria and dengue fever, reemerged in areas in which previously they had been eliminated. The telephone system had broken down, with a large number of telephones not functioning and no spare parts to repair them. Public transport became hazardous as the services of the state-owned Guyana Transport Services Limited (GTSL) collapsed due to a lack of spare parts and corruption. The state's transport policy allowed only itself to own and operate public bus networks. The private sector was debarred from operating in that area, although a number of privately owned taxis remained in operation. River and air transport also became a nightmare as those services became irregular and expensive.

The education system also performed below its traditionally high standards, as teachers were hired and fired for political reasons. Students were forced to participate in state sponsored political rallies, marches, and other events. The inclusion of participation in political activities organized by the ruling party in the evaluation of students distorted examination results. Course content was made fuzzy by the inclusion of state propaganda material on which students were evaluated. School children were forced to clean their schools in replacement of the workers who were retrenched.

The economic collapse affected the health and nutrition levels of the workers and their children. Crimes of all descriptions increased particularly armed robbery; in a significant number of cases the victims reported that their robbers were dressed in military uniforms and presented police identification cards. Crime became the order of the day at the level of the state bureaucracy as state officials exacted bribes and engaged in other forms of illicit rent seeking activities.

Surrendering to the IMF and World Bank

The worsening social and economic conditions in the country brought on by 'cooperative socialism' coupled with the mounting domestic political pressure that the crisis had helped to force the PNC government to implement a full-fledged IMF/World Bank Program in 1988 to its own peril. The forces of global capitalism had for years turned a blind eye to political repression in Guyana. But an anti-dictatorial movement emerged in the country that had sought international support in its struggle for democracy.

The global capitalist forces only engaged with the anti-dictatorial movement as the Cold War ended. The anti-dictatorial movement was an amalgamation of different political, civil, and class forces, which was dominated by individuals and groups that had a working-class outlook. The political agenda of the leading forces in the anti-dictatorial movement was heavily influenced by socialist ideals. But, by the time the post-colonial authoritarian state fell in 1992 the leading forces in the anti-dictatorial movement had fully embraced structural adjustment and neoliberal democratization in a remarkable turn of events.

Guyana had engaged with the IMF since the 1960s and 1970s, when the country negotiated several stand-by credit arrangements for Special Drawing Rights (Thomas, 1982). The first full-fledged World Bank-inspired structural adjustment program was implemented in 1981, to complement the IMF stabilization program (Thomas, 1982; Harrigan, 1991). The so-called abandonment of the structural adjustment program left the government with its annual budgets as the main means of economic management between 1981 and 1988. In that period the currency was devalued by 38 percent in 1984 and by 127 percent in 1987.

The government reduced the scope of price controls, increased public sector prices and tariffs to reflect the currency devaluations, and tried to rationalize the public enterprises. It made efforts to rehabilitate the bauxite industry, improve its managerial practices, and reduce its employment and operating cost. The state closed some sugar factories, and converted sugar lands into other uses (GOG, 1988).

To rationalize the tax system and raise revenue the government simplified the consumption tax by reducing the number of tax rates from twenty-nine to three, cutting the number of income tax brackets from ten to seven, and lowering the marginal income tax rate from 75 percent to 55 percent (GOG, 1988). Measures to improve incentives for the private sector included changes in the relative price structure and in the marginal income tax rates. The government extended the foreign exchange retention scheme to allow some private exporters to retain some of their foreign exchange earnings to buy imports and spare parts. There was also some liberalization of the foreign exchange market: registered private sector firms were allowed to export rice, and the Guyana Manufacturing and Industrial Development Agency (GUYMIDA) was established in 1984 to promote private investment.

The broad goals of the ERP implemented in 1988 were to bring about the recovery of the country's economy, and to lay the foundation for its self-sustained growth and development (GOG, 1989). To improve economic incentives, the ERP put into operation exchange-rate and domestic-pricing policies, exchange and trade restrictions, and measures to enhance the role of the private sector and to promote competition. It stipulated reforms in the agriculture, forestry, fisheries, mining, and manufacturing sectors.

The central government and public enterprises were reformed through fiscal policy and public sector measures. It instituted a public sector investment program (PSIP) to rehabilitate the basic infrastructure to increase exports and private investment. Its monetary measures enabled the Central Bank to pursue a credit policy consistent with the inflation and balance of payments targets. Its incomes policy retrained wages to increase employment, protect the external competitiveness of firms, and reduce inflation. The idea was to keep wage increases below the rate of inflation. Finally, the Social Impact Amelioration Program (SIMAP) was intended to help the poor to 'cushion' the social impact of the ERP. To this effect pensions were to be increased, school feeding and food for work programs implemented, as well as vocational training for young school leavers, and unemployed, unskilled and semi-skilled young people (GOG, 1989).

The framers of the ERP envisaged its finance by the multilateral financial agencies, the IMF, the World Bank and the Caribbean Development Bank (CDB), friendly traditional and non-traditional bilateral donor countries, the private sector, and the sale of Guyanese products and exports (GOG, 1989). A review of the economic and social data reveals that the conditions of working people had worsened despite the fact that the economy experienced reasonable growth (Canterbury, 1997).

The government's surrender to the IMF/World Bank structural adjustment program came at a high cost to working people due to increased inflation, declined wages, and increased taxes. Public sector debt increased dramatically, and the negative balance in the balance of payments worsened. The explicit aim of the social program to reverse the calamitous decline in the social services remained just a dream as the poverty rate skyrocketed. The malnutrition rate increased fourfold, life expectancy was the lowest in the Caribbean Community, infant mortality rate was on the rise, spending on education, health, social security, poverty alleviation increased marginally, and the sale of state enterprises had a negative impact on labor and employment conditions. The privatization program was almost a giveaway of public companies to favored private firms and individuals.

Labor and the anti-IMF/ERP struggle

The post-colonial authoritarian state dominated the trade union movement, as it did the private sector and civil society. The post-colonial authoritarian state had forged an unholy alliance with some labor unions in the country. This allowed the government to gain control over the Trades Union Congress (TUC) except for four militant unions in that organization at the time, the Guyana Agricultural and General Workers Union (GAWU), the National Association of Commercial and Industrial Employees (NAACIE), the Clerical and Commercial Workers' Union (CCWU), and the University of Guyana Workers Union (UGWU). The working-class struggle entailed the contest between these militant unions and the post-colonial authoritarian state for control of the TUC and the independence of labor unions.

The 1980s were characterized by a struggle for democracy by working people against the post-colonial authoritarian state. The government had blocked individual unions from negotiating for wages, a responsibility, which was granted solely to the TUC. The officials in the TUC fully supported the measure to strip unions of the right to negotiate for wages (Gopaul, 1997). The TUC sided with the government's position that the workers should not receive a 25 percent pay raise in 1982. The government and the TUC argued that the economy was incapable of supporting wage increases without there being large-scale retrenchment in the public sector.

The four militant unions in the TUC took a dissenting position and so the working-class struggle took on the form of independent trade unions versus a TUC/government alliance. The workers responded to the economic crisis with a number of intermittent strikes in 1981 and 1982 (Gopaul, 1997). An estimated number of 2,245 workers at Albion sugar estate struck over shortages of essential food items in 1981. In 1983 the bauxite workers decided to undertake protest demonstrations once weekly until the food shortage at Linden was corrected. The food demonstrations in the bauxite industry reached its high-point on May 18, when women and children came out in support of the workers. The government responded by sending out the Tactical Services Unit (TSU) of the Guyana Police Force that brutally broke up the protest, arrested twenty-four shop stewards, and severely beat two union organizers causing them to be hospitalized. Also, the state-owned Bauxite Company reduced the workweek from five to three days in thirty sections of the Linden operations, further punishing the workers.

The bauxite unions promptly called a general strike to protest the spiteful action of the state-owned company in reducing the workweek. The strike lasted for six weeks and the workers won as the bauxite management was forced to restore the five-day workweek. But the state struck back during those discussions by retrenching 1,721 union leaders and militant workers, including the President of the Guyana Bauxite Supervisors Union (GBSU) Gordon Griffith, and the Treasurer of the Guyana Mine Workers Union (GMWU), Malcolm Thompson. Having just come out of a six-week strike the workers were unable to respond effectively to the retrenchment of the most militant wing in the bauxite workforce and so the government had the final victory.

The TUC was under state control and it was incapable of effective retaliation against the crushing blow the state dealt to the bauxite unions. But the determination by the four unions to regain working-class control of the TUC was soon to create major problems for the post-colonial authoritarian state. The four unions launched a struggle for power within the TUC, which, through secret planning and organization, paid off at the TUC's 1984 elections when they delivered a stunning defeat to the state's candidate for the presidency of the organization. By 1984, the four unions had expanded to seven, to include the Guyana Public Service Union (PSU), the GMWU and the GBSU. George Daniels, the president of the PSU, was the alternative candidate for TUC president. The post-colonial authoritarian state mobilized its forces against Daniels who was bold enough to stand up in defiance of the government.

Despite serious efforts to the contrary several of the state's candidates were routed at the elections. The alternative candidates won positions as president, treasurer, organizing secretary, three vice-presidents, and two assistant secretaries. The post-colonial authoritarian state had lost its control of the TUC, which was now in the hands of the workers. Later in 1984 the new TUC executive organized a Special Delegates' Conference that passed a motion debarring state ministers from becoming executive members of their organization.

The government struck back when it mobilized the media, school children and public servants against the May Day rallies organized by the TUC in 1985 (Morrison, 1997). The state staged separate May Day rallies from those of the TUC, but the latter's workers' marches in Georgetown ended with a rally at the National Park. The rally was disrupted when the electricity to the public address system was mysteriously disconnected. The workers' activities however were very successful as they paraded through the streets of Georgetown demanding a minimum wage of $25 a day. The minimum wage at that time was $12.71. But while the government and the TUC were locked in negotiations on the minimum wage the former announced that the new minimum wage would be $15.10 a day.

The struggle for power in the TUC took another turn when the state-controlled unions moved to the courts and secured an injunction that restrained members of the GAWU and the PSU from voting in the elections at the organization's Annual Delegates Conference in 1985. The injunction barred forty delegates from voting including the TUC's president George Daniels. The result was that the conference never got around to discussing the business of the organization.

The post-colonial authoritarian state used its judicial arm to regain full control of the TUC in 1986. Also, it took over the worker's day parade from the labor unions. The challenge from the independent unions was temporarily subdued. Meanwhile, the economic conditions had gotten so bad that it was calculated that a minimum wage of $52 a day was needed to support a family of six in 1987. The workers were prepared to accept $30 or even $25 a day but the authoritarian state gave them only $23.75. On February 4, 1988 George Daniels wrote to the Permanent Secretary in the Public Service Ministry demanding that the increments due to the public service workers since 1977 be paid over to them. But the public service workers' demand that the state honored its contract with them fell on deaf ears.

The longstanding grievances the independent unions had with the TUC came to a head at the 1988 Annual Delegates Conference of the organization. The National Association of Agricultural, Commercial and Industrial Employees called on the TUC to change its rules to make them more democratic, so that the numerically larger unions are fairly represented in the executive of the organization. Matters came to a head in 1988 when the TUC fractured over that issue, forcing seven trade unions to break away from the TUC and to form the Federation of Independent Trade Unions of Guyana (FITUG).

The FITUG unions became very active in organizing the anti-IMF/ERP campaign but the TUC being in the control of the post-colonial authoritarian state stayed out. The Public Service Union came under tremendous pressure from the state for its decision to join the FITUG. Both the PSU and the post-colonial authoritarian state depended on the African segment of the population who dominated the public services sector for their support. The government felt threatened that the PSU was eroding its support base. Indeed, a faction of the PSU felt compelled to pledge their loyalty to the state for fear of reprisals after the PSU joined the FITUG.

The faction complained that the decision to take the PSU out of the TUC and to join the FITUG was undemocratic. The General Secretary of the union issued a statement however that the union had taken a democratic decision to join the FITUG. The state stepped up its pressure on the union by refusing to deduct union dues from public service workers and to pay them over to the PSU. The state justified its actions on the grounds that the union had not kept proper records and that its accounts were not audited.

In the meantime, the FITUG had called on the state for dialogue on the proposed economic recovery program. The FITUG organized a symposium attended by US Embassy officials and US State Department Representative Robert Hare, on November 15, 1988. The Minister of Finance did not acknowledge the FITUG's letter of invitation to participate in the symposium. In the absence of public discussion on the ERP when the news was made public that the state was about to sign an agreement with the IMF, the FITUG called for a day of protest on February 24, 1989.

There was a resounding response by bauxite and sugar workers to the day of protest. The state-owned Bauxite Company responded by de-recognizing the two bauxite unions and refused to deduct union dues from the members' wages and to hand them over to the unions. The bauxite unions called a strike in retaliation. The Guyana Agricultural and General Workers' Union, the NAACIE, and the University of Guyana Workers Union joined the strike in solidarity with the bauxite workers. The FITUG also threatened to call a strike on March 20, 1989 in support of the bauxite workers if the matter had not been resolved.

Meanwhile, in anticipation of a harsh ERP budget in 1989 the FITUG had begun to mobilize. Thus, when the budget debate commenced on April 6, thousands of workers gathered outside of the Parliament to demonstrate against the ERP. On April 5, the FITUG had issued a call to its affiliates to take immediate strike action against the ERP budget. But, the bauxite workers had spontaneously taken strike action on the day after the budget was read before their union officials called them out on strike. Also, university students staged a campus demonstration against the ERP budget.

In retaliation the state dismissed in excess of 300 workers in the public corporations for supporting the anti-ERP strike. Police harassment of union leaders, opposition politicians, religious leaders and university lecturers and students escalated. There were several arbitrary arrests and charges. The state-controlled media reported many incidents of arson in the sugar industry and in homes, and bottle bombs were thrown in residences and in a truck with strike-breakers.

The FITUG received worldwide support for its anti/ERP campaign. The Caribbean Congress of Labor (CCL), the World Federation of Trade Unions (WFTU), the Miners International Federation (MIF), and Solidarity of Poland expressed their solidarity with the Guyanese workers. The CCL called on the state to alleviate the agony of the striking workers and people of Guyana. The WFTU condemned the arbitrary arrest of trade union leaders in a cable it sent to the Minister of Labor. Lech Walesa of Solidarity sent a cable to the government appealing that it 'stop the repression against union leaders and the priests who are with them and to start negotiations with union leaders immediately' (Gopaul, 1997, p. 320). But the state's anti-working-class actions continued unabated.

In the meantime, the FITUG and opposition political parties were holding public anti-ERP meetings attended by large crowds in the city and countryside. On May 2, the FITUG held a public anti-ERP march attended by thousands including members of the Christians for Justice. In the midst of the strike the state eventually forced George Daniels the President of the PSU into exile under threats on his life. The PSU under new leadership pulled out of the FITUG during the seventh week of the strike after the state had finally orchestrated a coup in the union.

The economic crisis and the neoliberal structural adjustment medicine positively impacted the formation of working class consciousness in Guyana. Simultaneously with the introduction of the economic recovery program working-class action was stepped up. But, undoubtedly, political repression by the post-colonial authoritarian state in the 1970s had taken its toll on the working-class movement in the 1980s. Furthermore, the assassination of Walter Rodney dampened the working-class struggle in the 1980s.

Rodney and the Working People's Alliance (WPA) party had helped the working and middle classes to forge an alliance including across race lines, and to muster sufficient courage to resist the post-colonial authoritarian state. After the assassination of Walter Rodney much hope was placed on the Patriotic Coalition for Democracy (PCD), a broad association of opposition political organizations, to maintain the anti-dictatorial movement in the 1980s. But, the

PCD failed due to the power struggle in the alliance. On the other side of the equation the post-colonial authoritarian state formed an unholy alliance with a section of the labor movement in order to control the TUC.

The ERP served to reinforce and sharpen class difference by increasing poverty levels while at the same time growing the economy much to the benefit of the small local business community that align itself with international capital. State bureaucrats however found their positions threatened by the ERP that succeeded in lowering the level of employment in the public sector. Restructuring in the public sector therefore had the effect of depleting the numbers of the low-level state elites. Many of the retrenched workers forged themselves into a class of itinerant traders in the informal sector. Some of these traders secured state contracts to supply goods via the informal market to the state bureaucracy and maintained their class position in the society.

Also, the ERP stimulated working class consciousness reminiscent of the period of the early labor movement in the 1920s. The anti-ERP/IMF strike in 1989, however, took place in a post-colonial anti-dictatorial process quite unlike in the 1920s when the struggle was against the colonial authoritarian state as well as the global agricultural and industrial capitalists in the country.

Conclusion

The transition to center-periphery relations had taken the country on a roller-coaster ride down the road of authoritarianism serving in the interest of global capitalism in opposition to socialism/communism. Crisis in global capitalism necessitated further economic and political reforms, which set the post-colonial authoritarian state and its global capitalist financers on a path of conflict. Undoubtedly, the struggle for national ownership of natural resources, and the redistribution of income in the direction of the poor were prominent features of this process.

This process nonetheless is not linear, it fluctuates at times more favorably to working people and at other times unfavorably. Crisis in capitalism that produced the transition to center-periphery relations led to an anti-colonial struggle to control natural resources, with some degree of success. This has spawned pushback by global capitalism, which created certain dynamics in Guyana that led to internal political change. The cycle repeats itself with further crisis in global capitalism, with new struggles for national ownership and control of natural resources.

Notes

1 British Parliamentary Group on Human Rights (1980). Something to remember: The report of the international team of observers at the elections in Guyana, December.
2 Guyana Human Rights Association (1980). Human rights statement, Georgetown: Guyana, December 10.
3 The organizations and signatories to that statement were the Bishops of the Anglican and Roman Catholic Churches in Guyana, the Guyana Human Rights Association

(GHRA), the Guyana Bar Association, the Guyana Agricultural and General Workers Union, the Clerical and Commercial Workers Union, the National Association of Agricultural Commercial and Industrial Employees, and the University of Guyana Workers Union.

4 For detailed analyses of the principles of cooperative socialism see Thomas (1983), Thomas (1984a), and Canterbury (1991).

5 This development plan was drawn-up by the distinguished economist and Nobel Laureate the late Sir William Arthur Lewis under the title 'British Guiana development program, 1966–1972.' For appraisals of this plan see Brotherson (1983), Brewster (1966), Hope (1979), and Hope and David (1974).

6 These data were compiled from Government of Guyana. (1974). Economic survey of Guyana 1966–1973, Georgetown, Guyana: Statistical Bureau, and Bank of Guyana Annual Reports, 1966–1973, Georgetown, Guyana: Bank of Guyana.

7 These statistics were calculated from statistical data on Guyana 1981, Georgetown, Guyana: Ministry of Economic Planning and Finance.

8 The economic policies of 'cooperative socialism' were originally outlined in PNC (1970). Subsequently copying the Arusha Declaration in Tanzania, the PNC refined its policies in a document entitled Declaration of Sophia. See Tanganyika African National Union (1967) and Burnham (1974).

9 These statistics were calculated from Government of Guyana (1966), and Government of Guyana (1973).

10 These items were flour, bread, biscuits, chowmein, margarine, butter, evaporated, condensed and powdered milk, instant coffee, peanut butter, cheese, lard, ghee, onions, garlic, cubes, tomato pastes, icing sugar, jello, Horlicks, Chocolate, Complan, Ovaltine, Milo, Sago, Barley, Oats, Cereals, black-eye peas, split-peas, baby foods, fruit juices, canned soups and vegetables, vegetable juices, and chicken. Non-food items included hatching eggs, stock feed, cooking oil, kerosene, toilet paper, medical supplies (drugs, saline, dressing), cooking gas, newsprint, cement, matches, car and cycle tyres, batteries, paint, cigarettes, cellophane, and spare parts of all descriptions.

11 See Report of West India Royal Commission: The Moyne report (with introduction by Denis Benn) (2011). Kingston: Ian Randle Publishers.

12 See Page, S. (1980). 'Hmong refugees to start settlement in Guyana.' *The Stanford Daily*, 177 (37).

13 See Government of Guyana (1988, 1989, 1991, 1992, 1994, 1994a), Canterbury (1997), Commonwealth Advisory Group (1989), Report of a goodwill and fact-finding mission to Guyana. (1990). Georgetown: Guyana, October 5, World Bank (1992), Black and McKenna (1995), and Ferguson (1995).

14 These statistics were calculated from data obtained from Thomas (1982).

References

Alavi, H. (1972). 'The state in post-colonial societies: Pakistan and Bangladesh.' *New Left Review*, 1 (74), pp. 59–82.

Baker, J. L. (1994). Guyana: Strategies for reducing poverty. World Bank Report, Country Department III, Country Operations Division 2, Latin American and the Caribbean Region, April 14.

Bank of Guyana. Annual Reports, 1966–1973. Georgetown, Guyana: Bank of Guyana.

Bascom, W. O. (1970). 'The role of the Guyana national cooperative bank,' in People's National Congress, *Policy for the new co-op republic*. Georgetown: Guyana, April, pp. 83–87.

Bascom, W. O. (1969). The role of the Guyana national cooperative bank: Its relationship to the cooperative sector and the economy. (Address delivered during promotional work prior to the establishment of this national banking institution). Georgetown: Guyana.

Black, D. and McKenna, P. (1995). 'Canada and structural adjustment in the south: The significance of the Guyana case.' *Canadian Journal of Development Studies*, 16(1), pp. 55–78.

Brewster, H. (1966). 'Planning and economic development in Guyana,' in Girvan, N. and Jefferson, O. (eds) *Readings in the political economy of the Caribbean*. Kingston, Jamaica: New World, pp. 205–212.

British Parliamentary Group on Human Rights. (1980). Something to remember: The report of the international team of observers at the elections in Guyana, December.

Brotherson, L. (1983). 'The failure of Guyana's first development plan.' *Transition*, 8, pp. 55–77.

Burnham, L. F. S. (1983). Will to survive. (Address at the fifth biennial congress of the People's National Congress), Georgetown: Sophia, August 14–21.

Burnham, L. F. S. (1974). *Declaration of sophia*. Georgetown: Ministry of Information, Guyana.

Burnham, L. F. S. (1970). 'Planning for a new era,' in People's National Congress, *Policy for the new coop republic*. Georgetown: Guyana, April, pp. 5–23.

Burrowes, R. A. (1984). *The wild coast: An account of politics in Guyana*. Cambridge Schenkman.

Canterbury, D. C. (ed.) (1998). 'Guyana's gold industry: Evolution, structure, impacts and non-wage benefits.' *Transition Special Issue 27–28*, Georgetown: Institute of Development Studies, University of Guyana.

Canterbury, D. C. (1997). 'The impact of neoliberalism on labor in Guyana: A case from the Caribbean.' *Labor, Capital and Society*, (30) 2, pp. 260–289.

Canterbury, D. C. (1991). 'Guyana's debt crisis: Its meaning and effects,' in Jeffrey, H. and Menke, J. (eds) *Problems of development in the Guianas*. Paramaribo, Suriname: Anton de Kom University of Suriname, pp. 184–194.

Cardoso, F. H. (1979). 'On the characterization of authoritarian regimes in Latin America,' in Collier, D. (ed) *The new authoritarianism in Latin America*. Princeton: Princeton University Press, pp. 33–57.

Commonwealth Advisory Group. (1989). *Guyana: Economic recovery program and beyond*. Georgetown: Guyana, August 21.

d'Aguiar, P. (1965). Budget speech. First Session, First House of Assembly under the British Guiana (Constitution) Orders 1961–1965. Georgetown: Sessional Paper No. 2/65, April 14.

Darshan, S. (1984). 'General elections in Guyana 1953–1983: A study in the subversion of political participation (The decline of a nation).' *Transition*, 9, pp. 17–44.

Despres, L. A. (1967). *Cultural pluralism and nationalist politics in British Guiana*. Chicago: Rand McNally.

Ferguson, T. (1995). *Structural adjustment and good governance: The case of Guyana*. Georgetown: Public Affairs Consulting Enterprise.

Fitzpatrick, M. G. and Rockcliffe, L. O. (1991). *Report on the elections commission in Guyana*. Georgetown: Guyana, February 14.

Four Unions. (1977). The budget, the current economic situation and the interest of the working people (presentation by a 4-union delegation to the trades union congress). Georgetown: Guyana, January.

Gittens, T. (1982). 'The post-colonial state, class formation and social transformation: A return to theory.' *Transition*, 5, pp. 21–41.

Gopaul, N. K. (1997). *Resistance and change: The struggles of the Guyanese workers, 1964 to 1994*. New York: Inside News Publications.

Government of Guyana. (1994). Guyana: Enhanced structural adjustment facility, policy framework paper, 1994–1996, June 30.

Government of Guyana. (1994a). Guyana: Government policy orientation, presented at Caribbean Group for Cooperation and Economic Development Conference. Georgetown: Guyana, January 27–28.

Government of Guyana. (1992). Guyana: Enhanced structural adjustment facility, economic and financial policy framework, 1992–1994, November.

Government of Guyana. (1991). Guyana: Enhanced structural adjustment facility, economic and financial policy framework, 1991–1993, October 11.

Government of Guyana. (1989). The economic recovery program: Governmental developmental strategy. Georgetown: Ministry of Information, January.

Government of Guyana. (1988). Guyana: Economic and financial policy framework, 1988–1991, June 17.

Government of Guyana. (1981). Statistical data on Guyana 1981. Georgetown, Guyana: Ministry of Economic Planning and Finance.

Government of Guyana. (1980). The 1980 Guyana Constitution, Chapter 1:01, Georgetown: Guyana.

Government of Guyana (1979). The Guyana investment code. Georgetown: Ministry of Information, November.

Government of Guyana. (1974). Economic survey of Guyana 1966–1973. Georgetown, Guyana: Statistical Bureau.

Government of Guyana. (1973). Draft second development plan 1972–1976. Georgetown: Ministry of Economic Development.

Government of Guyana. (1966). Development program 1966–1972. Georgetown: Guyana Government Printers.

Greene, J. E. (1974). *Race versus politics in Guyana: Political cleavages and political mobilization in the 1968 general election*. Mona, Jamaica: Institute of Social and Economic Research, University of the West Indies.

Greenidge, C. B. (1985). Budget 1985: Developing within our means. Georgetown, Guyana: Ministry of Finance, January.

Guyana Human Rights Association. (1982). Guyana: Human rights report, July 1981–August 1982. Georgetown: GHRA.

Guyana Human Rights Association. (1980). Human rights statement. Georgetown: GHRA, December 10.

Guyana Trades Union Congress (GTUC). (1973). Confidential preliminary report to the trades union council on inflation, shortages and the working class interests in Guyana. Georgetown: Guyana.

Harrigan, J. (1991). 'Guyana,' in P. Mosley, J. Harrigan and J. Toye (eds) *Aid and power: The world bank and policy-based lending, Vol. II*. London and New York: Routledge.

Hope, K. R. (1979). *Development policy in Guyana: Planning, finance, and administration*. Boulder: Westview Press.

Hope, K. R. and David, W. L. (1974). 'Planning for development in Guyana: The experience from 1945–1973.' *Inter-American Economic Affairs*, 27, pp. 27–46.

Hoyte, D. (1979). A socialist economy through agricultural, industrial and technical development. (Paper presented at the third biennial congress of the people's national congress). Georgetown: Guyana, August 22–26.

Jack, H. (1970). 'The development of Guyana's hinterland,' in People's National Congress, *Policy for the new co-op republic*. Georgetown: Guyana, April, pp. 89–99.

Jagan, C. B. (1967). *The west on trial: My fight for Guyana's freedom*. New York: International Publishers.

Jeffrey, H. B. (1986). *Guyana: Politics, economics, and society beyond the Burnham era*. Boulder: Rienner.

Johnson, U. (1981). 'Co-operativism for people's development.' *Co-ops in Action Special*, 1 (1), pp. 1–2.

Lewis, W. A. (1955). *The theory of economic growth*. London: Allan and Unwin.

Lewis, W. A. (1950). 'The industrialization of the British West Indies.' *Caribbean Economic Review*, 2(1), pp. 1–51.

Leys, C. (1976). 'The "overdeveloped" post-colonial state: A re-evaluation.' *Review of African Political Economy*, 5, pp. 39–48.

Morrison, A. (1997). *Justice: The struggle for democracy in Guyana, 1952–1992*. Georgetown: Red Thread Women's Press.

Page, S. (1980). 'Hmong refugees to start settlement in Guyana.' *The Stanford Daily* 177(37), p. 2.

People's National Congress. (1970). *Policy for the new coop republic*. Georgetown: Guyana.

Petras, J. (1988). 'Rethinking the development of the state in the Caribbean,' in G. Schuyler and H. Veltmeyer (eds) *Rethinking Caribbean development*. Halifax: International Education Center.

Report of West India Royal Commission: The Moyne Report (with Introduction by Denis Benn). (2011). Kingston: Ian Randle Publishers.

Report of a goodwill and fact-finding mission to Guyana. (1990). Georgetown: Guyana, October 5.

Saul, J. (1974). 'The state in post-colonial societies: Tanzania,' in R. Miliband and J. Saville. (eds), *Socialist Register*. Merlin, London: Merlin, pp. 349–372.

Singer, H. (1997). 'The golden age of the Keynesian consensus.' *World Development*, 25 (3), pp. 293–295.

Tanganyika African National Union (TANU). (1967). *The Arusha declaration and TANU's policy on socialism and self-reliance*. Dar es Salaam: Tanzania.

Thomas, C. Y. (1984). *Plantations peasants and state: A study of the mode of sugar production in Guyana*. California: University of California, Center for Afro-American Culture and Society.

Thomas, C. Y. (1984a). *The rise of the authoritarian state in peripheral societies*. New York: Monthly Review.

Thomas, Clive Y. (1983). 'State capitalism in Guyana: An assessment of Burnham's cooperative "socialist republic",' in F. Ambursley and R. Cohen. (eds) *Crisis in the Caribbean*. New York: Monthly Review.

Thomas, C. Y. (1982). *Guyana: The IMF-World Bank group and the general crisis*. Georgetown: University of Guyana, November.

World Bank. (1992). *Guyana: From economic recovery to sustained growth*. World Bank Latin American and Caribbean Region, Report No. 10307-GUY, April 10.

9 The criminalized authoritarian state

In this chapter we analyze the rise of the criminalized authoritarian state, a degenerate form of the post-colonial authoritarian state in the period between 1992 and 2015. The political superstructure spawned by capitalist development in the Latin American and Caribbean periphery since the abandonment of extra-economic surplus extraction associated with the colonial slave mode of production has been inherently authoritarian. This dynamic authoritarianism nonetheless is not a homogeneous process it takes diverse forms at different historical conjunctures in the development of these peripheral capitalist countries. Authoritarianism varies in different historical time periods in a single country as well as in the region as a whole. It changes as crisis comes and goes in global capitalism, as was the case with the crises that produced anti-colonial struggles and neo-liberalism and the fight against it.

The state was an imposition by imperialist forces, which means that politics in the region was authoritarian from the onset. Since that time the countries have had various experiences with authoritarian regimes traversing between colonial and post-colonial authoritarianisms. Guyana, for example, had arrived at a criminalized authoritarian state as a super-structural institution to oversee the economy on behalf of criminal elements that came to dominate the economic affairs of the country especially in the period between 2000 and 2015.

This 'new' authoritarianism in Guyana is analyzed within the broader problematic of democratization in the twenty-first century. The question is: what is the relationship between democracy and authoritarianism in general and in Guyana in particular? It is argued that in general, democracy and authoritarianism are presented as two ends of a continuum – a country can either be democratic or authoritarian or somewhere in-between those two extremes.

The democratization of the colonial state meant granting the plebiscite to the locals by removing the property and literacy restrictions on voting. The post-colonial authoritarian state was meant to inhere democratic practices in the political fabric of Guyanese society. Neoliberalism was intended to democratize the post-colonial authoritarian state through free and fair national elections under the watchful eyes of overseas elections observers who would declare the elections result to be either free and fair or not. This is what we call neoliberal democratization.

Democratization of the neoliberal ilk that was instituted in Guyana produced a 'new' authoritarianism between 2000 and 2015, founded on what is termed, a 'criminalized authoritarian state.' This state mutated from the post-colonial authoritarian state that was supposedly democratized at the national elections held at the behest of the IMF/World Bank Group and under the direction of the Carter Center in 1992.

A central problem with this democratization was that rather than dismantling the institutional foundations of the post-colonial authoritarian state including the 1980 Guyana Constitution, the People's Progressive Party-Civic (PPP-C) chose to exercise power on the bases of the very constitution it protested against when it was in the political opposition. The reign of the PPP-C is divided into two parts for the purpose of analyses. The first being 1992 and 1997 under the leadership of Dr. Cheddi Jagan, and the second being the post-Jagan era up to 2015.

The criminalized authoritarian state is associated with the post-Jagan era, a historical period in which the state was used 'as a vehicle for criminal enterprise (Thomas, 2003, 2003a) combining criminality with authoritarianism. It was reported that investigators had found financial crimes associated with that state to the tune of G$300 billion (Chabrol, 2018). This state emerged after the death of Dr. Cheddi Jagan, when power passed to his wife and subsequently to her protégée Mr. Bharrat Jagdeo.

The criminalized authoritarian state was the political superstructure of the degenerate form that capitalist economic development took in Guyana between 2000 and 2015. Drawing on Thomas (2003, 2003a) the criminalized authoritarian state among other things was characterized by a ruling clique in which factions of organized crime bosses played an important role. Also, a large phantom economy emerged, which was a proxy for the economic might of organized crime. Corruption was another of its central features, which served as the willing and able handmaiden of organized crime. The criminalized authoritarian state engaged in extra-judicial murders, drug trafficking, corruption, money laundering and trafficking in persons.

As the principal large-scale gold mining company, the Canadian-owned Omai Gold Mines Limited, closed its doors in 2005, small-scale gold mining reclaimed its predominance in the Guyana-economy as the principal earner of foreign exchange between 2005 and 2015. Small-scale gold mining has had a long history in Guyana. It dates back to the native peoples who extracted gold for decorative purposes. It was evident in the period characterized by a colonial slave mode of production (Thomas, 1984). This was especially the case at times when the prosperity of sugar was under threat due to fluctuations in sugar-price on the world market. The threat to sugar profits forced the sugar planters to resort to gold mining on a limited scale to offset their losses from a fall in the price of sugar.

The gold mining activities of foreign extractive capital gives impetus to small-scale mining, as small-scale miners seek to cash-in on some of the profit generated in the process. Throughout the period that Omai Gold Mines Limited was in operations in Guyana small-scale gold miners held their own as the data showed. It was not surprising therefore that small-scale mining became dominant in the Guyana-economy after Omai ceased production. What was interesting from this development was the apparent correlation between the predominance of small-scale gold mining and the emergence of the criminalized authoritarian state.

In contrast, the developments in Latin America were much different as the neoliberal regimes were replaced by post-neoliberal regimes in the 2000s. This development in Latin America gave rise to the debate on neoextractivism, which seeks to come to terms with the development strategy of the post-neoliberal regimes and the new imperialism in the region. The development strategy favors taking control of the country's natural resources and the redistribution of income in favor of the poor. Veltmeyer and Petras (2014) argue that neoextractivism is a new form of imperialism based on 'primarization' and 'extractivism.' Others have described it as progressive extractivism because the governments who pursue the development strategy are considered to be on the left and the policies aim to redistribute income in the direction of working people (Gudynas, 2010).

Guyana did not witness the emergence of a post-neoliberal regime à la Latin America. Instead the PPP, which was overthrown twice in 1953 and 1964 on the accusation of being communist, made an about-turn to reorganize itself as the PPP-C to win power on a neoliberal agenda in 1992. The PPP-C government pursued an IMF-World Bank Group economic liberalization agenda. But, it found ways to turn that agenda to its own benefit utilizing whatever leverage it had over the small mining sector and the domestic and foreign investment process, including criminal means for the enrichment of state elites.

The PPP-C was able to hold on to power due to the class-race nature of politics in Guyana, which evolved in the course of the split in the nationalist anti-colonial anti-imperial movement in the 1950s. Since the 1950s regime change in Guyana has only came about with the intervention of foreign forces. Class-race-based politics has served in conjunction with foreign intervention to maintain the People's National Congress (PNC) and PPP-C in office – in the former case for twenty-eight years and in the latter for twenty-three years. In each of these periods, natural resources extraction played a significant role, as center-periphery relations deepened.

The PNC in the immediate post-colonial period took an approach to natural resources extraction that was similar to the progressive regimes in Latin America in the post-neoliberal period. The PNC pursued a policy of nationalization with the aim of socializing the income generated in the nationalized industries. This is quite similar to the neoextractivism that placed heavy emphasis on national ownership and or control of natural resources and the redistribution of income to working people through social programs. The PNC used the public enterprises to gain leverage over working people and to enrich the state elites. The PPP-C presided over the privatization of public entities, which commenced under the neoliberal agenda introduced by the PNC. To gain leverage over working people and enrich the state elites the PPP-C resorted to micromanagement of investment processes and converted the state into a criminal enterprise.

Dynamics and trajectory of politics and natural resources extraction

The dynamics and trajectory of politics and natural resources extraction in Guyana reflect the historical linkages and adaptations of the incumbent state elites and domestic political opposition to externally determined macro-political economy dialectical frameworks. These frameworks have been colonialism and anti-colonialism (nationalism), communism and anti-communism, neoliberalism and anti-neoliberalism, and post-neoliberalism and the current 'revenge of the right' as they push back against post-neoliberal regimes in Latin America.[1]

In each of these frameworks the class struggle to control state power involves foreign powers and domestic political forces. The domestic forces are usually divided between social strata that collaborate with foreign powers and the sub-groups that fight for national self-determination. Foreign powers seek to control the state apparatus to ensure it facilitates extractive capital and adapts to reforms in global capitalism. The incumbent state elites use the state apparatus to enrich its members and to redistribute the wealth through income transfers in the form of improved social programs.

Foreign intervention aimed at regime change is a key political dynamic in the fight to control the state. The political struggle for regime change in 1992 and 2015 has had two specific impacts on natural resources extraction, especially gold mining. First, foreign capital may invest in anticipation of a change in government, as we have seen with Canadian extractive capital when the structural adjustment program was pending implementation in Guyana. Second, foreign capital may explore for natural resources but await regime change before it commits to actual production, which seems to have been the case in the run-up to the national elections in 2015.

Omai Gold Mines Limited fits the bill in the first instance in terms of investing in anticipation of regime change in Guyana in 1992. When it became certain that due to Canadian intervention Guyana would sign a structural adjustment agreement with the IMF-World Bank Group, which would eventually lead to regime change due to the political conditionality in the program that the government holds 'free and fair,' Canadian extractive capital became busy in Guyana's natural resources sector.

In the second case, foreign extractive capital explored for minerals, but held back on investing in production until the political opposition gained a majority in parliament in 2011, while the presidency remained in the hand of the incumbent PPP-C party. But, when there was complete regime change through an opposition coalition that won a majority in the parliament and presidency in 2015, Canadian extractive capital again became the largest gold operation in the country.

The unique dynamics and trajectory of politics in Guyana are due to the class-race-structure of the country's population, and the superimposed externally determined macro-political economy frameworks. Nationalist politics commenced in earnest with trade-union-organized anti-colonial struggles to improve the working and living conditions for the masses, self-rule, and political independence. This led to the formation of nationalist-oriented political parties and economic policies, universal adult suffrage, the first democratically elected nationalist government, the imperial overthrow of that government on charges that it was communist, and the reinstatement of direct colonial rule from England in 1953. The colonial power changed the constitution, held fresh elections in 1957 and 1961, both of which were won by the PPP. Economic and political destabilization followed – US/British forces overthrew the PPP and installed an anti-communist PNC–United Force (UF) coalition government in 1964 (Agee, 1975; Schlesinger Jr., 2002).

The coalition government fractured in 1968, as the majority PNC party ousted the UF, its minority partner. The post-colonial authoritarian state emerged, as the PNC party held on to power through electoral fraud until 1992. The politics of the post-colonial authoritarian state supported by foreign capital produced its dialectical opposite in an anti-dictatorial movement. With the collapse of European communism in 1989 and the emergence of neoliberal globalization the US used IMF/World Bank structural adjustment political conditionalities to force the PNC to hold 'free and fair' elections in 1992. The PNC lost power to the PPP-C through this process, which is termed neoliberal democratization. A 'criminalized authoritarian state' emerged under the PPP-C, but there was regime change in 2015 again with the support of external political intervention.

Colonial politics and natural resources extraction

Colonial politics are the politics of direct rule of a colony by a foreign power or that of self-rule in a colony while the foreign power maintains a veto over the decisions of the self-rulers. Thomas (1988) and Mandel (1996) provided the raison d'être of the approach to natural resources extraction afforded by colonial politics. Mandel (1996) argues that the Caribbean's natural endowments were essential to its economic development. The idea is that countries like Guyana, Jamaica and Trinidad and Tobago had a comparative advantage in certain natural resources and therefore their economies should specialize in the extraction of those resources for sale to the manufacturing centers in Europe and North America. This argument however overlooks the limitations of comparative advantage amplified in the works of Singer (1992), Prebisch (1950), Lewis (1950), and more recently by Reinert (2007), and Chang (2008).

Thomas (1988), points to two commonly held views that shaped the colonial approach to natural resources extraction. The first being that there was insufficient domestic capital available to develop the region's natural resources hence capital will have to be imported. Second, the natural resources extractive industries would have to be 'export-oriented to be profitable' because of the small size of the domestic market. Foreign ownership and control of these industries was encouraged as a means of guaranteeing much needed capital, markets and profitability.

The political articulation of these commonly held colonial views heavily favored the attraction of foreign capital. It led the colonial powers to invite foreign capital to exploit the natural resources in their Caribbean colonies. A framework of laws, regulations, and institutions was established to minimize the risks of independent national economic policies and maximize capital and other resource flows between the Caribbean and the European powers (Thomas, 1972).

The result of this approach was that by the 1970s North American transnational corporations had the largest share of capital investments in natural resources extraction in the region (Thomas, 1988). According to Thomas (1988), at bauxite-alumina production in the West Indies was in the control of six American and one Canadian TNC by the end of the 1960s. Also, '98 percent of the region's bauxite and 57 percent of its alumina' were 'remitted to North America' (Thomas, 1988, p. 111). This pattern of ownership has persisted into the current period, after a brief phase of national ownership, with the arrival of extractive capital from emerging economies in particular China and Russia.

Nationalist politics and natural resources extraction

The regime of nationalist politics had two distinct phases – anti-colonial that led to self-rule and political independence, and post-colonial that led to the emergence of a post-colonial authoritarian state. Nationalist post-colonial or post-independence politics had five interrelated features. The first was the attempt to right a wrong committed by colonial politics in natural resources extraction. The Caribbean emerged as a significant area for extractive capitalism – the production of oil, bauxite, alumina, gold, and intermediate oil refineries. But, those extractive activities did not generate significant employment, tax revenues and foreign exchange for the region (Thomas, 1988).

The main grouse the local political elites had with the colonial approach to natural resources extraction was that the exploitation of the region's natural resources did not foster significant economic development in the mineral exporting countries. This fact stimulated domestic political agitation against foreign extractive companies. Thus, nationalist politics was driven by the fact that the Caribbean received a disproportionately small share of the surplus generated from the exploitation of its natural resources while at the same time the countries did not have sufficient revenue and foreign exchange to finance their development programs. This is the identical problem the advocates of the neoextractivism have with extractive capitalism. The problem persists not only in the Caribbean and Latin America, but in Africa as well.

The second related feature was that the grouse led to the promotion of an alternative approach to development based on national ownership of the commanding heights of the economy of which the natural resources sector is a central plank. The Trinidad and Tobago government for example purchased the operations of British Petroleum and Shell in the island. The Jamaica government introduced a levy set at 7.5 percent of the selling price of aluminum ingot on all ore mined or processed in the island (Thomas, 1988). The Guyana government undertook a 'mortgage-financed' takeover of the bauxite industry in the 1970s

– the Aluminum Company of Canada (ALCAN) that owned and operated the Demerara Bauxite Company Limited (DEMBA) at Linden and the Reynolds Metal Company, a US transnational that owned and operated the bauxite company at Kwakwani (Kwayana, 2012).

An important point to note here is that although these countries sought to develop alternative approaches to their economic development based on national ownership of natural resources, historical factors set Guyana apart from Jamaica and Trinidad and Tobago. These factors were responsible for the divergence in their respective domestic politics. Unlike Jamaica and Trinidad and Tobago, Guyana has not been able to develop a stable political system. A major historical factor in this connection has to do with the fact that the British colonial authorities overthrew the first democratically elected government in Guyana in 1953, after it was in office only for 133 days. Since that time regime change only came about in Guyana with US/UK military and political intervention. This situation makes it conducive for political dictatorships to emerge, as we have witnessed between 1964 and 1992 under the PNC and 1992 and 2015 under the PPP-C.

Another related historical factor is the racial politics in Guyana were the electorate votes in racial camps. This has been the case since the nationalist movement was split after the imperial overthrow of the PPP government in 1953. The African-Guyanese who vote for the PNC are a minority and could only win power through a coalition and proceed to hold on to power thereafter through nefarious means. The East Indian Guyanese who vote for the PPP constitute a majority and can therefore hold onto power indefinitely due to their race majority – unless the East Indian vote is split. It would seem that coalition politics in a multiparty system is the way forward to break the curse of race voting in Guyana. This is the prime reason that the PNC held power for twenty-eight years and the PPP-C for twenty-three years. A rupture in the PPP-C was the cause that the party lost its majority in the parliament in 2011, and ceded power to a coalition government in 2015.

The third feature had to do with the pushback by foreign extractive capital against the nationalizations. The extractive capitalists were swift in their reactions to Caribbean nationalism. This demonstrates the linkage between foreign extractive capital and the imperial state, which operates on its behalf. The home governments of the foreign extractive capitalists resorted to economic and political destabilization in Jamaica and Guyana (Payne, 1995). The foreign companies began to diversify out of the region (Thomas, 1988). This resulted in a rapid decline in Caribbean bauxite output as a proportion of total world output. The gains to the Caribbean economy brought about by nationalist politics all but disappeared by the mid-1980s (Thomas, 1988).

The fourth feature was that in Guyana nationalism morphed into a brand of dictatorial and authoritarian politics (Thomas, 1982, 1983). The doctrine of the 'paramountcy of the party' was instituted through which the governing political party placed itself above the institutions of state. A particularly egregious matter was that the ruling party flew its party flag over the Guyana Court of Appeal. The government controlled the media, banned essential foods, suppressed human rights, broke strikes, and undermined the labor movement. It repressed opposing political parties, sent its thugs to break-up opposition public meetings, and arrested and imprisoned opposition activists.

Working People's Alliance (WPA) political activists Ohene Koama and Edward Dublin were murdered by the police. And world-renowned historian Dr. Walter A. Rodney was assassinated on June 13, 1980 (Canterbury, 2005; Kwayana, 1988). It took thirty-four years, and after several key players were already dead, before a Commission of Inquire was launched into the assassination of Dr. Walter Rodney! The Commission of Inquire concluded that the leader of the ruling PNC party and prime minister was complicit in the murder of Dr. Rodney.

The politics of repression went hand-in-hand with the strategy of national ownership of the commanding heights of the economy. National ownership allowed the government to exercise considerable leverage over workers in the nationalized entities. Workers had to toe the line to keep their jobs and had their paychecks subjected to arbitrary deductions to provide financial support to state and PNC political party directed events. The government refused to hand over to the bauxite union dues deducted from workers' paychecks. Bauxite workers on strike were arrested, imprisoned and teargassed in their cells.

The fifth feature was the emergence of a broad-based anti-authoritarian politics in opposition to the government. Political opponents to the government came together to hold public rallies, and to forge opposition institutional structures in the struggle for democracy. However, the anti-authoritarian politics failed to produce the requisite political unity to remove the government from office. The result was that the various political entities that pretended towards a coalition contested the 1992 national elections as separate units.

There was much finger pointing as to why the anti-authoritarian politics failed to produce the desired unity to forge political change in Guyana. This was indicative of the power struggle within the opposition Patriotic Coalition for Democracy (PCD) alliance over issues such as the formula for distributing parliamentary seats in a coalition government and contesting the election under a single presidential candidate (Canterbury, 2005; Westmaas, 2004).

Extractive capitalism under the neoliberal regime

The neoliberal regime in Guyana encapsulates a number of significant events and processes, which began with the aborted IMF-World Bank adjustment policies with which the PNC government flirted but quickly abandoned in the mid-1980s. It involved the introduction of a full-fledged structural adjustment program in 1988; the Carter Center supervised national elections in 1992, which was declared 'free and fair' that led to regime change; the reign of the PPP-C government from 1992 to 2015; and regime change between 2011 and 2015. Each of these historical events had particular effects on natural resources extraction in Guyana. In essence the politics of the neoliberal regime represented the opening-up of the natural resources sector to foreign extractive capital.

There is burgeoning literature on the politics of structural adjustment (Simutanyi, 1996; Olukoshi, 1992; Haggard and Kaufman, 1989). We have the narrow focus on politics in Guyana and natural resources extraction. In Guyana, politics in the neoliberal period merged the anti-dictatorial struggle against the post-colonial authoritarian state with the political conditionalities of structural adjustment in a pro-democracy movement. The anti-dictatorial struggle aimed to rid Guyana of the PNC post-colonial authoritarian state and build a just, democratic and egalitarian society (Thomas, 1976).

It was the politics of structural adjustment that led to regime change in 1992. The primary goals of that politics were the opening-up of the Guyana-economy to foreign capital, 'free trade,' and to place domestic politics in the control of foreign powers. This has been the essence of the political economy of structural adjustment – regime change, free market fundamentalism, penetration by foreign capital of liberalized economies, and external control of domestic political processes (Petras and Veltmeyer, 2001). But, as the structural adjustment agenda became dominant after the change in government, and the platform of the anti-dictatorial struggle subsided, a mad scramble began for the country's natural resources.

Initial phase of neoliberal regime

The neoliberal structural adjustment period commenced around 1988 when the post-colonial authoritarian state implemented its economic recovery program (ERP). The ERP marked the beginning of the end of the post-colonial authoritarian state-led by the PNC and the subsequent emergence of a new authoritarian state under the domination of the PPP-C. As the years went by the new authoritarian state gradually became criminalized. Natural resources extraction featured in a unique manner as the political transformation took place from the post-colonial authoritarian state to the criminalized authoritarian state. The mind-boggling scale of the state as a criminal enterprise under the Jagedo administration is currently being revealed through the Asset Recovery Unit of the current A Party for National Unity-Alliance for Change (APNU+AFC) coalition administration and forensic audits that are being carried out at government departments.

Neoliberal politics removed from the extractive capitalists the fear of nationalization of their assets in Guyana. Privatization is a central plank in the economic agenda of neoliberal structural adjustment. Nationalization was replaced with privatization. This situation therefore provided foreign extractive capital with a sense of security to resume investment activity in Guyana. This observation is based on two historical developments, the Canadian government's decision to sponsor Guyana's re-entry into the fold of the IMF and World Bank (Black and McKenna, 1995), and the privatization program of structural adjustment. Prior to these developments Guyana was not attracting foreign capital.

The prevalent neoliberal idea was that democracy has a positive effect on foreign direct investment (Kucera and Principi, 2014), and Guyana was rightly considered as an undemocratic state. The idea on the relationship between democracy and economic progress echoes a longstanding view that democracy associated with enlightened politics unleashes positive economic forces leading to economic prosperity, while authoritarianism has a constraining effect on economic progress (Canterbury, 2005). Thus, the impending democratization of Guyana stimulated the flow of foreign direct investment into the country.

The post-colonial authoritarian government first implemented a full-fledged structural adjustment program in mid-1980s, which it soon abandoned. Thereafter, Guyana became an outcast from the global community of countries dominated by the International Monetary Fund (IMF)/World Bank Group's structural adjustment program. Guyana held that outsider status until Canadian sponsorship of its re-entry into the IMF/World Bank system of global domination in 1988. In hindsight the reality was that the Canadian government represented the interest of Canadian extractive capital in Guyana. The Canadian-owned Omai Gold Mines Limited became the largest gold mining operations in the country and on the South American Continent. The Canadian government's actions restored Canadian extractive capital to Guyana. The payoff to Canada for its services to bring Guyana back into the fold of the global capital market was the reopening of Guyana's natural resources to exploitation by Canadian extractive capital. Simultaneously, Canada represented Guyana to the IMF/World Bank Group, Canadian extractive capital began to explore for gold in Guyana.

In 1985, two Canadian firms, Golden Star Resources Limited and Cambior secured rights to undertake a joint venture partnership with the Guyana government in gold mining (Mars, 1998). There were at least ten overseas firms that commenced undertakings or pilot explorations in Guyana during the late 1980s (Merrill, 1992). The three largest of these firms were Golden Star Resources and Placer Dome of Canada, and Brazil's Paranapanema (Merrill, 1992). Three other top mining companies in operation in the country were Giant Resources of Australia, Homestake Mining of the United States, and the UK's Robertson Group (Merrill, 1992).

Cambior Inc., Golden Star Resources, and the Guyana government were the principal shareholders in the high-tech Omai Gold Mines Limited. The Guyana government equity interest in Omai was only 5 percent. The gold mining sector became the leading earner of foreign exchange above agriculture and bauxite/alumina (Thomas, 1998). This was due to the size of Omai Gold Mines Limited in Guyana's mineral production declared between 1993 and 2005. Omai was the largest gold producer, although it began to wind down its operations from 2003. The production of bauxite a principal mineral export was almost in a free fall.

However, Omai capitalized on the political conditions in Guyana in the early days of the structural adjustment program. It began producing gold in 1993 the year after the new PPP-C government was installed and ceased production in 2005 two years before the 2007 national election. The political climate had begun to heat-up against the new government and possibly in anticipation of political instability due to electoral violence becoming a reality in the next elections cycle foreign extractive capitalists began to cut back on their activities.

Declared diamond production dramatically increased from 2001 until 2004. This coincided with the early period of the Kimberley Process 'the principal international initiative established' in 2000 'to develop practical approaches to stemming the global flow of conflict diamonds.'[2] Guyana is not classified as a 'conflict diamonds' state but the sharp decline in diamonds production declared in 2005, could possibly be attributed to the domestic political climate, which influenced the exit of foreign extractive capital. Second, the Kimberley Process Certification Scheme that started from January 2003 to 'increase transparency and oversight in the diamonds industry in order to eliminate trade in conflict diamonds'[3] may have had an effect on production, due to the increased regulation and paperwork for producers to be in compliance.

Agriculture (sugar and rice) and mining (bauxite and gold) competed for the position of largest contributor to major exports in percentage terms between 1993 and 2005. But, bauxite and gold had more years (seven) when they were the principal export compared with sugar and rice (five years), with one year where the two were even. The US dollar earnings of major exports commodities portrayed a similar pattern. The earnings from bauxite and gold were greater than that earned from the export of sugar and rice in eight years, compared with five years for the latter commodities.

The structural adjustment program created a more liberal economic framework for natural resource extraction. Its divestment and privatization component meant that the government was prepared to resell to private companies the nationalized natural resources entities. The first action to liberalize the natural resources sector was the institution of the Mining Act in 1989. This was coupled with 'the establishment of pro forma mineral agreement, and the creation of the medium-scale mining sector by the passing of subsidiary legislation in October 1992' (Guyana Mineral, Mining Sector Investment and Business Guide, 2013). A primary goal of the structural adjustment model was the privatization of natural resources extraction. This involved the creation of the legal framework to encourage the growth in the private sector.

The economic recovery program involved opening-up the natural resources sector to private investors, and widespread retrenchment and reduction in workers' benefits. In the bauxite industry the responsibility for workers' benefits were transferred from the bauxite company to the central government, a new local government authority was created, local government taxes were introduced, and the management of the bauxite company at Linden was privatized, and central and local government taxes were increased.

Political change and natural resources extraction

The newly elected PPP-C government approached the Carter Center in 1993 for help to formulate a National Development Strategy (NDS) for Guyana. The Carter Center gave financial and technical support to that process and a first draft NDS was completed in 1996.[4] The parliamentary opposition PNC objected to the first draft of the NDS on the grounds that there was not sufficient local input into its preparation.

The second draft of the NDS completed with acceptable local inputs states in the section on origins and methodology that 'although many Guyanese experts contributed to the preparation of the series of documents which comprised the Strategy,' the process was not managed by Guyana's civil society. It stated that many well-qualified individuals did not have the opportunity to participate. The PNC argued that the plan should not be put forward as a national strategy because the PPP, which was the party in government would use it as 'its manifesto for the elections which were due in the following year.'[5] The mining policy in the first draft NDS was contained in Chapter 32 entitled 'Mining Policy,' while in the second draft NDS the mining policy was outlined in Chapter 16. The NDS remains a draft, as it was never tabled before the parliament for approval.

The NDS took an approach to the extractive industry that was similar to the neoliberal regimes in Africa.[6] The tax regime, the main source of government revenue from mining was regarded as too repressive to attract foreign investment. The NDS identified two key problems with the tax regime in the extractive sector that it sought resolve. The first was that the percentage of pre-tax mining revenues, which accrued to government was 48.16 percent in Guyana, the second highest to Australia's 50 percent. The lowest was in Chile, 15 percent. Second, the government's share of the profits repatriated to shareholders abroad was 55.9 percent. These two concerns were identified as placing Guyana at a comparative disadvantage in terms of the country's capacity to attract investment in mining.

The NDS placed the royalty rate for gold on a sliding scale based on a maximum of 3 percent of the prevailing price of gold. It advocated a half percent royalty payment from the existing royalty stream, to go into an Amerindian Development Fund for exploitation of Amerindian lands, and a corporate income tax rate fixed at 30 percent for all mining projects. It promoted the reduction to zero of export duties on minerals, a 10 percent cost, insurance and freight (CIF) consumption tax on fuel, a zero-rate consumption tax and duty on mining equipment, spares and supplies, and withholding tax on repatriated dividends fixed at 6.25 percent for Omai, rather than the 15 percent rate that was normally applicable. Also, the rental rates on mineral land during exploration stage was fixed at US$0.12/acre – Yr1; US$0.175/acre – Yr2; US$0.225/acre – Yr3; US$0.275/acre Yr4; and US$0.325/acre – Yr5.[7]

The NDS therefore called for a reduction in duties on inputs for mining, a lessening of royalty paid by mining companies, and a decrease in corporate taxes in the mining sector.

Post-neoliberal politics and natural resources extraction

Post-neoliberal politics is understood in two contexts – first it refers to the politics associated with the push back against neoliberalism in Latin America in the early 2000s. Second it denotes the shift from free market fundamentalism to state interventionism in the US and European Union (EU) in the aftermath of the 2008 financial crash. It includes the alterations to the policy prescriptions that the developed capitalist states push on the developing countries, and the changes in those policies demanded by the developing countries. Post-neoliberal politics entails the impetuous rejection of IMF/World Bank policies in both developed and developing countries after the financial crash in 2008.

Two observable developments in Latin American and Caribbean politics that impact natural resources extraction were first the 'left' turn in national politics, which gave a new momentum to the role of natural resources extraction in economic development (Veltmeyer and Petras, 2014). It was typified by politics in opposition to neoliberal structural adjustment and the promotion of natural resources extraction as a means to stimulate economic growth, social inclusion and reduce inequality (Veltmeyer and Petras, 2014). The second was the emergence of a 'criminalized authoritarian state,' which fed on micromanagement and political control of natural resources extraction.

Veltmeyer and Petras (2014) correctly argue that in reality post-neoliberal politics is merely the latest twist and turn in the politics, of the new extractivism. It represents a capitalist development dynamic, which is based on an expanding extractive frontier inclusive of intensified social conflicts over territorial rights, land, water and associated natural resources (Veltmeyer and Petras, 2014). These conflicts are the forms that class struggle takes in the extraction process (Veltmeyer and Petras, 2014). Its consequences include the pillage of natural and human resources, simultaneously with environmental destruction, and devastation of livelihoods of local communities. This leads to widespread resistance and a new and virulent form of class conflict (Veltmeyer and Petras, 2014). The post-neoliberal state rallies to the defense of extractive capital due to the fact that its economic interests are congruent with profit for the corporations and royalties and taxes for the government (Veltmeyer and Petras, 2014).

In Guyana the politics were of a 'criminalized authoritarian' nature and a struggle for democracy within the framework of neoliberal political conditionalities. Extra-judicial murders, drug trafficking, corruption, money laundering, and trafficking in persons typified the state. Natural resources extraction played a big part in the activities of the 'criminalized authoritarian state.' The indigenous peoples of Guyana have absorbed the brunt of this process through its debilitating impact, environmental destruction, and intensified conflict situations with small miners, and women (Canterbury, 2013, 2014).

The essential features of the criminalized authoritarian state

Was Guyana characterized by a criminalized state or a criminalized authoritarian state in the first decade and a half of the twenty-first century? Thomas (2003, 2003a) argues that a criminalized state – the use of the state as a vehicle for criminal enterprise – emerged under the reign of the PPP-C regime, and that it grew out of the authoritarian state, which was its historical antecedent. While Thomas' (2003, 2003a) observations on the nature of the criminalized state are correct, we argue that the state in Guyana under the PPP-C was both criminalized and authoritarian. This state form developed out of two sets of historical factors, the hitherto authoritarian predisposition of the state in Guyana due to its colonial origins, and the operation of the state as a criminal enterprise under the PPP-C government. The state is therefore more appropriately classified as a criminalized authoritarian state. Its authoritarianism was a product of Guyana's colonial history and the conditions of neoliberal democratization – national elections held under the direction of the IMF/World Bank/Carter Center (Canterbury, 2005).

The historical trajectory of the authoritarian state in Guyana is as follows – colonial, post-colonial, neoliberal, and post-neoliberal. The criminalized authoritarian state was merely a degenerate form of the post-colonial authoritarian state. It was an anomaly rather than the norm and was the first of its kind to emerge in the English-speaking Caribbean. How did it come about?

Rather than dismantling the foundations of the post-colonial authoritarian state namely the 1980-Guyana Constitution, the PPP-C chose to exercise power on the bases of the very authoritarian constitution. It was only in the period characterized as post-neoliberal in Latin America that criminality came to dominate the operations of the state in Guyana. What were some of the main features of the criminalized authoritarian state? Drawing on Thomas' analysis of the 'criminalized state' in Guyana we develop our argument on the criminalized authoritarian state, focusing on five sets of interrelated factors.

The first set of factors involved its characterization by extra-judicial murders, drug trafficking, corruption, money laundering, and trafficking in persons, which typified the state. The crime driven activities were located in the underground economy, remittances, and were enabled by the tax administration facilitates.

The state was a state for itself – a state whose leaders had no other vocation but doing and seeing what they can grab for themselves (Thomas, 2003). The state became a self-fulfilling entity, with the principal aim not to drive any national vision and national development. Its sole purpose was to 'bring benefits to those who controlled and occupied it'. In Thomas' view the state was not simply a kleptocracy or a failed state – it was worse than that. It was a state for itself because it had no higher altruistic purpose. The state pursued no advocation, no vision, no attempt to transform the society into something better or of a higher order (Thomas, 2003).

The state had a heavy dependence on natural resources extraction, and controlled the increased revenue from mining, which it used to enrich its members. This was unlike in Latin America, where there was a higher ideal to use revenue from resource extraction to improve the social and economic conditions of the poor. With impunity the state cabal engaged in illegal activities in the natural resources sector to enrich themselves. For example, the notorious Knights Templar, a Mexican drug cartel allegedly financed four gold mining operations in Guyana linked to the Minister of Natural Resources and the Environment (Adonis, 2014). It was reported that the Minister profited from two mining companies funded by the Knights Templar (Adonis, 2014).

The state represented a form of backward capitalism that depended on pre-globalization forms of economic specialization dominated by natural resources intensive primary products that overshadowed commodity production and exports; and a rudimentary services sector characterized by low technology, low skills and low value-added services (Thomas, 2003a). It maintained rather small, thin, and weak private markets. The criminal capital accumulated in the phantom economy, constantly sought to transmute itself into legitimate capital (Thomas, 2003a).

Perceivably , the regulatory authorities in Guyana were held hostage by the enterprises they were supposed to regulate (Thomas, 2003a). The effect of crime and corruption distorted the incentive framework (Thomas, 2003). The Economic governance was very poor, and the country was in the strong grip of the International Financial Institutions (IFIs) in key areas of economic policy-making. In particular, the IFIs dictated the macroeconomic standards and policy and public sector reform. Furthermore, they exerted control over the tax structure, public expenditure and wage policy in the public sector (Thomas, 2003).

The second set of factors involved the establishment of the appropriate superstructure of institutions and laws to facilitate foreign capital in Guyana and the subversion of those laws by criminal activity and authoritarian behavior. The infrastructure was designed to attract foreign direct investment (FDI), legally protect such assets, and guarantee the repatriation of profits. But, the state elites systematically subverted those institutions and laws to serve their own interests. The government elites were accused by their political opponents of using state institutions to engage in activities such as corruption, nepotism, xenophobia, bigotry, and of dispensing rewards to their supporters and punishing their opponents (Kaieteur News, 2012; Kaieteur News, 2012a; Lall, 2012).

The US State Department expressed its displeasure at those developments. It claimed that although Guyana had the legal infrastructure in support of foreign direct investment, the political micromanagement of FDI constituted a major deterrent to foreign investors. The US government had also expressed concerns about the Guyana government not enforcing a number of laws to counter money laundering and drug trafficking (Chabrol, 2013). This, it claims further hinders the arrival of direct foreign investment in the country.

The Bureau of Economic and Business Affairs in the US State Department declared in its investment climate statement on Guyana in 2014 that the investment climate had taken a downturn in 2013. This was due to political impasse and infighting that hold back Guyana's development in several areas. The Bureau stated that the Amaila Falls Hydropower Project , the largest capital project in Guyana's history, had collapsed after Sithe Global, the US equity partner involved withdrew from the multinational development team in August 2013. The failure was due to the company's concerns with the political risk associated with objections to the venture by the largest parliamentary opposition party (US State Department, 2014). Although the government continued to encourage foreign investment, it had failed to attract much investments outside of the gold mining sector. Indeed, some of the primary barriers to foreign investment included perceived corruption, inefficient government, inadequate infrastructure, and crime (US State Department, 2014).

As evidenced by the above quote from the US State Department, the foreign capitalist was reluctant to invest in Guyana, except in its natural resources sector. However, foreign extractive capital seemed to express a preference for exploration for gold, oil, rare earth minerals, uranium, manganese, etc., rather than production. Why is it that foreign extractive capitalists from the traditional capitalist countries held back on investing in actual production? The most probable answer to this question was that they were awaiting a change in government, and for more measures favorable to them to be put into operation before they commenced production. It would seem that foreign investors wanted less government micromanagement of foreign direct investment.

Guyana was blacklisted by the Caribbean Financial Action Task Force (CFATF) for its failure to control money laundering. Also, the CFATF action was based on the fact that the government had failed to pass legislation to strengthen anti-money laundering laws (US State Department, 2014; Rambarran, 2015). The international Financial Action Task Force could have taken actions that would increase the cost and delays in processing Guyana's international financial and trade transactions (US State Department, 2014).

The third set of factors concerned the conflict situations that emerged in the natural resources sector. The conflicts involved the government, small miners, bauxite union, workers, the community, indigenous people, and women in their struggle to find a place in the extractive sector as miners and other than as domestic and sex workers. The government's decision to increase electricity tariff in the bauxite community has been the most serious of the conflicts. The state brutally repressed the uprising of bauxite workers and community members against the rate hikes. The conflict evoked the most extreme form of state violence, when on July 18, 2012, the police opened fire on a crowd of peaceful demonstrators killing three of them – twenty-four-year-old Shemroy Bouyea, forty-six-year-old Allan Lewis, and seventeen-year-old Ron Somerset – and wounding many others.

The Russian-owned Bauxite Company of Guyana Inc. (BCGI) and the Guyana government were on the same side, in a conflict with the Guyana Bauxite and General Workers' Union (GB&GWU) and working people over the BCGI's union busting tactics. The BCGI moved to derecognize the union, issued suspension and dismissal letters to workers, after they had resorted to industrial action over wages and working conditions (Barbados Underground, 2010, 2010a; Kaieteur News, 2010; Sinclair, 2010; National Workers Union, 2010; UhuruNews, 2010).

Conflicts with indigenous peoples, small miners, and women included issues such as sexual exploitation, prostitution, use of illegal drugs, trafficking in persons, murders, suspected murders, disappearances, armed robberies, rape and abuse in the gold fields, and the use of toxic chemicals in mining (Griffiths and Anselmo, 2010). The forestry preservation deal that the Guyana government signed with the government of Norway to receive up to US$250 million over a five-year period has led to regulatory measures such as a moratorium on the issue of new permits for gold and diamond mining in its rivers (Green, 2012), and the entrenching of political racialization and state patronage (Bulkan, 2014; Green, 2012; Thomas, 2010).

The Guyana Gold and Diamonds Mining Association (GGDMA) opposed the proposed six-month moratorium and approved a vote of no confidence in the Minister of Natural Resources and the Environment's management of the mining sector, and raised millions of Guyana dollars to fund a campaign against the temporary moratorium (GGDMA Press Release: Miners fight the proposed imposition of a six-month moratorium on mining http://guyanaminers.org; GGDMA Press Release: GGDMA approve no confidence vote in Natural Resources Minister, http://guyanaminers.org).

Also, indigenous peoples and small miners were subjected to the criminal activities of state officials. For example, the police arrested the Toshao (indigenous chief) of Moco-Moco village in the Rupununi for sexual assault. But, Toshao Mark George claimed that the real reason for his arrest was because of his failure to accommodate President Ramotar's visit to his village (*Demerara Waves*, 2015).

The fourth set of factors concerned the disinclination of miners to sell their gold to the state-owned Guyana Gold Board, the role of extractive capital from the emerging economies, and the proliferation of exploration for metals, minerals and oil. The gold was smuggled to Venezuela, Suriname, and Brazil. Gold smuggling, illegal mining and corruption made for the gross understatement of gold production declared in Guyana. Reportedly, as much as half of the gold produced at that time was smuggled out of the country by miners in search of a higher return on their output, and by illegal miners from Brazil known as garimpeiros. The government estimated that about half of the 600,000-plus ounces of gold produced by small- and medium-scale miners was smuggled to Suriname across the Corentyne River (Edmonds, 2013).

Extractive capital from the traditional capitalist countries engaged in exploration, while those from the emerging economies – China and Russia – became involved in bauxite production. Small-scale miners funded by domestic capital dominated in the gold mining sector. The natural resources landscape in Guyana became characterized by extractive capital from non-traditional sources such as China and Russia engaged in the bauxite industry, Malaysia and India in forestry extraction, and Chinese in gold mining. Paulo Cesar Quartiero a large-scale Brazilian rice producer expressed interest in buying-up lands in a land grab for agricultural purposes in Guyana (GRAIN, 2010).

Rare Earth Elements International, Inc., (REEI) a US based mineral exploration company acquired a rare earth property at Port Kaituma, Guyana in 2012 (Marketwire 2012). The property comprised forty-four square miles with over 200 concessions. The Guyana Geological and Mines Commission estimated in 2009 that the initial deposit of Colimbite-Tantalite in the ground was in excess of US$10 million at current market price.

U308 Corporation a Canadian mining company based in Toronto explored the Roraima Basin, in which it obtained uranium exploration rights to approximately

1.3 million ha. Argus Metals Corp. of Vancouver, British Columbia in Canada acquired license to explore for uranium at Port Kaituma (Mining.Com, 2012). Reunion Manganese Inc. the wholly owned subsidiary of Reunion Gold Corporation of Canada explored for manganese at Matthews Ridge. Tullow Oil, a British Company, which has a joint venture with REPSOL of Spain, started drilling in the Guyana–Suriname Basin, and CGX of Canada resumed exploration under its Corentyne Petroleum Prospecting License (PPL) (Thomas, 2012).

The exploration for oil also moved apace with ExxonMobil's US$600 million exploration project in the Lisa Area or Stabroek Block Area measuring approximately 26,806 square kilometers over 100 miles offshore Guyana. Drilling, which will be at 1,750 meters in depth that reach up to 3,000 meters, was expected to begin in March 2015 (Guyana Times International, 2015). Several other companies engaged in oil exploration including the Spanish oil company Repsol Exploration Guyana S.A., CGX Resources Inc., ESSO Exploration and Production Guyana Ltd, Ratio Oil Exploration Ltd., Petroleum, Anadarko Petroleum Corporation (Guyana Company), Pacific Rubiales, and Tullow Oil Plc., and Nabi Oil and Gas Inc. (Kaieteur News, 2013).

ExxonMobil is preparing to begin commercial oil production at the Lisa 1 Field offshore in early 2020. The 2016 Petroleum Agreement made public after mounting pressure on the government to do so, revealed that ExxonMobil will be exempt from a range of taxes and duties when production starts. The 2016 Petroleum Agreement states that the company will pay no tax, value added tax, excise tax, duty, fee, charge or other impost, when production starts. Neither shall those be levied from time to time thereafter on ExxonMobil or affiliated companies' petroleum income or property from authorized or contemplated transactions or activities for any purpose. According to the Minister of Natural Resources, Guyana stands to earn US$80 billion in years to come from oil and gas production, at a rate of at least US$1 million daily or just over US$300 million annually (Chabrol, 2017).

The fifth set of factors involved the US interpretation of the political micromanagement of FDIs and degenerate activities of the 'criminalized authoritarian state' as a breakdown in democracy and good governance. The US called for a deepening of democracy in Guyana, which meant, in principle, regime change. Critics pointed to the fact that neoliberal democratization did not bring about democracy in countries where it was implemented but rather resulted in the emergence of semi-authoritarian (Ottaway, 2002), and new authoritarian states (Canterbury, 2005).

The promoters of neoliberal democratization also came to the realization that democracy is not established merely by free and fair national elections. Projects to deepen democracy in the developing countries have become a focal point at the current historical conjuncture characterized by the transmutation of neoliberalism into post-neoliberalism. The US State Department became deeply involved in the process to 'expand' democracy in Guyana through the controversial Leadership and Democracy (LEAD) project. The LEAD project indicated the direction of post-neoliberal politics in the country, a politics that facilitated regime change in 2015.

Conclusion

In conclusion, we have combined two concepts of the state – the 'authoritarian state,' which is a historical phenomenon in the Caribbean, with the 'criminalized state,' a recent phenomenon in Guyana as identified by Thomas (2003), to describe the rule of the PPP-C in the 2000s as the 'criminalized authoritarian state.' This state depended heavily on natural resources extraction to enrich its members, rather than to use the revenues from resource extraction to improve the lot of the poor as was the case in Latin America. It expanded the frontiers of capitalism in the region albeit in a degenerate form in the center-periphery relations in which it existed. Analysis of this form of degeneration of the state requires further analysis for it to be understood in a better way in order to thwart its future emergence.

In a Caribbean context this state is unique to Guyana, based on its origins, race and class character in addition to its modus operandi. It was based on free and fair national elections that, due to racial voting, only a single political party could win.[8] Also, it was characterized by some of the traits of the post-colonial authoritarian state. Finally, the state became a criminal enterprise, while simultaneously operating within a historical authoritarian framework. It was against that 'criminalized authoritarian state' that working people's struggle for genuine bottom-up people's participatory democracy was conducted that led to regime change in 2015.

What does the future hold for politics in Guyana? In answer to this question the Guyanese people and political parties need to take into consideration a number of factors. First, the role of global capitalist forces in Guyanese domestic politics must be studied and clearly understood. Second, historical evidence supports the idea that the state in Guyana originated in authoritarian circumstances, which it has not been able to shake off. The issue of authoritarianism is a matter of degree since the state in peripheral or mature capitalist societies is a coercive power in general. Third, the future of political arrangements must be characterized by coalition politics.

Notes

1 See Burges, S. (2016). 'Revenge of the Right in Brazil?' Council on Hemispheric Affairs (COHA), Washington, DC, May 16.
2 www.nrcan.gc.ca/mining-materials/kimberley-process/8222.
3 www.state.gov/e/eb/tfs/tfc/diamonds/index.htm.
4 Guyana National Development Strategy, Ministry of Finance, Georgetown, Guyana, 1996, www.guyana.org/NDS/NDS.htm).
5 National Development Strategy: Eradicating Poverty and Unifying Guyana, A Civil Society Document, www.ndsguyana.org.
6 For elaboration on neoliberalism in the mining sector in Africa see *Mining Journal*, 1997; Hilson and Potter, 2005; Chachage, Ericsson, and Gibson, 1993; and on Latin America see Veltmeyer and Petras, 2014.
7 National Development Strategy, www.ndsguyana.org.
8 Ottaway's (2003) work on semi-authoritarianism supports this idea. Indeed, she argues that race, cultural, and religious differences are some of the main reasons why authoritarianism persists in the midst of neoliberal democratization.

References

Adonis, D. (2014). 'Guyana's alleged 'mineral-smuggling minister' furious over Oslo Times article.' *Epoch Times*, December 9.

Agee, P. (1975). *Inside the company: CIA diary*. London: Penguin Books Ltd.

Barbados Underground. (2010). Bauxite company of Guyana (BCGI) formed workers committee as illegal substitute for GB&GWU April 3, 2010 https://barbadosunderground.wordpress.com/2010/04/03/bauxite-company-of-guyana-bcgi-formed-workers-committee-as-illegal-substitute-for-gbgwu/.

Barbados Underground. (2010a). GB&GWU takes case to London to fight to restore the rights of BCGI workers, August 22, 2010a https://barbadosunderground.wordpress.com/2010/08/22/gbgwu-takes-case-to-london-to-fight-to-restore-the-rights-of-bcgi-workers/.

Black, D. and McKenna, P. (1995). 'Canada and structural adjustment in the south: The significance of the Guyana case.' *Canadian Journal of Development Studies*, VXI (1), pp. 55–78.

Bulkan, J. (2014). 'REDD letter days: Entrenching political radicalization and State patronage through the Norway-Guyana REDD-plus agreement.' *Social and Economic Studies*, 63 (3 and 4), pp. 249–279.

Burges, S. (2016). 'Revenge of the right in Brazil?' Council on Hemispheric Affairs (COHA), Washington, DC, May 16.

Canterbury, D. C. (2014). 'Extractive capitalism and the resistance in Guyana,' in J. Petras and H. Veltmeyer, H. (eds) *Extractive imperialism in the Americas: Capitalism's new frontier*. Leiden and Boston: Brill, pp. 147–175.

Canterbury. D. C. (2013). 'El capitalismo extractivo: El caso de Guyana.' *Estudios Críticos del Desarrollo*, 3 (4), pp. 145–189.

Canterbury, D. C. (2005). *Neoliberal democratization and new authoritarianism*. Aldershot, UK and Burlington, VT: Ashgate.

Chabrol, D. S. (2018). 'Sloth in investigating financial crimes totaling almost GY$300 billion - UK advisor to SOCU.' *Demerara Waves*, January 9.

Chabrol, D. S. (2017). 'ExxonMobil gets generous tax concessions: Guyana stands to earn US$7.5 billion in 20 years.' *Demerara Waves*, December 28.

Chabrol, D. S. (2013). 'USAID agreement breached over governance and democracy project.' *Demerara Waves*, December.

Chachage, S. L., Ericsson, M. and Gibbon, P. (1993). *Mining and structural adjustment: Studies on Zimbabwe and Tanzania*. Uppsala, Sweden: The Scandinavian Institute of African Studies.

Chang, H. J. (2008). *Bad samaritans: The myth of free trade and the secret history of capitalism*. New York: Bloomsbury Press.

Demerara Waves. (2015). 'Toshao's alleged rape of teenage girl occurred long before Ramotar's planned visit,' February 20.

Edmonds, K. (2013). Everything that glitters isn't green in Guyana. North American Congress on Latin America, July 13.

GRAIN. (2010). Land grabbing in Latin America. March 29 www.grain.org/ article/entries/3995-land-grabbing-in-latin-america.

Green, J. (2012). Guyana suspends gold and diamond mining permits, *Earth Time*, July 8, www.earthtimes.org/pollution/guyana-suspends-gold-diamond-mining-permits/2075/.

Griffiths, T. and Anselmo, L. (2010). *Indigenous peoples and sustainable livelihoods in Guyana: An overview of experiences and potential opportunities*. Georgetown, Guyana,

United Kingdom, and Ottawa, Canada: Amerindian People's Association, Forest People Program, and The North-South Institute, June.

Gudynas, E. (2010). 'The new extractivism of the 21st century: Ten urgent these about extractivism in relation to current South American progressivism.' Washington, DC: Center for International Policy, January 21.

Guyana: Mineral, Mining Sector Investment and Business Guide. (2013). Strategic information and regulations, international business publication, Volume 1. USA, Washington, DC – Guyana.

Guyana Times International. (2015). 'ExxonMobil to invest US$600M into oil exploration in Guyana,' February.

Haggard, S. and Kaufman, R. (1989). 'The politics of stabilization and structural adjustment,' in J. D. Sachs (ed.) (1989). *Developing country debt and the world economy*. Chicago: University of Chicago Press, pp. 263–274.

Hilson, G. and Clive Potter, C. (2005). 'Structural adjustment and subsistence industry: Artisanal gold mining in Ghana.' *Development and Change*, 36 (1), pp. 101–131.

Kaieteur News. (2013). 'Oil exploration companies meet tomorrow in US to update Guyana,' December 19.

Kaieteur News. (2012). 'Guyana most corrupt country in English-speaking Caribbean,' December 12.

Kaieteur News. (2012a). 'Re-migrant launches incisive publication on corruption in Guyana,' August 12.

Kaieteur News. (2010). 'President Jagdeo must prove government is not anti-union – GB&GWU,' February 16.

Kucera, D. and Principi, M. (2014). 'Democracy and foreign direct investment at the industry level: Evidence for US multinationals.' *Review of World Economics*, 150 (3), pp. 595–617.

Kwayana, E. (2012). *The bauxite strike and the old politics*. Atlanta Georgia: On Our Own Authority!

Kwayana, E. (1988). *Walter Rodney*. Georgetown, Guyana: Working People's Alliance.

Lall, G. H. K. (2012). *Guyana: A national cesspool of greed, duplicity and corruption*. Georgetown: Guyana.

Lewis, W. A. (1950). 'The industrialization of the British West Indies.' *Caribbean Economic Review*, 2 (1), pp. 1–51.

Mandle, J. R. (1996). *Persistent underdevelopment: Change and economic modernization in the West Indies*. Amsterdam: Gordon and Breach.

Marketwire. (2012). 'REE International acquires rare earth property with estimated value of $10 Million.' *Mining and Metals*, March 20.

Mars, P. (1998). 'Socio-political impact of large scale gold mining in Guyana: Resolving tensions between capital and labor,' in D. C. Canterbury (ed.) *Guyana's gold industry: Evolution, structure, impacts and non-wage benefits*, *Transition*. Special Issue 27–28, pp. 57–70.

Merrill, T. (ed.) (1992). *Guyana: A country study*. Washington: GPO for the Library of Congress.

Mining.Com. (2012). Argus receives title, and uranium license for the large-scale, drill-ready Kaituma uranium/gold project, www.mining.com/argus-receives-title-and-uraniumlicence-for-the-large-scale-drill-ready-kaituma-uraniumgold-project/.

Mining Journal. (1997). Namibia: Abundant exploration opportunities, Country Supplement, London, October 10.

National Workers Union. (2010). 'Guyana bauxite dispute: Union reports dispute to Recognition and certification board,' Trinidad and Tobago.

Olukoshi, A. O. (ed.) (1992). *The politics of structural adjustment in Nigeria.* Oxford: James Currey.

Ottaway, M. (2002). *Democracy challenged: The rise of the semi-authoritarian state.* Washington, DC: The Carnegie Endowment for International Peace.

Payne, A. (1995). *Politics in Jamaica.* London: Palgrave Macmillan.

Petras, J. and Veltmeyer, H. (2001). *Globalization unmasked: Imperialism in the twenty first century.* London: Zed Books.

Prebisch, R. (1950). *The economic development of Latin America and its principal problems.* New York: United Nations.

Rambarran, R. (2015). The economic and social implications of the anti-money laundering and countering the financing of terrorism act on a small, developing economy, University of Hyderabad, November 15, MPRA Paper No. 68056.

Reinert, E. S. (2007). *How rich countries got rich and why poor countries stay poor.* New York: Public Affairs.

Schlesinger, Jr., A. M. (2002). *A thousand days: John F. Kennedy in the white house.* New York: Mariner Books.

Simutanyi, N. (1996). 'The politics of structural adjustment in Zimbabwe.' *Third World Quarterly*, 17 (4), pp. 825–389.

Sinclair, C. (2010). 'A deepening of collusion between government and BCGI.' *Kaieteur News*, May 23.

Singer, H. (1992). 'Lessons of post-war development experience, 1945–1988,' in S. Sharma (ed.) *Development policy.* New York: St. Martin Press, pp. 35–80.

Thomas, C. Y. (2012). *Guyana: Economic performance and outlook – The recent scramble for natural resources.* Georgetown, Guyana: University of Guyana, April.

Thomas, C. Y. (2010). 'Norway's deception: Partnership or capture of Guyana's rainforest.' Georgetown Guyana: *Sunday Stabroek*, reprinted in 'The LCDS Guyana-Norway agreement and environmental issues related to global warming and climate change.' Sunday Stabroek News Columns November 29, 2009 – August 1, 2010, Georgetown, Guyana: University of Guyana.

Thomas. C. Y. (2003). 'More theses on the criminalized state: Guyana and the wider world.' *Sunday Stabroek*, Georgetown: Guyana, August 17.

Thomas, C. Y. (2003). 'Guyana and the wider world,' *Sunday Stabroek*, Georgetown: Guyana, March 9.

Thomas, C. Y. (1998). 'Omai's gold production in Guyana,' in D. C. Canterbury (ed.) Guyana's gold industry: Evolution, structure, impacts and non-wage benefits, *Transition* Special Issue 27–28, Georgetown, Guyana: Institute of Development Studies, University of Guyana, pp. 37–56.

Thomas, C. Y. (1988). *The poor and the powerless: Economic policy and change in the Caribbean.* New York: Monthly Review Press.

Thomas, C. Y. (1984). *Plantations peasants and state: A study of the mode of sugar production in Guyana.* California: University of California, Center for Afro-American Culture and Society.

Thomas, C. Y. (1983). 'State capitalism in Guyana: An assessment of Burnham's cooperative 'socialist republic,' in F. Ambursley and R. Cohen (eds) *Crisis in the Caribbean.* New York: Monthly Review.

Thomas, C. Y. (1982). 'From colony to state capitalism: Alternative paths of development in the Caribbean,' *Transition*, 5, pp. 1–20.

Thomas, C. Y. (1976). *Bread and justice: The struggle for socialism in Guyana*. Georgetown: Guyana, February.

Thomas, C. Y. (1972). *The structure, performance and prospects of central banking in the Caribbean*. Kingston, Jamaica: Institute of Social and Economic Research, University of the West Indies.

UhuruNews. (2010). 'Black workers in Guyana struggle against neocolonial state and foreign bosses,' August 26.

US State Department. (2014). Investment climate statement – Guyana. Bureau of Economic and Business Affairs, June.

Veltmeyer, H. and Petras, J. (2014). *The new extractivism: A post-neoliberal development model or imperialism in the twenty-first century*? London: Zed Books.

Westmaas, N. (2004). 'Resisting orthodoxy: Notes on the origins and ideology of the Working People's Alliance.' *Small Axe*, 8 (1), pp. 63–81.

10 Political change and foreign intervention

This chapter analyzes the issue of political change in natural resources rich peripheral capitalist countries as center-periphery capitalist relations deepens in the historical period marked by the transition from neoliberalism to post-neoliberalism. The main argument here is as follows: neoliberal democratization represented regime change in post-colonial authoritarian states, but these states are subjected to further imperial intervention under the guise of deepening democracy. The reality is that center-periphery capitalist relations are further deeply embedded in the resource-rich countries, as the imperial powers continue to intagliate their evolving brand of peripheral capitalism on the political economy of those states. As if neoliberal democratization did not bring sufficient democracy to the post-colonial authoritarian states, there is need for further action by foreign powers in collaboration with their domestic allies to bring more democracy to these states. This phenomenon, is distinctly associated with capitalist development in the periphery. Developing countries visited by political change through neoliberal democratization are subjected to further imperial intervention allegedly to strengthen democracy.

In Guyana, neoliberal democratization represented regime change – the surrendering of the post-colonial authoritarian state to the International Monetary Fund (IMF)/World Bank/Carter Center. But then a new form of authoritarianism emerged described as a criminalized authoritarian state. This development prompted further foreign intervention to bring about regime change but this time under the ruse of strengthening democracy. Thus, bringing democracy and strengthening democracy in peripheral countries are both ruses for foreign intervention in peripheral states to control their natural resources. The real situation in Guyana however was that the criminalized authoritarian state was not working fully in the interest of the imperial powers, namely the US. As such the US needed to bring about regime change to put in place a government that would pay more attention to the interests of foreign capital.

The politics of natural resources extraction has shifted a gear in the developing countries in recent years. But while scholars and observers of politics in these states have been focusing their attention on a number of pertinent issues such as governance and stability, they have overlooked this key political development that is taking place in those natural resources rich states. Neoliberal democratization has brought about political change in these countries by installing a political cabal supposedly to preside over the dismantling of nationalist economic and post-colonial authoritarian state policies, and to implement neoliberal economic programs. The discharge of these economic measures was mainly to serve the interest of neoliberal capital.

As the years rolled on the new rulers have failed to fully serve the interests of neoliberal capitalism. Instead, they have implemented appropriate superstructures comprising institutions and laws as dictated by neoliberal capital through the IMF and World Bank. But, the ruling elites have found ways to subvert those institutions and laws through corruption, nepotism, and bigotry to let them serve their own interests. The US State Department expressed its discontent at the fact that the Guyana government had the legal infrastructure in place to support foreign direct investment, but continued to politically micromanage foreign investment. In the view of the US administration that constituted a hindrance to foreign investors (US State Department, 2012). Also, the Guyana government failed to enforce the laws to counter money laundering and drug trafficking (Chabrol, 2013).

As a consequence, a significant change took place in the political relationships between the US, the incumbent state elites in natural resources rich developing countries, and their domestic political opposition. This change is examined here in the context of the US turning on the People's Progressive Party-Civic (PPP-C) government it had installed through neoliberal democratization measures overseen by the IMF, World Bank and the Carter Center at the national elections in 1992, and the method to have the PPP-C government removed from office in the national elections in 2011 and 2015. The change epitomizes a kind of politics, which seeks to rationalize foreign control over the natural resources rich peripheral capitalist countries through the cyclically adjusting of their domestic elite forces that hold state power. This is the political context for the 'new extractivism' outlined by Veltmeyer and Petras (2014).

Undoubtedly, Guyana is currently pursuing a development strategy that is based on natural resources extraction. The evidence of this is suggested by the fact that there is a significant amount of foreign direct investment in the country in exploration for gold, manganese, uranium, rare earth minerals, and oil and natural gas. The government has been explicitly pursuing foreign direct investment in the Guyana's natural resources sector. Gold mining is currently the leading contributor to the country's gross national product, surpassing sugar. The production of oil and natural gas is set to soon overtake the gold mining sector when production commences in 2020.

The response by global capital under such conditions is to change gear by calling for more democracy in countries such as Guyana. Inevitably, this means political change in the natural resource rich developing countries either by the ruling elites undergoing significant reforms in their conduct of the economic affairs of the country, or their removal from office and the installation of a new set of rulers, who will carry out the wishes of neoliberal capital. But, the dynamism of this situation implies that since the scales have fallen off the eyes of peoples in the developing world, there is no way that foreign capital will be able to exercise total domination of these countries.

The future of state politics in the natural resources rich peripheral capitalist countries is one in which at periodic intervals foreign capital will intervene to install state elites favorable to foreign capital, but the locals will find ways to subvert the process to make it benefit the new ruling elites. This would lead to foreign intervention to change the government, and the cycle will continue. This in essence is a basic theory of state politics in natural resource rich peripheral capitalist countries. Political change comes about through foreign intervention, the new state elites are favored for a time until they begin to subvert the political and economic institutions to serve their own interests. They are then replaced by a new set of state elites. This is representative of the process of capitalist development in the periphery.

The current political situation in Guyana is a perfect illustration of this theory of state politics in peripheral capitalist development. The PPP-C Guyana government initially secured state power through foreign intervention, namely neoliberal democratization. The PPP-C government proceeded to dismantle the economic institutions established by its predecessor the post-colonial authoritarian state. It then established new economic institutions and laws to facilitate neoliberal capital. Then it proceeded to progressively subvert those institutions and laws in the interest not of the country, but of the ruling elites and their collaborators. Most often this process of subversion becomes possible because of racial allegiance. Primarily, individuals called East Indians, who serve the interest of the East Indian political elites in power, staff the state bureaucracy.

In the light of these developments the US responded by resorting to a program to fund the expansion of democracy in Guyana. A quarrel ensued between the US authorities and the PPP-C Guyana government over the US funding of democracy expansion in Guyana. This quarrel became a public affair in December 2013. There were four sides who were involved in this quarrel – the PPP-C, the Alliance for Change (AFC), APNU, and the US government.

The purpose here is to examine the change in international and domestic politics, which was revealed at the point of intersection of foreign capital and domestic political forces in struggle to control state power in a natural resources rich peripheral capitalist country. It is proposed first that the politics of natural resources extraction involves a struggle between foreign capital and domestic political forces to control state power in the natural resources rich peripheral capitalist countries. The smooth operations of foreign capital in these countries necessitate that politicians favorable to foreign capital occupy the seat of government. Although domestic political forces contend for state power in their own right, there is always a point at which they have to contend with the forces of foreign capital that seek to influence political outcomes in their self-interests.

Second, this feature of the politics of natural resources extraction in the peripheral capitalist countries is caused by the fact that the principal economic activities that gave rise to the state in these countries have never been in the control of domestic capitalist forces. The colonial economies were created by absentee capitalist classes – mercantile, industrial, and extractivist that owned and operated their principal means of production. These included agricultural production, trading outlets, manufacturing, and natural resources extraction. Now that the colonies have become independent states, the struggle for state power inevitably involves domestic and foreign forces.

Third, in the absence of a strong domestic capitalist class there is a strong tendency for the political elites that control the state to use their power to enrich themselves through corruption, rent extraction, or taking ownership and control of the principal production operations. These activities inevitably place the ruling political elites at odds with foreign capital. To counteract this tendency of the state to go rogue on foreign capital, the capitalist powers maintain a political presence – influencing the outcomes of national elections by providing financial support to selective domestic political forces vying for state power. Money is funneled to the political entities trusted by foreign capital to carry out its bidding, when in power. Thus, the contest for state power becomes one between three distinct sets of political actors – the government, the political opposition and foreign capital. These are not necessarily homogenous entities but may be quite heterogeneous.

Fourth, the domestic political actors financed by foreign capital usually secure state power, and those that do not remain in the political opposition. But, there is always a tendency for those that secure state power to go rogue on their financial masters. This tendency is a domestic factor that stimulates further foreign intervention to promote political change. Historically, the process – coups, military invasion, social unrest through destabilization, strikes, etc. – by which political change is brought about varies by the degree of the conflict between foreign capital and the domestic political elites and how much foreign capital is embedded in the country. This phenomenon is recognizable across Africa, Asia, the Caribbean, Latin America, and in the Middle East. Political elites that win power with the support of foreign capital run afoul of their financial masters and are routinely replaced.

Fifth, the above fact is ever present in politics in the natural resource rich developing countries and needs to be understood. The politics of natural resources extraction take place at the point of intersection of foreign capital and domestic political forces in their struggle to control state power. This is what needs to be understood in the study of political change in natural resources rich peripheral capitalist countries.

Finally, the preferred method of political change in the current period is expected to come about through what is variously referred to as 'strengthening democracy,' 'deepening democracy,' 'expanding democracy,' etc. This takes the form of political mobilization that leads to social unrest to replace an incumbent state that is out of favor with foreign capital. Terminology such as 'strengthening democracy' is used because these states have already been 'democratized' as a political conditionality of structural adjustment. Although 'democratization' has tightened the grip of foreign capital on the natural resources in the natural resources rich peripheral capitalist countries, it has not gone far enough. There is a need to 'strengthen democracy' in the furtherance of the capitalists' scramble for natural resources. All this is a ruse to maintain foreign domination of resources-rich countries in the capitalist periphery.

Outlining the problems of political change – old and new

Political change brought about by neoliberal democratization in the 1980–1990s is now being subjected to further alteration and modification with the stated objective of strengthening democracy. The idea about strengthening democracy nonetheless is merely reflective of an old problem faced by the rich capitalist states. Taking measures to create in the capitalist periphery the appropriate state bureaucracy to buttress the uninhibited extraction of natural resources by foreign-owned extractive capital. The imperial powers have resolved this age-old problem in different ways in the past including political assassinations, the overthrow of democratically elected governments, political and economic destabilization, and sanctions. The domestic state elites are not absolutely dependent on foreign capital but in their self-interest seek to exercise some degree of independence. This sets them on a collision course with the forces of foreign capital. The ebb and flow of the contest to control state power therefore tends to vary between the extremes of pro- and anti-foreign capital.

Factors such as corruption, rent collection, crime, bureaucratic red tape, strong-arm politics, electoral malpractices, state control of the media, etc. in the peripheral capitalist state and society tend to compound the problems faced by foreign capital. These problems tend to interfere with the smooth operations of foreign capital in the peripheral capitalist countries. These issues are highlighted in support of the idea that there is a need to strengthen democracy in the state. The agents of foreign capital in conjunction with elements in the political opposition then formulate interventionist programs to strengthen democracy with or without the support of the state elites.

The problem to effect political change by reigning in the excesses in state and society that hinder foreign capital is manifested as a conflict between the domestic state on one side and foreign capital represented by the most dominant capitalist countries and global institutions, and domestic political opposition on the other. The global institutions in the control of foreign capital are used as fronts in this conflict to take the lead in helping to bring about the relevant political changes in the state. The strategies used to cause various interest groups to turn on the government and to strengthen opposition groups usually have a heavy focus on youths and women, and on social issues such as health, HIV-Aids, education, and community service. The recalcitrant regime is forced to undertake major reforms to correct the conditions that hinder foreign capital. Alternatively, it is destabilized through, among other things, social unrest, economic sanctions, and sabotage, leading to its loss of power.

The dilemma of the political left

There seems to be public support, including that which is provided by the political left for US intervention to bring about political change in developing countries inflicted for extended periods of time by a criminalized authoritarian state or other forms of authoritarianisms. The left also supported foreign intervention through neoliberal democratization to bring about political change. In the present moment the following three reasons seem to be at play for this public support for foreign intervention in domestic politics in a developing country.

First, the incumbent state elites installed through US involvement have consolidated their political power. This results in the domestic political opposition being banished in the political wilderness for an excessive number of years with no end in sight to their exile from power. Political power does not change hands at regular intervals due to the charade it is in, for example, in places like the US, the two-party system has a stranglehold on the state, and the Democratic and Republican parties are merely two sides of the same coin.

Second, the cash-strapped domestic political opposition end up either directly taking US government money to fund their campaigns, or indirectly benefiting from the favorable domestic political conditions such monies create. These conditions would include foreign financed programs to educate the electorate to vote on issues rather than on race allegiance, bringing to the fore many of the social ills in state and society, among other pathologies. The government elites on the other hand have a huge war chest – they use state resources and tributes from the domestic economic strata for favors and protection, to finance their party-political operations against their opponents, thereby holding onto power for many years.

Third, the masses blame the government for their poor social and economic conditions. They are therefore in the mood for political change, albeit they are conscious and weary of foreign intervention in the political affairs of their country.

The dilemma of left domestic civil and political forces is that they lack the finances to mount a serious challenge for power against such an entrenched authoritarian government. But, if they take US government money to fund their campaigns to secure power they will be collaborating with US imperialism. During the Cold War they might have gone to the communist bloc for financial support. Meanwhile they have no source of finance to match those of the incumbent ruling political party. In their weak state and dire need for political change due to the criminal nature of the state and its repression and authoritarian measures, the left parties fall prey to US initiatives to strengthen democracy in their countries. Given the weak state in which they find themselves, the real issue would seem to be whether as a tactic the left parties could embrace US initiatives for regime change to win power from incumbent authoritarian governments after which they pursue a progressive economic agenda.

An illustration from politics in Guyana

Politics in Guyana provides a perfect example of the dynamic scenario described above concerning the struggle for state power in a natural resources rich peripheral capitalist country as center-periphery relations continue to be deepen. The PPP-Civic government, which ascended into power in 1992 on a neoliberal democratization ticket, was on the one side of the conflict, and on the other the political opposition and US government seeking to finance the political opposition to effect political change. The political change engendered by neoliberal democratization has seen the installation of a political cabal supposedly to preside over the dismantling of nationalist economic policies of the post-colonial authoritarian state, and the implementation of new measures founded on neoliberal economic and political doctrine.

There is evidence based on the sudden influx of Canadian extractivist capital in the gold industry in conjunction with the implementation of structural adjustment in Guyana in the 1990s that the discharge of these measures was mainly to serve the interest of neoliberal capital. Indeed, a primary goal of structural adjustment was the achievement of economic growth based on the attraction of foreign direct investment into a stagnant and cash-starved economy. As time went by after the introduction of structural adjustment, the new rulers had failed and needed to do more to fully serve the interests of neoliberal capitalism, enriching themselves instead, much to the displeasure of the US authorities.

The response by global capital

Global capital responds to situations such as those in Guyana by calling for a deepening of the democratic process in the country. Deepening democracy means the creation of the appropriate political superstructure to facilitate foreign capital's extraction of natural resources and transfer of wealth from the developing countries to the advanced capitalist states. Indeed, the critics have pointed to the fact that neoliberal democratization has not brought about democracy in countries where it was applied but has resulted in the emergence of semi-authoritarian and new authoritarian regimes (Ottaway, 2002; Canterbury, 2005). Meanwhile, the perpetrators of neoliberal democratization came to the realization that democracy is not established by merely holding national elections that are considered 'free and fair.' Thus, projects to deepen democratic structures have become a focal point at the current evolutionary phase of neoliberal democratization.

The US State Department is deeply involved in the push to deepen democracy in states that have been faltering, since the 'third wave' of democratization that replaced authoritarian states in the developing countries during the 1990s. This means that the US will support political change in these states rich in natural resources. The ruling elites will either reform the conduct of the economic affairs of the countries or be removed through foreign intervention and replaced with rulers, who will carry out the wishes of neoliberal capitalists. These reforms will be in addition to those already implemented through structural adjustment and neoliberal democratization.

The Leadership and Democracy project (LEAD)

In the struggle by foreign capital to control state power, the US proposed the Leadership and Democracy (LEAD) project to fund the expansion of democracy in Guyana. The LEAD program was funded by the US Congress, to the tune of US$1,250,000 for the period April 2013 to April 2015. It was executed through the notorious International Republican Institute (IRI) in collaboration with domestic political forces. Mr. Glenn Bradbury, a 'democracy specialist' with impressive credentials, was appointed as the 'Chief of Party' of the LEAD project.

Mr. Bradbury is a highly skilled operator who at the time had served as a senior parliamentary advisor and senior policy advisor to various Canadian parliamentarians, in excess of twenty years. The PPP-C government revoked Mr. Bradbury's visa on the accusation that the LEAD favored the political opposition and would lead to the overthrow of the government (USAID, 2013; USAID, 2013a; Kaieteur News, 2015).

The LEAD had four program components supposedly to strengthen political and consensus building and skills. The four components were first joint non-partisan work with all political parties to assist the National Assembly, as a representative deliberative body to effectively carry out its functions. Second, was to strengthen the National Assembly and boost citizen engagement and understanding of Parliament. Third, was to motivate youth and women to become more politically and civically involved. Fourth was to promote civic and voter education in support of implementing local government reforms and local elections (USAID, 2013).

The LEAD program allowed US operatives to become involved in a wide variety of political activities in Guyana. These include intra-party and cross-party negotiations and political party collaboration. It involved legislative research and drafting, the development of legislative agendas, the establishment of a Women's Parliamentary Caucus, increasing citizen's engagement by disseminating information to the public through social media, etc., about the workings of the parliament, and parliamentary oversight. The LEAD proposed to motivate university and secondary school students to become involved in political and civic processes, and for them to become engaged in civic voter education to implement local government reform and local elections (USAID, 2013).

The IRI is well known for destabilizing governments in Latin America and the Caribbean (COHA, 2008a; Agee, 2003). It had a major role in the overthrow of President Aristide in Haiti (Goodman, 2004; Bernsein, 2006; COHA, 2008). It was implicated along with the US State Department and the US Embassy in Venezuela in the failed coup against the late President Hugo Chávez in April 2002 (Leight, 2004; Golinger, 2006; James, 2006). It is regarded as an institution that is a front organization to promote unscrupulous ultraconservative Republican foreign policy agenda (Leight, 2004). It is supposed to be a research institution, but it is really a cloak-and-dagger operation (Leight, 2004). The overthrow of the democratically elected Morsi government in Egypt is a recent example of the IRI at work through the US democracy assistance program (Aljazeera, 2013). The IRI's tactics of 'party building' and 'educational seminars' employed in Haiti and Venezuela were quite similar to those of the LEAD project in Guyana.

Regime change took place in Guyana in 2015 and the LEAD project exited the country (Kaieteur News, 2015). The Aurora Gold Mine began producing gold in August 2015. ExxonMobil is set to begin pumping oil after its large offshore discovery, but the political risk became very high after the Maduro administration in Venezuela claimed the approximately US$40 billion Exxon oil find as belonging to Venezuela (McDonald, 2016). ExxonMobil has since made additional offshore oil discoveries in Guyana since that time.

The LEAD project controversy

A public quarrel ensued between the US authorities and the Guyana government over the US funding of democracy in Guyana. The Guyana Trades Union Congress, the opposition A Party for National Unity (APNU), and the Alliance for Change (AFC), among others, supported the LEAD without reservations. The PPP-C government and the Private Sector Commission opposed the implementation of the LEAD without it being renegotiated. The government stated that it would not renegotiate the LEAD while the program was in operation. The Guyana government wanted the US administration to halt the program before it engaged in any negotiations on the matter.

The PPP and PPP-C government positions

The ruling PPP-C government claimed that the US had breached the agreement between the USAID and the government of Guyana in the manner in which the LEAD project, was being implemented without the government's full knowledge (Chabrol, 2013a). The Guyana government objected to the LEAD project on the following six grounds. First, the Guyana government claimed that it was not properly consulted and so it disapproved of the project, but that the US government in violation of Guyana's sovereignty was going ahead to implement the LEAD project.

Second, the US administration conceptualized the LEAD, approved its funding, and contracted the IRI to execute the project, before engaging with the Guyana government on the matter. The IRI receives funding from the National Endowment for Democracy and the US Agency for International Development. The neoconservative John Bolton of the American Enterprise Institute, the Project for a New American Century, the Republican National Committee, and former US Ambassador to the United Nations, described the USAID as an arm of the CIA that promotes the political and economic needs of the US government through its foreign financial assistance programs (Leight, 2004).

Third, the LEAD provided funds directly to opposition political parties that would give those organizations an advantage over the PPP-C. Fourth, the project engaged opposition political parties in policy formulation that could lead to constitutional reform in Guyana. Fifth, the Guyana government prefers that political parties were engaged by the LEAD through the National Assembly or other such institutions. Sixth, the project violates an agreement between the USAID and the Guyana government on the procedures for engaging the Guyana government and on the implementation of projects in Guyana (Chabrol, 2014).

The Guyana government contended that the US had long approved the funds for the LEAD project, designed it and hired the IRI to execute it. The US claimed however that the Guyana government had been properly consulted. Furthermore, as a party the PPP accused the US of using the LEAD to boost the fortunes of the political opposition in Guyana (*Demerara Waves*, 2013; Guyana Chronicle Online, 2014). Mr. Clement Rohee the then General Secretary of the PPP claimed that the PPP and the PPP-C government held the same position on the LEAD project. Rohee said that the PPP's and government's position were the same on the matter (Guyana Chronicle Online, 2014). Rhoee echoed the Head of the Presidential Secretariat Roger Luncheon that the government was prepared to enter into talks with the US authorities on the LEAD project but that the project must first be put on hold because the government cannot be negotiating the project and implementing it simultaneously (Guyana Chronicle Online, 2014).

The PPP accused the US of attempting to destabilize the Guyana government by financing the activities of the political opposition through the US$1.250 million project that government had disapproved (*Demerara Waves*, 2013). The PPP said in a statement it issued that there was deep suspicion in political circles to corroborate the view that the project was intended to strengthen the position of the opposition political parties in Guyana (*Demerara Waves*, 2013). The PPP argued that the opposing political parties and the media were enamored with the project. According to the PPP, LEAD money funded trips by the political opposition to the interior of Guyana and bought those parties radio and television time. The PPP argued that the LEAD funded the activities of the opposition political parties to give them political advantage over the PPP (*Demerara Waves*, 2013).

The Guyana government dispensed with the LEAD project on the grounds that it was not properly consulted, and that individual political parties were being engaged and resourced to carry out political activities (*Demerara Waves*, 2013). In the wake of concerns by the PPP and the PPP-C government that the US embassy, USAID and/or the contracted IRI were still executing aspects of the project, the US Ambassador Mr. Brent Hardt was quoted in the privately owned *Stabroek News* newspaper as saying that the US was going ahead with the project (*Demerara Waves*, 2013; Guyana Chronicle Online, 2014). The PPP expressed fear that Guyana had returned to the 1962–1964 period when opposition Trade Unions and political parties were funded by the American Congress of Labor and Congress of Industrial Organizations (AFL-CIO) to destabilize the PPP government (*Demerara Waves*, 2013).

The Head of the Presidential Secretariat, Dr. Roger Luncheon pointed out that, Regions Three and Four were a hive of activities involving the LEAD program and that Cabinet members have reported that activities involved political parties and their mobilization, women and children, but that there were no reports of the PPP's involvement in any of those activities (*Demerara Waves*, 2013a).

The PPP pledged nonetheless to use its historical experience to pushback politically against the new challenge and its adversaries. The PPP stated that it stood fully behind the government's efforts to defend Guyana's national interests and sovereignty, and to resist the abuse of diplomatic privilege by any foreign mission in the country that interferes in the domestic political process in the country (*Demerara Waves*, 2013a). The PPP-C government had expressed the view that the LEAD project should go through established institutions such as the national parliament rather than go directly to political parties because Guyana does not have a system that finances political parties (Chabrol, 2014a).

Meanwhile, the US embassy had declined to respond to a series of questions emerging from ongoing criticisms by the Guyana government. US Ambassador Brent Hardt said that the project benefitted from extensive consultations with the Donald Ramotar-led administration. Despite government's disapproval of the project, Ambassador Hardt said that the project would go ahead, a move that has prompted the Foreign Ministry to write the US State Department to register its concerns (*Demerara Waves*, 2013a).

The APNU and AFC positions

The political opposition A Partnership for National Unity (APNU) and the Alliance for Change (AFC) constituted a parliamentary majority at the time. The PPP-C government was therefore a minority, since the national elections in 2011, when it lost the majority in parliament but won the Presidency. The APNU and AFC had a different position on the LEAD than the PPP and the PPP-C government. The leader of the APNU Mr. David Granger criticized the PPP's claim that the LEAD project violated Guyana's sovereignty, but acknowledged that it could help the political opposition in the country (*Demerara Waves*, 2013a). Mr. Granger said that the LEAD project was helping the Guyanese citizens particularly the youth to become more aware of the issues confronting the country and the opposition would benefit because the project will help them to make the right decision in selecting the country's leaders (Chabrol, 2013).

According to Chabrol (2013) Mr. Granger confirmed that the APNU had benefited from the LEAD project targeting youths in Anna Regina. The leader of the APNU said that young people were starved of information but that the IRI facilitated discussion and free passage of ideas among youths in Guyana (Chabrol, 2013). According to Chabrol (2013) there were many eligible voters who were not born in 1994 when the last local government election was held. However, although the IRI was not an element of decision making in Guyana, it could become a catalyst for ideas about local elections.

Mr. Granger dismissed the PPP's claims that the LEAD project is similar to that of the AFL-CIO's through which the US administration in its anti-communist campaign funneled funds to the Guyana Trades Union Congress in the 1960s to topple the Cheddi Jagan government in Guyana. Mr. Granger said that the allegations that the LEAD project would destabilize Guyana and breach its sovereignty were a diversion by the PPP to prevent needed help from coming to the country Chabrol (2013). Chabrol (2013) reported that the APNU's Chairman said that the LEAD must go head, the government cannot stop it, and that he believed and the IRI had a legitimate role to play since he did not think the IRI's role was subversive. Furthermore, Mr. Granger contended the PPP appeared locked in old ideas from the former Soviet Union, but that times had changed (Chabrol, 2013).

The AFC also endorsed the LEAD project and supported the position taken by the US to go ahead with it even in the absence of approval by the Guyana government (*Demerara Waves*, 2013b). The AFC stated that it supported the US government and embraced the positive contribution the project would make to improve democracy in Guyana (*Demerara Waves*, 2013b). With regards to the accusation by the PPP and the Guyana government that the US disregarded Guyana's state power and violated the country's sovereignty the AFC stated that it believed any effort to promote democracy, does not undermine sovereignty, but rather enhances it. The AFC held the view that because there have not been local government elections in fourteen years and the country was being ruled by a minority government that was constantly at odds with the legislative arm of the state the LEAD was welcomed. Its view is that the LEAD improved and brought more people into the decision making process of the country a development which was necessary (*Demerara Waves*, 2013b).

The AFC noted that the PPP was conveniently forgetting the fact that Dr. Cheddi Jagan its late leader actively sought and secured the support of former US President Carter in efforts to enhance democracy in Guyana in 1992. The AFC stated that it was confused about the changes that came about that made the support of US President Carter to enhance democracy an effort, while the US-supported LEAD project was a challenge to sovereignty (*Demerara Waves*, 2013b).

The Private Sector Commission

The Private Sector Commission (PSC), which was regarded as a mouthpiece of the PPP and PPP-C government, took the government's position by calling for the LEAD project to be put on hold until it was renegotiated by the US and the Guyana government (Chabrol, 2014a). The PSC organized a delegation that met separately with the head of the US embassy in Georgetown and a Guyana government delegation led by President Donald Ramotar, as a fact-finding mission about issues concerning the LEAD. The PSC arrived at the conclusion that the LEAD must be renegotiated in order to avoid political instability that could affect the business climate (Chabrol, 2014a).

The PCS sided with the government against the attempts by the majority parliamentary opposition to curtail government corruption. The opposition used its majority in the parliament to vote down a number of projects, and the anti-money laundering and financing terrorism bill, because of the corruption surrounding them. These projects included the construction of an approximately US$1 billion hydro power plant, rehabilitation of the Cheddi Jagan International Airport, and a Speciality Hospital (Chabrol, 2014a). Also, the PSC spoke out against the opposition for its voting against the amendments to the Anti Money Laundering and Countering of Financing Terrorism Act, the non-implementation of which caused Guyana to be blacklisted by the Caribbean Financial Action Task Force (CFATF).

The PSC subsequently announced nonetheless that the US Embassy in Guyana and the Guyana government were preparing for talks to resolve their differences on the LEAD project (*Demerara Waves*, 2014). A statement issued by the PSC said that it after reviewing the project document the agency concluded that there was merit in the objectives of the LEAD project, but that the USAID should not proceed with its implementation without the full agreement and sanction of the government of Guyana (*Demerara Waves*, 2014).

Other public comments on the LEAD

Sara Bharrat (2014), in a Guest Opinion piece in the *Demerara Waves* published on January 11, 2014 called on the PPP-C government to release its files on the LEAD project so that the public could get a more balanced view of the situation concerning the problem. Ms. Bharrat's purpose was to expose the contradictory position taken by the government against the LEAD. Bharrat (2014) quoted from correspondences between the US Embassy and the Guyana government on the LEAD to show that the government was in on the discussions since October 2012. In fact, President Ramotar met with the USAID representatives on the matter on October 29, 2012, and the US Ambassador wrote to President Ramotar on November 29, 2012, thanking him for the meeting.

The letter from the US Ambassador to President Ramotar said in part that the government had provided helpful information that allowed for the finalization of the LEAD project (Bharrat, 2014). A letter to the President of Guyana, dated October 18, 2012, Ambassador Hardt wrote pointed out that the USAID was planning to implement the LEAD project that would have a role in improving democracy and democratic governance in Guyana. The letter further states that Mr. Hardt was 'writing to solicit (Government's) support in coordinating a meeting with appropriate leaders within (the PPP-C) to hear your insights' (Bharrat, 2014). Thus, opposition to the LEAD project on the grounds that the US failed to consult with the government contradicts the evidence presented in the correspondences between the two sides, as revealed by Bharrat (2014).

Former PPP-C government minister Dr. Henry Jeffrey welcomed the LEAD project and pointed out that it targets race-based voting in Guyana by helping the electorate to vote on issues rather than race allegiance (Chabrol, 2014). Speaking on *Roundtable*, a National Communication Network (NCN) television program in Guyana Dr. Jeffrey observed that the government had found itself in a difficult situation because it was a minority in the parliament. Accordingly, the PPP-C administration, which is known to be dominated by East Indians was very uncomfortable with the LEAD project that could move people away from racial voting (Chabrol, 2014). The former minister noted that if the PPP-C government objects to the LEAD project that the US could reformulate it and give the monies to non-governmental organizations to achieve the same results.

The Georgetown Chambers of Commerce and Industry also came out in full support of the LEAD project. The Chamber urged the PPP-Civic government and the US authorities to resume discussion on the project in order to identify mutually feasible and pragmatic grounds for the implementation of the project. The Chamber fully endorsed the objectives of the LEAD project since it strengthened political institutions and enhanced citizens' understanding in how they could participate in civic actions in the country (iNews Guyana, 2014).

The PPP's broad left, progressive democratic front strategy

Meanwhile, in the midst of the controversy over the LEAD project the PPP announced that it had embarked on a broad left, progressive, democratic front electoral strategy for the 2015 national elections to win back a majority in the parliament. The new political strategy was intended to get more people to vote for the PPP and for the party to win back a majority at the general and regional elections (Chabrol, 2014b). According to Mr. Clement Rhoee, the party had intended to establish a national Democratic State by bringing together working people, farmers, intellectuals, professionals, the business community and NGOs (Chabrol, 2014b).

The former PPP General Secretary pointed out that the strategy would touch on every social strata of Guyanese society desirous of playing a role in nation building. People in this front may not be members of the PPP, or left-leaning, but merely patriots and nationalists who admire the idea (Chabrol, 2014b). According to Chabrol (2014) the PPP had conceded that it needed to work hard to regain its simple majority, due to younger voters, short memories by older voters of PNC rule, complacency and apathy (Chabrol, 2014b).

Undoubtedly, the PPP-C government's decision to launch a Commission of Inquiry into the assassination of the late Dr. Walter Anthony Rodney the world-renowned scholar and political activist was a tacit dimension of this strategy to win the votes of non-members. The Rodney Commission of Inquiry (RCI) was thirty-four years late, but was welcomed to bring closure to this vexing case. But, the PPP-C used it as a part of its strategy to win back the parliament and a majority at the local government elections. The PPP-C's thinking was that the RCI would possibly achieve three things to enhance its electoral strategy.

First, it would rupture the APNU alliance that forms part of the parliamentary majority. The APNU is a coalition comprising, among others, the Working People's Alliance, Rodney's party, and the PNC, which was responsible for Rodney's assassination. The RCI was definitely opening-up old wounds that would place a serious strain on the WPA–PNC-R alliance. Second, there was a category of voters that the PPP-C was eying. These were former WPA supporters who were disaffected with the party because of its alliance with the PNC-R. The RCI could potentially stimulate these individuals to vote for the PPP-C. Third, the concerned electorate would hail the PPP-C as a champion of justice for finally holding the RCI. These individuals might see the PPP-C as deserving of their votes.

It is ironic that the PPP resorted to a strategy that was attempted against the PNC authoritarian regime in the 1990s. Then, the opposition came together against the post-colonial authoritarian state. The absurdity of the PPP-C's strategy was that it advocated a coalition against its political opponents. The problem nonetheless is that the PPP is living in the shadow of its past when it embraced the Marxist ideology. Radical elements in the PPP that espoused Marxism caused the party to be removed from office by imperialist forces in 1953. The PPP was in the camp of the Soviet-led socialist bloc in the 1960s and that caused it to be again out maneuvered from office in 1964.

But, the party has now morphed into something else other than Marxist to regain power in 1992. It has since governed in Guyana on a neoliberal agenda following the dictates of the International Monetary Fund (IMF) and World Bank. Simultaneously, it established a race-based criminalized authoritarian state in a similar vein to the race-based authoritarian state from which it secured power, with the aid of imperialist forces in 1992.

The PPP claimed that it would resort to a broad left, progressive, democratic front strategy for the 2015 national elections that would have included working people, farmers, intellectuals, professionals, the business community, and NGOs. This was the very strategy that the political opposition used against the PNC dictatorship that led to a change in government in 1992. But, the PPP proceeded to govern in its own way ignoring those who helped form that broad alliance against the PNC dictatorship. The PPP did not set out post-1992 to establish a socialist state but instead it has presided over the establishment of what Thomas (2003, 2003a) characterized as a 'criminalized state,' while holding on to power through race-based voting.

After ruling Guyana in excess of twenty continuous years and establishing a criminalized authoritarian state rather than a socialist state, the PPP saw the need to have a broad alliance with progressive forces to build a National Democratic State. The PPP claimed in its campaign in the 2015 national elections that the political opposition took money from foreign forces to overthrow the PPP-C government. It played on the sympathies of the progressive forces by claiming that the PPP continues to be the victim of US imperialism, having been twice overthrown in the past by foreign powers.

But, the struggle by the PPP against the LEAD and to regain a parliamentary majority was not to maintain a socialist state against US imperialism such as was the case in Cuba and Venezuela. The PPP was struggling to maintain a criminalized authoritarian state through which the ruling elites due to corruption, theft from the public treasure, money laundering, trafficking in persons, drug trafficking, and the exercising of control over the natural resources sector especially small-scale gold mining, secured an economic base from which to rule. The PPP is invoking its Marxist past to win the sympathy of the progressive forces globally, in its fight to maintain a criminalized authoritarian state.

This is a tactic that the PPP has learned from the PNC when that party ruled Guyana. The PNC sometime after it was installed by US imperialism, declared itself socialist, and successfully ingratiated itself with the international progressive movement, as it sought to isolate the left in Guyana from those circles. But, in the same way that the progressive forces saw through the PNC tactic for what it really was, so too they had unveiled the tricks of the PPP to prolong their stay in power.

It is a well-known historical fact that the US intervened in Guyana to overthrow the democratically elected PPP government in the 1960s. Guyana is a country in which politics has been dominated by the political left since the nationalist movement emerged in earnest with the formation of the Guyana Labor Union (GLU) in 1919. For this reason, foreign intervention in Guyana is something that is generally abhorred by the locals. But, the real politics has been that historically, foreign intervention has been involved in decisive political change in Guyana from since 1953. It has either taken the form of direct military invasion, destabilization, or arranged deals, such as in 1992. It was therefore easy for the PPP to use the foreign intervention bogie as a tactic against its political opponents.

Citizens of a country tend to close ranks against foreign enemies, in demonstration of their nationalism. This observation that Machiavelli made has been tested and proven throughout modern times. Governments that are in trouble with the electorate deliberately start foreign wars to create national solidarity, diverting attention away from the problematic domestic issues. The PPP used this same tactic to drum-up support against its domestic opponents. The political opposition in Guyana therefore faced a peculiar dilemma. The PPP government openly received financial support from the US administration and continues to implement US dictated economic policies. But, because of the historic role that the US played in destabilizing the PPP government in the 1960s, if the cash-strapped political opposition in Guyana receives any funding from the US administration, the PPP accuses the opposition and the US of colluding to destabilize and overthrow the government. Compounding matters is the fact that the very PNC political party that collaborated with the US to destabilize the PPP government in the 1960s is leading the APNU the main political opposition, which had endorsed the LEAD project.

The PPP was in the bosom of the US imperialism since it secured power in 1992 through a US sponsored democratization project that the Carter Center supervised. When the PNC government was removed through foreign intervention, namely by the political conditionality of structural adjustment, there was no talk of foreign intervention and destabilization. Desmond Hoyte, the then leader of the PNC dictatorship played a role similar to that of Frederik Willem de Klerk in South Africa. Rather than choosing to hold on to a crumbling apartheid system he surrendered power to the African National Congress (ANC). Similarly, rather than holding on to a crumbling post-colonial authoritarian state President Hoyte surrendered to the IMF/World Bank/Carter Center allowing the PPP-C to secure power. The PPP became a creature of the US government, which supported it, financially. But, the PPP accused its opponents of colluding with the US administration to overthrow the Guyana government at the national election in 2015.

However, the PPP was in a better position to cry foul against US money going to the political opposition in Guyana. This was because the democratically elected PPP government was overthrown through similar means in the 1960s. The PPP government's accusations had great merit, because of the role of the US in its overthrow in the 1960s, but that was a very different PPP. Also, the very institution, the IRI that executed the LEAD project in Guyana, is notorious for its nefarious activities in Latin America and the Caribbean, and more recently in Honduras and Egypt.

The PNC now leading the APNU did not have a similar claim, although US money and pressure had a role in its removal from office in 1992. The PNC was initially put in power by US money and its government became a dictatorship. However, the PNC surrendered to the IMF and World Bank amidst the anti-dictatorial struggle in Guyana and external pressure from the IMF and World Bank. Also, the PPP-C government degenerated into a dictatorship and then it was faced with a similar situation to that of the PNC, namely US support to the political opposition that would unseat it at democratic elections.

The challenge that Guyana poses to the US today is not really about communism or terrorism. It is about keeping Guyana in line with US policies that would allow foreign extractivist capital free and easy entry and exit from the country. To stay in line with US policies would include the enforcement of US anti-terrorism policies through legislation to counteract terrorism, money laundering, trafficking in persons, drug trafficking, environmental degradation, and removal of all hindrances to foreign direct investment. The US promotion of 'democratic' change in Guyana has nothing to do with which political party is in power in the country. The US merely wants its policy agenda to be adhered to by the Guyanese state.

Conclusion

The incumbent state elites who advocate the extractivist model of development in Guyana are under serious political challenge by the forces of post-neoliberal capital. The model was championed by the PPP-C state elites, who attained control of the state through neoliberal democratization. But, the US wanted to 'expand democracy' in the country that would lead to the removal of the PPP-C from office and strengthen center-periphery relations in the country. Undoubtedly, the state elites that replaced the PPP-C would govern in the interest of post-neoliberal capital. The reasons for wanting to remove the PPP-C from office were first that the extractivist model of development it advocated had become a humbug to foreign direct investment. Second, the PPP-C had also been in power in excess of twenty years, which does not augur well for the democratization model, the US proffers.

The political change envisioned was intended to take place through a USAID funded democracy project being led by the notorious IRI. The IRI is known for its overthrow of democratic governments in Africa, Latin America and the Caribbean. The PPP-C, which had abandoned its socialist ideology in favor of the neoliberal doctrine, was seeking to hold on to power through various means, including a new broad left strategy. But, the political opposition in Guyana argued that the PPP-C government could not stop the US-funded democracy project. The US plays an integral role in politics in Guyana, which seemingly influenced political change in the country in roughly twenty-year cycles – 1964, 1992 and 2015.

Meanwhile, the PPP-C has completely caved on its opposition to the LEAD project. It revoked the visa of Mr. Glenn Bradbury in protest against his activities in Guyana. But, the private sector mounted pressure on the government for its action, pointing out the hardships that could be heaped on Guyana due to its action. The government and US commenced discussions on the LEAD and the US Ambassador announced that the talks were going well. Then dramatically, the government announced that it had withdrawn its disapproval of the LEAD project, because it will be given an opportunity to input on its design (Chabrol, 2014c).

References

Aljazeera. (2013). US bankrolled anti-Morsi activists: Documents reveal US money trail to Egyptian groups that pressed for president's removal, www.aljazeera.com/indepth/features/2013/07/201371011352248980l.html.

Agee, P. (2003). Former CIA agent tells: How US infiltrates 'civil society' to overthrow governments, www.informationclearinghouse.info/ article4332.htm.

Bernsein, D. (2006). 'Interviews Jeb Sprague: IRI election manipulation in Haiti.' *Third World Traveler*, February 7.

Bharrat, S. (2014). 'Release government files on US-funded democracy project.' *Demerara Waves*, January 11.

Canterbury, D. C. (2005). *Neoliberal democratization and new authoritarianism*. Aldershot, UK and Burlington, VT: Ashgate.

Chabrol, D. S. (2014). 'US-funded democracy project targets race-based voting – former minister.' *Demerara Waves*, January 5.

Chabrol, D. S. (2014a). 'PSC backs negotiation of US-funded democracy project.' *Demerara Waves*, January 14.

Chabrol, D. S. (2014b). 'PPP embarks on 'broad-left' electoral strategy.' *Demerara Waves*, January 3.

Chabrol, D. S. (2014c). 'Guyana government withdraws disapproval of LEAD project.' *Demerara Waves*, May 22.

Chabrol, D. S. (2013). 'US-funded democracy project not destabilizing but helpful to opposition.' *Demerara Waves*, December 27.

Chabrol, D. S. (2013a). 'USAID agreement breached over governance and democracy project.' *Demerara Waves*, December 24.

COHA (Council on Hemispheric Affairs). (2008). The bridge in the coup: The IRI in Venezuela, August 5.

COHA (Council on Hemispheric Affairs). (2008a). A hidden agenda: John McCain and the IRI, June 25.

Demerara Waves. (2014). 'US, Guyana preparing for talks on democracy project,' January 16.

Demerara Waves. (2013). 'PPP accuses US of boosting opposition fortunes,' December 24.

Demerara Waves. (2013a). 'US still executing abandoned democracy project – Luncheon,' December 18.

Demerara Waves. (2013b). 'AFC endorses US funded project that PPP opposes,' December 26.

Golinger, E. (2006). *The Chavez code: Cracking US intervention in Venezuela*. London: Pluto Press.

Goodman, A. (2004). Interviews Max Blumenthal, did the Bush administration allow a network of right-wing republicans to foment a violent coup in Haiti? *DemocracyNow*, July 20.

Guyana Chronicle Online. (2014). 'Ruling party and government hold similar position on LEAD project,' January 16.

iNews Guyana. (2014). 'GCCI comes out in full support of USAID LEAD Project; urges productive dialogue,' January 14. Available at: www.inewsguyana.com/gcci-comes-out-in-full-support-of-usaid-lead-project-urges-productive-dialogue/.

James, I. (2006). 'Chavez government probes U.S. funding.' *Associated Press*, August 27.

Kaieteur News. (2015). 'The exit of USAID's leadership and democracy (LEAD) program,' July 14. www.kaieteurnewsonline.com/2015/06/14/the-exit-of-usaids-leadership-anddemocracy-lead-programme/.

Leight, J. (2004). The international republican institute: Promulgating democracy of another variety. Washington: Council on Hemispheric Affairs, Memorandum to the Press 04.40, July 15.

McDonald, M. (2016). 'ExxonMobil's large offshore discovery faces political risk,' January 24. http://oilprice.com/Energy/Crude-Oil/ExxonMobils-Large-Offshore-Discovery-Faces-Political-Risk.html.

Ottaway, M. (2002). *Democracy challenged: The rise of the semi-authoritarian state*. Washington, DC: The Carnegie Endowment for International Peace.

Thomas, C. Y. (2003). 'Guyana and the wider world.' *Sunday Stabroek*, Georgetown: Guyana, March 9.

Thomas. C. Y. (2003a). 'More theses on the criminalized state: Guyana and the wider world.' *Sunday Stabroek*, Georgetown: Guyana, August 17.

US State Department. (2012). Investment climate statement – Guyana. Bureau of Economic and Business Affairs, June.

USAID. (2013). USAID leadership and democracy program (LEAD) total funding: US$1,250,000 implementation period: April 2013–April 2015 https://photos.state.gov/libraries/guyana/19452/pdfs/2013–08–22_USAID_LEAD_Program_Document-1.pdf.

USAID. (2013a). Remarks Ambassador D. Brent Hardt USAID leadership and democracy (LEAD) project reception to welcome chief of party, Wednesday July 24, 2013a, Cara Lodge, Quamina Street, Georgetown Guyana. http://photos.state.gov/libraries/guyana/461177/speechpdf/2013–07–24_ambassador-remarks-to-usaid-lead-reception.pdf.

Veltmeyer, H. and Petras, J. (2014). *The new extractivism: A post-neoliberal development model or imperialism in the twenty-first century*? London: Zed Books.

Conclusion

To conclude, the story of capitalist development has been told in many places before comprising many varieties of expositions on how the system came into existence and works at various stages of its evolution.[1] The emergence of theories of imperialism[2] nonetheless, a phenomenon that is an outgrowth of the expansion of capitalism, represented a landmark shift in the way the story of capitalist development is told. It now has to incorporate the countries which have become known as the capitalist periphery to which capital from the mature capitalist states have expanded. The stories of the complex relations of pillage, exploitation and debauchery, which embodies that expansion, is best told through the imperialist relationships that continue to evolve between those countries and the mature capitalist states.

An important point of clarification is that there is a distinction to be made between the stories about how the capitalist system has developed, including its imperialist dimensions and the deliberate theories that set out since the 1940s to bring about capitalist development to the capitalist periphery. These development theories are not about how the capitalist system has evolved over time but are better characterized as tool boxes that the former colonies must draw on to achieve the same level of economic prosperity and social development as the mature capitalist countries. Thus, the literature that focus on the story of capitalist development are not to be placed in the same category as the literature on development theory.

This book sought to expand on those stories of capitalist development by focusing on the role of development theory in that process. In particular, the concern is with the role of development theory in the expansion and consolidation of the capitalist system in the natural resources rich capitalist periphery. The development theory in vogue is neoextractivism, which is understood as a constituent element in the deepening of center-periphery imperialist relations in the natural resources rich peripheral capitalist countries in the Latin American and Caribbean region. Neoextractivism is the current attempt to bring about peripheral capitalist development, which is adjoined and cannot be divorced from the litany of theoretical formulations on the economic development of the region. However, it is merely one small link in the story of capitalist development.

The advocates of neoextractivism utilize tools of analyses that have their theoretical foundations and applications in the ideas espoused by the French Physiocrats, and in classical political economy, neoclassical economics, Keynesianism, development theory, and neoliberalism. Furthermore, the primary goal of neoextractivism has not gone past the ideal established by the French Physiocrats, and has subsequently been embraced by classical political economy and the theories it has spawned concerning the accumulation of wealth. Undoubtedly, the belief in that theoretical tradition is that the wealth generated from economic activity in agriculture, manufacturing and free trade within and among nation-states inevitably lays the foundation of social development.

Marx (1963) was adamant nonetheless that the analysis of capital from a bourgeois perspective was basically the work of the Physiocrats. For this reason Marx (1963) believed that the Physiocrats were the true fathers of political economy.[3] Marx (1963) noted however that the problem with the Physiocrats and their successors was that they separated capital from its social conditions in the sphere of production, that is the labor process in general independently of its social form thereby making capitalist production appears natural (Marx, 1963). The bourgeois forms of production therefore appear as natural forms of production. Thus, to the Physiocrats the natural forms of production were independent of anyone's will and of politics, they were material laws. But, in Marx's (1963) view the gravest mistake of the Physiocrats was that they conceived material law as an abstract law, whereas the former was of a definite historical social stage that could not abstractly govern equally all forms of society. In reality each historical social stage produces its own laws, to match the material conditions of the times.

Due to this focus on capitalist production as a natural phenomenon it became necessary for there to be invented a system of distribution to enhance social development. Should the market or the state take responsibility for the enhancement of social development, or should they combine to take responsibility? The accumulation of wealth in the hands of the few however, does no good for social development, unless the wealth is redistributed to find its way down to the poorest in society. Hence, in more recent times a central critique in development theory of capitalist development took the form of the idea of 'redistribution with growth.'[4] This means that the problem in the capitalist system is that wealth accumulates only in the hands of the few and unless it is redistributed social development will only be minimal. This problem has created the urgent need to redistribute wealth to the sundry population through social programs. For sure, this is basically the same goal of neoextractivism in which the state that transfers wealth generated from natural resources extraction to protect the most vulnerable in society through its social spending and cash transfers.

The neoextractivism ideal that marries social protection and social development might be traced to the 'laissez faire' doctrine at the time of the early beginnings of political economy. It is an idea that rests on the doctrine of the natural rights of the individual. According to this doctrine all individuals were born with the same natural rights, but they did not possess equal capabilities. It was necessary therefore for individuals to form a social union or contract as a mechanism to protect those who are weak and vulnerable due to their capabilities.

The social contract however limits the natural freedom of the individual insofar as such freedom may be in conflict with the rights of others (Ingram, 2015). Government appointed by the consent of individuals therefore was regarded as a 'necessary evil' that on the one hand took care through its social programs of the issue of social inequality that stems from the individual's capabilities. But on the other hand, the government should refrain from too much interference unless it is necessary to secure the fulfilment of the contract (Ingram, 2015).

In this line of reasoning, the form of government necessary to fulfill the social contract may be characterized as a type of 'legal despotism,' which combines the legislative and executive functions of the state. That form of government was considered necessary for the implementation of public programs without the hindrances associated with divergent opinions in government and hampered by constitutional checks and balances (Ingram, 2015). How far has the Physiocratic ideal about the social contract been removed from the current domain of neoliberal capitalism?

The role of the state under neoliberal capitalism in the fulfillment of the social contract has been minimized. The social contract envisioned by the founders of the capitalist system has been broken under neoliberal capitalism. The individual is left to fend for his/herself, as social programs are removed from the state. Neoliberalism was invented in response to capitalist crisis and to post-colonial authoritarian states that sought to own and or control their natural resources by recourse to nationalizations, and legal and tax reforms. This latter action would exacerbate the crisis as it would cut in even further on capitalist profit. The goal of state ownership and or control of natural resources in the post-colonial authoritarian state was to increase the state's revenue so that it would have more money to spend on social programs to improve the social and economic conditions of the poor. The same goal is true of neoextractivism in the transition from neoliberalism to the post-neoliberalism period.

The problem however is that neoextractivism is regarded as something new whereas it is a historical phenomenon that has been identified in different historical periods in the Latin American and Caribbean region. The argument that neoextractivism is a phenomenon that is historically specific the post-neoliberalism is therefore misleading. This mistake has serious implications for the class struggle against capitalism in the current period. The political activist must be aware that he/she is not struggling against a historically specific phenomenon, that would go away after it is vanquished. The political struggle against a historically specific phenomenon of necessity must take a different form and outlook compared with the struggle against a cyclical phenomenon. The former is reformist while the latter seeks to bring about transformative change to abolish the system that perennially creates those conditions. Neoextractivism is not historically specific to post-neoliberalism, it was also present in the post-colonial period in the struggle against colonialism.

Undoubtedly, development theory represents nothing other than the formulations in bourgeois social sciences about how to spread and embed capitalism in general and in the peripheral capitalist countries. As a development theory therefore neoextractivism merely represents a particular case of capitalist development. But, the advocates of the new extractivism regard it as a new progressive model of development that improves the economic and social conditions of the poor. The critique of neoextractivism was undertaken in the context of an appraisal of development theory or theories of development that are catalysts for the spread and development of capitalism.

Of critical importance is that development theory since the 1940s has strengthened the grip that capitalism has on the peripheral capitalist states. This is because these theories are all concerned with how to have the peripheral capitalist countries imitate the developed capitalist states in their political economy affairs. The focus of development theory claiming to be something other than classical political economy, have gone no further than to analyze the very categories that the classical political economists were concerned about namely the acquisition of wealth by the European nation-states. Besides, development theory continues to take the lead from theoretical advances in the developed capitalist countries. The debate on financialization is a recent example which is analyzed in the context of the mature capitalist economies. However, this phenomenon is now being analyzed in terms of development in the peripheral capitalist countries.

In essence, the debate on extractivism and neoextractivism is really about the dynamics of capitalist development. But, development continues to be elusive in the countries in the capitalist periphery, despite the fact that they are well endowed with natural resources. This is the evidence that capitalist development has failed to produce the necessary socio-economic transformations in the capitalist periphery desired by development theorists. Furthermore, the debate in the literature on extractivism and neoextractivism is very much contradictory and misguided since what it represents is merely a surface manifestation of a dynamic capitalist development process. A fundamental flaw in neoextractivism is that it pretends to redistribute income in favor of the poor, but in reality, foreign extractive capital continues to be the main beneficiaries.

In addition, neoextractivism is a myth in the sense that it pretends to reverse a particular situation namely halting the siphoning off by the transnational corporations of the wealth produced in the natural resources sector. The reality nonetheless is that it is business as usual in the natural resources sector in that although neoextractivism secures an increased share of the wealth which could be shared with the poor, the transnational corporations continue to siphon off the bulk of the wealth. Another myth of neoextractivism is that it is a new phenomenon, which is dispelled by the historical political economy data on the transformation from colonies to independent nation-states in the capitalist periphery. Historically, these countries have had very intense class struggles with colonial authorities and transnational corporations to control their natural resources.

The contradiction in capitalist production between the purchase and sale of commodities produces crisis in the mature capitalist countries. The ruling elites in the capitalist periphery are inspired by the crisis to step up their demand to recapture their natural resources from the transnational corporations. The ensuing class struggle results in the mature capitalist states using their political and economic leverage over the peripheral states to implement policies that roll-back nationalist measures designed to bring about national ownership and or control of natural resources.

Political change is inspired by foreign intervention as the imperialist forces regain control over the natural resources rich peripheral capitalist countries. The struggle between the imperialist forces and domestic economic and political elites to control power becomes fierce. It must be borne in mind that the state is the executive committee of the ruling class in the Latin American and Caribbean region. It is therefore the role of the state to facilitate the operations of the transnational corporations in the extractive industries.

Some ideas on the way forward for natural resource rich peripheral capitalist states

In the first instance, scholars, political activists, social movements, and working people engaged in the struggle for state power must be clear what it is they are fighting for and against. The key is the disentanglement of the class, economic, political, environmental, and social complexities at the domestic, geopolitical, and global levels. By so doing they will achieve clarity even through the trial and error of the goal ahead of them.

Second, these class forces need to step up their searches for alternatives to capitalist development. This has been a long and arduous task, but it must be pursued especially in the light of the vast power being accumulated by the capitalist and their deliberate marginalization and immiserization of the poor. The extremely naked neoliberal capitalism of the twenty-first century is a particular turn in the story of capitalist development that is unprecedented. Never before has the gap between the rich and poor been so pronounced. It must be resisted and halted.

Third, undoubtedly, the natural resources rich peripheral capitalist states need to take coordinated actions in their self-interest against the global transnational corporations. This strategy need not be only at the level of the governments engaged in the negotiations of contracts. Working people, their organizations and representatives must coordinate their resistance to those exploitative organizations. There is a need for the greater promotion of international solidarity among natural resources rich peripheral capitalist states.

Finally, as a tactic, working-class struggle for transformative change must be both reformist and revolutionary. Given the current disadvantaged position in which working people find themselves today their struggles must as matter of tactic combine the struggle for reform with that of transformative change. While reforms will bring temporary relief to the wretched conditions of the poor, the fundamental transformation of the capitalist system promises to bring a fresh start by revolutionizing the power dynamics in society currently founded on capitalist production and property relations.

Notes

1 See for example Rapley (2017), Sweezy (1942), Baran (1957), Polanyi (2001), Dobb (2007), Appleby (2011).
2 Noonan (2017) has categorized the theories of imperialism into three phases, 'classical,' 'neo-Marxist,' and 'globalization-era Marxist' theories of imperialism.
3 See Marx, K. (1963). *Theories of surplus value*. Moscow: Progress Publishers.
4 For an elaboration on redistribution with growth see Chenery, H., Ahluwalia, M. S., Bell, C. L. G., Duloy, J. N. H. and Jolly, R. (1974). *Redistribution with growth*. Oxford: Oxford University Press.

References

Appleby, J. (2011). *The relentless revolution: A history of capitalism*. New York: W. W. Norton and Company.
Baran, P. A. (1957). *The political economy of growth*. New York: Monthly Review Press.
Chenery, H., Ahluwalia, M. S., Bell, C. L. G., Duloy, J. N. H. and Jolly, R. (1974). *Redistribution with growth*. Oxford: Oxford University Press.
Dobb. M. (2007). *Studies in the development of capitalism*. Montana: Kessinger Publishing.
Ingram, J. K. (2015). *A history of political economy*. Ontario, Canada: Scholar's Choice.
Marx, K. (1963). *Theories of surplus value*. Moscow: Progress Publishers.
Noonan, M. (2017). *Marxist theories of imperialism: A history*. London and New York: I. B. Tauris.
Polanyi, K. (2001). *The great transformation: The political and economic origins of our time 2nd edition*. New York: Beacon Press.
Rapley, J. (2017). *Twilight of the money gods: Economics as a religion and how it all went wrong*. London and New York: Simon and Schuster.
Sweezy, P. A. (1942). *The theory of capitalist development: Principles of Marxian political economy*. New York: Monthly Review.

Index

Acosta, A. 54–5, 58, 69, 72
Acts and Regulations, Guyana Independence Constitution 164
AFC 196, 213, 219, 221–2; *see also* Alliance for Change
Africa 15, 38, 49, 54, 59, 61–2, 65, 83, 91, 140, 145, 193, 199, 214, 228; and the diaspora in Guyana 126; and the former European colonies in 38, 49; and the Guyanese-based PNC 161; and the middle classes 145; and new extractivism in 62; and the overthrow of democratic governments in 228; slaves in 30, 148
African Manganese Company 131
agricultural capitalism 30, 114, 125
'agricultural imperialism' 109
Aguilar, C. 55–6, 61, 71–2
Allende, Salvador 145
Alliance for Change 196, 213, 219, 221–2
Amaila Falls Hydropower Project 202
anti-colonialism 20, 25, 31, 143, 158, 191, 193; antecedents 141; and anti-dictatorial struggles in Guyana 31; sentiments 10; trade-union-organized struggle 188, 191
anti-communism 11, 159, 191; hysteria 10, 158; propaganda 158
anti-dictatorial struggles 31, 196, 227
anti-globalization 10, 141
anti-neoliberal politics 11
anti-privatization movements 87
APNU 196, 213, 219, 221, 225–7; *see also* A Party for National Unity
Argosy 152
Ayelazuno, J.A. 61–2
Azamar, A. 55–7

Barima Gold Mining Company 124, 129, 131
bauxite 85, 121, 125, 149, 154, 166, 181, 193, 197–8; companies 86, 179, 181, 194, 198; deposits 130–1; dried 151; extraction 130; and forestry subsectors 120, 124, 137; and gold 198; in Guyana 130–1, 151; industry 86, 130–1, 138, 176–7, 179, 193, 198, 204; and kaolin 121; management 179; and manganese mining industries 149; mining 125, 131; ore 130; production 131, 151, 197, 204; striking workers 195; unions 179–81, 195, 203; workers 179–82, 203
Bauxite Company of Guyana Inc. 203
BCGI 203; *see also* Bauxite Company of Guyana Inc
Bentham, Jeremy 17
BGLU 85; *see also* British Guiana Labor Union
Bradbury, Glenn 218, 228
Brazil 15, 60, 63, 65, 84, 104, 106, 147, 204; government of 60; and the Paranapanema company 197; and the penetration of the economy by imperial multinational corporations 106; and South Africa 72
Britain 27, 84, 86, 131, 135; and administrations in opposition to the PPP 155; and colonial rule 27, 93, 103, 123, 144, 166, 194; government of 27, 120–1, 126, 130, 132–3, 137–8, 143–4, 152, 155; mining companies 126, 130; and the powers of the appointed governor 146; and the Venezuelan government 30
British Aluminum Company 130
British Guiana 27, 85, 122–4, 126–9, 131–7, 144, 155; as a colonial power 149; Dutch colonies of Essequibo, Berbice and Demerara named 120

British Guiana Consolidated Goldfields Limited 143
British Guiana Gold Company 125–6
British Guiana Labor Union 85
British Guyana *see* Guiana
British Parliamentary Group on Human Rights 165
Brotherson, L. 166–7
Brown, Andrew Benjamin 124
Buchholz, P. 15–16, 65
Burnham, Forbes 142, 144, 148, 154, 172, 174–5

capital 4, 28–30, 36, 41–3, 49, 66–7, 91, 102, 105, 111–13, 120–1, 126, 128–9, 146, 192, 231–2; anti-foreign 215; criminal 202; domestic Guyanese 131; exporting 113; financial 1, 87, 103, 110, 113; foreign extractivist 227; international 183; investments 193; and labor 78, 81, 125–6; and labor relations in capitalist development 66; markets 110, 114, 162, 166; private 56, 143; social 129; transnational 70; variable 36, 112
capital accumulation 4, 7, 27–8, 35, 37, 42, 44–5, 53, 57, 63, 89, 101, 107, 110–15, 137; buttressed 30; maintaining 111; perpetuating 101; primitive 19; process of 45, 102, 113; purposes of 58, 109
Capital Gains Tax 153
capitalism 4, 6–9, 18–25, 27–9, 35–8, 40–1, 43–9, 71, 77–82, 94–5, 99–102, 107, 109–15, 119, 137–8, 233–4; agricultural 30, 114, 125; alternatives to 24–5; and capitalist development 111–12; colonial 10, 82, 85; contradictions of 81; crisis prone nature of 112; current 100, 110–11; development of 6–7, 28–9, 36, 48, 119, 125, 234; era of extractive 100, 110; evolution of 21, 27, 35, 48–9, 80, 94–5; extractive 5, 8–9, 63, 67, 99–100, 102, 104–8, 110–14, 119, 137, 191, 193, 195, 197, 200, 204; free market 40, 103, 123; global 1, 6–7, 9, 15, 18–21, 24–5, 30–1, 68, 72, 80–1, 83, 85, 160, 174, 177, 183; and imperialism 9, 99–101, 103, 105, 107, 109–11, 113–15, 119; mercantile 6, 35, 88, 113; neoliberal 7–8, 15, 20–1, 55, 73, 79, 82–3, 87–8, 94–6, 104, 119, 149–50, 212, 217, 233, 235; peripheral 28, 120, 140, 211; post-neoliberalism 69; and socialism/communism 47; in terms of incomes 23
capitalist center 8, 48, 77–8, 102, 111, 161; developed 43; emergent global 29; periphery relations 10, 120, 122, 137
capitalist classes 45, 112; absentee 214; domestic 214; transnational 109
capitalist countries 54, 72, 231, 235; advanced 42; developed 3, 82, 234; dominant 215; resources-rich 19, 78; traditional 203–4; underdeveloped peripheral 77; wealthy 49
capitalist crisis 15, 18–19, 21, 27, 80, 84, 233; heightens nationalist struggles 6, 19; and reforms 15–16, 19, 27; responses to 233
capitalist development 3–8, 10–12, 15–19, 21–5, 29–31, 35–49, 62–4, 68, 72–3, 77–8, 80–4, 111–13, 119–20, 124–5, 231–2, 234–5; in British Guiana 144; in Guyana 29; models 8, 24, 53, 79; of nation-states 43; and natural resources extraction 120; neoliberal 60; peripheral 83, 123, 137–8, 213, 231; process 42–3, 112, 169; promotion of 1; struggle for 78; suppressing 125; theory of 38, 41, 47, 49
capitalist exploitation 5, 8, 21–2, 64, 77
capitalist markets 4, 15–16, 25, 36, 48, 54, 58, 64, 68, 121
capitalist modes of production 25, 28–9, 38, 47–8, 58, 100, 102, 107, 114; backward 27; exploitative 5; and private ownership 38
capitalist nation-states 20, 42, 46
capitalist production 5–6, 23, 25, 28, 46, 66–7, 80, 94, 96, 100, 102, 108, 137, 156, 232, 235–6
capitalist relations 44, 78, 120–1, 123, 125, 127, 129, 131, 133, 135, 137; center-peripheral 19, 31, 120, 138, 211; deepening of 10; and natural resources extraction 119–38; peripheral 146–7; transition to 137
capitalist society 3, 18, 21, 31, 78, 94, 101, 109; developed 82; exploitation of labor in 21; mature 206; peripheral 67, 78–80, 83, 87, 140; and the transformation of power relations in 31
capitalist states 28, 69–70; advanced 217; developed 234; mature 82, 112, 231, 235; peripheral 12, 19, 87, 215, 234; rich 78, 90, 215, 235
capitalist system 3–6, 8, 16–17, 19, 21, 24, 28, 31, 40–2, 45, 77, 79–80, 84, 91, 102, 231–3; crisis-prone 63; exploitative 5;

global 15, 17, 24, 28–9, 58; industrial 113; of production 5, 7, 45, 114
capitalists 5–7, 9–10, 16–18, 22–3, 28, 38, 42–5, 47, 69, 81–3, 89, 91–2, 94, 99–103, 108–9, 121; agricultural 114, 124; commercial 114; domestic 108; foreign 44, 149, 203; private 91; resource-rich 92, 95; and wealth appropriate for personal and class accumulation 37
Caribbean 16–18, 21–2, 24, 36, 38, 41, 43–4, 65–6, 68, 79, 81, 84–5, 93, 192–3, 206, 227–8; bauxite output 194; colonies 193; community 178; contributions to development theory 44; countries 25, 31, 43–4, 57, 84, 113; development 42–4; economies 57, 194; nation-states 43; nationalism 194; politics 200
Caribbean Congress of Labor 182
Caribbean Development Bank 178
Caribbean Financial Action Task Force 203, 223
Caribbean Food and Nutrition Institute 169
CCL *see also* Caribbean Congress of Labor
CCWU *see also* Clerical and Commercial Workers' Union
CDB 178; *see also* Caribbean Development Bank
CFATF 203, 223; *see also* Caribbean Financial Action Task Force
CFNI 169; *see also* Caribbean Food and Nutrition Institute
Chabrol, D. 189, 202, 205, 212, 219–24, 228
charcoal 121, 132–4, 169
Chavez, Hugo 145
class struggle 8–9, 22, 40–1, 77, 83, 99, 105, 107, 112, 114–15, 148, 191, 200, 233; domestic 105; existing 47; increased 63; intense 234
Clerical and Commercial Workers' Union 179
coalition 161–4, 194–5, 225; administration 196; politics 159, 161, 164, 194, 206
coalition government 151, 155, 160–3, 192, 194–5; anti-communist 11; anti-Jagan 155; in Guyana 151
coffee 136, 153–4
Cold War 163, 174, 177, 216
Colimbite-Tantalite deposit 204
colonial authorities 44, 120, 137, 142–6, 148–50, 156, 163, 234; and domestic middle-class pressure 125; and transnational corporations 234
colonial capitalism 10, 82, 85
colonial capitalists 142, 150
colonial politics 192–3
colonial powers 120, 124, 158, 192
'colonial slave mode of production' 9–10, 19, 21, 27–31, 67, 120–1, 124, 126, 128–9, 136–8, 140, 146, 148, 151, 161, 188–9; to center-periphery relations 67, 124, 137, 140; to full-fledged capitalist production relations 29; and neoliberal capitalism 21
colonialism 7, 28, 38, 80, 83–5, 87, 141, 143, 149, 159–60, 191, 233
colonies 1, 8, 24, 27, 40–2, 54, 78–80, 91, 95, 119–22, 137, 142, 144, 192, 214, 234; advancing to nation-state status 95; British 27; Dutch 27, 120; Essequibo, Demerara and Berbice 27, 31, 120; former 3, 24, 40, 44, 48, 78–80, 83, 93, 95, 231; former European 1, 8, 20, 38, 41–3, 47–9, 102; separate 27
commodities 3–4, 16–17, 35–8, 59, 65, 72, 81, 88–9, 94, 100–1, 110, 114, 131, 138, 151–2, 171–2; imported 154; manufactured 4, 35, 48, 91; natural resources 100; primary 17, 72, 113; production of 3, 58, 88, 94, 100; sale of 81, 96, 110, 235
communism 29, 144, 191, 227
communist bloc 151, 162, 216
communists 144–5, 154, 156, 190, 192
companies 57, 59, 79, 85–6, 123, 125, 127, 131, 153, 161, 202, 205; bauxite-mining 86; British mining 126, 130; extractive 31, 57, 80, 193; foreign-owned 20, 59, 80, 84, 86, 123, 131, 141, 149–50, 194; gold 30, 129–30, 189; insurance 152; joint-stock 172; mineral exploration 204; mining 57, 62, 125, 199, 201; non-tax-holiday 153; state-owned 87, 179
'conflict diamonds' 198
conflicts 27, 56–7, 66–7, 94, 109, 144, 146, 175, 183, 200, 203, 214–15, 217, 233; between the forces and relations of production 112; citizen 68; institutional 167; manipulated race 146; political 107
cooperative socialism 86, 166, 168–9, 171–3, 175, 177; rhetoric 170; state-led economic policies of 168, 170; *see also* socialism

corruption 11, 26, 92, 162, 172, 176, 189, 200–2, 204, 212, 214–15, 223, 226; and illegal mining 204; perceived 203
costs 27, 30, 55, 91, 122–3, 129, 150, 170–1, 199, 203; economic 72; environmental 68, 72; operating 171, 177; shipping 151; social 68
countries 15–17, 19–20, 24–7, 39–43, 53–5, 67–9, 82–93, 119–25, 134–7, 140–3, 145–51, 158–60, 168–70, 173–5, 212–14, 226–8; bauxite-producing 86; conquered 112; developed 42, 72, 78; foreign 31; former imperialist 101; former socialist/communist 47; lower-middle-income 61; mineral-rich 95; for national ownership 15; non-traditional bilateral donor 178; poor 43, 48, 69, 71, 88; semi-peripheral 101; socialist 171
Court of Justice 27
Court of Policy 27, 124
criminal enterprises 11, 26, 189–90, 196, 200–1, 206

The Daily Chronicle 151–2
Daniels, George 180–1
'deepening democracy' 214
Demerara (former Dutch colony) 27, 120, 136
Demerara Bauxite Company 131, 166, 194
Demerara River 130, 133–4, 151
democracy 4, 11–12, 24, 36, 71, 142, 177, 179, 188, 195–7, 200, 205, 211–12, 217, 219, 222; and authoritarianism 11, 188; deepening 12, 205, 217; and economic progress 197; expanding 205, 214, 227; in Guyana 205, 213, 218–19, 222; projects 218, 228; strengthening of 12, 211, 215–16; struggle for 177, 179, 195, 200
development planning 141, 163, 166, 168
development strategies 10, 15, 31, 59, 64, 66, 87, 103, 107–8, 166, 190, 212; common 104; economic 11, 64, 103; endogenous 70; resources-led 10, 64–5; state-led 103
development theories 1, 4–7, 23–4, 35–6, 38–49, 73, 119, 231–2, 234; and capitalism 119; and capitalist development 35–49; and policy reform 21
diamonds 120–4, 129, 135, 137–8; fields 125–6, 129; and gold 123, 138; mining of 124, 129, 204; production of 198
Dos Santos, T. 44, 70–1
Dublin, Edward 195
East Indians 26, 126, 137, 145, 147–9, 154, 161, 194, 213, 224; and African middle classes 145, 148–9; and PPP 141–5, 148, 151, 154–6, 160–6, 190, 192, 194, 199, 219–22, 224–7
ECLAC School 42–3
Economic Commission for Latin America 104
economic independence 10, 19, 21, 78–80, 95–6, 140, 148, 168
economic institutions 171–2, 213
economic management 90, 92, 177
economic policies 16, 29, 44, 105, 156, 160–2, 167–8, 170, 173–5, 192, 217; to build an airport 86; dictated by the US 226; independent national 193; international 31; and practices 44
Economic Recovery Program 160, 175, 178, 181–3, 196, 198
economic surplus 6, 8, 20–3, 25, 37, 69, 77, 80, 84, 115, 141–2, 156
Ecuador 63, 71, 104
EGCI 92–3; *see also* Energy Governance and Capacity Initiative
elections 155, 161, 164–6, 180, 195, 199; democratic 227; and fraud 145, 164, 192; free and fair 145, 192; general 155, 165–6; local government 218, 222, 224; national 24, 141–2, 145–6, 163–5, 189, 191, 195, 197, 201, 212, 214, 221, 224–5, 227; regional 224; results of 12, 188; *see also* national elections
Elections Commission 164
Energy Governance and Capacity Initiative 92–3
Engels, F. 37–8, 46
ERP 160, 175, 178, 181–3, 196, 198; *see also* Economic Recovery Program
ETB 171–2; *see also* External Trade Bureau
European nation-states 39–42, 44, 82, 234
'expanding democracy' 214
exploitation of labor 21–2, 103, 113
exports 7, 43, 53–5, 58, 60–1, 70, 86, 102–3, 106, 131–5, 150–3, 161, 169, 178, 198, 202; agrarian 106; bauxite 131, 151, 197, 204; commodity 105, 107; diamonds 120–4, 129, 135, 137–8; manufacturing 106; mineral 62, 197; of natural resources 70, 152; nature and character of commodity 105, 198; sugar 154; value of 150–1
External Trade Bureau 171–2

extraction 9–10, 17, 22, 35–7, 55–9, 61, 64, 66, 70, 72, 77, 100, 106–7, 114–15, 121, 136–7; activities 25, 55–8, 60, 67, 100, 193; agro-mineral 105–6; bauxite 130; of gold 30, 128; mineral 30, 54, 88, 126; of natural resources for export 55, 61, 121; resource 3–4, 8, 15–16, 22, 31, 35, 53, 62–6, 70, 201, 206
extractive capitalism 5, 8–9, 63, 67, 99–100, 102, 104–8, 110–14, 119, 137, 191, 193, 195, 197, 200, 204; analysis of 119; benefits of 106; class struggle in 105; in Colombia 106; costs of 63, 104; and extractive imperialism 9, 99–100, 109–10, 114; foreign 11, 31, 64, 90, 105, 132, 138, 189, 191, 194–8, 203, 234; in Guyana 197; labor and capital in 67
extractive companies 31, 57, 80, 193
extractive sector 7, 15–16, 55, 63–5, 67, 90–1, 100, 103, 130, 137, 199, 203
extractivism 5, 7, 9, 53–5, 57–60, 63, 65–7, 99–100, 102–3, 140–1, 143, 145, 147, 149, 151, 153; classical 103, 107; and neoextractivism 5, 7, 37, 53, 55, 57–9, 61, 63, 65, 67, 69, 71, 73, 119, 234; old 66, 68; post-colonial 6, 10; predatory 55, 71; progressive 63–4, 66, 104, 190; prudent 56

FDI 62–3, 102, 108, 196–7, 202–3, 212, 217, 227–8; *see also* foreign direct investment
Federation of Independent Trade Unions of Guyana 181–2
FITUG 181–2; *see also* Federation of Independent Trade Unions of Guyana
food 122–3, 127, 135, 155, 171, 175, 178; banned essential 194; imported 172; milk-based infant 153, 171; nutritional 169; production of 169, 172; production zones 56
foreign capital (*see also* foreign extractive capital) 31, 56, 61, 67, 91–2, 103, 106, 124–5, 131, 149, 159, 161, 191–3, 196, 213–15, 218
foreign extractive capital 11, 31, 64, 90, 105, 132, 138, 189, 191, 194–8, 203, 234
foreign intervention 6, 10, 12, 120, 141, 145, 158, 190–1, 211, 213–17, 219, 221, 223, 225–7, 235; and destabilization 227; in Guyana 226; imperialist 154; and political change 6, 12, 120, 211, 211–28; primary goal of 12; ruses for 12, 211
foreign investment 55, 62–3, 102, 104, 108–9, 196–7, 199, 202–3, 212, 217, 227–8
foreign powers 79, 85, 96, 143, 191–2, 196, 211, 225
forestry products 20, 30, 121, 132, 134, 136–7
forestry sector 132–3, 137
forestry workers 124, 127
forests 55, 61, 124, 132–3, 135
free trade 3, 42, 44, 48, 82, 196, 232
French Revolution 27
fuel wood 121, 132–4; *see also* woods

gas production 54, 71–2, 92–3, 205
GAWU 179–80; *see also* Guyana Agricultural and General Workers Union
GBSU 179–80; *see also* Guyana Bauxite Supervisors Union
GDF 165; *see also* Guyana Defense Force
Guyana Agricultural and General Workers Union 179–81, 203
Georgetown 129, 152, 15
GGDMA 204; *see also* Guyana Gold and Diamonds Mining Association
Girvan, N. 44–5, 130
global capitalism 1, 6–7, 9, 15, 18–21, 24–5, 30–1, 68, 72, 80–1, 83, 85, 160, 174, 177, 183; crisis and reform in 1, 6–7, 9, 18–21, 31, 35, 81, 85, 183; current era of 15, 110; decolonization phase of 68; evolutionary development of 30; forces of 24, 177; hegemonic position in 72; and political change 24; reforms in 19, 68, 83, 160, 191
global capitalists 25–6, 174, 176
GLU 226; *see also* Guyana Labor Union
GMWU 179–80; *see also* Guyana Mine Workers Union
GNCB 171–2; *see also* Guyana National Cooperative Bank
gold 30, 88, 120–4, 126–9, 135, 137–8, 193, 197–9, 203–4, 212; bullion 126–7; companies 30, 129–30, 189; and diamond mining 124, 204; industry 122, 126–7, 217; miners 30, 127, 130; mines 129–30; production 30, 128, 204; production in Guyana 30; and silver mining 88; smuggling of 204; workers 130

gold mining 30, 79, 122–3, 125, 128–9, 143, 189, 191, 197, 201–2, 204, 212; operations in Guyana 201; small-scale 11, 189–90, 226; stimulated by the depression in England in the 1880s 126
goldfields 122, 129–30
government 2, 25, 84–7, 124, 135–6, 145–7, 160, 162, 166, 168–77, 179–82, 190–2, 194–205, 211–16, 218–28, 233; authoritarian 216; bureaucracy 133, 162–3; democratic socialist 85; destabilizing of 218; elected 143, 192, 194, 215, 219; expenditure 166; financing 173; incumbent authoritarian 216; inefficient 203; left leaning 59, 66, 68; minority 222; post-colonial authoritarian 197; regulations 65; revenues 87, 93, 154, 199; revolutionary 86; spending 22, 85, 162, 170, 176
Granger, David 221
Graulau, J. 88–9
Griffith, Gordon 179
GTSL 176; *see also* Guyana Transport Services Limited
GTUC 170–2, 219, 222; *see also* Guyana Trades Union Congress
Gudynas, Eduardo 58–60, 66–8, 71–2, 190
Guyana 9–12, 25, 27–31, 83–6, 96, 119–21, 125–38, 140–3, 145–9, 151, 155–6, 158–61, 188–92, 194–206, 211–13, 217–28; and British imperialist forces 11, 155, 159; and Capital Gains Tax 153; and the Carter Center 96; colonial history of 201; democracy in 205, 213, 218–19, 222; destabilized by the LEAD project 222; economy of 86, 128–30, 135, 141, 147, 149–50, 166, 189–90, 196; and the forestry sector 132; mistaken for a small island in the Caribbean Sea 121; nationalism 194; natural resources extraction in 6, 126, 191, 195; overseeing US covert operations in 155; political opposition in 220, 226–8; previously called British Guiana 27, 120; and the privatization program of structural adjustment 196; and the re-entry into the fold of the IMF and World Bank 196; and the role of Canada 197; ruled by the PNC Party 226; set apart from Jamaica and Trinidad and Tobago 194; sovereignty of 219, 221; and Venezuela 126; and workers of 182
Guyana Bauxite Supervisors Union 179–80
Guyana Constitution 1980 168, 189
Guyana Court of Appeal 194
Guyana Defense Force 165
Guyana Gold and Diamonds Mining Association 204
Guyana government 84, 92, 96, 131, 145, 174–5, 193, 197, 202–3, 212–13, 219–23, 227; accuses the US of financing the activities of the political opposition 220; delegation led by President Donald Ramotar 222; equity interest in Omai Gold Mines 197; and gold mining 197; *see also* PPP-Civic Guyana government
Guyana Labor Union 226
Guyana Manufacturing and Industrial Development Agency 178
Guyana Mine Workers Union 179–80
Guyana National Cooperative Bank 171–2
Guyana Trades Union Congress 170–2, 219, 222
Guyana Transport Services Limited 176
GUYMIDA 178; *see also* Guyana Manufacturing and Industrial Development Agency

Haiti 218–19
Hardt, Brent 220, 223
hardwoods 133
Harrigan, J. 175, 177
Harvey, David 29
health 3, 20, 56, 59, 62, 123, 166, 168, 175–8, 215
health services 67, 170, 174
Hilson, G. 61–2
Holloway, Perry 96
housing 62, 166, 168–9, 175; authority 167; sector 167; shortage 173; units 168–9
Howell-Jones, B. 124
Hoyte, Desmond 169–70, 227
Hubbard, H.J.M. 146–7
Huber, M. 61
human labor power 3, 22, 28, 36–7, 101, 103, 123
Hunt, Diana 38

IFIs 111, 202; *see also* International Financial Institutions
IMF 15–16, 62, 64–5, 95, 160, 163, 174–8, 181, 197, 211–12, 225; *see also* International Monetary Fund

imperialism 5, 8–9, 23–4, 58, 61–5, 99–105, 107–15, 119, 144, 190, 231; and capitalism 9, 99–101, 103, 105, 107, 109–11, 113–15, 119, 144; displaces free competition 109; historical 109; secures the conditions needed for capital accumulation 111
industrialization 1–3, 43–4, 70; facilitated by reforms 43; and import substitution 16, 22, 43, 64, 91, 103, 106
inflation 45, 170, 178
Ingram, J.R. 1–3, 233
International Financial Institutions 111, 202
International Monetary Fund 15–16, 62, 64–5, 95, 160, 163, 174–8, 181, 197, 211–12, 225
International Republican Institute 218–22, 227–8
IRI 218–22, 227–8; *see also* International Republican Institute

Jagan, Dr Cheddi 142, 145, 148, 151, 154–5, 166, 189, 222
Jamaica 84–6, 151–2, 192, 194; bauxite sector in 85; economic and political destabilization in 194; economy of 85; government of 85–6, 193; independence and nationhood 85; political democracy in 85
Jamaica Bauxite Institute 86
Jeffrey, Dr Henry 161, 224
Josiah, B.P. 30, 124–5

Kaieteur News 202–3, 205, 218–19
kaolin 121
Keynesian Consensus 174
Keynesianism 38, 232
King, Sidney 142
Knowledge Sharing Institute 171–2
Koama, Ohene 195
KSI 171–2; *see also* Knowledge Sharing Institute
Kwayana, Eusi 142, 194–5

labor 2–4, 9, 21–3, 28, 30, 36–8, 66–7, 78, 103, 108, 113, 120–1, 124–6, 137–8, 146, 178–9; and capital 4, 41, 66–7, 128, 148; exploitation of 21–2, 103, 113; manual 133–4; processes 91, 108, 232; reforms 124; slave 29–30; unions 124, 155, 169, 179–80; unpaid 108
labor power 3, 22, 28, 36–7, 101, 103, 123; *see also* human labor power
laborers 28, 57, 122, 126–7, 129–30, 135; employed for three to four months at a time 134; indentured 147; indentured Portuguese 147; ordinary 122; wage 28–9
Latin America and Caribbean region 28–9, 43, 55–6, 58–60, 66–7, 69, 71, 80–3, 99–100, 102–3, 107, 110–11, 114–15, 138, 140–3, 159–60; becomes dominated by neo-liberal policies 114; and extractive capitalism 105; and neoliberal extractivism 69; and the organized power of the ruling classes to oppress the working classes 114; and the rise of the criminalized authoritarian state 188; and the role of scholars 42; and the role of structuralism 89
LEAD 205, 218–26, 228; *see also* Leadership and Democracy project
leaders 18–19, 143–5, 152, 154–6, 158, 161–2, 174, 195, 201, 221, 227; middle-class 84, 145; new 154, 182; progressive 105; radical 143–4; religious 182; renegade 158
leadership 145, 154, 165, 189, 218; controversial 205; nationalist 145
Leadership and Democracy Project 205, 218–26, 228
Leight, J. 218–20
Levitt, K. 39, 41, 44–5
Lewis, W.A. 43–5, 108, 167, 192
Lewis plan 108, 166–8
'logging imperialism' 109
The London Times 151
Luncheon, Dr Roger 221

mahogany 132–3, 136
manganese production 131–2, 151
Manley, Michael 85
Manley government (Jamaica) 85–6
manufacturing 1–2, 4, 35, 46, 106, 111, 132, 135, 153, 169, 214, 232; commodities 4, 35, 48, 91; exports 106; and free trade 232; industry 2; local 161; sectors 178
markets 3–5, 17, 41–2, 48, 66–8, 88, 100, 111, 132–4, 136, 151, 192, 232
Mars, Perry 197
Marx, K. 22, 28–9, 36–7, 45, 49, 81, 100, 108, 112, 144, 232
mercantile capitalism 6, 35, 88, 113
Milanez, B. 70–1

minerals 2, 15, 30, 54, 88–92, 94–5, 106, 120–1, 128–30, 191, 193, 199, 204; exports of 62; extraction of 30, 54, 88, 126; and forestry industries 120; production of 94; rare earth 203, 212; trade in 88; in wealth creation and accumulation 89
miners 30, 122, 128, 130, 138, 203–4
mineworkers 122, 130
mining 29–31, 60, 62, 88–91, 94–5, 106, 121–5, 128, 133, 138, 153, 175, 178, 198–9, 201, 203–4; in developing countries 88; districts 122–3, 126–8; industry 29, 61, 64, 122, 124; policies 199; quartz 126, 128; regulations 30, 122–3; revenues 90, 95, 199; sector 90, 92–3, 95, 106, 124–5, 137–8, 199, 204
monopolies 2, 71–2, 109
Myrdal, Gunnar 41

Napoleonic Wars 27
nation-states 1, 3–4, 23, 35, 38–49, 78–9, 82, 88–9, 232, 234; accumulation of wealth in 45, 88–9; capitalist 20, 42, 46; European 39–42, 44, 82, 234; independent 20, 38–40, 44, 48, 234; peripheral 40, 81
National Development Strategy for Guyana 198–9
national elections 24, 141–2, 145–6, 163–5, 189, 191, 195, 197, 201, 212, 214, 221, 224–5, 227; fair 11, 188, 205–6; holding of 217; rigged 11, 159–60, 164; supervised 195
national ownership 9–10, 15, 19–20, 25, 83–4, 87, 96, 143, 147, 149, 155, 158, 183, 190, 193, 195; agendas 83; claim for 10; and control of natural resources 8, 79, 82–5, 96, 149, 158, 183, 194; demands for 19, 83; implementing 83; levers of state power to agitate for 25; nationalist struggle for 9, 19; political independence and 20; strategies 84, 195
National Workers Union 203
nationalism 105, 191, 226
nationalists 8, 20–1, 77, 104–5, 142, 149–50, 224; agenda 158; experiments in Guyana 84, 145; politics 191, 193–4; post-colonial politics 193
nationalizations 11, 20, 59, 68, 80, 85–6, 131, 146, 149, 158–9, 166, 190, 194, 196, 233; mortgage-finance type 84
natural gas 212
natural resources extraction 4–11, 20–2, 29–30, 53–4, 56–61, 63, 67–72, 77, 79–80, 94–6, 100–1, 119–21, 190–3, 195–6, 198–201, 211–14; in agriculture 20; to buttressed capital accumulation 30; and capitalist development 119; and capitalist relations 119–38; current focus on 110; development impact of 8, 79, 94, 119; encroachment of 56; endowment 58; to enrich its members 206; and expanded capitalist relations 9, 119–20; exploitation 22, 63; for export 61, 161; and the Guyana experience 29; in mining 71; in political economic structures 57; for sale 54; for sale in capitalist markets 54; in social programs 60; to stimulate economic development 96
NDS 198–9; *see also* National Development Strategy
Negro Progress Convention 124
neo-colonialism 7, 102, 109, 124
neo-developmentalism 56, 70–1
neoextractivism 5–11, 16–24, 26–8, 30–2, 35–8, 40, 42, 44, 46, 53–74, 77–96, 100–2, 119, 159–60, 190, 231–4; and capitalist development 5–6, 15, 17–19, 21, 23, 25, 27, 29, 31; and center-periphery relations 120, 122, 124, 126, 128, 130, 132, 134, 136, 138, 142, 144, 146, 148, 150, 152; concepts of 70; critical examination of 5; critique of 6, 234; deliberations on 60; exponents of 22; fundamental flaw in 234; goal of 232; idea of 58; in Latin America and the Caribbean 5, 10–11, 16–18, 29, 140; myth of 234; and neo-developmentalism 70–1; post-colonial 120; post-neoliberal 44, 156; struggle for 24; subject of 5, 24, 53–4; theory of 9
neoliberal capitalism 7–8, 15, 20–1, 55, 73, 79, 82–3, 87–8, 94–6, 104, 119, 149–50, 212, 217, 233, 235
neoliberal democratization 12, 177, 188, 192, 201, 205, 211, 213, 215–18, 227; conditions of 201; current evolutionary phase of 217; perpetrators of 217; and structural adjustment 177, 218
neoliberal policies 62, 64, 82–3, 107, 145; changing 83; dismantling of 83; draconian 59; failed 16; implemented 160
neoliberalism 11–12, 40, 42, 44, 55, 65, 69–71, 80–4, 87, 106, 140, 143, 156, 159, 188, 232–3

new extractivism 15–17, 58–70, 77, 79–81, 83–4, 87, 95, 99–100, 102–4, 107–9, 120, 140–1, 149, 155–6, 160, 168; in Latin America 65, 99, 120; Latin American and Caribbean region and the emergence of 59; policies of 66; post-colonial 140–1
New York Times 151
Newman, P. 132, 149–51, 154
newspapers 151–2, 220; *Argosy* 152; *The Daily Chronicle* 151–2; *Kaieteur News* 202–3, 205, 218–19; *The London Times* 151; *New York Times* 151; *Thunder* 142
NGOs 64, 224–5; *see also* non-governmental organizations
non-communists 145
non-governmental organizations 64, 224–5
NPC 124; *see also* Negro Progress Convention
Nurkse, Ragnar 41

oil 54, 70–2, 87, 92–3, 96, 106, 132, 136, 193, 203–5, 212; commercial quantities in Guyana 92; exploration 205; extraction 92; offshore discoveries 219; production 96, 193, 205, 212; revenues 60
Omai Gold Mines Limited 189, 191, 197

parliament 162, 164–5, 182, 191, 194, 199, 218, 221, 223–4; and the distribution of seats 165; national 221; and the opposition 165, 198, 202, 223
A Party for National Unity (APNU) 196, 213, 219, 221, 225–7
Patriotic Coalition for Democracy 182–3, 195
PCD 182–3, 195; *see also* Patriotic Coalition for Democracy
People's National Congress 141, 145, 154–5, 160–6, 168–9, 171–4, 190, 192, 194–6, 199, 225–7
People's Progressive Party 141–5, 148, 151, 154–6, 160–2, 164–6, 190, 192, 194, 199, 219–22, 224–7
peripheral capitalist countries 8, 10, 20–1, 54, 77, 87, 90, 95–6, 112, 158, 188, 213, 215, 234; and the control over natural resources 19, 78; imitating the developed capitalist states 234; nationalize private companies to improve social welfare 160–1; rich 19, 95, 211–14, 217, 231, 235
Petras, James 9, 17, 23–5, 61–4, 87, 99–114, 160, 190, 196, 200, 212
plantations 27, 30, 147; agriculture 9, 29–30, 79, 121; agro-extractivism 79; established 136; experimental rubber 121, 136; sugar 121, 124
planters 27, 30, 121, 125, 137
PNC 141, 145, 154–5, 160–6, 168–9, 171–4, 190, 192, 194–6, 199, 225–7; *see also* People's National Congress
PNC - United Force coalition government 151, 155, 161–2, 164, 192
policies 55–7, 59, 62–3, 70, 72, 83, 85, 92, 104–5, 107, 110–12, 124–5, 169, 171, 174, 190; capitalist 156; change in capitalist 156; coalition government 163; economic 16, 29, 44, 105, 156, 160–2, 167–8, 170, 173–5, 192, 217; government 61, 146; neoliberal 62, 64, 82–3, 107, 145; political 39, 168; price control 171; production 55; to recapture control over the natural resources 96; social development 64
political change 6, 12, 21, 24, 81–2, 120, 145, 168, 195, 211–17, 226, 228, 235; in developing countries 216; due to 'strengthening democracy' 12, 211, 214–15; in Guyana 145, 195, 226; internal 183; in natural resources 214; and natural resources extraction 198; preferred method of 214; through 'deepening democracy' 214; through 'expanding democracy' 214
political economy 1–3, 5, 10, 17, 28, 39, 84, 100, 111–12, 140, 196, 211, 232; of capitalist development and class formation 111; circumstances in Guyana 158; conditions 6, 10, 102; conditions in Guyana 10; development of 2; goals 46; of Guyana 27, 29; relations 6, 29, 140; situations 103–4; of structural adjustment 196
political opposition 66, 105, 141, 159, 164–5, 167, 189, 191, 214–15, 217–18, 220–1, 225–8; cash-strapped 216, 226; domestic 191, 212, 215–16; in Guyana 220, 226–8
political parties 141, 155, 160, 182, 194–5, 206, 216, 218, 220–1, 226–7; dominant 141; and Guyanese people 206, 220; nationalist-oriented 192; Portuguese-based UF party 152; pro-West 152; single 148, 163, 206
political power 49, 59, 113–14, 168, 216

politics 29, 63, 112, 146–7, 149, 159–61, 188, 191–2, 195–6, 199–200, 205, 211–12, 214, 217, 226, 232; anti-authoritarian 195; anti-neoliberal 11; coalition 159, 161, 164, 194, 206; colonial 192–3; domestic 196, 206, 213, 216; in Guyana 141, 145, 161, 190, 196, 206, 217, 228; of natural resources extraction 211, 213–14; post-neoliberal 199–200, 205; of structural adjustment 196
Portugal 101, 147–8, 155
post-colonial 24, 44, 140–1, 143, 145, 147, 149, 151, 153, 155, 159, 193, 201; authoritarian state in Guyana 6, 10–12, 29, 120, 140, 155–6, 158–83, 188–9, 192–3, 196, 201, 206, 211–13, 217, 225, 233; authoritarianism 11, 159, 188; extractivism 6, 10; societies 81, 160; state authoritarian economic policies 168
post-colonialism 46, 80, 83, 85, 143
post-development theorists 47
post-extractivism 70–3
post-neoliberal policies 83
post-neoliberal politics 199–200, 205
post-neoliberal regimes 21, 70, 190–1
post-neoliberalism 7, 12, 16, 39, 47, 69, 71, 80–1, 83, 140, 143, 156, 159, 205, 211, 233; and capitalism 69; period 233
PPP 141–5, 148, 151, 154–6, 160–2, 164–6, 190, 192, 194, 199, 219–22, 224–7; claims 221–2; and colonial forces 161; government 151, 155, 160, 194, 221, 226–7; involvement in the LEAD program 221; leaders and leadership 142–4; left-leaning 162; and PNC 145; radical 145; united 154; *see also* People's Progressive Party
PPP-Civic Guyana government 213, 217, 224; launches a Commission of Inquiry into the assassination of Dr. Walter Anthony Rodney 224; strategy 225
Prebisch, Raul 41
primary commodities 17, 72, 113
privatization 20, 61, 87, 106, 160–1, 190, 196, 198; of natural resources extraction 198; policies 20; program of structural adjustment 196; programs 178, 196
production 2–3, 9, 16–17, 27–31, 36–8, 45–9, 56–8, 94–5, 100–2, 107, 114–15, 120–1, 124–6, 131, 135–8, 232; activities 9, 81, 91, 99–100, 102, 109, 114, 120; of commodities 3, 58, 88, 94, 100; industrial 3; process 7, 36, 53, 68, 91, 100, 110, 126; for profit 47, 92; systems 17, 70, 81, 101
production relations 100, 112; expanding capitalist 79; expansion of center-periphery capitalist 155; exploitative capitalist 90, 140; new non-capitalist 23; peripheral capitalist 10, 29, 79, 140, 146–7; pre-capitalist 113
progressive governments 21, 25, 55, 59–60, 66, 68; agendas of 25; neoliberalism by 55; self-proclaimed 58
PSC 164, 222–3; *see also* Public Service Commission
PSU 180–2; *see also* Public Service Union
Public Service Commission 164, 222–3
Public Service Union 180–2

Quamina, O.T. 130–1
quarrying 138, 175
quartz milling 123, 128

race 10, 126, 140–1, 145–8, 155, 158, 161, 206; and class character 145, 206; and class conflicts 155; and class divisions 148; and class groups 147–8; voting in Guyana 194
radicals 141–4, 149, 151; domestic 149; to power in Guyana 141
Rambarran, R. 203
raw materials 2–3, 24, 36, 54, 60, 69–70, 72, 88, 91, 95, 101, 132, 135, 138, 158, 161; demands by European capitalist powers for 54; exporting of 55, 69–71; importing 72; production of 54
RCI 224–5; *see also* Rodney Commission of Inquiry
reforms 1, 6–7, 15–16, 18–21, 23, 25, 27, 29, 35, 43, 68, 83, 92, 107, 217–18, 235; constitutional 27, 220; economic 143, 148; in global capitalism 19, 68, 83, 160, 191; implementing local government 218; labor 124; neoliberal 18–19, 21; and policies 92; political 183; public sector 202; social 125; tax 233
regime changes 12, 31, 190–2, 195–6, 205–6, 211, 216, 219; complete 191; facilitated 205; in Guyana 190–1; in post-colonial authoritarian states 12
Regina, Anna 221
resources 4–5, 7–8, 10, 17, 19, 29, 31, 35–6, 53–4, 57, 59, 68–9, 73, 105, 108, 112; economic 149; extraction 3–4, 8,

15–16, 22, 31, 35, 53, 62–6, 70, 201, 206; human 63, 200; national 84; non-renewable 72; offshore oil and gas 92; primary 69; to rummage for gold 127; scarce 77; and wealth and transferring 112
revenues 16, 31, 59–60, 62, 64–5, 87, 90, 92–3, 106, 162, 177, 193, 201, 206; collection 31; for economic development 16; government 87, 93, 154, 199; management 92; mining 199
Rhoee, Clement 220, 224
Ricardo, David 17, 89
rich countries 48, 90, 92
riffles 127–8, 152
Robertson Commission 1954 142–5, 148
Robertson Constitution 1956 and 1961 155
Rodney, Walter A. 195
Rodney Commission of Inquiry 224–5
Ruiz-Marrero, C. 69–70

self-government for British Guiana 142, 144
SIDS 78; *see also* Small Islands Developing States
slave labor 29–30
slaves 22, 27–8, 30, 148
'sluice' 126–8
Small Islands Developing States 78
Smith, Adam 17
social development 17–18, 23, 29, 44–6, 56, 59–60, 62, 64–5, 84, 231–2; foundation of 232; policies 64; redistribution of 232
social movements 7, 10, 20, 24–5, 57, 59, 68, 105, 125, 141, 143, 145, 163, 235; in Guyana 68; in Latin America 10; left-leaning 11, 159; radical 53
social programs 20, 22, 37, 45, 58, 60, 64, 66, 69, 80–1, 85, 154, 166, 178, 190, 232–3
social unrest 19, 81, 141, 143–4, 151, 154, 214–15
socialism 29, 46, 60, 63, 86, 107, 113; building of 85–6; communitarian 56; cooperative 86, 166, 168–9, 171–3, 175, 177; democratic 85
socialists 104, 143–5, 154, 156, 226; cooperative 172; self-sufficient 44
sociologists 39, 45
Somerset, Ron 203
South Africa 72, 227
South America 9, 68, 132, 145, 197
state power 8, 21, 25–6, 31, 59, 77, 112, 141, 146, 212–14, 217, 235; class-based 113; control of 8, 31, 77, 149, 191, 213–15, 218; and foreign capital seeking to control 218; in Latin America 21; object of 146; projection of 113; secured 79, 213; seized 163; struggle for 8, 77, 214, 217, 235
state violence 203
'strengthening democracy' 12, 211, 214–15
structural adjustment program (1980) 175–8, 191, 197–8
Stürmer, M. 15–16, 65
sub-Saharan Africa 16, 62
sugar 29–30, 151, 154, 171, 189, 198, 212; estates 126, 136; factories 177; industry 149, 182; plantations 121, 124; planters 30, 189; prices 189; profits 121, 189
Suriname 151, 204
surplus labor 108, 167; exploitation of 107–8; necessary 108; rural 103
surplus value 28, 94, 100–3, 114; extraction of 102–3; production of 101, 114; system of production of 101; usurper of 94
sustainable development 16, 36, 47, 65, 83, 95, 107

taxes 27, 66, 86, 128, 154, 173, 176, 200, 205; annual 153; corporate 199; direct 150; excise 205; gift 153; increasing 105, 178; local government 198; withholding 199
Thomas, C.Y. 11, 26, 28–9, 44–5, 86–7, 120, 160, 175, 177, 189, 192–4, 196–7, 200–2, 204–6, 225
Thompson, Malcolm 179
Thunder 142
timber 132–5, 151; and cabinet woods 132; exports of 151; grants 134; industries 121; production 133–4
Tobago 21, 84–5, 87, 192, 194
trade 1–4, 16, 35, 48, 58, 65, 73, 88–9, 91, 111, 150, 167, 171, 198; domestic 2; foreign 86; illegal drug 111; import 171; import-export 56; international 72, 89, 113; losses 153; practices 48; and production 89; protective 48; restrictions 178
trade unions 85, 179, 181–2; *see also* unions
Trades Union Congress 179–81, 183, 219, 222
Trinidad 84–5, 87, 192–4

TUC 179–81, 183, 219, 222; *see also* Trades Union Congress

UGWU 179, 181; *see also* University of Guyana Workers Union
underdeveloped countries 39
unemployment 166–7, 169, 173
union leaders 179, 182
unions 169, 179–82, 203; bauxite 179–81, 195, 203; independent 180–1; militant 179; *see also* trade unions
University of Guyana Workers Union 179, 181
US 11–12, 72, 93, 96, 113, 131–2, 134–5, 143, 155, 159, 161, 204–5, 211–13, 216–20, 222–4, 226–8; administration 85, 155, 175, 212, 219, 222, 226–7; and anti-terrorism policies 227; authorities 130, 213, 217, 219–20, 224; and British administrations 155; and British imperial forces 161; and European Union 200; funded democracy project 228; government 92, 155, 202, 213, 217, 220, 222, 227; imperialism 63, 99, 101, 110, 148, 216, 225–6; money 216
US State Department 92–3, 202–3, 205, 212, 217–18, 221

value 2–3, 6, 36–7, 44, 94, 100, 103, 127, 129, 134–5, 150, 154, 205; aggregated 36; exchangeable 3; market 129; potential 132; surplus 28, 94, 100–3, 114; total 127, 129, 134–5
Veltmeyer, Henry 9, 17, 23–5, 61–4, 99–100, 102–4, 107–14, 190, 196, 200, 212
violence 26, 62, 66, 144, 146; electoral 197; state 203
voters 155, 164–5, 221, 224–5
voting 11, 180, 188, 223; military personnel 165; race-based 206, 224–5; rights 163–4

Waddington Constitutional Commission 142, 146
Waddington Report 142
wages 4, 23, 108, 122, 129, 147, 153, 171, 178–9, 181, 203; daily 134; increased 22, 106; minimum 180; policies 163, 202; social 23
Wallerstein, I. 101
wars 5, 21, 27, 73, 81–3, 102, 125, 144, 150, 170, 173; foreign 226; resource 107; secret 173; stimulated 20
Washington Consensus 61, 63–4, 103–4, 174
wealth 3–4, 18, 21–2, 37–8, 41–2, 44–6, 64, 80, 82, 85, 88–90, 106–7, 112, 158–60, 232, 234; accumulation of 41, 44–5, 94, 232; acquisition of 88, 234; concentration 70; creation 22, 88–9; financial 111; gap 20; generation 4; of nations 46, 88; natural 55, 59; and power 107; redistribution of 45, 232; significant natural resources 69; transferring of 20, 160, 232
WFTU 182; *see also* World Federation of Trade Unions
Willem, Frederik 227
Williams, Eric 27–8
Wong, Clinton 144
woods 132–4, 169
workers 20, 22–3, 28–9, 94, 107–8, 129, 147, 152, 168, 170–1, 175–7, 179–80, 182, 195, 198, 203; clerical 133; estate 148; exploitation of 7, 114; forestry 124, 127; gold 130; Guyanese 182; militant 179; and people of Guyana 182; public service 181; retrenched 183; rural landless 105; sex 203; sugar 181; underpaid 174; unemployed industrial 105
Workers' Party 84
working classes 1, 45, 114, 148, 152; African and East Indian 148; struggles of 106, 179, 182, 235
Working People's Alliance 182, 195, 225
World Federation of Trade Unions 182
World War I 125
WPA 182, 195, 225; *see also* Working People's Alliance